Yamaha
Raptor 660 & 700 ATVs
Service and Repair Manual

by Alan Ahlstrand

Models covered

YFM660 Raptor 660, 2001 through 2005
YFM70R Raptor 700, 2006 through 2012

ABCDE
FGHIJ
KLMNO
PQRST

ISBN-13: **978-1-56392-977-9**
ISBN-10: **1-56392-977-5**

Library of Congress Control Number 2012940698
Printed in the USA

Haynes Publishing
Sparkford, Nr Yeovil, Somerset BA22 7JJ, England

Haynes North America, Inc
861 Lawrence Drive, Newbury Park, California 91320, USA

© **Haynes North America, Inc. 2012**
With permission from J.H. Haynes & Co. Ltd.

A book in the **Haynes Service and Repair Manual Series**

12-240

Contents

LIVING WITH YOUR YAMAHA ATV

Introduction

Daily (pre-ride) checks

MAINTENANCE

Routine maintenance and servicing

Contents

REPAIRS AND OVERHAUL

Engine, transmission and associated systems

Chassis and bodywork components

Wiring diagrams

REFERENCE

Index

Yamaha
Musical instruments to Motorcycles

The Yamaha Motor Company

The Yamaha name can be traced back to 1889, when Torakusu Yamaha founded the Yamaha Organ Manufacturing Company. Such was the success of the company, that in 1897 it became Nippon Gakki Limited and manufactured a wide range of reed organs and pianos.

During World War II, Nippon Gakki's manufacturing base was utilised by the Japanese authorities to produce propellers and fuel tanks for their aviation industry. The end of the war brought about a huge public demand for low cost transport and many firms decided to utilise their obsolete aircraft tooling for the production of motorcycles. Nippon Gakki's first motorcycle went on sale in February 1955 and was named the 125 YA-1 Red Dragonfly. This machine was a copy of the German DKW RT125 motorcycle, featuring a single cylinder two-stroke engine with a four-speed gearbox. Due to the outstanding success of this model the motorcycle operation was separated from Nippon Gakki in July 1955 and the Yamaha Motor Company was formed.

The YA-1 also received acclaim by winning two of Japan's biggest road races, the Mt. Fuji Climbing race and the Asama Volcano race. The high level of public demand for the YA-1 led to the development of a whole series of two-stroke singles and twins.

Having made a large impact on their home market, Yamahas were exported to the USA in 1958 and to the UK in 1962. In the UK the signing of an Anglo-Japanese trade agreement during 1962 enabled the sale of Japanese lightweight motorcycles and scooters in Britain. At that time, competition between the many motorcycle producers in Japan had reduced numbers significantly and by the end of the sixties, only the big-four which are familiar with today remained.

Yamaha Europe was founded in 1968 and based in Holland. Although originally set up to market marine products, the Dutch base is now the official European Headquarters and distribution centre. Yamaha motorcycles are built at factories in Holland, Denmark, Norway, Italy, France, Spain and Portugal. Yamahas are imported into the UK by Yamaha Motor UK Ltd, formerly Mitsui Machinery Sales (UK) Ltd. Mitsui and Co. were originally a trading house, handling the shipping, distribution and marketing of Japanese products into western countries. Ultimately Mitsui Machinery Sales was formed to handle Yamaha motorcycles and outboard motors.

The FS1-E - first bike of many sixteen year olds in the UK

Based on the technology derived from its motorcycle operation, Yamaha have produced many other products, such as automobile and lightweight aircraft engines, marine engines and boats, generators, pumps, ATVs, snowmobiles, golf cars, industrial robots, lawnmowers, swimming pools and archery equipment.

Two-strokes first

Part of Yamaha's success was a whole string of innovations in the two-stroke world. Autolube engine lubrication, pressed steel monocoque frame, electric starting, torque induction, multi-ported engines, reed valves and power valves kept their two-strokes at the forefront of technology.

In the 1960s and 70s the two-stroke engined YAS3 125, YDS1 to YDS7 250 and YR5 350 formed the core of Yamaha's range. By the mid-70s they had been superseded by the RD (Race-Developed) 125, 250, and 350 range of two-stroke twins, featuring improved 7 port engines with reed valve induction. Braking was improved by the use of an hydraulic brake on the front wheel of DX models, instead of the drum arrangement used previously, and cast alloy wheels were available as an option on later RD models. The RD350 was replaced by the RD400 in 1976.

Running parallel with the RD twins was a range of single-cylinder two-strokes. Used in a variety of chassis types, the engine was used in the popular 50 cc FS1-E moped, the V50 to 90 step-thrus, RS100 and 125, YB100 and the DT trail range.

The air-cooled single and twin cylinder RD models were eventually replaced by the

The distinctive paintwork and trim of the RD models

LC series in 1980, featuring liquid-cooled engines, radical new styling, spiral pattern cast wheels and cantilever rear suspension (Yamaha's Monoshock). Of all the LC models, the RD350LC, or RD350R as it was later known, has made the most impact in the market. Later models had YPVS (Yamaha Power Valve System) engines, another first for Yamaha - this was essentially a valve located

in the exhaust ports which was electronically operated to alter port timing to achieve maximum power output. The RD500LC was the largest two-stroke made by Yamaha and differed from the other LCs by the use of its vee-four cylinder engine.

With the exception of the RD350R, now manufactured in Brazil, the LC range has been discontinued. Two-stroke engined models have given way to environmental pressure, and thus with a few exceptions, such as the TZR125 and TZR250, are used only in scooters and small capacity bikes.

The Four-strokes

Yamaha concentrated solely on two-stroke models until 1970 when the XS1 was produced, their first four-stroke motorcycle. It was perhaps Yamaha's success with two-strokes that postponed an earlier move into the four-stroke motorcycle market, although their work with Toyota during the 1960s had given them a sound base in four-stroke technology.

The XS1 had a 650 cc twin-cylinder SOHC engine and was later to become known as the XS650, appearing also in the popular SE custom form. Yamaha introduced a three cylinder 750 cc engine in 1976, fitted in a sport-tourer frame and called the XS750, TX750 in the USA. The XS750 established itself well in the sport tourer class and remained in production with very few changes until uprated to 850 cc in 1980.

Other four-strokes followed in 1976, with the introduction of the XS250/360/400 series twins. The XS range was strengthened in 1978

The XS650 led the way for Yamaha's four-stroke range

Yamaha's XS750 was produced from 1976 to 1982 and then uprated to 850 cc

by the four-cylinder XS1100.

The 1980s saw a new family of four-strokes, the XJ550, 650, 750 and 900 Fours. Improvements over the XS range amounted to a slimmer DOHC engine unit due to the relocation of the alternator behind the cylinders, electronic ignition and uprated braking and suspension systems. Models were available mainly in standard trim, although custom-styled Maxims were produced especially for the US market. The XJ650T was the first model from Yamaha to have a turbo-charged engine. Although these early XJ models have now been discontinued, their roots live on in the XJ600S and XJ900S Diversion (Seca II) models.

The FZR prefix encompasses the pure sports Yamaha models. With the exception of the 16-valve FZR400 and FZR600 models, the FZ/FZR750 and FZR1000 used 20-valve engines, two exhaust valves and three inlet valves per cylinder. This concept was called Genesis and gave improved gas flow to the combustion chambers. Other features of the new engine were the use of down-draught carburetors and the engine's inclined angle in the frame, plus the change to liquid-cooling. Lightweight Deltabox design aluminium frames and uprated suspension improved the bikes's handling. The Genesis engine lives on in the YZF750 and 1000 models.

The vee-twin engine has been the mainstay of the XV Virago range. Since 1981 XVs have been produced in 535, 700, 750, 920, 1000 and 1100 engine sizes, all using the same basic air-cooled sohc vee-twin engine. Other uses of vee engines have been in the XZ550 of the early 1980s, the XVZ12 Venture and the mighty VMX-12 V-Max.

Anti-lock braking, engine management and catalytic converters are all features found on present-day models, ensuring that Yamaha remains at the forefront of technology.

Yamaha's entry into the field of four-stroke off-road competition came in 1998 with the introduction of the YZ400F motocrosser and its companion, the WR400F enduro bike. The WR was basically the same as the YZ, but with lights and wide-ratio transmission gears (hence the WR designation). Since the introduction, the four-strokes have enjoyed growing success.

Yamaha entered the ATV market in 1980 with the YT125 Tri-Moto three-wheeler. A competitor to Honda's ATC (All-Terrain Cycle) models, the Tri-Moto featured a 123cc air-cooled 2-stroke engine, five-speed transmission with reverse, and chain drive. Several other three-wheel models were added over the next five years. Production of three-wheelers was discontinued by all ATV manufacturers after the 1985 model year.

The company's first four-wheeler was the 1985 YFM200, introduced in 1984. The engine was a 196cc four-stroke single with an overhead cam. Power was transferred to the five-speed transmission by an automatic centrifugal clutch, and from the transmission to the rear wheels by a driveshaft. The transmission included reverse gear.

The first automatic transmission ATV was the Breeze in 1986. A centrifugal clutch transferred engine power to a continuously variable belt-drive transmission. The Breeze also had reverse gear.

The YFZ450, built around the engine/transmission unit from the YZF450 motocross bike, was a significant addition to Yamaha's sport ATV line, beginning in 2004. The YFZ450 continued mostly unchanged for several years. In 2009 the YFZ450R, a motocross

A new family of four-strokes was released in 1980 with the introduction of the XJ range

variant of the YFZ450, was introduced, with fuel injection replacing the carburetor and significant modifications to the chassis.

The Raptor 660 gave Yamaha's ATV line its first big-bore sport quad, beginning in 2001. Its large-displacement, single cylinder engine, equipped with Yamaha's unique five-valve cylinder head design and twin carburetors, offered a considerable increase in power for sports such as hill climbing. It was replaced in 2006 by the Raptor 700, which used a similar chassis design together with a higher-displacement, fuel injected engine.

Acknowledgements

Our thanks to GP Sports of Santa Clara and San Jose, California, for supplying the ATVs used in the photographs throughout this manual; to David Guy, service manager, for arranging the teardowns and fitting them into GP Sports' busy schedule; and to Kevin Wood, service technician, for providing valuable technical information.

About this manual

The aim of this manual is to help you get the best value from your motorcycle. It can do so in several ways. It can help you decide what work must be done, even if you choose to have it done by a dealer; it provides information and procedures for routine maintenance and servicing; and it offers diagnostic and repair procedures to follow when trouble occurs.

We hope you use the manual to tackle the work yourself. For many simpler jobs, doing it yourself may be quicker than arranging an appointment to get the vehicle into a dealer and making the trips to leave it and pick it up. More importantly, a lot of money can be saved by avoiding the expense the shop must pass on to you to cover its labor and overhead costs. An added benefit is the sense of satisfaction and accomplishment that you feel after doing the job yourself.

References to the left or right side of the vehicle assume you are sitting on the seat, facing forward.

We take great pride in the accuracy of information given in this manual, but motorcycle manufacturers make alterations and design changes during the production run of a particular motorcycle of which they do not inform us. No liability can be accepted by the authors or publishers for loss, damage or injury caused by any errors in, or omissions from, the information given.

Engine and frame numbers

The frame serial number is stamped into the left side of the frame. The engine number is stamped into the crankcase and is visible from the left side of the machine. Both of these numbers should be recorded and kept in a safe place so they can be given to law enforcement officials in the event of a theft.

The frame serial number and engine serial number should also be kept in a handy place (such as with your driver's license) so they are always available when purchasing or ordering parts for your machine.

The following table lists frame numbers where they are available. If frame numbers are not available, the model code is listed instead. The model code is printed on a sticker attached to the top of the air cleaner housing.

Year and model	Initial vehicle identification
2001 YFM660RN	JY4AM013*1A000052
2001 YFM660RNC (California)	JY4AM013*1A000002
2002 YFM660RP	JY4AM01Y*2C003061
2003 YFM660RR	Not available (model code 5LPC)
2003 YFM660RRLER (Black Limited Edition)	Not available (model code 5LPC)
2004 YFM660RS	JY4AM01Y*4C045660
2005 YFM660RT	JY4AM01Y*5C064904
2006 YFM700RV	JY4AM07Y*6C000021
2007 YFM70RW	JY4AM07Y*7C026475
2007 YFM70RSEW (Special Edition)	Not available (model code 1S3A)
2007 YFM70RSE2W (Special Edition 2)	JY4AM07Y*7C044028
2007 YFM70RSEW-B (GYTR Edition)	Not available (model code 1S3D)
2008 YFM70RX	JY4AM14Y*8C000004
2008 YFM70RSPX (Special Edition)	JY4AM14Y*8C002085
2008 YFM70RSP2X, YFM70RSPX-B (Special Edition II)	Not available (model code 1S3S)
2009 YFM70RY	JY4AM14Y*9C015814
2009 YFM70RSEY, YFM70R-B (Special Edition)	JY4AM14Y*9C017478
2010 YFM7RSEZ (Special Edition)	Not available (model code 1AS4)
2011 YFM7RAL, YFM7RAW	Not available (model code 1AS7)
2011 YFM7RSEA	Not available (model code 1ASA)
2012 YFM7RBL, YFM7RBW	Not available (model code 1ASD)
2012 YFM7RSEB (Special Edition)	Not available (model code 1ASG)

Buying spare parts

Once you have found all the identification numbers, record them for reference when buying parts. Since the manufacturers change specifications, parts and vendors (companies that manufacture various components on the machine), providing the ID numbers is the only way to be reasonably sure that you are buying the correct parts.

Whenever possible, take the worn part to the dealer so direct comparison with the new component can be made. Along the trail from the manufacturer to the parts shelf, there are numerous places that the part can end up with the wrong number or be listed incorrectly.

The two places to purchase new parts for your motorcycle – the accessory store and the franchised dealer – differ in the type of parts they carry. While dealers can obtain virtually every part for your ATV, the accessory dealer is usually limited to normal high wear items such as shock absorbers, tune-up parts, various engine gaskets, cables, chains, brake parts, etc. Rarely will an accessory outlet have major suspension components, cylinders, transmission gears, or cases.

Used parts can be obtained for considerably less than new ones, but you can't always be sure of what you're getting. Once again, take your worn part to the salvage yard for direct comparison.

Whether buying new, used or rebuilt parts, the best course is to deal directly with someone who specializes in parts for your particular make.

The engine number is stamped into the top of the crankcase

The frame serial number is stamped into the left frame rail forward of the footrest

Professional mechanics are trained in safe working procedures. However enthusiastic you may be about getting on with the job at hand, take the time to ensure that your safety is not put at risk. A moment's lack of attention can result in an accident, as can failure to observe simple precautions.

There will always be new ways of having accidents, and the following is not a comprehensive list of all dangers; it is intended rather to make you aware of the risks and to encourage a safe approach to all work you carry out on your bike.

Asbestos

● Certain friction, insulating, sealing and other products - such as brake pads, clutch linings, gaskets, etc. - contain asbestos. Extreme care must be taken to avoid inhalation of dust from such products since it is hazardous to health. If in doubt, assume that they do contain asbestos.

Fire

● Remember at all times that gasoline is highly flammable. Never smoke or have any kind of naked flame around, when working on the vehicle. But the risk does not end there - a spark caused by an electrical short-circuit, by two metal surfaces contacting each other, by careless use of tools, or even by static electricity built up in your body under certain conditions, can ignite gasoline vapor, which in a confined space is highly explosive. Never use gasoline as a cleaning solvent. Use an approved safety solvent.

● Always disconnect the battery ground terminal before working on any part of the fuel or electrical system, and never risk spilling fuel on to a hot engine or exhaust.

● It is recommended that a fire extinguisher of a type suitable for fuel and electrical fires is kept handy in the garage or workplace at all times. Never try to extinguish a fuel or electrical fire with water.

Fumes

● Certain fumes are highly toxic and can quickly cause unconsciousness and even death if inhaled to any extent. Gasoline vapor comes into this category, as do the vapors from certain solvents such as trichloro-ethylene. Any draining or pouring of such volatile fluids should be done in a well ventilated area.

● When using cleaning fluids and solvents, read the instructions carefully. Never use materials from unmarked containers - they may give off poisonous vapors.

● Never run the engine of a motor vehicle in an enclosed space such as a garage. Exhaust fumes contain carbon monoxide which is extremely poisonous; if you need to run the engine, always do so in the open air or at least have the rear of the vehicle outside the workplace.

The battery

● Never cause a spark, or allow a naked light near the vehicle's battery. It will normally be giving off a certain amount of hydrogen gas, which is highly explosive.

● Always disconnect the battery ground terminal before working on the fuel or electrical systems (except where noted).

● If possible, loosen the filler plugs or cover when charging the battery from an external source. Do not charge at an excessive rate or the battery may burst.

● Take care when topping up, cleaning or carrying the battery. The acid electrolyte, even when diluted, is very corrosive and should not be allowed to contact the eyes or skin. Always wear rubber gloves and goggles or a face shield. If you ever need to prepare electrolyte yourself, always add the acid slowly to the water; never add the water to the acid.

Electricity

● When using an electric power tool, inspection light etc., always ensure that the appliance is correctly connected to its plug and that, where necessary, it is properly grounded. Do not use such appliances in damp conditions and, again, beware of creating a spark or applying excessive heat in the vicinity of fuel or fuel vapor. Also ensure that the appliances meet national safety standards.

● A severe electric shock can result from touching certain parts of the electrical system, such as the spark plug wires (HT leads), when the engine is running or being cranked, particularly if components are damp or the insulation is defective. Where an electronic ignition system is used, the secondary (HT) voltage is much higher and could prove fatal.

Remember...

✗ **Don't** start the engine without first ascertaining that the transmission is in neutral.

✗ **Don't** suddenly remove the pressure cap from a hot cooling system - cover it with a cloth and release the pressure gradually first, or you may get scalded by escaping coolant.

✗ **Don't** attempt to drain oil until you are sure it has cooled sufficiently to avoid scalding you.

✗ **Don't** grasp any part of the engine or exhaust system without first ascertaining that it is cool enough not to burn you.

✗ **Don't** allow brake fluid or antifreeze to contact the machine's paintwork or plastic components.

✗ **Don't** siphon toxic liquids such as fuel, hydraulic fluid or antifreeze by mouth, or allow them to remain on your skin.

✗ **Don't** inhale dust - it may be injurious to health (see Asbestos heading).

✗ **Don't** allow any spilled oil or grease to remain on the floor - wipe it up right away, before someone slips on it.

✗ **Don't** use ill-fitting wrenches or other tools which may slip and cause injury.

✗ **Don't** lift a heavy component which may be beyond your capability - get assistance.

✗ **Don't** rush to finish a job or take unverified short cuts.

✗ **Don't** allow children or animals in or around an unattended vehicle.

✗ **Don't** inflate a tire above the recommended pressure. Apart from overstressing the carcass, in extreme cases the tire may blow off forcibly.

✔ **Do** ensure that the machine is supported securely at all times. This is especially important when the machine is blocked up to aid wheel or fork removal.

✔ **Do** take care when attempting to loosen a stubborn nut or bolt. It is generally better to pull on a wrench, rather than push, so that if you slip, you fall away from the machine rather than onto it.

✔ **Do** wear eye protection when using power tools such as drill, sander, bench grinder etc.

✔ **Do** use a barrier cream on your hands prior to undertaking dirty jobs - it will protect your skin from infection as well as making the dirt easier to remove afterwards; but make sure your hands aren't left slippery. Note that long-term contact with used engine oil can be a health hazard.

✔ **Do** keep loose clothing (cuffs, ties etc.

and long hair) well out of the way of moving mechanical parts.

✔ **Do** remove rings, wristwatch etc., before working on the vehicle - especially the electrical system.

✔ **Do** keep your work area tidy - it is only too easy to fall over articles left lying around.

✔ **Do** exercise caution when compressing springs for removal or installation. Ensure that the tension is applied and released in a controlled manner, using suitable tools which preclude the possibility of the spring escaping violently.

✔ **Do** ensure that any lifting tackle used has a safe working load rating adequate for the job.

✔ **Do** get someone to check periodically that all is well, when working alone on the vehicle.

✔ **Do** carry out work in a logical sequence and check that everything is correctly assembled and tightened afterwards.

✔ **Do** remember that your vehicle's safety affects that of yourself and others. If in doubt on any point, get professional advice.

● If in spite of following these precautions, you are unfortunate enough to injure yourself, seek medical attention as soon as possible.

1 Engine/transmission case oil level check

⚠️ **Warning: On models with an oil level dipstick, never remove the dipstick to check oil level immediately after hard or high-speed riding. Hot oil could spurt out and cause burns. Let the engine cool to approximately 70-degrees C (150-degrees F) before removing the dipstick.**

Before you start:

✔ The engine and transmission share a common oil supply, which is checked through the oil tank filler plug/dipstick.

✔ Park the vehicle in a level position, then start the engine and allow it to reach normal operating temperature. **Caution:** *Do not run the engine in an enclosed space such as a garage or shop.*

✔ Stop the engine and allow the machine to sit undisturbed in a level position for about five minutes.

Vehicle care:

● If you have to add oil frequently, you should check whether you have any oil leaks. If there is no sign of oil leakage from the joints and gaskets the engine could be burning oil (see *Troubleshooting*).

The correct oil

● Modern, high-revving engines place great demands on their oil.
It is very important that the correct oil for your bike is used.
● Always top up with a good quality oil of the specified type and viscosity and do not overfill the engine.

Oil type

API grade SG or higher meeting JASO standard MA - the MA standard is required to prevent clutch slippage. See Chapter 1 for viscosity ratings.

1 The engine must be completely cooled down before starting this procedure, so that oil can return from the engine to the oil tank. After the engine has cooled down, run it for several minutes to warm it to normal operating temperature, let it idle for 10 seconds, shut it off and let the oil settle for several minutes. Unscrew the dipstick from the oil tank - this is a 660 . . .

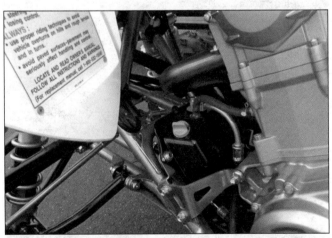

2 . . . and this is a 700. Wipe the dipstick with a clean rag and put it back in the tank (don't screw it in - just let it rest on the threads). Pull the dipstick out and check the oil level on the dipstick scale.

3 If the oil level is low on a 700, unscrew the oil filler cap. On 660 models, oil is added through the dipstick hole. Add enough oil of the specified grade and type to bring the level on the dipstick up to the upper mark. Do not overfill.

2 Coolant level check

 Warning: DO NOT remove the radiator cap while the engine is warm or scalding coolant will spray out. Let the engine cool down before removing the cap.

 Warning: Antifreeze is poisonous. Do not leave open containers of coolant about.

 Warning: Do not run the engine in an enclosed space such as a garage or workshop.

Before you start:

✔ Make sure you have a supply of coolant available (a mixture of 50% distilled water and 50% corrosion inhibited ethylene glycol antifreeze is needed).
✔ Always check the coolant level when the engine is cold.

✔ Make sure the motorcycle is on level ground while checking the coolant level.

Vehicle care:

● Use only the specified coolant mixture. It is important that antifreeze is used in the system all year round, and not just in the winter. Do not top the system up using only water, as the system will become too diluted.
● Do not overfill the reservoir tank. If the coolant is significantly above the F (full) level line at any time, the surplus should be siphoned or drained off to prevent the possibility of it being expelled out of the overflow hose.
● If the coolant level falls steadily, check the system for leaks (see Chapters 1 and 3). If no leaks are found and the level continues to fall, it is recommended that the machine is taken to a Yamaha dealer for a pressure test.

1 Check coolant level in the reservoir under the left rear fender (660) . . .

2 . . . or at the left front of the vehicle (700). It should between the Low and Full marks with the engine warmed up. If it's low, reach under the fender, pull off the cap, top off the reservoir with a 50/50 mixture of ethylene glycol-based antifreeze and distilled water, then reinstall the cap.

3 Brake fluid level check

> **⚠ Warning: Brake fluid can harm your eyes and damage painted or some plastic surfaces, so use extreme caution when handling and pouring it and cover surrounding surfaces with rag. Do not use fluid that has been standing open for some time, as it absorbs moisture from the air which can cause a dangerous loss of braking effectiveness.**

Before you start:

✔ Make sure the vehicle is on level ground.
✔ Make sure you have the correct brake fluid. DOT 4 is recommended. Never reuse old fluid.

✔ Wrap a rag around the reservoir to ensure that any spillage does not come into contact with painted surfaces.

Vehicle care:

● The fluid in the front or rear master cylinder reservoir will drop slightly as the brake pads wear down.

● If the fluid reservoir requires repeated topping-up this is an indication of a hydraulic leak somewhere in the system, which should be investigated immediately.

● Check for signs of fluid leakage from the hydraulic hoses and components – if found, rectify immediately.

● Check the operation of the front and rear brakes before taking the machine on the road; if there is evidence of air in the system (spongy feel to lever), it must be bled as described in Chapter 7.

1 With the front brake reservoir as level as possible, check that the fluid level is above the LOWER line next to the inspection window. If the level is below the LOWER line, remove the cover screws (arrows) and lift off the cover and diaphragm. Top up fluid to the upper level line; don't overfill the reservoir, and take care to avoid spills (see WARNING above). Compress the diaphragm, reinstall the diaphragm and cover, and tighten the cover screws securely.

2 On 660 models, check rear brake fluid level through the translucent reservoir. It should be between the upper and lower lines. If it's low, unbolt the protective cover for access to the reservoir cap. Add the specified brake fluid until the level is up to the upper line on the reservoir, then install the cap and tighten it securely.

3 On 700 models, remove the seat. Remove the screw and bolt that secure the rear portion of the fender and pull it out slightly for access to the reservoir. If the level is below the lower line, unscrew the cap and lift it off. Add the specified brake fluid until the level is up to the upper line on the reservoir, then install the cap and tighten it securely. Install the fender fasteners and seat.

3 Tire checks

The correct pressures:

● The tires must be checked when **cold**, not immediately after riding. Note that low tire pressures may cause the tire to slip on the rim or come off. High tire pressures will cause abnormal tread wear and unsafe handling.
● Use an accurate pressure gauge. Clean any dirt from the gauge and tire valve before measuring.
● Proper air pressure will increase tire life and provide maximum stability and ride comfort.

Tire care:

● Check the tires carefully for cuts, tears, embedded nails or other sharp objects and excessive wear. Operation of the motorcycle with excessively worn tires is extremely hazardous, as traction and handling are directly affected.
● Check the condition of the tire valve and ensure the dust cap is in place.
● Pick out any stones or nails which may have become embedded in the tire tread. If left, they will eventually penetrate through the casing and cause a puncture.
● If tire damage is apparent, or unexplained loss of pressure is experienced, seek the advice of a tire fitting specialist without delay.

Tire tread depth:

The minimum tread depth for these vehicles is 3 mm (1/8 inch). To maintain good performance and handling, check the profile of the knobs on the tires as well as the tread depth.

When the knobs begin to get excessively rounded on their edges, the tire should be replaced.

Tire pressures

Standard	4.0 psi (27.5 kPa)
Minimum	3.6 psi (24.5 kPa)
Maximum	4.4 psi (30.5 kPa)*

Yamaha specifies a maximum pressure for 660 models only.

1 Unscrew the cap from the tire valve and measure air pressure with a gauge designed for the low pressures used in ATV tires

2 Measure tread depth with a depth gauge or tape measure

Chapter 1
Tune-up and routine maintenance

Contents

Degrees of difficulty

Easy, suitable for novice with little experience

Fairly easy, suitable for beginner with some experience

Fairly difficult, suitable for competent DIY mechanic

Difficult, suitable for experienced DIY mechanic

Very difficult, suitable for expert DIY or professional

Specifications

660 models

Engine

Spark plug
- Type ... NGK DPR8EA-9
- Gap ... 0.8 to 0.9 mm (0.031 to 0.035 inch)

Valve clearance
- Intake ... 0.10 to 0.15 mm (0.004 to 0.006 inch)
- Exhaust ... 0.15 to 0.20 mm (0.006 to 0.008 inch)

Engine idle speed ... 1450 to 1550 rpm

Chassis

Brake pad thickness (limit) ... 1.0 mm (0.04 inch)
Front brake lever freeplay ... Zero
Rear brake pedal height ... 4 mm (0.16 inch) below footpeg
Throttle lever freeplay ... 3 to 5 mm (0.12 to 0.20 inch)
Clutch lever freeplay ... 5 to 10 mm (0.20 to 0.39 inch)
Drive chain slack ... 30 to 45 mm (1.18 to 1.77 inches)
Speed limiter screw setting ... Do not back out more than 12 mm (0.47 inch)
Minimum tire tread depth ... See "Daily (pre-ride) checks"
Tire pressures (cold) ... See "Daily (pre-ride) checks"
Front wheel toe-in ... 0 to 10 mm (0 to 0.4 inch)

Torque specifications

Coolant drain bolt	10 Nm (84 inch-lbs)
Oil drain bolt	
Crankcase	30 Nm (22 ft-lbs)
Oil tank	25 Nm (18 ft-lbs)
Oil pressure check bolt	7 Nm (61 inch-lbs)
Oil filter cartridge	17 Nm (144 inch-lbs)
Spark plugs	13 Nm (113 inch-lbs)
Tie rod locknuts	
660	15 Nm (11 ft-lbs)
700	18 Nm (13 ft-lbs)

Recommended lubricants and fluids

Engine oil	
Type	Yamalube 4-CW or Yamalube 4 or equivalent API Service SG or higher, meeting JASO Standard MA*
Viscosity	
50-degrees F (10-degrees C) or above	20W-50
10-degrees to 110-degrees F (-10 to 40-degrees C)	10W-40
30-degrees F (0-degrees C) or below	5W-30
Capacity	
At oil change (without filter replacement)	1.9 liters (2.01 quarts)
At oil change (with filter replacement)	1.95 liters (2.06 quarts)
After engine overhaul	2.3 liters (2.43 quarts)
Air filter oil	Yamaha foam air filter oil, or 10W-30 engine oil
Cooling system	
System capacity	1.3 liters (1.37 quarts)
Reservoir tank capacity	0.29 liter (0.31 quart)
Miscellaneous	
Wheel bearings	Medium weight, lithium-based multi-purpose grease
Swingarm pivot bearings	Medium weight, lithium-based multi-purpose grease
Steering shaft bushings	Medium weight, lithium-based multi-purpose grease
Cables and lever pivots	Medium weight, lithium-based multi-purpose grease
Brake pedal/shift lever/throttle lever pivots	Medium weight, lithium-based multi-purpose grease

To avoid clutch slippage, do not use oils rated diesel CD or Energy Conserving II.

700 models

Engine

Spark plug	
Type	NGK CR8E
Gap	0.6 to 0.7 mm (0.024 to 0.028 inch)
Valve clearance	
Intake	0.09 to 0.13 mm (0.0035 to 0.0051 inch)
Exhaust	0.16 to 0.20 mm (0.0063 to 0.0079 inch)
Engine idle speed	1500 to 1700 rpm

Chassis

Brake pad thickness (limit)	1.0 mm (0.03 inch)
Front brake lever freeplay	Zero
Throttle lever freeplay	2 to 4 mm (0.08 to 0.16 inch)
Clutch lever freeplay	5 to 10 mm (0.20 to 0.39 inch)
Drive chain slack	25 to 35 mm (1.0 to 1.38 inches)
Speed limiter screw setting	Do not back out more than 12 mm (0.47 inch)
Minimum tire tread depth	See "Daily (pre-ride) checks"
Tire pressures (cold)	See "Daily (pre-ride) checks"
Front wheel toe-in	2 to 12 mm (0.08 to 0.47 inch)

Torque specifications

Coolant drain bolt	10 Nm (84 inch-lbs)
Oil drain bolt	
Crankcase	23 Nm (17 ft-lbs)
Oil tank	19 Nm (168 inch-lbs)
Oil pressure check bolt	10 Nm (84 inch-lbs)
Oil filter drain and cover bolts	10 Nm (84 inch-lbs)
Spark plugs	13 Nm (113 inch-lbs)
Tie rod locknuts	18 Nm (13 ft-lbs)

Recommended lubricants and fluids

Engine oil
   Type .... Yamalube 4 or equivalent API Service SG or higher, meeting JASO Standard MA*

   Viscosity
      50-degrees F (10-degrees C) or above 20W-50
      10-degrees to 110-degrees F (-10 to 40-degrees C) 10W-40
      30-degrees F (0-degrees C) or below... 5W-30
   Capacity
      At oil change (without filter replacement) .... 1.75 liters (1.85 quarts)
      At oil change (with filter replacement) .... 1.85 liters (1.96 quarts)
Air filter oil.. Yamaha foam air filter oil or equivalent
Cooling system
   System capacity .... 1.61 liters (1.7 quarts)
   Reservoir tank capacity .... 0.25 liter (0.26 quart)
Miscellaneous
   Wheel bearings .... Medium weight, lithium-based multi-purpose grease
   Swingarm pivot bearings .... Medium weight, lithium-based multi-purpose grease
   Steering shaft bushings .... Medium weight, lithium-based multi-purpose grease
   Cables and lever pivots.. Medium weight, lithium-based multi-purpose grease
   Brake pedal/shift lever/throttle lever pivots .... Medium weight, lithium-based multi-purpose grease

*To avoid clutch slippage, do not use oils rated diesel CD or Energy Conserving II, and do not use chemical additives.

Right side maintenance points

1	Front brake fluid reservoir	
2	Front tire valve	
3	Front suspension grease points (three; behind wheel)	
4	Water pump weep hole	
5	Rear brake light switch adjuster	
6	Rear brake pedal height adjuster	

1   Front brake fluid reservoir
2   Front tire valve
3   Front suspension grease points (three; behind wheel)
4   Water pump weep hole
5   Rear brake light switch adjuster
6   Rear brake pedal height adjuster

7   Rear tire valve
8   Parking brake cable adjuster
9   Spark arrester (inside muffler)
10 Battery (under seat)
11 Rear brake fluid reservoir (under seat on 700 models); 660 reservoir behind external cover)

12 Clutch cable mid-line adjuster
13 Spark plug (700 shown; 660 at front of engine)
14 Throttle lever
15 Oil filter (700 shown; 660 has an external filter in the same location)

Left side maintenance points

1   Clutch lever adjuster
2   Air filter (under seat)
3   Coolant reservoir location (660 models)
4   Drive chain
5   Engine oil filler cap/dipstick (700 shown; 660 on opposite side)
6   Coolant reservoir (700 models)
7   Headlight adjuster (left side shown; right similar)

1 Routine maintenance intervals

Note: *The pre-ride inspection outlined in the owner's manual covers checks and maintenance that should be carried out on a daily basis. It's condensed and included here to remind you of its importance. Always perform the pre-ride inspection at every maintenance interval (in addition to the procedures listed). The intervals listed below are the shortest intervals recommended by the manufacturer for each particular operation during the model years covered in this manual. Your owner's manual may have different intervals for your model.*

Daily or before riding

- [ ] Check the operation of both brakes - check the brake lever and pedal for correct freeplay
- [ ] Check the throttle for smooth operation and correct freeplay
- [ ] Make sure the engine kill switch works correctly
- [ ] Check the tires for damage, the presence of foreign objects and correct air pressure
- [ ] Check the engine oil level
- [ ] Check the fuel level and inspect for leaks
- [ ] Check the air cleaner drain tube and clean it if necessary
- [ ] If the drain tube is clogged, clean the air filter element
- [ ] Inspect the drive chain
- [ ] Make sure the steering operates smoothly
- [ ] Verify that the headlight and taillight are operating satisfactorily
- [ ] Check all fasteners, including wheel nuts and axle nuts, for tightness
- [ ] Check the underbody for mud or debris that could start a fire or interfere with vehicle operation

Every 20 to 40 operating hours

- [ ] Clean the air filter element and replace it if necessary*

More often in dusty or wet conditions.

Every three months

- [ ] Clean and gap and, if necessary, replace the spark plug
- [ ] Check idle speed and adjust it if necessary
- [ ] Inspect the fuel tap (carbureted models) and fuel line (all models)
- [ ] Inspect the front and rear brake discs
- [ ] Check brake operation and brake lever and pedal freeplay
- [ ] Lubricate and inspect the drive chain, sprockets and rollers
- [ ] Check all chassis fasteners for tightness
- [ ] Inspect the front and rear suspension
- [ ] Lubricate the rear suspension linkage
- [ ] Check steering system operation and freeplay
- [ ] Inspect the cooling system
- [ ] Check the throttle for smooth operation and correct freeplay
- [ ] Lubricate the cables and lever pivot points

Every six months

- [ ] Check valve clearance and adjust it if necessary
- [ ] Check the exhaust system for leaks and check fastener tightness
- [ ] Change the engine oil and filter
- [ ] Clean the spark arrester
- [ ] Check choke operation (carbureted models)
- [ ] Check the clutch for smooth operation and correct lever freeplay
- [ ] Lubricate the steering shaft and front suspension
- [ ] Inspect the wheels and tires
- [ ] Check the wheel bearings for looseness or damage
- [ ] Check the skid plates for looseness or damage

Every 18 months

- [ ] Replace the spark plug

2.1 Decals on the vehicle include maintenance and safety information

4.4 Press the brake pedal to bring the pads out where you can see the friction material - replace the pads if they're worn to or near the wear indicators

2 Introduction to tune-up and routine maintenance

This Chapter covers in detail the checks and procedures necessary for the tune-up and routine maintenance of your vehicle. Section 1 includes the routine maintenance schedule, which is designed to keep the machine in proper running condition and prevent possible problems. The remaining Sections contain detailed procedures for carrying out the items listed on the maintenance schedule, as well as additional maintenance information designed to increase reliability. Maintenance information is also printed on decals, which are mounted in various locations on the vehicle (see illustration). Where information on the decals differs from that presented in this Chapter, use the decal information.

Since routine maintenance plays such an important role in the safe and efficient operation of your vehicle, it is presented here as a comprehensive check list. These lists outline the procedures and checks that should be done on a routine basis.

Deciding where to start or plug into the routine maintenance schedule depends on several factors. If you have a vehicle whose warranty has recently expired, and if it has been maintained according to the warranty standards, you may want to pick up routine maintenance as it coincides with the next mileage or calendar interval. If you have owned the machine for some time but have never performed any maintenance on it, then you may want to start at the nearest interval and include some additional pro-

cedures to ensure that nothing important is overlooked. If you have just had a major engine overhaul, then you may want to start the maintenance routine from the beginning. If you have a used machine and have no knowledge of its history or maintenance record, you may desire to combine all the checks into one large service initially and then settle into the maintenance schedule prescribed.

The Sections that describe the inspection and maintenance procedures are written as step-by-step comprehensive guides to the actual performance of the work. They explain in detail each of the routine inspections and maintenance procedures on the check list. References to additional information in applicable Chapters is also included and should not be overlooked.

Before beginning any actual maintenance or repair, the machine should be cleaned thoroughly, especially around the oil filler plug, spark plug, engine covers, carburetor or throttle body, etc. Cleaning will help ensure that dirt does not contaminate the engine and will allow you to detect wear and damage that could otherwise easily go unnoticed.

3 Fluid levels - check

Check, and if necessary, top up, the front brake fluid, rear brake fluid, engine oil and coolant as described in "Daily (pre-ride) checks" at the front of this manual.

4 Brake system - general check

1   Always inspect the brakes before riding! A routine pre-ride general check will ensure that problems are discovered and remedied before they become dangerous.
2   Inspect the brake lever and pedal for loose pivots, excessive play, bending, cracking and other damage. Replace any damaged parts (see Chapter 7). Make sure all brake fasteners are tight.
3   Squeeze the front brake lever so that the brake pads protrude from the calipers and look at the wear indicators. If the pad material has been worn down so that the wear indicators touch the disc - or are getting close to the disc - it's time for new pads (see Chapter 7).
4   Depress the rear brake pedal so that the pads protrude from the caliper and look at the wear indicators (see illustration). Again, if the pad material is worn down so that the indicators are at or near the disc, install new pads (see Chapter 7).
5   If you have difficulty determining whether the pads are excessively worn because the wear indicator is hard to see (or you have aftermarket pads that don't have any kind of indicator), remove the pads (see Chapter 7), measure the thickness of the pads and compare your measurements to the pad thickness limits listed in this Chapter's Specifications.
6   Verify that the parking brake system will hold the vehicle on an incline. If it won't, adjust the parking brake (see Chapter 7).
7   These vehicles are equipped with a brake light which is activated by a brake light

4.7a The front brake light switch (lower arrow) can't be adjusted, but lever position on 700 models can - loosen the locknut (upper left) and turn the adjuster (upper right) to change lever position

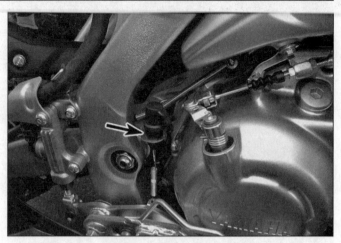

4.7b The brake light switch is adjusted by turning the adjusting nut

switch at the front brake lever or rear brake pedal **(see illustrations)**. Make sure that the brake light works when the lever or pedal is applied (it should come on just before the brake begins to work). The front brake light switch is not adjustable. If it doesn't activate the brake light, check the switch and brake light circuit (see Chapter 5). If the brake pedal doesn't activate the brake light, adjust the switch. To do this, hold the body of the brake light switch so that it doesn't turn, and rotate the switch adjusting nut as necessary.

5	Brake levers and pedal - check and adjustment

Front brake lever freeplay

1   Operate the brake lever and measure freeplay at the tip of the lever **(see illustration 4.7a)**. There shouldn't be any (zero freeplay). If there is freeplay, bleed the front

brakes (see Chapter 7). If this doesn't work, check the master cylinder and calipers for wear and check the brake lines for leaks (see Chapter 7). Front brake freeplay is not adjustable.
2   The position of the front brake lever can be adjusted to suit rider preference. To make the adjustment, loosen the adjuster locknut **(see illustration 4.7a)** while pushing the brake lever toward the front of the vehicle. While holding pressure on the lever, turn the adjusting bolt until the lever is where you want it to be.
3   Tighten the adjuster locknut securely and recheck the lever position.

Rear brake pedal height

4   The upper side of the rear brake pedal should be the specified distance (listed in this Chapter's Specifications) below the top of the footpeg **(see illustration)**.
5   If the pedal height is incorrect, loosen the locknut on the adjusting bolt **(see illustration)**. Turn the adjusting bolt to obtain the

correct pedal height, then tighten the locknut.

Caution: The distance between the locknut and the hex on the adjusting bolt must not exceed the value listed in this Chapter's Specifications. If it does, check the master cylinder and pedal for wear.

6   After making the adjustment, jack up the rear of the vehicle, spin the rear wheels and check for brake drag. If the brake drags, repeat the height adjustment.

Parking brake lever

7   With the parking brake released, measure the length of the cable between the measurement points **(see illustrations)**. If it's not within the range listed in this Chapter's Specifications, adjust it as described below.

Early 660 models

8   These vehicles have a parking brake cable adjuster at the handlebar lever, next to the clutch cable adjuster.
9   Loosen the locknut on the adjusting bolt

5.4 Measure brake pedal height from the top of the footpeg to the top of the pedal

5.5 Loosen the locknut and turn the adjusting bolt to adjust pedal height

5.7a Parking brake cable details (early 660 models)

A   Adjusting bolt
B   Locknut
C   Cable length
     measurement points

5.7b Parking brake cable measurement points -
late 660 and 700 (700 shown)

5.10a At the handlebar on early 660
models, pull back the cover from the
parking brake and clutch
cable adjusters . . .

5.10b . . . loosen the adjuster locknut and
turn the adjusters to change
cable freeplay

A   Clutch cable adjuster locknut
B   Clutch cable adjuster
C   Parking brake cable adjuster locknut
D   Parking brake cable adjuster

5.16 The parking brake cable adjuster is
on the right side of the swingarm; loosen
the locknut (lower arrow), hold the cable
end (upper right arrow) with a wrench and
turn the adjuster (upper left arrow)

at the parking brake lever on the rear caliper **(see illustration 5.7a)**.

10   Pull back the rubber cover for access to the parking brake cable adjuster at the handlebar lever **(see illustrations)**.

11   Loosen the adjuster locknut, turn the adjuster to obtain the specified cable length measurement at the rear caliper, then tighten the locknut.

12   At the caliper, turn the adjusting bolt in until it feels tight, then back it out 1/8 turn and tighten the locknut.

13   At the handlebar cable adjuster, slide the cover back over the adjuster.

14   After making the adjustment, jack up the rear of the vehicle, spin the rear wheels and check for brake drag. If the brake drags, repeat the height adjustment.

Late 660 and all 700 models

15   These vehicles do not have a cable adjuster at the parking brake lever on the handlebar.

16   Locate the mid-line adjuster in the parking brake cable on the right side of the vehicle **(see illustration)**. Pull the cover toward the front of the vehicle to expose the adjuster. Loosen the adjuster locknut, turn the adjuster to obtain the specified cable length at the caliper **(see illustration 5.7b)**, then tighten the locknut.

17   At the mid-line cable adjuster, slide the cover back over the adjuster.

18   After making the adjustment, jack up the rear of the vehicle, spin the rear wheels and check for brake drag. If the brake drags, repeat the height adjustment.

6   Steering system - inspection and toe-in adjustment

Inspection

1   These vehicles are equipped with bearings at the upper and lower ends of the steering shaft. These can become dented, rough or loose during normal use of the machine. In extreme cases, worn or loose parts can cause steering wobble that is potentially dangerous.

2   To check, block the rear wheels so the vehicle can't roll, jack up the front end and support it securely on jackstands.

3   Point the wheel straight ahead and slowly move the handlebar from side-to-side. Dents or roughness in the bearing will

6.11a Loosen the locknuts at the tie rod inner ends . . .

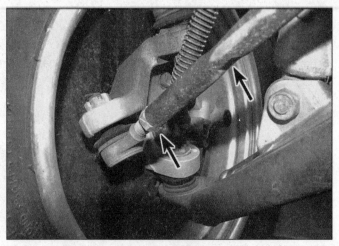

6.11b . . . and at the outer ends (left arrow); use a wrench on the flat (right arrow) to hold and turn the tie rod

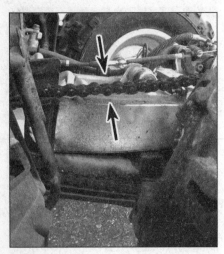

8.3 Measure drive chain slack along the upper chain run

be felt and the bars will not move smoothly. **Note:** *Make sure any hesitation in movement is not being caused by the cables and wiring harnesses that run to the handlebar.*

4   If the handlebar doesn't move smoothly, or if it has excessive lateral play, remove and inspect the steering shaft bushings (see Chapter 6).

5   Look at the tie-rod ends (inner and outer) while slowly turning the handlebar from side-to-side. If there's any vertical movement in the tie-rod balljoints, replace them (see Chapter 6).

Toe-in adjustment

6   Roll the vehicle forward onto a level surface and stop it with the front wheels pointing straight ahead.

7   Make a mark at the front and center of each tire, even with the centerline of the front hub.

8   Measure the distance between the marks with a toe-in gauge or steel tape measure.

9   Have an assistant push the vehicle backward while you watch the marks on the tires. Stop pushing when the tires have rotated exactly one-half turn, so the marks are at the backs of the tires.

10   Again, measure the distance between the marks. Subtract the front measurement from the rear measurement to get toe-in.

11   If toe-in is not as specified in this Chapter's Specifications, hold each tie-rod with a wrench on the flats and loosen the locknuts **(see illustrations)**. Turn the tie-rods an equal amount to change toe-in. When toe-in is set correctly, tighten the locknuts to the torque listed in this Chapter's Specifications.

7 Suspension - check

1   The suspension components must be maintained in top operating condition to ensure rider safety. Loose, worn or damaged suspension parts decrease the vehicle's stability and control.

2   Lock the front brake and push on the handlebars to compress the front shock absorbers several times. See if they move up-and-down smoothly without binding. If binding is felt, the shocks should be inspected (see Chapter 6).

3   Check the tightness of all front suspension nuts and bolts to be sure none have worked loose.

4   Inspect the rear shock absorber for fluid leakage and tightness of the mounting nuts and bolts. If leakage is found, the shock should be replaced.

5   Raise the rear of the vehicle and support it securely on jackstands. Grab the swingarm on each side, just ahead of the axle. Rock the swingarm from side to side - there should be no discernible movement at the rear. If there's a little movement or a

slight clicking can be heard, make sure the swingarm pivot shaft is tight. If the pivot shaft is tight but movement is still noticeable, the swingarm will have to be removed and the bearings replaced (see Chapter 6).

6   Inspect the tightness of the rear suspension nuts and bolts.

8 Drive chain and sprockets - check, adjustment and lubrication

1   A neglected drive chain won't last long and can quickly damage the sprockets. Routine chain adjustment isn't difficult and will ensure maximum chain and sprocket life.

2   To check the chain, support the vehicle securely on jackstands with the rear wheels off the ground. Place the transmission in neutral.

3   Push down and pull up on the top run of the chain and measure the slack midway between the two sprockets **(see illustration)**, then compare the measurements to the value listed in this Chapter's Specifications. As wear occurs, the chain will actually stretch, which means adjustment is necessary to remove some slack from the chain. In some cases where lubrication has been neglected, corrosion and galling may cause the links to bind and kink, which effectively shortens the chain's length. If the chain is tight between the sprockets, rusty or kinked, it's time to replace it with a new one. **Note:** *Repeat the chain slack measurement along the length of the chain - ideally, every inch or so. If you find a tight area, mark it with felt pen or paint and repeat the measurement after the machine has been ridden. If the chain's still tight in the same areas, it may be damaged or worn. Because a tight or kinked chain can damage the transmission countershaft bearing, it's a good idea to replace it.*

4   Check the entire length of the chain for

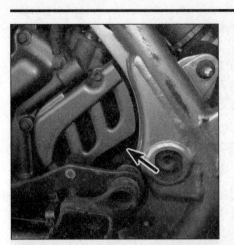

8.5a Inspect the front sprocket teeth for excessive wear; on 600 models, you can get a good view of the sprocket from behind the cover . . .

8.5b . . . and on 700 models, look through the slots in the cover - make sure there's no play in the sprocket

8.6a Check the chain upper roller and slider . . .

damaged rollers or O-rings, loose links and loose pins.

5   Look through the slots in the engine sprocket cover and inspect the engine sprocket **(see illustrations)**. Check the teeth on the engine sprocket and the rear sprocket for wear (see Chapter 6). Refer to Chapter 6 for the sprocket replacement procedure if the sprockets appear to be worn excessively. **Note:** *Never install a new chain on old sprockets and never use the old chain if you install new sprockets - replace the chain and sprockets as a set.*

6   Check the chain roller and slider **(see illustrations)**. If a roller or slider is worn, replace it (see Chapter 6).

Adjustment

7   Rotate the rear wheels until the chain is positioned with the least amount of slack present.

8   On 660 models model, loosen the upper and lower rear hub bolt nuts **(see illustrations)**. Loosen the adjusting bolt locknuts **(see illustration)** and turn the adjusting

8.6b . . . and the lower roller (660 shown)

bolt on each side of the swingarm evenly until the proper chain tension is obtained **(see illustration)**. Turn the adjusters evenly to keep the wheel in alignment, using the indicator scales stamped into the hub to make

8.8a Loosen the upper hub nut (accessible through holes in the brake disc) and bolt

sure they're set evenly **(see illustration)**. If the adjusters reach the end of their travel, the chain is excessively worn and should be replaced with a new one (see Chapter 6).

8.8b Loosen the lower hub nut and bolt (accessible though the brake disc)

8.8c Loosen the locknuts and turn the adjusting bolts to set chain tension

8.8d Use the chain adjuster marks to set the adjusters evenly

8.9a Loosen the hub pinch bolts (outer two bolts first, then the inner two)

8.9b Insert a rod (a Phillips screwdriver will work) into one of the three adjusting holes (hidden behind the sprocket) and roll the vehicle to turn the hub inside the swingarm and adjust chain slack

9   On 700 models, loosen the pinch bolts at the rear edge of the swingarm **(see illustration)**. Loosen the outer two bolts first, then loosen the inner two. Insert a rod into one of the holes in the hub from the left side, through the sprocket (there are three holes) **(see illustration)**. The rod will lock the hub to the sprocket so they rotate together. Make sue the transmission is in Neutral, then pull or push the vehicle to rotate the hub inside the swingarm (the hub is an eccentric shape, so rotating it will change the drive chain slack). Once the slack is adjusted correctly, remove the rod and tighten the pinch bolts. Tighten the inner two bolts first, then the outer two.

Lubrication

Note: *If the chain is dirty, it should be removed and cleaned before it's lubricated (see Chapter 6).*
10   The best time to lubricate the chain is after the vehicle has been ridden. When the chain is warm, the lubricant will penetrate the joints between the side plates to provide lubrication. Yamaha specifies SAE 30 to 50 engine oil only; do not use chain lube, which may contain solvents that can damage the chain's rubber O-rings. Apply the oil to the area where the side plates overlap - not to the middle of the rollers.
11   Apply the lubricant along the top of the lower chain run, so that when the machine is ridden centrifugal force will move the lubricant into the chain, rather than throwing it off.
12   After applying the lubricant, let it soak in a few minutes before wiping off any excess.

9   Tires/wheels - general check

1   Routine tire and wheel checks should be made with the realization that your safety depends to a great extent on their condition.
2   Check the tires carefully for cuts, tears, embedded nails or other sharp objects and excessive wear. Operation of the vehicle with excessively worn tires is extremely hazardous, as traction and handling are directly affected. Measure the tread depth at the center of the tire and replace worn tires with new ones when the tread depth is less than that listed in this Chapter's Specifications.
3   Repair or replace punctured tires as soon as damage is noted. Do not try to patch a torn tire, as wheel balance and tire reliability may be impaired.
4   Check the tire pressures when the tires are cold and keep them properly inflated; see "Daily (pre-ride) checks" at the front of this manual. Proper air pressure will increase tire life and provide maximum stability and ride comfort. Keep in mind that low tire pressures may cause the tire to slip on the rim or come off, while high tire pressures will cause abnormal tread wear and unsafe handling.

Caution: ATV tires operate at very low pressures. Over-inflation may rupture them.

5   Make sure the tires are installed on the correct side of the vehicle. ATV tires are directional; that is, they are designed to rotate in only one forward direction. The direction of forward rotation is indicated by an arrow molded into the tire sidewall **(see illustration)**.

Caution: On these vehicles, it's possible to install one or more wheels with the inner side out, so that even if the tire is mounted correctly on the wheel, it will rotate backwards when the vehicle is ridden. The tire inflation valves face outward when the wheels are installed correctly.

6   The wheels used on this machine are virtually maintenance free, but they should be kept clean and checked periodically for

9.5a Be sure the directional arrow points in the forward rotating direction of the tire

9.5b Some tires also have words such as THIS SIDE FACING OUTWARDS to indicate the side that faces away from the vehicle

10.3 Rock the wheel and tire from side-to-side to check wheel bearing play

11.3 Lubricating a cable with a pressure lube adapter (make sure the tool seats around the inner cable)

cracks, bending and rust. Never attempt to repair damaged wheels; they must be replaced with new ones.

7   Check the valve stem locknuts to make sure they're tight. Also, make sure the valve stem cap is in place and tight. If it is missing, install a new one made of metal or hard plastic.

10 Front wheel bearings - check

1   Raise the front of the vehicle and support it securely on jackstands.
2   Spin the front wheels by hand. Listen for noise, which indicates dry or worn wheel bearings.
3   Grasp the top and bottom of the tire and try to rock it back-and-forth (see illustration). If there's more than a very small amount of play, the wheel bearings are in need of adjustment or replacement. Refer to Chapter 7 for service procedures.

11 Lubrication - general

1   Since the controls, cables and various other components of an ATV are exposed to the elements, they should be lubricated periodically to ensure safe and trouble-free operation.
2   The throttle lever, brake levers and brake pedal should be lubricated frequently. Yamaha recommends 10W-30 motor oil inside cables and for the pivot points of levers and pedals. Multi-purpose lithium grease is recommended for cable ends and other lubrication points, such as suspension and steering bushings. In order for the lubricant to be applied where it will do the most good, the component should be disassembled. However, if chain and cable lubricant is being used, it can be applied to the pivot joint gaps and will usually work its way into the areas where friction occurs. If motor oil or light grease is being used, apply it spar-

ingly as it may attract dirt (which could cause the controls to bind or wear at an accelerated rate). **Note:** *One of the best lubricants for the control lever pivots is a dry-film lubricant (available from many sources by different names).*
3   The throttle and clutch cables should be removed and treated with a commercially available cable lubricant which is specially formulated for use on ATV control cables. Small adapters for pressure lubricating the cables with spray can lubricants are available and ensure that the cable is lubricated along its entire length (see illustration). When attaching a cable to its handlebar lever, lubricate the barrel-shaped fitting at the end with multi-purpose grease.
4   To lubricate the cables, disconnect one end, then lubricate the cable with a pressure lube adapter (see illustration 11.3) (clutch cable, see Chapter 2A; throttle cable, see Chapter 4).
5   Refer to Chapter 6 for the following lubrication procedures:

  a) *Steering shaft bushings*
  b) *Swingarm bearings and dust seals*

6   Refer to Chapter 7 for the following lubrication procedures:

  a) *Rear brake pedal pivot*
  b) *Front wheel bearings*

7   Using a grease gun, lubricate the front and rear suspension bushings through the grease nipples (see illustrations).

12 Fasteners - check

1   Since vibration of the machine tends to loosen fasteners, all nuts, bolts, screws, etc. should be periodically checked for proper tightness. Also make sure all cotter pins or other safety fasteners are correctly installed.
2   Pay particular attention to the following:
    Spark plug(s)

11.7a There are three grease fittings on each pair of front suspension arms

11.7b The rear suspension has two grease fitting accessible from above . . .

11.7c . . . and a third fitting at the pivot point of the suspension linkage and frame

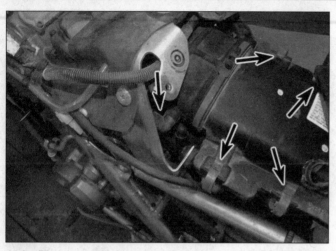

14.2a Disconnect the hose from the intake duct, release the clips and lift the cover off the air cleaner housing (660 models)

14.2b Remove the housing together with the intake duct; turn the retainer 1/4-turn and remove the cap from the rear end of the filter (660 models)

14.3a The OUT SIDE marking on the cap faces away from the filter when the cap is installed (660 models)

Engine oil drain plug
Gearshift pedal
Brake pedal
Footpegs
Engine mount bolts
Shock absorber mount bolts
Front axle nuts
Rear axle nuts
Skid plate bolts

3   If a torque wrench is available, use it along with the torque specifications at the beginning of this, or other, Chapters.

13 Skid plates - check

1   Check the skid plates under the vehicle for damage (see Chapter 8). Have damaged plates repaired, or else replace them.

2   Make sure the skid plate fasteners are all in position and tightly secured.

14 Air filter element and drain tube - cleaning

Element removal

1   Remove the seat (see Chapter 8).

660 models

2   Pull back the four cover clips (see illustration). Disconnect the breather hose from the left side of the air cleaner intake nozzle and lift the cover off (see illustration).
3   Twist the retainer 1/4 turn and remove the cap from the air filter element (see illustration). Remove the air filter element (see illustration) and separate the element from the element guide (see illustration).

14.3b Lift the air filter out of the air cleaner housing (660 models)

14.3c Separate the filter element from the guide (660 models)

14.4 Remove the clips and lift the air filter cover off the housing (700 models)

14.5 Turn the wing bolt 1/4 turn, pull the filter to the rear and lift it out, then separate the filter from its frame (700 models)

700 models

4   Pull back the cover clips **(see illustration)**.
5   Unscrew the wing bolt until it's loose **(see illustration)**. Lift the filter element and wing bolt out of the air filter housing together, then separate the bolt, filter element and frame.

Element cleaning and installation

6   Clean the element and guide in a high flash point solvent, squeeze the solvent out of the foam and let the guide and element dry completely.
7   Soak the foam element in the foam filter oil listed in this Chapter's Specifications, then squeeze it firmly to remove the excess oil. Don't wring it out or the foam may be damaged. The element should be thoroughly oil-soaked, but not dripping.
8   Reassemble the element and guide.
9   Installation is the reverse of removal.

Drain tube cleaning

10   Check the air cleaner housing drain tube for accumulated water and oil **(see illustration)**. If oil or water has built up in the tube,

squeeze its clamp, remove the tube from the air cleaner housing and clean it out. Install the drain tube on the housing and secure it with the clamp. **Note:** *A drain tube that's full indicates the need to clean the filter element and the inside of the case.*

15 Fuel system - inspection

⚠️ *Warning: Gasoline is extremely flammable, so take extra precautions when you work on any part of the fuel system. Don't smoke or allow open flames or bare light bulbs near the work area, and don't work in a garage where a gas-type appliance (such as a water heater or clothes dryer) is present. Since gasoline is carcinogenic, wear fuel-resistant gloves when there's a possibility of being exposed to fuel, and if you spill any fuel on your skin, rinse it off immediately with soap and water. Mop up any fuel spills immediately and do not store fuel-soaked rags where they could ignite. When you*

perform any kind of work on the fuel system, wear safety glasses and have a fire extinguisher suitable for class B type fires (flammable liquids) on hand.

Carbureted models

1   Check the fuel tank, the fuel tap, the fuel line and the carburetors for leaks and evidence of damage **(see illustration)**.
2   If carburetor gaskets are leaking, the carburetors should be disassembled and rebuilt (see Chapter 4).
3   If the fuel tap is leaking, tightening the screws may help. If leakage persists, the tap should be disassembled and repaired or replaced with a new one.
4   If the fuel line is cracked or otherwise deteriorated, replace it with a new one.
5   Place the fuel tap lever in the Off position. Remove and drain the fuel tank. Remove the screws and detach the tap from the tank **(see illustration 15.1)**.
6   Clean the strainer with solvent and let it dry.

14.10 Check the drain tube on the underside of the air cleaner housing for accumulated water and oil

15.1 Inspect the fuel line and the fuel tap for leaks; if the fuel tap is leaking, remove its screws and separate the tap and strainer from the tank

15.8 If the vehicle will be stored for more than a month, loosen the float chamber drain screws to drain the fuel from the carburetors

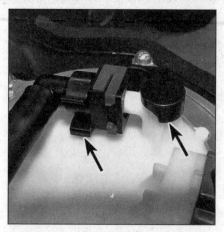

15.11a Check that the fuel line at the tank outlet is in good condition and the retaining clip is securely attached at both ends

15.11b Make sure the fuel line retainer at the fuel rail inlet is securely attached

16.1a On 660 models, work the spark plug cap back and forth to free its seal from the cylinder head . . .

16.1b . . . then twist and pull the cap to free it from the spark plug, but don't use pliers or a screwdriver

7   Installation is the reverse of removal. Use a new O-ring. Hand-tighten the screws firmly, but don't overtighten them. If you do, the

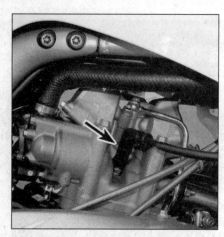

16.2 On 700 models, the spark plug cap is out in the open, on the right-hand side of the engine; twist and pull the cap to free it from the spark plug

O-ring will be distorted, which will result in fuel leaks. Run the engine and check for fuel leaks.
8   Any time the vehicle is going to be stored for a month or more, remove and drain the fuel tank. Also loosen the float chamber drain screws (in the bottom of each carburetor, facing the left-hand side of the vehicle) and let the fuel drain from the carburetors through the drain hoses **(see illustration)**.
9   Inspect the condition of the crankcase breather hose. Replace it if it's cracked, torn or deteriorated.

Fuel injected models

10   Remove the fuel tank cover (see Chapter 8).
11   Check the fuel line from the tank to the throttle body for leaks and evidence of damage **(see illustrations)**. If problems are visible, replace the line (see Chapter 4).

⚠ *Warning: Refer to precautions in Chapter 4 regarding disconnecting of fuel injection system lines before disconnecting the fuel line.*

12   Check the fuel tank breather hose that runs from the fuel filler cap to the handlebar. Replace it if it's cracked or deteriorated.
13   Inspect the condition of the crankcase breather hose. Replace it if it's cracked, torn or deteriorated.

16 Spark plug - inspection, cleaning and gapping

1   On 660 models, work the spark plug cap back and forth to free it from the valve cover, twist it to free it from the plug, then lift the spark plug cap out of the spark plug well **(see illustrations)**.
2   On 700 models, twist the spark plug cap to free it from the plug and pull it off **(see illustration)**.
3   If available, use compressed air to blow any accumulated debris from around the spark plug. Remove the plug with a spark plug socket.
4   Inspect the electrodes for wear. Both the

16.7a Spark plug manufacturers recommend using a wire type gauge when checking the gap - if the wire doesn't slide between the electrodes with a slight drag, adjustment is required

16.7b To change the gap, bend the side electrode only, and be very careful not to crack or chip the ceramic insulator surrounding the center electrode

17.3a Remove the drain plug from the bottom of the oil tank (700 shown)

center and side electrodes should have square edges and the side electrode should be of uniform thickness. Look for excessive deposits and evidence of a cracked or chipped insulator around the center electrode. Compare your spark plugs to the color spark plug reading chart on the inside back cover. Check the threads, the washer and the ceramic insulator body for cracks and other damage.

5   If the electrodes are not excessively worn, and if the deposits can be easily removed with a wire brush, the plug can be regapped and reused (if no cracks or chips are visible in the insulator). If in doubt concerning the condition of the plug, replace it with a new one, as the expense is minimal.

6   Cleaning the spark plug by sandblasting is permitted, provided you clean the plug with a high flash-point solvent afterwards.

7   Before installing a new plug, make sure it is the correct type and heat range. Check the gap between the electrodes, as it is not preset. For best results, use a wire-type gauge rather than a flat gauge to check the

gap (see illustration). If the gap must be adjusted, bend the side electrode only and be very careful not to chip or crack the insulator nose (see illustration). Make sure the washer is in place before installing the plug.

8   Since the cylinder head is made of aluminum, which is soft and easily damaged, thread the plug into the head by hand. Slip a short length of hose over the end of the plug to use as a tool to thread it into place. The hose will grip the plug well enough to turn it, but will start to slip if the plug begins to cross-thread in the hole - this will prevent damaged threads and the accompanying repair costs.

9   Once the plug is finger tight, the job can be finished with a socket. If a torque wrench is available, tighten the spark plug to the torque listed in this Chapter's Specifications. If you do not have a torque wrench, tighten the plug finger tight (until the washer bottoms on the cylinder head) then use a spark plug socket to tighten it an additional 1/4 turn. Regardless of the method used, do not over-tighten it.

10   Push the cap down onto the plug and make sure it's seated securely.

17 Engine oil and filter - change

1   Consistent routine oil and filter changes are the single most important maintenance procedure you can perform on a vehicle. The oil not only lubricates the internal parts of the engine, transmission and clutch, but it also acts as a coolant, a cleaner, a sealant and a protectant. Because of these demands, the oil takes a terrific amount of abuse and should be replaced often with new oil of the recommended grade and type.

2   Before changing the oil and filter, warm up the engine by running it for several minutes so the oil will drain easily. Be careful when draining the oil, as the exhaust pipe, the engine and the oil itself can cause severe burns.

3   Place a clean drain pan under the vehicle, positioned underneath the two drain plugs (see illustrations).

4   Remove the dipstick from the oil tank

17.3b On 660 models, the oil drain plug is on the left side of the engine, just forward of the shift pedal linkage

17.3c On 700 models, the oil drain plug is in the underside of the crankcase and can be reached through a hole in the skid plate

17.4 Remove the dipstick from the oil tank (660 shown)

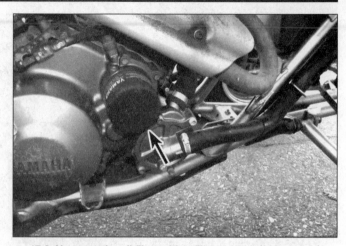

17.6 Unscrew the oil filter with a filter wrench (660 models)

17.10 Remove the lower bolt to drain the oil from the filter housing, then remove the upper bolts

to vent the crankcase and act as a reminder that there is no oil in the engine (see illustration).

5   Remove the drain plug from the engine (660 models, see illustration 17.3b; 700 models, see illustration 17.3c) and allow the oil to drain into the pan.

660 models

6   These vehicles use a screw-on cartridge oil filter, located on the right-hand side of the engine just above the water pump (see illustration).

7   Place a rag beneath the filter to catch dripping oil, then unscrew the filter from the engine, using a filter wrench if necessary.

8   Wipe any remaining oil out of the filter housing area of the crankcase and make sure the oil passage is clear. If the old filter gasket stuck to engine, remove it and thoroughly clean the gasket contact area on the engine.

9   Make sure the gasket is in place on the new filter, then coat the gasket with clean engine oil and thread the filter onto the engine fitting. Tighten it, using the filter wrench and a torque wrench, to the torque listed in this Chapter's Specifications. **Note:** *If there's a torque setting printed on the filter, use it instead.*

700 models

10   Remove the lower bolt from the oil filter cover and let the oil filter drain (see illustration).

11   Remove the remaining cover bolts, take the cover off and remove the filter element (see illustrations). If additional maintenance is planned for this time period, check or service another component while the oil is allowed to drain completely.

17.11a Remove the cover with its O-ring; the open side of the filter faces into the engine

17.11b Remove the O-ring from the lower bolt hole and the rubber washer from the inside of the filter housing

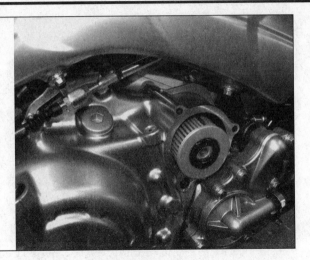

17.14 The open end of the filter element goes into the engine first; the closed end (with attached rubber washer) faces outward

be disposed of. Check with your local refuse disposal company, disposal facility or environmental agency to see if they will accept the oil for recycling. Some disposals companies provide containers that you can put the oil in for recycling, as well as disposal bags for used filters. Don't pour used oil into drains or onto the ground. After the oil has cooled, it can be drained into a suitable container (capped plastic jugs, topped bottles, milk cartons, etc.) for transport to one of these disposal sites.

18 Cooling system - inspection and coolant change

12 Wipe any remaining oil out of the filter housing area of the crankcase and make sure the oil passage is clear.
13 Check the condition of the filter plug threads and the O-rings.
14 Install the filter element with its closed end facing out (see illustration).

Caution: The filter must be installed facing the correct direction or oil starvation may cause severe engine damage.

15 Install the cover with a new O-ring and tighten the bolts to the torque listed in this Chapter's Specifications.

All models

16 Before refilling the engine, check the old oil carefully. If the oil was drained into a clean pan, small pieces of metal or other material can be easily detected. Also check the filter - foreign material can become trapped in it. If the oil is very metallic colored, then the engine is experiencing wear from break-in (new engine) or from insufficient lubrication. If there are flakes or chips of metal in the oil, then something is drastically wrong internally and the engine will have to be disassembled

for inspection and repair.
17 If there are pieces of fiber-like material in the oil, the clutch is experiencing excessive wear and should be checked. Black, fine-grained material in the oil or trapped in the filter may indicate burned clutch plates from excessive slippage.
18 If the inspection of the oil turns up nothing unusual, refill the crankcase to the proper level with the recommended oil and install the dipstick/filler cap.
19 Start the engine and let it run for two or three minutes. Shut it off, wait a few minutes, then check the oil level. If necessary, add more oil to bring the level up to the upper level mark on the dipstick. Check around the drain plugs and filter canister (660 models) or filter cover (700 models) for leaks.
20 Loosen the oil gallery plug on the cylinder head slightly (see illustrations). Start the engine and let it idle. Oil should seep from the plug within one minute. If not, oil is not flowing properly. Shut the engine off and find the problem before running it further. Make sure the oil filter is installed in the proper direction.
21 The old oil drained from the engine cannot be reused in its present state and should

Inspection

1 The cooling system should be carefully inspected at the recommended intervals. Look for evidence of leaks, check the condition of the coolant, check the radiator for clogged fins and damage and make sure the fan operates when required.
2 Examine each of the rubber coolant hoses along its entire length. Look for swelling, cracks, abrasions and other damage. Squeeze each hose at various points. They should feel firm, yet pliable, and return to their original shape when released. If they are dried out or hard, replace them.
3 Look for leaks at each cooling system joint. Tighten the hose clamps carefully to halt minor leaks. If a hose is seriously cracked or torn at a hose clamp, tightening the clamp won't stop the leak; it might even accelerate it. If a hose leaks after tightening the hose clamp, drain the coolant (see Steps 13 through 16), loosen the clamp, pull off the hose and inspect it closely. If the damage is close to the end of the hose, cut off the damaged end and reattach the hose. If the damage is too far from the end of the hose, cutting off the end of the hose is not an option; replace the hose.

17.20a On 660 models, the oil gallery bolt is located in the camshaft end plug on the right-hand side of the engine

17.20b On 700 models, the oil gallery bolt is on the right-hand side of the engine above the spark plug - it has a copper washer

18.4a Water pump has a weep hole location - if coolant has been leaking from it, the water pump seal should be removed and inspected (660 models)

18.4b On 700 models, check for coolant inside the water pump breather hose

4   Check for leaks at the water pump weep hole or breather **(see illustrations)** and water pump gaskets. Also check for leaks at the coolant drain plug(s). Replace water pump or drain plug gaskets if they've been leaking. If coolant has been leaking from the weep hole, it's time for a new water pump seal (see Chapter 3).

5   Inspect the radiator for evidence of leaks and other damage. Radiator leaks usually produce tell-tale deposits or stains on the surface of the core below the leak. If the radiator is leaking, remove it (see Chapter 3) and have it repaired by a radiator shop or replace it.

Caution: Do NOT use a liquid leak-stopping compound to try to repair leaks.

6   Inspect the radiator cooling fins for mud, dirt and insects. Debris stuck in the fins can impede the flow of air through the radiator. If the fins are dirty, force water or low-pressure compressed air through the fins from the backside of the radiator. If any of the fins are bent or distorted, straighten them carefully with a screwdriver.

7   Remove the radiator cover.

8   Remove the radiator cap as follows: Turn it counterclockwise until it reaches the first detent. If you hear a hissing sound (indicating there is still pressure in the system), wait until it stops. Then press down on the cap and continue turning it counterclockwise until it's free.

9   Inspect the condition of the coolant in the radiator. If it's rust-colored, or if accumulations of scale are visible in the radiator, drain, flush and refill the system with new coolant. Inspect the cap gaskets for cracks and other damage. Have the cap tested by a dealer service department or replace it with a new one. Install the cap by turning it clockwise until it reaches the first detent, then push down on the cap and continue turning it until it stops.

10   Analyze the condition of the antifreeze in the coolant with an antifreeze hydrometer. Sometimes coolant may look like it's in good condition, but might be too weak to offer adequate protection. If the hydrometer indicates a weak mixture, flush and refill the cooling system (see Steps 17 through 27).

11   Start the engine and let it reach normal operating temperature, then check for leaks again. As the coolant temperature increases,

the fan should come on automatically and the temperature should begin to drop. If it doesn't, check the fan and fan circuit (see Chapter 3).

12   If the coolant level is constantly low, but there is no evidence of leaks, have the system pressure checked by a Yamaha dealer service department, ATV repair shop or service station.

Coolant change

⚠️ *Warning: Don't allow antifreeze to come into contact with your skin or with painted surfaces of the vehicle. Rinse off spills immediately with plenty of water. Antifreeze is highly toxic if ingested. Never leave antifreeze in an open container or in puddles on the floor; children and pets are attracted by its sweet odor and may drink it. Check with local authorities regarding the proper disposal of used antifreeze. Many communities have collection centers that can dispose of antifreeze safely. Finally, antifreeze is combustible, so don't store it or put it near open flames.*

⚠️ *Warning: Let the engine cool completely before performing this Step. Opening the radiator cap while the engine is hot will allow scalding coolant to spray out.*

Draining

13   On 660 models, remove the front cover. On 700 models, remove the seat and front fender (see Chapter 8).

14   Put a shop rag over the radiator cap **(see illustrations)**. Slowly rotate the cap counterclockwise to the first detent and allow any residual pressure to escape. When the hissing sound ceases, push down on the cap, turn it counterclockwise again and remove it.

15   Place a large, clean drain pan under the engine, remove the drain plug **(see illustrations)** and drain the coolant into the con-

18.14a On 660 models, the radiator cap is beneath the front cover

18.14b On 700 models, the radiator cap is behind the radiator grille

18.15a Coolant drain plug location (660 models)

18.15b Coolant drain plug location (700 models)

tainer. If you didn't remove the radiator cap earlier, the coolant will dribble out, then flow quickly when the cap is removed.

 HAYNES HiNT *The coolant will rush out with considerable force, so be prepared to quickly readjust the position of the drain pan.*

16 Remove the coolant reservoir (see Chapter 3) and drain it. Wash out the reservoir with clean water. Install the reservoir.

Flushing

17 Flush the system with clean tap water by inserting a garden hose into the radiator filler neck. Allow the water to run through the system until it is clear when it exits the drain bolt holes. If the radiator is extremely corroded, remove it (see Chapter 3) and have it cleaned by a radiator shop.
18 Using a new gasket, install the drain bolt and tighten it to the torque listed in this Chapter's Specifications.
19 Fill the cooling system with clean water mixed with a flushing compound. Make sure the flushing compound is compatible with

aluminum, and follow the manufacturer's instructions carefully.
20 Start the engine and allow it to reach normal operating temperature. Let it run for about ten minutes.
21 Stop the engine. Let the machine cool for awhile, then cover the radiator cap with a heavy rag and turn it counterclockwise to the first stop, releasing any pressure that may be present in the system. Once the hissing stops, push down on the cap and remove it completely.
22 Drain the system.
23 Fill the system with clean water, then repeat Steps 20, 21 and 22.

Refilling

24 On 700 models, remove the bleed bolt from the thermostat housing **(see illustration)**.
25 Install the drain bolt on the water pump, using a new gasket.
26 Pour the correct coolant mixture (listed in this Chapter's Specifications) into the radiator. Fill the system to the top of the radiator cap filler neck and install the radiator cap. Fill the reservoir to the FULL mark and install the reservoir cap. On 700 models, reinstall the bleed

bolt, using a new gasket and tighten it to the torque listed in this Chapter's Specifications.
27 Run the engine for several minutes, checking for leaks. Shut it off, let the coolant level settle for several minutes, then recheck the level in the reservoir. Top up as needed.

19 Clutch lever freeplay - check and adjustment

1 The clutch cable is adjusted at the clutch lever. Clutch freeplay can also be adjusted at the crankcase end of the clutch cable if adjustment at the handlebar doesn't bring freeplay within the specified range.

Adjusting clutch lever freeplay at the handlebar

2 Operate the clutch lever and check freeplay at the lever tip.
3 If freeplay isn't within the range listed in this Chapter's Specifications, loosen the adjuster locknut, turn the adjuster to set freeplay **(see illustration)** and tighten the locknut.

18.24 On 700 models, remove the bleed bolt and its copper washer when filling the radiator

19.3 To adjust clutch freeplay, loosen the locknut (right arrow) and turn the adjuster (left arrow)

19.4 If freeplay can't be adjusted at the handlebar, loosen the locknut and adjusting nuts, reposition the cable in the bracket to set freeplay, then tighten the nuts

20.3a Throttle stop (idle speed) screw location (660 models)

20.3b Throttle stop (idle speed) screw location (700 models)

Adjusting clutch freeplay at the crankcase

4   If necessary, pull the cover back from the adjuster on the right-hand side of the engine **(see illustration)**.

5   Loosen the adjuster locknut, then turn the adjuster in or out until clutch freeplay is within the limits listed in this Chapter's Specifications.

6   Tighten the locknut securely and slide the cover back over it.

---

20 Idle speed - check and adjustment

1   Before adjusting the idle speed, make sure the spark plug gap is correct (see Section 16). Also, turn the handlebars back-and-forth and note whether the idle speed changes. If it does, the throttle cable may be incorrectly routed. Correct this problem before proceeding.

2   Start the engine and warm it up to its normal operating temperature. Make sure the transmission is in Neutral, then hook up an inductive-type tachometer.

3   Turn the idle speed adjustment screw **(see illustrations)** to bring the idle speed within the range listed in this Chapter's Specifications. Turning the screw in increases the idle speed; backing it out decreases the idle speed.

4   Snap the throttle open and shut a few times, then recheck the idle speed. If necessary, repeat the adjustment procedure.

5   If a smooth, steady idle can't be achieved, the fuel/air mixture may be incorrect. Refer to Chapter 4 for additional fuel system information.

---

21 Throttle cable and speed limiter - check and adjustment

Throttle cable

1   Before proceeding, check and, if necessary, adjust the idle speed (see Section 20).

2   Make sure the throttle lever moves easily from fully closed to fully open with the front wheel turned at various angles. The lever should return automatically from fully open to fully closed when released. If the throttle sticks, check the throttle cable for cracks or kinks in the housing. Also, make sure the inner cable is clean and well-lubricated.

3   Measure freeplay at the throttle lever **(see illustration)**. If it's within the range listed in this Chapter's Specifications, no adjustment is necessary. If not, adjust it as follows.

4   Pull the rubber boot to expose the adjuster at the carburetor or throttle body end of the throttle cable **(see illustrations)**. Loosen the adjuster locknut. Turn the adjuster to set freeplay, then tighten the locknut.

5   If freeplay can't be brought within the specified range by adjusting it at the carburetor, pull back the rubber boot from the adjuster at the handlebar end of the throttle cable **(see illustration)**. Loosen the adjuster locknut. Turn the adjuster to set freeplay, then tighten the locknut.

6   Reposition the rubber boot(s) over the adjuster(s).

Speed limiter

7   The speed limiter **(see illustration)** can be used to restrict maximum throttle opening. Turning the screw in reduces the maximum throttle opening; backing it out increases maximum throttle opening.

8   To change the speed limiter screw setting, loosen the locknut, turn the screw in or out as necessary and tighten the locknut. Screw length is measured from the underside of the screw head to the throttle housing.

21.3 Check throttle lever freeplay at the lever tip

21.4a On 660 models, adjust the throttle cable at the carburetors by loosening the locknut (right) and turning the adjusting screw (left)

21.4b On 700 models, adjust the throttle cable at the throttle body by loosening the locknut (right) and turning the adjusting screw (left)

21.5 To adjust the throttle cable at the handlebar, loosen the locknut (right) and turn the adjuster (left)

21.7 To adjust the throttle limiter, loosen the locknut and turn the adjusting screw

22.3 Unscrew the choke valve from the carburetor, operate the choke lever and measure the stroke of the plunger

⚠ *Warning: Do NOT back out the speed limiter screw farther than the maximum setting listed in this Chapter's Specifications; doing so will affect throttle lever operation.*

4   Operate the choke lever and measure the plunger stroke, from fully retracted to fully extended. If it isn't as listed in this Chapter's Specifications, loosen the locknut on the cable, turn the adjuster to obtain the correct stroke, then tighten the locknut **(see illustration)**.

⚠ *Warning: Always disconnect the negative cable first and reconnect it last to avoid sparks which could cause a battery explosion.*

22 Choke (carbureted models) - operation check and adjustment

1   Operate the choke lever and note whether it operates smoothly.
2   If the choke lever doesn't operate smoothly, inspect the choke system (see Chapter 4).
3   If the choke lever has too much play or doesn't seem to have full travel, unscrew the choke plunger from the carburetor with the cable attached **(see illustration)**. Don't remove the choke plunger from the cable.

23 Battery - check

1   All models use a sealed, maintenance-free battery. Periodic checking of the electrolyte specific gravity is not possible. Inspect the battery (see Chapter 5).
2   If the vehicle will be stored for an extended time, fully charge the battery, then remove it. Disconnect the negative cable and remove the battery retainer strap. Disconnect the positive cable and vent tube and lift the battery out.

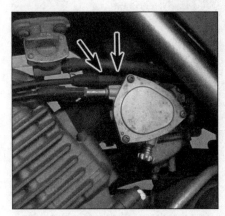

22.4 If necessary, loosen the locknut (right) and turn the adjuster (left) to adjust the choke plunger

24.4a Remove four Allen bolts and take off the intake valve adjusting hole cover

24.4b Unscrew the two exhaust valve adjusting hole covers with a wrench or socket

3   Store the battery in a cool dark place. Check open circuit voltage (see Chapter 5) at least once a month and recharge the battery if it's low.

24.5 Unscrew the crankshaft end plug and timing hole plug, using a tool like this or a coin gripped with pliers

24 Valve clearance - check and adjustment

660 models

Check

1   The engine must be cool to the touch for this maintenance procedure, so if possible let the machine sit overnight before beginning.
2   Remove the seat, front fender and fuel tank (see Chapters 8 and 4).
3   Remove the spark plug (see Section 16). This will make it easier to turn the crankshaft.
4   Remove the valve adjusting hole covers **(see illustrations)**.
5   Unscrew the crankshaft end plug and timing hole access plug **(see illustration)**.

 TOOL TiP *Use a coin gripped with pliers if you don't have a screwdriver big enough to fit the slots .*

6   Make sure the transmission is in Neu-

tral. Using a socket on the crankshaft rotation bolt (inside the crankshaft end plug hole), turn the engine to position the piston at Top Dead Center on the compression stroke. **Note:** *Rotate the crankshaft counterclockwise.* When this occurs, the timing mark on the rotor will align with the notch in the crankcase cover **(see illustration)**. To make sure the piston is on the compression stroke, not the exhaust stroke, wiggle the rocker arms with your fingers. There should be some play. If there isn't any play, rotate the crankshaft one full turn, so the crankshaft timing mark again aligns with the notch.
7   With the engine in this position, all five valve clearances can be checked. There are five valves, three intakes and two exhausts.
8   Insert a feeler gauge of the same thickness as the valve clearance listed in this Chapter's Specifications between each of the valve adjusting screws and the valve stem beneath it **(see illustrations)**.
9   Pull the feeler gauge out slowly - you should feel a light drag. If there's no drag, the clearance is too loose. If there's a heavy drag, the clearance is too tight.

24.6 Align the timing mark with the notch - if the piston is on the compression stroke, there should be play in the rocker arms

24.8a Check the clearance of all three intake valves with a feeler gauge - slip the feeler gauge between the rocker arm and valve stem

24.8b Check the clearance of both exhaust valves

24.10a If adjustment is necessary, loosen the adjusting screw locknut . . .

24.10b . . . and turn the adjusting screw while holding the locknut steady - you can use a small open-end wrench if you don't have this Yamaha special tool

Adjustment

10   To adjust a clearance, loosen the locknut on the adjusting screw (see illustration). Turn the adjusting screw to change the clearance (see illustration), then retighten the locknut.

11   Check and adjust clearances on the remaining valves.

12   The remainder of installation is the reverse of removal. Use new O-rings on the adjusting hole covers.

700 models

Check

13   The engine must be cool to the touch for this maintenance procedure, so if possible let the machine sit overnight before beginning.

14   Remove the seat, front fender and fuel tank (see Chapters 8 and 4).

15   Remove the spark plug (see Section 16). This will make it easier to turn the crankshaft.

16   Remove the valve adjusting hole covers (see illustrations).

17   Unscrew the crankshaft end plug and timing hole access plug with an Allen wrench (see illustration).

24.16a Exhaust valve cover hex bolt locations (700 models)

24.16b Exhaust valve cover bolt locations (700 models)

18   Unbolt the camshaft end cap and take it off the engine (see illustrations).

19   Make sure the transmission is in Neutral. Using a socket on the crankshaft rotation bolt (inside the crankshaft end plug

hole), turn the engine to position the piston at Top Dead Center on the compression stroke. Note: Rotate the crankshaft counterclockwise. When this occurs, the timing mark on the alternator rotor will align with the notch

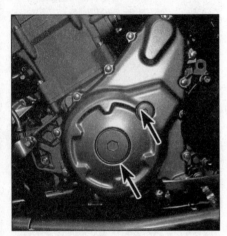

24.17 Unscrew the crankshaft end plug and timing hole plug with an Allen wrench

24.18a Remove the camshaft end cover bolts . . .

24.18b . . . and remove the cover, together with its O-ring

24.19a Turn the crankshaft with a socket on the alternator nut until the timing mark and notch align . . .

24.19b . . . and the mark on the camshaft aligns with the pointer cast in the cylinder head - if the camshaft mark is not visible, rotate the crankshaft one full turn to align the marks

in the crankcase cover **(see illustration)**. To make sure the piston is on the compression stroke, not the exhaust stroke, look at the timing marks on the camshaft sprocket and cylinder head **(see illustration)**. If the tim-

24.21 Measure the clearances of both valves with a feeler gauge

ing mark on the cam sprocket isn't aligned with the cast pointer on the cylinder head as shown, rotate the crankshaft one full turn so the marks on the alternator rotor and cam sprocket align as described.

20   With the engine in this position, all four valve clearances can be checked. There are two intake valves and two exhaust valves.

21   Insert a feeler gauge of the same thickness as the valve clearance listed in this Chapter's Specifications between each of the valve adjusting screws and the valve stem beneath it **(see illustration)**.

22   Pull the feeler gauge out slowly - you should feel a light drag. If there's no drag, the clearance is too loose. If there's a heavy drag, the clearance is too tight.

Adjustment

23   To adjust a clearance, loosen the locknut on the adjusting screw **(see illustration 24.10a)**. Turn the adjusting screw to change the clearance, then retighten the locknut.

24   Check and adjust clearances on the remaining valves.

25   The remainder of installation is the

reverse of removal. Recheck the valve clearances to make sure they're within the Specifications.

25 Exhaust system - inspection

1   Periodically inspect the exhaust system for leaks and loose fasteners.

2   The exhaust pipe flange nuts at the cylinder head are especially prone to loosening, which could cause damage to the head (see Chapter 4). Check them frequently and keep them tight. If tightening the flange nuts fails to stop the leak, replace the gasket (see Chapter 4).

3   The spark arrester should be removed and cleaned at the specified intervals.

> ⚠ *Warning: To avoid burns, be sure the exhaust system has cooled down before you start this procedure.*

> ⚠ *Warning: To avoid carbon monoxide poisoning, run the engine in a well-ventilated area.*

4   Unbolt the spark arrester. Remove three bolts from the rear end of the tailpipe **(see illustration)**.

5   Pull the spark arrester out of the muffler. Tap it lightly with a soft-faced mallet to loosen any deposits, then clean the deposits off with a wire brush. Also clean any deposits from the inside of the muffler, again using a wire brush.

6   Reinstall the spark arrester and tighten the bolt(s) to the torque listed in this Chapter's Specifications.

7   Remove the purging bolt from the underside of the muffler **(see illustration)**. Start the engine and rev it 20 or more times to blow out any remaining deposits. Shut the engine off, let it cool down again, and reinstall the purging bolt.

25.4 The tailpipe/spark arrester is secured by three bolts

25.7 Remove the purging bolt and rev the engine to blow any remaining residue out of the exhaust system

Chapter 2 Part A
Engine, clutch and transmission

Contents

Degrees of difficulty

Easy, suitable for novice with little experience	**Fairly easy,** suitable for beginner with some experience	**Fairly difficult,** suitable for competent DIY mechanic	**Difficult,** suitable for experienced DIY mechanic	**Very difficult,** suitable for expert DIY or professional

Specifications

Note: *Refer to Part B of this Chapter for clearances and wear tolerances.*

660 models

General

Bore	100 mm (3.94 inches)
Stroke	84 mm (3.31 inches)
Displacement	660 cc
Compression ratio	9.2 to 1

Torque specifications

Valve cover bolts	10 Nm (86 inch-lbs)
Camshaft end cap bolt	10 Nm (86 inch-lbs)
Oil pressure check bolt	See Chapter 1
Cylinder head main bolts (1)	38 Nm (27 ft-lbs)
Cylinder head small bolts	10 Nm (86 inch-lbs)
Oil tube union bolts (metal tubes)	
Front corner of engine	20 Nm (168 inch-lbs)
Back of engine	18 Nm (156 inch-lbs)
Oil pipe/hose compression fittings	35 Nm (25 ft-lbs)
Oil pipe/hose flange fitting bolts to back of engine	10 Nm (86 inch-lbs)
Cam chain guide bolts	8 Nm (70 inch-lbs)
Cam chain tensioner body bolts	10 Nm (86 inch-lbs)
Cam chain tensioner cap bolt	22 Nm (16 ft-lbs)
Cylinder main bolts	42 Nm (30 ft-lbs)
Cylinder base bolts	10 Nm (86 inch-lbs)
Crankcase bolts	10 Nm (86 inch-lbs)
Crankcase cover bolts	10 Nm (86 inch-lbs)
Oil filter canister fitting to crankcase	63 Nm (45 ft-lbs)
Oil pump mounting bolts	10 Nm (86 inch-lbs)
Oil pump assembly screw	Not specified
Oil strainer mounting bolts (in crankcase)	7 Nm (61 inch-lbs)
Clutch boss nut (1)	90 Nm (65 ft-lbs)
Clutch spring bolts	8 Nm (70 inch-lbs)
Shift drum segment bolt	30 Nm (22 ft-lbs)
External shift linkage stopper lever bolt	10 Nm (86 inch-lbs)
External shift linkage shift guide bolts (2)	10 Nm (86 inch-lbs)
Shift pedal linkage pinch bolt	10 Nm (86 inch-lbs)
Primary drive gear/balancer drive gear nut (1)	150 Nm (110 ft-lbs)
Balancer driven gear nut (1)	140 Nm (100 ft-lbs)
Engine mounting bolts/nuts	
Upper bracket to frame	33 Nm (24 ft-lbs)
Upper bracket to engine	40 Nm (29 ft-lbs)
Front bracket to frame	56 Nm (40 ft-lbs)
Front bracket to engine	56 Nm (40 ft-lbs)

700 models

General

Bore	102 mm (4.02 inches)
Stroke	84 mm (3.31 inches)
Displacement	686 cc
Compression ratio	9.2 to 1

Torque specifications

Cylinder head main bolts (1)	35 Nm (25 ft-lbs)
Cylinder head underside bolts (2)	38 Nm (27 ft-lbs)
Cylinder head small bolts	10 Nm (86 inch-lbs)
Oil pressure check bolt	See Chapter 1
Oil tube union bolts (metal tube)	20 Nm (168 inch-lbs)
Oil tube retaining bolt to engine	10 Nm (86 inch-lbs)
Lower oil pipe/hose compression fitting to engine	35 Nm (25 ft-lbs)
Upper oil pipe/hose flange fitting to engine	10 Nm (86 inch-lbs)
Oil pipe/hose flange fitting to oil tank (top and bottom)	10 Nm (86 inch-lbs)
Camshaft sprocket cover bolts	10 Nm (86 inch-lbs)
Camshaft sprocket bolts	20 Nm (172 inch-lbs)
Decompressor to camshaft bolts	20 Nm (172 inch-lbs)
Cam chain guide bolts	10 Nm (86 inch-lbs)
Cam chain tensioner body bolts	10 Nm (86 inch-lbs)
Cam chain tensioner cap bolt	20 Nm (168 inch-lbs)
Cylinder main bolts	
Step 1	15 Nm (132 inch-lbs)
Step 2	50 Nm (36 ft-lbs)
Cylinder base bolts	10 Nm (86 inch-lbs)
Crankcase bolts	10 Nm (86 inch-lbs)
Crankcase cover bolts	10 Nm (86 inch-lbs)
Oil pump mounting bolts	10 Nm (86 inch-lbs)

(1) Use a new lockwasher.
(2) Apply non-permanent thread locking agent to the threads.

700 models (continued)

Torque specifications

Oil pump assembly screw	7 Nm (61 inch-lbs)
Oil pump outer baffle screws (2)	4 Nm (35 inch-lbs)
Oil pump inner baffle bolts	10 Nm (86 inch-lbs)
Oil strainer mounting bolts (in crankcase)	10 Nm (86 inch-lbs)
Clutch boss nut (3)	95 Nm (68 ft-lbs)
Clutch spring bolts	8 Nm (70 inch-lbs)
Shift drum segment bolt	30 Nm (22 ft-lbs)
External shift linkage shift guide bolts (2)	10 Nm (86 inch-lbs)
Shift pedal pinch bolt	16 Nm (132 inch-lbs)
Primary drive gear/balancer drive gear nut (4)	110 Nm (110 ft-lbs)
Balancer driven gear nuts (5)	60 Nm (43 ft-lbs)
Engine mounting bolts/nuts	
Upper bracket to frame	33 Nm (24 ft-lbs)
Upper bracket to engine	40 Nm (29 ft-lbs)
Front bracket to frame and engine	66 Nm (48 ft-lbs)
Lower through-bolt and nut	66 Nm (48 ft-lbs)

(1)   Use a new lockwasher
(2)   Apply non-permanent thread locking agent to the threads
(3)   Replace the nut with a new one
(4)   Apply molybdenum disulfide grease to the threads
(5)   Apply engine oil to the threads

1 General information

The Raptor 660 and 700 engine/transmission units are of the liquid-cooled, single-cylinder four-stroke design.

660 models have five valves (three intake and two exhaust). 700 models have four valves (two intake and two exhaust). The valves are operated by a single overhead camshaft, which is chain driven off the crankshaft.

The engine/transmission assembly is constructed from aluminum alloy. The crankcase is divided vertically.

The crankcase incorporates a dry sump, pressure-fed lubrication system which uses a gear-driven rotor-type oil pump and an oil filter. An external oil tank is mounted in front of the engine.

A wet, multi-plate clutch connects the crankshaft to the transmission. Engagement and disengagement of the clutch is controlled by a lever on the left handlebar through a cable.

The transmission has five forward gears and one reverse gear.

2 Operations possible with the engine in the frame

The components and assemblies listed below can be removed without having to remove the engine from the frame. If, however, a number of areas require attention at the same time, removal of the engine is recommended.

Starter motor
Starter reduction gears
Starter clutch
Alternator rotor and stator
Clutch
External shift mechanism
Cam chain tensioner
Camshafts and lifters
Cylinder head
Cylinder and piston
Oil pump
Balancer gears

3 Operations requiring engine removal

It is necessary to remove the engine/transmission assembly from the frame and separate the crankcase halves to gain access to the following components:

Crankshaft and connecting rod
Transmission shafts
Shift drum and forks

4 Major engine repair - general note

1   It is not always easy to determine when or if an engine should be completely overhauled, as a number of factors must be considered.
2   High mileage is not necessarily an indication that an overhaul is needed, while low mileage, on the other hand, does not preclude the need for an overhaul. Frequency of servicing is probably the single most important consideration. An engine that has regular and frequent oil and filter changes, as well as other required maintenance, will most likely give many miles of reliable service. Conversely, a neglected engine, or one which has not been broken in properly, may require an overhaul very early in its life.
3   Exhaust smoke and excessive oil consumption are both indications that piston rings and/or valve guides are in need of attention. Make sure oil leaks are not responsible before deciding that the rings and guides are bad. Perform a cylinder compression check to determine for certain the nature and extent of the work required (see Chapter 2B).
4   If the engine is making obvious knocking or rumbling noises, the connecting rod and/or main bearings are probably at fault.
5   Loss of power, rough running, excessive valve train noise and high fuel consumption rates may also point to the need for an overhaul, especially if they are all present at the same time. If a complete tune-up does not remedy the situation, major mechanical work is the only solution.
6   An engine overhaul generally involves restoring the internal parts to the specifications of a new engine. During an overhaul the piston rings are replaced and the cylinder walls are bored and/or honed. If a rebore is done, then a new piston is also required. Generally the valves are serviced as well, since they are usually in less than perfect condition at this point. While the engine is being overhauled, other components such as the carburetor and the starter motor (if equipped) can be rebuilt also. The end result should be a like-new engine that will give as many trouble-free miles as the original.
7   Before beginning the engine overhaul, read through all of the related procedures to familiarize yourself with the scope and requirements of the job. Overhauling an engine is not all that difficult, but it is time consuming. Plan on the vehicle being tied up for a minimum of two weeks. Check on the availability of parts and make sure that any necessary special tools, equipment and supplies are obtained in advance.
8   Most work can be done with typical shop hand tools, although a number of precision measuring tools are required for inspecting parts to determine if they must be replaced. Often a dealer service department or repair shop will handle the inspection of parts and offer advice concerning reconditioning and

5.11 Disconnect the oil tank and crankcase breather hoses (700 shown, 660 similar)

replacement. As a general rule, time is the primary cost of an overhaul so it doesn't pay to install worn or substandard parts.
9   As a final note, to ensure maximum life and minimum trouble from a rebuilt engine, everything must be assembled with care in a spotlessly clean environment.

5 Engine - removal and installation

 Warning: Engine removal and installation should be done with the aid of an assistant to avoid damage or injury that could occur if the engine is dropped.

Removal

1   Remove the seat, left footrest, both fenders and engine skid plate (see Chapter 8).
2   Disconnect the negative cable from the battery (see Chapter 5).
3   Remove the fuel tank, its heat shield and the exhaust system (see Chapter 4).
4   Drain the engine oil and coolant (see Chapter 1).
5   Disconnect the radiator hoses from the engine (see Chapter 3).
6   Remove the carburetors (660) or throttle body (700) (see Chapter 4).
7   Disconnect the clutch cable from the engine (see Section 14).
8   Disconnect the spark plug wire (see Chapter 1).
9   Disconnect the starter motor cable (see Chapter 5).
10   Remove the drive sprocket from the engine (see Chapter 6).
11   Disconnect the oil tank and crankcase breather hose(s) **(see illustration)**.
12   Disconnect the external oil hoses from the engine (see Section 12).
13   Label and disconnect the harness connectors above the left side of the engine.
14   Remove the speed sensor from the back of the engine (see Chapter 5).

5.16a On 660 models, the ground cable is attached to the left side of the engine above the engine sprocket

5.16b On 700 models, the ground cable is attached to the back of the engine near the speed sensor

5.20a To remove the top engine mount, remove the nut (lower arrow) and pull out the through-bolt, then unbolt the bracket from the frame (upper arrows) (660 models)

5.20b To remove the front engine mount, remove the upper nut and through-bolt (upper right arrow), then the lower nut and through-bolt, then unbolt the bracket from the frame (660 models)

15 Label and disconnect the following wires:
   CDI magneto and alternator
   Neutral switch
   Reverse switch
16 Disconnect the engine ground cable **(see illustrations)**.
17 Disconnect the parking brake cable (see Chapter 7).
18 Support the engine securely from below.
19 Remove the swingarm pivot bolt partway (see Chapter 6).

 The swingarm pivot bolt acts as an engine mounting bolt. Pull out the bolt just far enough to free the engine, but leave it in far enough to support one side of the swingarm.

20 Remove the engine mounting bolts, nuts and brackets at the lower front and top **(see illustrations)**. On 700 models, remove the through-bolt from the underside of the engine.

5.20c To remove the top engine mount, remove the nut (lower arrow) and pull out the through-bolt, then unbolt the bracket from the frame crossmember (700 models)

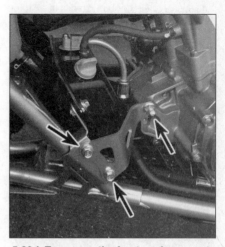

5.20d To remove the front engine mount, remove the nut (right arrow) and pull out the through-bolt, then unbolt the brackets from the engine (there's a separate bracket on each side) (700 models)

6.2 A selection of brushes is required for cleaning holes and passages in the engine components

6.3 An engine stand can be made from short lengths of lumber and lag bolts or nails

21 Have an assistant help you support the engine. Remove it from the left side.

22 Slowly lower the engine to a suitable work surface.

Installation

23 Check the engine supports for wear or damage and replace them if necessary before installing the engine.

24 Make sure the vehicle is securely supported so it can't be knocked over during the remainder of this procedure.

25 With the help of an assistant, lift the engine up into the frame. Install the mounting nuts and bolts at the rear, front and top. Be sure the mount brackets are installed on the correct sides of the bike (refer to their L and R marks). Finger-tighten the mounting bolts, but don't tighten them to the specified torque yet.

26 Tighten the engine mounting bolts and nuts evenly to the torques listed in this Chapter's Specifications.

27 The remainder of installation is the reverse of removal, with the following additions:

a) *Use new gaskets at all exhaust pipe connections.*

b) *Adjust the throttle cable, clutch cable and parking brake cable (see Chapter 1).*

c) *Fill the engine with oil and coolant (see Chapter 1). Run the engine and check for oil, coolant and exhaust leaks.*

6 Engine disassembly and reassembly - general information

1 Before disassembling the engine, clean the exterior with a degreaser and rinse it with water. A clean engine will make the job easier and prevent the possibility of getting dirt into the internal areas of the engine.

2 In addition to the precision measuring tools mentioned earlier, you will need a torque wrench, a valve spring compressor, oil gallery brushes **(see illustration)**, a piston ring removal and installation tool, a piston ring compressor. Some new, clean engine oil of the correct grade and type, some engine assembly lube (or moly-based grease) and a tube of RTV (silicone) sealant will also be required.

3 An engine support stand made from short lengths of 2 x 4s bolted together will facilitate the disassembly and reassembly procedures **(see illustration)**. If you have an automotive-type engine stand, an adapter plate can be made from a piece of plate, some angle iron and some nuts and bolts.

4 When disassembling the engine, keep mated parts together (including gears, rocker arms and shafts, etc.) that have been in contact with each other during engine operation. These mated parts must be reused or replaced as an assembly.

5 Engine/transmission disassembly should be done in the following general order with reference to the appropriate Sections.

Remove the cam chain tensioner
Remove the camshaft and rocker arms
Remove the cylinder head
Remove the cylinder
Remove the piston
Remove the clutch
Remove the balancer gears
Remove the oil pump
Remove the external shift mechanism
Remove the alternator rotor
Remove the starter reduction gears
Separate the crankcase halves
Remove the shift drum and forks
Remove the transmission gears and shafts
Remove the crankshaft and connecting rod

6 Reassembly is accomplished by reversing the general disassembly sequence.

7 Valve cover and rocker arms (660 models) - removal, inspection and installation

Removal

1 Remove the seat, fuel tank cover and front fender (see Chapter 8).

2 Remove the fuel tank and rubber cover (see Chapter 4A).

3 Remove the spark plug (see Chapter 1).

4 Remove the upper engine mount **(see illustration 5.20a or 5.20c)**.

5 Disconnect the oil tank breather hose from the engine **(see illustration 5.11)**.

6 Remove the front oil pipe (see Section 12).

7 Remove the valve adjusting hole covers (see Chapter 1).

8 Place the engine at Top Dead Center (TDC) on the compression stroke (see Chapter 1, Section 24).

9 You'll need to remove the camshaft end cover to replace its O-ring. You can unbolt it now and remove the cover, together with the oil pressure check bolt and its sealing washer **(see illustration)**. If it's difficult to remove, leave it in place and lift it off together with the valve cover.

10 Loosen the cover bolts evenly, in several stages, working in a criss-cross pattern **(see illustration)**. Once they're all loose, remove them.

11 Lift the valve cover off the cylinder head **(see illustration)**. If it's stuck, don't attempt to pry it off - tap around the sides of it with a plastic hammer to dislodge it.

12 Locate the cover dowels (they may have stayed in the cover or the cylinder head) **(see illustration 7.11)**. Remove all traces of sealant from the cover and cylinder head mating surfaces.

7.9 Remove the Allen bolt (upper arrow) and pull the end plug and O-ring out of the valve cover - the oil pressure check plug (lower arrow) can be left in the end plug

7.10 Remove the valve cover Allen bolts

Inspection

13   Note how the rocker arms are installed. Remove the bolts that locate the exhaust rocker shaft **(see illustration)**.

14   The ends of the rocker shafts have internal threads. Thread a 6mm bolt (one of the cover bolts will do) into the end of each intake rocker shaft, then hook a slide hammer to the bolt and pull on it to pull the shaft out of the cover **(see illustrations)**. For access to the left exhaust rocker shaft, you'll need to unscrew the plug from the cover **(see illustration)**. **Note:** *The intake rocker shaft is secured by two of the valve cover bolts, which pass through notches in the shaft. If you placed the valve cover bolts back in their holes for storage after removing the valve cover, pull them out.*

7.11 Lift the valve cover off the cylinder head and locate the dowels

7.13 The exhaust rocker shafts are secured by Allen bolts

7.14a Thread a bolt into the end of the rocker shaft (one of the Allen bolts will do) and hook a slide hammer to it . . .

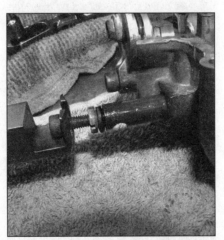

7.14b . . . and yank on the slide hammer weight to pull the rocker shaft out of its bore

7.14c Unscrew the plug for access to the intake rocker shaft

7.15 Remove the rocker shafts and wave washers

8.1a Tensioner cap bolt (upper arrow) and tensioner body Allen bolt (lower arrows) locations

8.1b Remove the tensioner cap, spring and sealing washer

15   Once the shafts are removed, remove the rocker arms and wave washers **(see illustration)**.

16   Inspect the rocker arms and shafts (see Chapter 2B).

17   Check the camshaft bearing surfaces in the cover for wear or damage. If problems are found, remove the camshaft (see Section 9) and check the bearing surfaces in the cylinder head. Check the camshaft journals (see Chapter 2B).

18   If you haven't removed the camshaft end plug, unscrew the oil pressure check bolt (this will be easier to do while the end plug is bolted to the valve cover). Remove the end plug bolt and take it out of the valve cover.

Installation

19   Installation is the reverse of removal, with the following additions:

a)   *Use new O-rings on the exhaust rocker shafts, rocker shaft plug and camshaft end plug.*

b)   *Install a wave washer next to each rocker arm* **(see illustration 7.15)**. *The exhaust wave washers go toward the inboard sides of the rocker arms. The intake wave washers go toward the left side of the engine when the valve cover is in the installed position.*

c)   *Lubricate the rocker shafts with engine oil and the camshaft surfaces of the rocker arms with molybdenum disulfide grease.*

d)   *Install the rocker shafts with their bolt notches vertical, so the bolt notches will align with the bolt holes in the valve cover. There's a slot in the end of each shaft so you can use a screwdriver to twist the shaft into the correct installed position if necessary.*

e)   *Apply a thin coat of Quick Gasket sealant or equivalent to the mating surfaces of the cylinder head and cover.*

f)   *Tighten the cover bolts evenly, in two or three stages, to the torque listed in this Chapter's Specifications.*

g)   *Use new sealing washers on the external oil pipe.*

8   Cam chain tensioner - removal and installation

Caution: *Once you start to remove the tensioner Allen bolts, you must remove the tensioner all the way and reset it before tightening the bolts. The tensioner extends and locks in place, so if you loosen the bolts partway and then tighten them, the tensioner or cam chain will be damaged.*

1   Unscrew the tensioner cap bolt and remove the sealing washer and spring **(see illustrations)**.

2   Remove the tensioner body Allen bolts and remove the tensioner body.

3   Clean all old gasket material from the tensioner body and engine.

4   Place a new gasket on the tensioner body.

5   Lift the latch on the tensioner body and press the piston into the tensioner. Release the latch to hold the piston in the retracted position **(see illustrations)**.

6   Position the tensioner body on the cylinder, making sure the raised dot faces the center of the engine **(see illustration)**. Install the bolts, tightening them to the torque listed in this Chapter's Specifications.

7   Install the cap bolt with a new sealing washer and tighten it to the torque listed in this Chapter's Specifications.

9   Camshaft, chain and guides - removal, inspection and installation

Removal
Camshaft

1   Place the engine at Top Dead Center (TDC) on the compression stroke (see Chapter 1, Section 24).

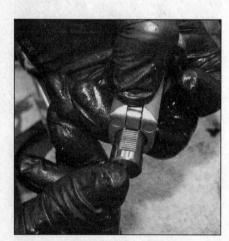

8.5a With the tensioner extended as shown here, lift the latch, push the piston into the tensioner body . . .

8.5b . . . and release the latch to hold the tensioner piston in the retracted position

8.6 The raised dot on the tensioner body faces toward the center of the engine

9.3a Turn the crankshaft until the two punch marks on the sprocket are aligned with the cylinder head surface . . .

9.3b . . . and the punch mark underneath the decompressor retainer is at the top

660 models

2   Remove the valve cover and rocker arms (see Section 7).
3   Verify that the engine is at top center on the compression stroke by checking the positions of the alignment marks on the camshaft sprocket **(see illustrations)**. There should be two punch marks on the sprocket aligned with the cylinder head surface, and a third punch mark straight up (you'll need to unbolt the decompressor retainer and take it off the sprocket to see the third mark). If the third mark isn't visible, reinstall the decompressor retainer, then rotate the crankshaft one full turn (which will cause the camshaft to rotate 1/2 turn), until the two punch marks align with the cylinder head surface again. Remove the other decompressor retainer and make sure the upper mark is straight up.
4   Remove the cam chain tensioner (see Section 8).
5   Tie the cam chain up with wire so it can't fall into the chain cavity. Unbolt the sprocket from the camshaft and remove it.

6   Unbolt the sprocket from the camshaft **(see illustration)**. Disengage it from the chain and remove it.
7   Lift the camshaft out of its saddles.

700 models

8   Loosen the locknuts on the valve adjusting screws and back the screws off all the way.
9   Remove the cylinder head (see Section 10).
10   Unbolt the camshaft retainer from the cylinder head **(see illustration)**. Care-

fully remove the camshaft from the cylinder head, together with the sprocket-end bearing. Don't try to remove the bearing from the camshaft.
11   Reach into the camshaft bore and remove the remaining camshaft bearing from the cylinder head.
12   Hold each rocker arm in turn and remove its shaft from the cylinder head, then out lift the rocker arm. Slip the shaft back into the rocker arm so the intake and exhaust shafts don't get mixed up. Mark the rocker arms so they and their shafts can be returned to the correct sides of the cylinder head.

9.6 Unbolt the sprocket from the camshaft

9.10 Camshaft and rocker arms (700 models)

1   Camshaft retainer
2   Rocker shafts
3   Rocker arms
4   Valve adjusting screws and locknuts
5   Camshaft (with integral bearing)
6   Decompressor lever
7   Decompressor lever pin
8   Camshaft bearing

9.14 On 660 models, the exhaust side chain guide can be removed with the cylinder head in position

9.15 Unbolt the intake side chain guide from the crankcase

9.19 If the rotor has been removed, align the keyway with the cast pointer to place the piston at TDC

Timing chain and guides

13 On 700 models, remove the cylinder head if you haven't already done so (see Section 10).

14 Lift the front (exhaust) cam chain guide out of the engine with needle-nosed pliers **(see illustration)**.

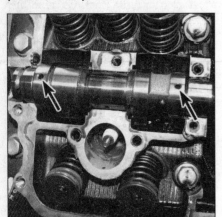

9.22 Position the camshaft with the oil holes upward

15 The rear (intake) guide is bolted at the bottom, so the left crankcase cover and alternator rotor will have to be removed for access if the guide or the cam chain need to be removed (see Section 13 and Chapter 5). Once this has been done, unbolt the guide from the crankcase and lift it out of the engine **(see illustration)**.

16 Lower the cam chain and disengage it from the crankshaft sprocket **(see illustration 9.15)**.

17 Stuff clean rags into the cam chain opening so dirt, small parts or tools can't fall into it.

18 Inspect the cam chain, sprockets and guides (see Chapter 2B).

Installation
660 models

19 Make sure the piston is still at TDC on the compression stroke (see Chapter 1, if necessary). If the alternator rotor is off the engine (so you can't use the timing marks on the rotor), you can position the crankshaft by aligning the rotor keyway with the pointer cast in the crankcase **(see illustration)**.

20 Install the cam chain on the crankshaft sprocket, then install the chain guides.

21 Coat the bearing surfaces of the camshaft with moly-based grease.

22 Install the camshaft in the cylinder head with the oil holes upward **(see illustration)**.

23 Place the decompressor cam guide plates on the cam sprocket (if they were removed) **(see illustrations)**.

24 Engage the chain with the cam sprocket, then install the sprocket on the camshaft. Two of the three punch marks in the cam sprocket must be aligned with the mating surface of the cylinder head and valve cover; the remaining mark must be straight up **(see illustrations 9.3a and 9.3b)**.

25 Install the camshaft sprocket bolts and tighten them to the torque listed in this Chapter's Specifications.

26 The remainder of installation is the reverse of removal.

27 Rotate the crankshaft two full turns and make sure the timing marks still line up correctly.

28 Check the valve clearances (see Chapter 1). This is necessary to make sure none of the shims has slipped out of position.

29 Refill the engine oil and coolant (see Chapter 1).

9.23a Engage the decompressor notches with the pins . . .

9.23b . . . install the retainers and bolt them to the sprocket

10.3a Unscrew the bolt from the left rear corner of the cylinder head . . .

10.3b . . . the underside of the head on the intake side . . .

700 models

30 Installation is the reverse of removal. Use thread locking agent on the threads of the camshaft retainer bolts.

---

10 Cylinder head - removal, inspection and installation

Removal

660 models

1 Remove the carburetors and exhaust system (see Chapter 4).
2 Remove the valve cover, rocker arms and camshaft (see Sections 8 and 9).
3 Loosen the cylinder head bolts in the specified sequence, 1/4 turn at a time, until all are loose, then remove them. The sequence is as follows:

a) *Allen bolt on the left rear corner of the cylinder head* **(see illustration)**
b) *Hex bolt on the underside of the head on the intake side* **(see illustration)**

10.3c . . . and the underside of the head on the exhaust side (660 models)

c) *Hex bolt on the underside of the head on the exhaust side* **(see illustration)**
d) *Main head bolts, in a criss-cross pattern* **(see illustration)**.

4 Lift the cylinder head off the cylinder **(see illustration)**. If it's stuck, don't attempt

10.3d Loosen the four main bolts in a crisscross pattern until they're loose, then remove the bolts and their washers (660 models)

to pry it off - tap around the sides of it with a plastic hammer to dislodge it.
5 Locate the dowels **(see illustration)**. The dowels may be in the cylinder or they

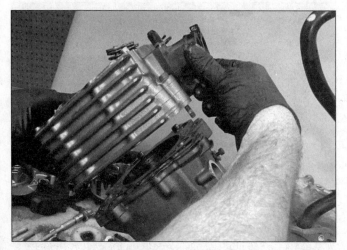

10.4 Lift the head off the cylinder

10.5 Locate the dowels and remove the gasket

10.13 Camshaft sprocket bolts (upper arrows) and decompressor bolts (lower arrows) (700 models)

10.14a Cylinder head small bolts (upper arrows) and cylinder small bolts (lower arrows) (700 models)

may have come off with the head.

6   Remove the old head gasket from the cylinder or head **(see illustration 10.5)**.

7   Inspect the cylinder head and valves (see Chapter 2B).

10.14b Left rear main bolt (right arrow) and left front main bolt (left arrow) (700 models)

700 models

8   Remove the spark plug (see Chapter 1). Place the engine at Top Dead Center (TDC) on the compression stroke (see Chapter 1, Section 24).

9   Remove the thermostat and coolant temperature sensor (see Chapter 3).

10   Remove the throttle body (see Chapter 4).

11   Remove the cam chain tensioner (see Section 8).

12   Remove the external oil line that connects the cylinder head to the crankcase (see Section 12).

13   Unbolt the cam sprocket and decompressor unit from the camshaft **(see illustration)**.

14   Loosen the cylinder head bolts 1/2 turn at a time, in the following sequence:

   a) *Two small bolts beneath camshaft sprocket* **(see illustration)**.
   b) *Underside of cylinder head at the rear of the engine*
   c) *Underside of cylinder head at the front of the engine*
   d) *Left rear corner main bolt* **(see illustration)**

   e) *Right front corner main bolt* **(see illustration)**
   f) *Left front corner main bolt* **(see illustration 10.14b)**
   g) *Right rear corner main bolt* **(see illustration 10.14c)**

15   Once all of the bolts are loose, remove them from the engine.

16   Lift the cylinder head off the cylinder. If it's stuck, don't attempt to pry it off - tap around the sides of it with a plastic hammer to dislodge it.

17   Locate the dowels. There are two of them, both located on the left side of the engine. The dowels may be in the cylinder or they may have come off with the head.

Installation

18   Make sure the two dowel pins are in position, then place the new head gasket on the cylinder **(see illustration 10.5)**. Never reuse the old gasket and don't use any type of gasket sealant. On 660 models, there's a cutout on the head gasket that spells the word UP - it should be upright when the gasket is installed **(see illustration)**. On 700

10.14c Right rear main bolt (left arrow) and right front main bolt (right arrow) (700 models)

10.18 On 660 models, the word UP on the gasket should be upright

11.3 Cylinder base bolts (660 models)

11.4a On 660 models, remove the cylinder bolts (arrows) . . .

models, the side of the gasket that goes toward the front of the engine has coolant passages; the rear side does not. The coolant passages in the gasket must line up with the passages in the cylinder.

19   Carefully lower the cylinder head onto the cylinder.

 It's helpful to have an assistant support the cam chain with a piece of wire so it doesn't fall and become kinked or detached from the crankshaft. When the head is resting on the cylinder, wire the cam chain to another component to keep tension on it.

20   Install the washers on the four main head bolts and install the bolts finger-tight. Install the other three head bolts and tighter them finger-tight.

21   On 660 models, tighten all of the bolts, in two stages, in the reverse of the loosening sequence (see Step 3), to the torque listed in this Chapter's Specifications.

22   On 700 models, apply molybdenum disulfide grease to the threads and the undersides of the bolt heads of the four main bolts. Apply engine oil to the threads and the undersides of the bolt heads of both the bolts that install from underneath the head.

23   On 700 models, tighten the bolts, in two stages, in the reverse of the loosening sequence (see Step 14), noting that there are three different torque settings for the different bolts.

24   The remainder of installation is the reverse of removal. Change the engine oil and check the valve clearances (see Chapter 1).

11 Cylinder - removal, inspection and installation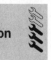

Removal

1   Remove the cylinder head (see Section 11). Make sure the engine is at Top Dead Center (TDC) (see Chapter 1, Section 24).

2   Disconnect the water pump outlet hose from the cylinder (see Chapter 3). **Note:** *If the hose is difficult to remove, you may find it easier to unbolt the hose fitting from the cylinder, leaving the hose connected.*

3   Remove the Allen bolts securing the base of the cylinder to the crankcase **(660 models, see illustration; 700 models, see illustration 10.14a).**

4   Unscrew the four main cylinder bolts **(see illustration).** Lift the bolts and washers out of the cylinder **(see illustration).**

5   Lift the cylinder straight up to remove it **(see illustration).** If it's stuck, tap around its perimeter with a soft-faced hammer. Don't attempt to pry between the cylinder and the crankcase, as you'll ruin the sealing surfaces.

6   Locate the cylinder base O-ring and the dowels (they may have come off with the cylinder or still be in the crankcase)

11.4b . . . and their washers

11.5 Lift the cylinder straight off

11.6a Locate the cylinder base O-ring (arrow) . . .

11.6b . . . and the dowels (arrows) - they may have come off with the cylinder or stayed in the crankcase

(see illustrations). There are two dowels, located next to the timing chain cavity. Be careful not to let these drop into the engine. Stuff rags around the piston and remove the gasket and all traces of old gasket material from the surfaces of the cylinder and the crankcase.

7 To inspect the cylinder and piston, as well as for piston removal and installation procedures, refer to Chapter 2B.

Installation

8 Lubricate the cylinder bore with plenty of clean engine oil. Apply a thin film of moly-based grease to the piston skirt.

9 Install the dowel pins, then install a new cylinder base gasket and O-ring (see illustrations 11.6a and 11.6b).

10 Attach a piston ring compressor to the piston and compress the piston rings. A large hose clamp can be used instead - just make sure it doesn't scratch the piston, and don't tighten it too much.

11 Install the cylinder and carefully lower it

down until the piston crown fits into the cylinder liner. While doing this, pull the camshaft chain up, using a hooked tool or a piece of stiff wire. Push down on the cylinder, making sure the piston doesn't get cocked sideways, until the bottom of the cylinder liner slides down past the piston rings. A wood or plastic hammer handle can be used to gently tap the cylinder down, but don't use too much force or the piston will be damaged.

12 Remove the piston ring compressor or hose clamp, being careful not to scratch the piston.

13 The remainder of installation is the reverse of removal.

12 Oil tank and lines - removal and installation

1 660 models have the following tank and line components:

a) Combined oil pipe/hoses connecting the oil tank to the left side of the engine (see illustration)
b) Oil tank mounted on the frame forward of the engine (see illustration)
c) External oil tubes at the right front and right rear of the engine (see illustrations)

700 models have the following tank and line components:

a) Combined oil pipe/hoses connecting the oil tank to the left side of the engine (see illustration)
b) An external oil tube connecting the top of the engine to the front

Oil lines

2 Follow the lines from one end to the other and determine what type of connection they use at each end. Note the locations of any retainers.

3 To disconnect an oil pipe/hose from the engine, remove its mounting bolt(s) and pull the fitting off, or unscrew the compression fitting (see illustrations). Free the pipe

12.1a On 660 models, the oil pipe/hoses run along the left side of the engine . . .

12.1b . . . there's one hose connected to the top of the oil tank (shown) and another connected to the bottom

12.1c On the right front corner of the engine, a metal tube connects the top of the engine to the crankcase (660 shown, 700 similar)

12.1d On the right rear of the engine, another tube connects the oil filter housing to the crankcase (660 shown, 700 similar)

12.1e On 700 models, the upper oil pipe/hose (upper arrow) connects the top of the oil tank to the left side of the engine; the lower pipe/hose (lower arrow) connects the bottom of the oil tank to the left side

12.3a Unbolt the flange fitting at the rear of the oil tube (660 models)

12.3b The banjo fitting at the front end of the oil tube has a sealing washer on each side of the fitting

12.3c Location of the lower oil hose compression fitting

12.3d Unscrew the fitting and remove the O-ring - the upper pipe/hose is secured by a retainer bolted to the engine

12.3e On 700 models, the upper pipe/hose is secured by one bolt; unscrew the bolt, pull off the fitting and remove the dowel and O-ring

from its retainers (or unbolt the retainers from the engine) and take the oil pipe/hose off the engine.

4   To disconnect an oil pipe/hose from the oil tank, unscrew the compression fitting (660) or unbolt the flange fitting (700) and pull it straight up or straight down (see illustration 12.1b or 12.1e). Remove the fitting dowel and O-ring.

5   To disconnect the oil tank vent hose, loosen its clamp and carefully pry it off the fittings (see illustration 12.1b or 12.1e).

6   To remove an external oil pipe, remove the banjo bolts and sealing washers (if equipped) from each of the fittings (see illustrations 12.1c, 12.1d and the accompanying illustration). If you're removing the pipe at the right front of the engine (the right front pipe on 660 models, and the only pipe on 700 models), unbolt its retainer from the engine. Take the pipe off. If the fitting is an O-ring type, remove the O-ring (see illustration).

7   Installation is the reverse of removal, with the following additions:

a) Replace the sealing washers whenever the union bolts or hose fittings are loosened.
b) Replace O-rings whenever they are removed.
c) Tighten the union bolts and tube retaining bolt to the torques listed in this Chapter's Specifications.

Oil tank

Removal

8   Drain the oil tank (see Chapter 1).

9   Disconnect the hoses from the tank (see Step 4).

10   Remove the tank mounting bolts and lift the tank from the frame (see illustrations).

Installation

11   Check the mounting bushings for damage or deterioration and replace them as needed.

12   Position the tank on the frame and tighten the mounting bolts. Connect the hoses (see Step 7).

13   Change the engine oil (see Chapter 1).

13 Crankcase covers - removal and installation

Right crankcase cover

Removal

1   Drain the engine oil and remove the oil filter (see Chapter 1).

2   Drain the cooling system and remove the water pump (see Chapters 1 and 3). Water pump removal is necessary because one of the crankcase cover bolts is located inside the water pump housing.

3   Remove the metal oil pipes from the right front corner of the engine (all models) and right rear corner of the engine (660) (see Section 12).

4   Remove the engine from the vehicle (see Section 5).

5   Remove the cover bolts (see illustrations). Loosen the bolts evenly in a crisscross pattern, then remove them.

12.6a The front oil tube is secured at upper and lower ends by banjo fittings (660 model upper fitting shown)

12.6b The rear fitting on the rear tube (660) and the bottom fitting on the oil tank (700) are sealed with an O-ring

12.10a Mounting bolt and grommet location (660 models)

12.10b Mounting bolt and grommet location (700 models)

13.5a Right crankcase cover bolts . . .

13.5b . . . this bolt is behind the water pump (660 models)

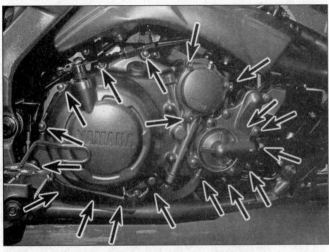

13.5c Right crankcase cover bolts . . .

13.5d . . . here's another view of the three rear bolts (700 models)

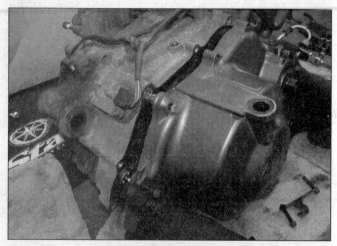

13.6 Separate the cover from the crankcase and locate the dowels

13.8a Inspect the clutch shift lower bearing . . .

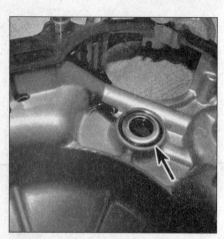

13.8b . . . and the seal that fits over the outer end of the crankshaft

6   Pull off the cover **(see illustration)**. Tap it with a rubber mallet if it won't come off easily. Don't pry the cover off or the gasket surfaces will be damaged.
7   Locate the cover dowels **(see illus-**

tration 13.6)**. They may have stayed in the crankcase or come off with the cover.
8   Remove all traces of the old gasket from the cover and crankcase. Check the clutch lifter lever lower bearing and inner seal **(see illustrations)**. Replace them if their condition is in doubt.

Installation

9   Installation is the reverse of removal. When installing the inner cover, use a new gasket, coated on both sides with gasket sealer. Be sure the dowels are installed.
10   Tighten the cover bolts evenly to the torque listed in this Chapter's Specifications.

Left crankcase cover
Removal

11   Drain the engine oil (see Chapter 1).
12   Remove the shift pedal linkage (see Section 17).
13   Disconnect the oil pipe/hose from the bottom left of the engine (see Section 12).
14   Follow the alternator wiring harness to the electrical connector and disconnect it (see Chapter 5).

15   Remove the starter slipper clutch (see Chapter 5). One of the crankcase cover bolts is hidden behind the slipper clutch.
16   Remove the cover bolts **(see illustrations)**. Loosen the bolts evenly in a criss-cross pattern, then remove them.
17   Pull off the cover. Tap it with a rubber mallet if it won't come easily. Don't pry the cover off or the gasket surfaces will be damaged.
18   Locate the cover dowels. They may have stayed in the crankcase or come off with the cover.
19   Remove all traces of the old gasket from the cover and crankcase.

Installation

20   Installation is the reverse of removal. Use a new gasket, coated on both sides with gasket sealer. Be sure the dowels are installed. Don't forget to refill the engine oil (see Chapter 1).
21   Tighten the cover bolts evenly to the torque listed in this Chapter's Specifications.

13.16a Left crankcase bolt locations (660 models)

13.16b Left crankcase cover bolt locations (660 models)

14.1 Align the three slots (in the adjuster, its locknut and the clutch lever), pull the cable end out of the adjuster and swing the cable out of the lever

14.2a Unbolt the cable bracket . . .

14.2b . . . and the retainer on the engine (if equipped)

14 Clutch and release mechanism - removal, inspection and installation

Cable and handlebar lever
Removal

1   Loosen the midline cable adjuster or handlebar cable adjuster all the way to create slack (see Chapter 1). Rotate the cable so the inner cable aligns with the slot in the lever, then slip the cable and fitting out of the lever **(see illustration)**.
2   Unbolt the cable bracket from the top of the crankcase **(see illustration)**. On 660 models, unbolt the cable brackets from the right rear of the engine as well **(see illustration)**.
3   Swing the cable clockwise (viewed from the top) until its end slides out of the slot in the release lever. Pull the cable end out of the release lever.
to align it with the slot in the lever and lift the cable end out of the lever.
4   Free the cable from the hook on the cylinder head, then remove it **(see illustration)**. Separate the cable from the brackets if necessary.
5   To remove the lever from the handlebar bracket, unscrew the pivot bolt locknut, then unscrew the pivot bolt **(see illustration)**. To remove the bracket from the handlebar, undo the clamp bolts **(see illustration)**. The parking brake lever will come off with the clutch lever bracket.

Inspection

6   Slide the inner cable back and forth in the housing and make sure it moves freely. If it doesn't, try lubricating it as described in Chapter 1. If that doesn't help, replace the cable.

14.4 Release the cable from the hook at the right front corner of the engine

14.5a Unscrew the locknut from the pivot bolt, then unscrew the pivot bolt from the lever

14.5b Remove the clamp bolts and take the lever off the handlebar

14.9a On 660 models, remove the retaining bolt . . .

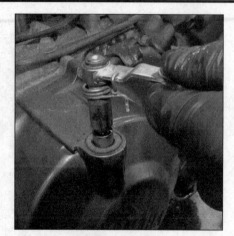

14.9b . . . and lift the lever shaft out of the crankcase cover

14.10 Inspect the seal and the bearing below it

Installation

7 Installation is the reverse of removal. Adjust clutch freeplay (see Chapter 1).

Lifter lever

Removal

8 The lifter lever, which engages with the clutch pull rod through a pinion gear, pulls

14.12 Remove the snap-ring, upper washer, lever and lower snap-ring

the pull rod against the clutch center to disengage the clutch. The lifter lever on all models can be removed with the right crankcase cover installed. The 660 lifter lever shaft is secured by a retaining bolt that's accessible from outside the crankcase cover, so the shaft can be removed with the crankcase cover installed. The 700 lifter lever shaft is secured by a snap-ring on the bottom end of the shaft inside the right crankcase cover, so the crankcase cover must be removed to remove the shaft. To remove the pull rod on all models, remove the right crankcase cover (see Section 13) and refer to the clutch removal procedures later in this Section.

9 Note how the spring ends engage the lever and the crankcase cover. On 660 models, remove the retaining bolt and lift the lever shaft out of the crankcase cover (see illustrations). On 700 models, remove the snap-ring from the bottom of the shaft and lift the shaft out.

10 Check for visible wear or damage at the contact points of the lifter lever and pull rod (use a small flashlight to look into the hole that the lever shaft came out of and inspect the gear teeth on the pull rod, as well as the

needle roller bearings) (see illustration). Replace any parts that show problems. If you need to replace the pull rod or the lower bearing, remove the right crankcase cover (see Section 13).

11 Pry the lifter shaft seal out of the crankcase cover. If the upper needle bearing is worn or damaged, pull it out. Pack the needle bearing with grease, install it in the crankcase cover and press in a new seal.

12 If necessary, remove the snap-ring and washer and slide the lever off the shaft (see illustration). Remove the spring and lower washer. Replace any worn or damaged parts with new ones, then reinstall them, using a new snap-ring.

Installation

13 Installation is the reverse of removal. Engage the gear teeth on the lifter lever with the gear teeth on the pull rod (see illustration). Position the lever so its alignment mark will be lined up with the mark on the crankcase after the clutch cable is connected (see illustration). Hook the release lever spring to the crankcase.

14 Adjust clutch freeplay (see Chapter 1).

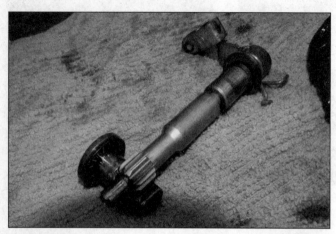

14.13a The gears on the lever shaft and pull rod engage like this

14.13b Position the lever shaft in the crankcase cover so that the marks will align after the cable is installed

Clutch

Removal

15   Remove the right crankcase cover (see Section 13).

16   Hold the clutch from turning.

 HAYNES HiNT *You can wedge a copper washer or penny between the primary drive gear and clutch housing driven gear to keep the clutch housing from turning while you loosen the clutch spring bolts and clutch housing nut (see illustration).*

17   Refer to the **accompanying illustrations** to remove the clutch.

14.16 Slip a copper washer or penny between the gears at this point to keep the clutch from turning while you remove the pressure plate bolts

14.17a Remove the pressure plate bolts and springs

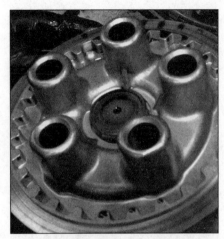

14.17b Remove the pressure plate

14.17c Remove the pull rod and its bearing

14.17d Remove the bearing washer

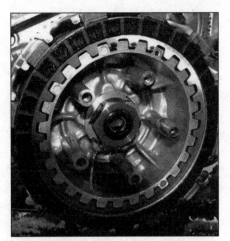

14.17e Note how the tabs of the clutch plates fit in the slots of the clutch center . . .

14.17f . . . and the slots in the clutch housing

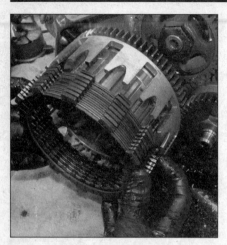

14.17g Pull off the plates

14.17h Bend back the lockwasher tab

14.17i Hold the clutch with a holding tool (or wedge the gears with a copper washer or penny as described earlier) and unscrew the nut

14.17j Pull off the lockwasher, noting how its tabs engage the slots in the clutch center

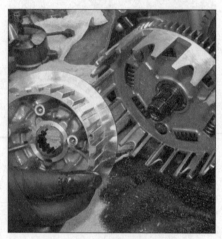

14.17k Pull off the clutch center . . .

14.17l . . . and the clutch housing

14.19a Install a new lockwasher so its tabs fit into the clutch center notches

14.19b Wedge the gears from above with a copper washer or penny, tighten the locknut and bend the lockwasher's locking tabs against the nut

Inspection

18   Refer to Chapter 2B for clutch inspection procedures.

Installation

19   Installation is the reverse of removal, with the following additions:

a) Install a new lockwasher and position its tabs in the clutch center notches (see illustration). Tighten the clutch nut to the torque listed in this Chapter's Specifications, then bend the lockwasher tabs against two of the flats on the nut. If you don't have a clutch holder tool, wedge the gears from the top with a copper washer or penny (see illustration).

b) Coat the friction plates with clean engine oil before you install them.

14.19c On 700 models, install the damper spring and its seat first, then install a friction plate (on 660 models [shown], install a friction plate first)

14.19d Install a metal plate

c) On 700 models, install the damper spring seat, then install the damper spring with the OUT SIDE mark facing away from the engine. Install a friction plate, then a metal plate and secure them with a new wire ring.

d) Install a friction plate, then the remaining metal and friction plates until they're all installed (see illustrations). Friction plates go on first and last, so the friction material contacts the metal surfaces of the clutch center and the pressure plate. On 660 models, the two narrower friction plates go on second and last, with a damper spring inside the narrower friction plate in the second position (see illustration).

e) Lubricate the release bearing (the ball bearing in the pressure plate) with clean engine oil. Lubricate the pull rod with multipurpose grease.

15 Primary drive gear and balancer gears - removal, inspection and installation

1   The primary drive gear and balancer gears are mounted on the right-hand side of the crankcase, inside the right crankcase cover. The primary drive gear and balancer drive gear are on the end of the crankshaft (see illustration). The balancer drive gear on 660 models, and upper balancer drive gear on 700 models, is mounted on the balancer in the top of the crankcase. 700 models have a second balancer, mounted low in the front of the crankcase. On 660 models, the primary drive gear drives the clutch housing and the water pump. On 700 models, the water pump is driven by the water pump drive gear, which is mounted on the crankshaft outboard of the primary drive gear.

14.19e On 660 models install the damper spring and the narrow friction plate . . .

14.19f . . . and position the damper inside a narrow friction plate like this; on 700 models, install the wire ring that secures the damper spring and seat, first friction plate and metal plate. On all models, install the remaining plates

15.1 660 models have one balancer driven gear (top), with the balancer drive gear and primary drive gear on the crankshaft (bottom); 700 models have an additional balancer at the lower front and a water pump drive gear on the crankshaft outboard of the primary drive gear

15.3 Align the marks on the balancer driven gear (top) and driven gear (bottom); on 700 models, the mark on the lower balancer's driven gear must line up with its corresponding mark on the drive gear

15.4 Wedge the gears from the left side, bend back the lockwasher tab and unscrew the nut from the balancer

15.5a Wedge the gears from the other side, bend back the lockwasher tabs . . .

15.5b . . . and unscrew the nut; on 700 models, use the same method to remove the lower balancer nut

Removal

2   Remove the clutch (see Section 14).
3   Turn the crankshaft so the match marks on the balancer drive and driven gears align **(see illustration)**.
4   Bend back the tab on the balancer driven gear lockwasher **(see illustration)**.
5   Wedge a copper washer or penny between the teeth of the balancer drive and driven gears to prevent them from turning. Loosen the driven gear nut. If you plan to remove the primary drive gear or balancer drive gear, wedge the gears from the other side **(see illustration)**. Bend back the lockwasher tab and loosen the primary drive gear nut **(see illustration)**.
6   Unscrew the nuts and remove the lockwashers.
7   Slide off the balancer driven gear **(see illustration)**.
8   Remove the primary drive gear and balancer drive gear, then remove the Woodruff keys from the crankshaft and balancer shaft **(see illustrations)**.
9   On 660 models, remove the plate and washer from the crankshaft, noting how their tabs fit in the crankshaft slot **(see illustrations)**.

Inspection

10   Check the gears for worn or damaged teeth and replace them as a set if problems are found.
11   On 660 models, check the balancer drive gear for damaged or loose buffer springs or missing pins (there should be a pin inside each of the six buffer springs) **(see illustration)**. Don't disassemble the balancer drive gear unless necessary, but if any problems are found, slip the inner and outer portions of the gear apart and remove the springs and pins for further inspection. The pins and springs are available separately, but the inner and outer parts of the gear are available only as a set. If you do separate the inner and outer parts, be sure to realign the alignment marks when you put the gear back together. The 700 balancer drive gear doesn't have buffer springs.
12   Check the remaining components for wear and damage and replace any worn or damaged parts. Replace the lockwasher with a new one whenever it's removed.
13   Inspect the balancer and crankshaft ball bearings to the extent possible without disassembling the crankcase. If wear, looseness or roughness can be detected (especially if there's any side play in the balancer shaft or crankshaft), the crankcase will have to be disassembled to replace the bearings.

Installation

14   Installation is the reverse of removal. Align the balancer and crankshaft timing marks **(see illustration 15.3)**. Wedge the gears as described in Step 5 and tighten the nuts to the torque listed in this Chapter's Specifications. Bend the lockwasher tabs to secure the nut(s).

15.7 Slide the balancer gear off the shaft and remove the key from its slot

15.8a Slide the water pump gear (700 only), primary drive gear and balancer gear off the crankshaft . . .

15.8b . . . then remove the key . . .

15.9a . . . the plate . . .

15.9b . . . and the washer behind it

15.11 On 660 models, the balancer drive gear has inner and outer segments, with springs and pins between them

16.2 Oil pump and drive gear details (700 models)

1 Outer baffle
2 Snap-ring
3 Drive gear
4 Inner baffle
5 Oil pump
6 Gasket
7 O-rings

16 Oil pump - removal, inspection and installation

Removal

1 Remove the clutch (see Section 14).

2 On 700 models, remove the outer oil baffle **(see illustration)**.

3 Remove the snap-ring (and washer on 660 models only) and take the oil pump drive gear off its shaft **(see illustrations)**.

4 Remove the oil pump mounting bolts and take it off the engine (together with the inner oil baffle on 700 models) **(see illustrations)**.

5 Remove the oil pump O-rings **(see illustration)**.

16.3a Remove the snap-ring (and washer on 660 models only)

16.3b Remove the drive gear from the oil pump

16.4a Remove the mounting bolts . . .

16.4b . . . and pull the pump out of the engine

16.5 Remove the O-rings

16.6a Remove the assembly screw to disassemble the pump

16.6b Disassemble the oil pump; don't forget to install the drive pin (arrow) on assembly

16.6c Oil pump components (700 models)

1 Scavenge rotor cover and oil seal
2 Outer scavenge rotor
3 Scavenge rotor drive pin
4 Inner scavenge rotor
5 Feed rotor cover and oil seal
6 Dowels
7 Pump shaft
8 Feed rotor drive pin
9 Inner feed rotor
10 Outer feed rotor
11 Pump body

16.8 Align the rotor match marks when assembling the pup

Disassembly

6   Remove the pump assembly screw, take off the cover and separate the components (see illustrations).

7   Wash all the components in solvent, then dry them off. Inspect the pump (see Chapter 2B).

8   Reassemble the pump by reversing the disassembly steps, with the following additions:

a) Before installing the cover, pack the cavities between the rotors with petroleum jelly - this will ensure the pump develops suction quickly and begins oil circulation as soon as the engine is started.

b) Make sure the drive pin is in position (see illustration 16.6b).

c) Position the rotor alignment marks as shown (see illustration).

d) Tighten the cover screw to the torque listed in this Chapter's Specifications.

Installation

9   Installation is the reverse of removal, with the following additions:

17.1 On 660 models, make alignment marks on the shift shaft and linkage, remove the bolt and slide the linkage off the shaft

a) Use new O-rings and a new gasket without sealer.

b) Tighten the oil pump mounting bolts to the torque listed in this Chapter's Specifications.

17 External shift mechanism - removal, inspection and installation

Shift pedal and linkage
Removal

660 models

1   Look for alignment marks on the end of the shift linkage lever and shift shaft (see illustration). If they aren't visible, make your own marks with a felt pen or sharp punch. Remove the pinch bolt completely (it fits in a groove in the shaft) and slide the lever off the shaft.

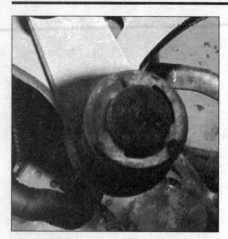

17.2 Remove the circlip to detach the pedal from the bracket

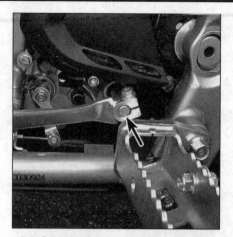

17.3 On 700 models, the shift pedal bolts directly to the shaft; make alignments marks (if necessary), remove the pinch bolt and slip off the pedal

17.11a Note how the return spring pin fits between the ends of the spring, and how the shift shaft lever fits over the roller

2   If you need to remove the pedal and linkage from the vehicle, unbolt the left footpeg from the frame (see Chapter 8). Remove the

17.11b Remove the circlip from the shift shaft on the other side of the engine

circlip that secures the pedal and separate it from the footpeg **(see illustration)**.

700 models
3   The pedal connects directly to the shift shaft without a linkage. To remove it, Look for alignment marks on the end of the shift pedal and shift shaft **(see illustration)**. If they aren't visible, make your own marks with a felt pen or sharp punch. Remove the pinch bolt completely (it fits in a groove in the shaft) and slide the pedal off the shaft.

Inspection
4   Check the shift pedal for wear or damage such as bending. Check the splines on the shift pedal and shaft for stripping or step wear. Replace the pedal or shaft if these problems are found.
5   Check the shift shaft seal in the alternator cover for signs of leakage. If the seal has been leaking, remove the left crankcase cover (see Section 13). Pry the seal out of

the cover, then tap in a new one with a seal driver or socket the same diameter as the seal.

Installation
6   If you removed the pedal from the footpeg, lubricate it with molybdenum disulfide grease and install it, using a new snap-ring.
7   Install the shift linkage lever. Line up its punch marks and tighten the pinch bolt to the torque listed in this Chapter's Specifications.
8   Check shift pedal height and adjust the shift linkage (see Chapter 1).

External shift linkage
Removal
9   Remove the shift pedal and linkage (see Steps 1 through 3).
10   Remove the clutch (see Section 14).
11   Refer to the **accompanying illustrations** to remove the linkage.

17.11c Disengage the shift shaft lever . . .

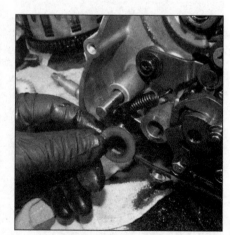

17.11d . . . and pull the shift shaft out of the engine (on 700 models, the stopper lever fits over the shift shaft)

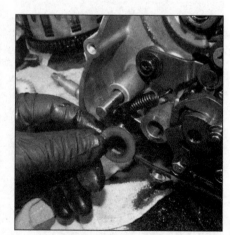

17.11e Remove the washer . . .

17.11f . . . and the pin

17.11g Note how the shift guide fits over the pawl assembly . . .

17.11h . . . then unbolt the shift guide from the crankcase and remove it

17.11i Remove the pawl assembly from the shift drum cam

17.11j Remove the bolt from the center of the shift drum cam

17.11k Remove the cam; the notch fits over a dowel pin

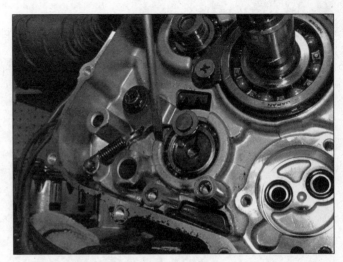

17.11l On 660 models, unhook the lower end of the stopper lever spring, then unbolt the lever and remove it from the engine

18.11a Crankcase bolt locations: lower right front . . .

18.11b . . . top right . . .

Inspection

12   Check the shift shaft for bends and damage to the splines. If the shaft is bent, you can attempt to straighten it, but if the splines are damaged it will have to be replaced. Check the condition of the return spring, shift arm and the pawl spring. Replace the shift shaft if they're worn, cracked or distorted.

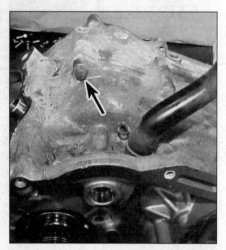

18.11c . . . top left . . .

Installation

13   Installation is the reverse of removal, with the following additions:

a) *Tighten the stopper arm bolt and shift drum segment bolt to the torques listed in this Chapter's Specifications.*

b) *Check the engine oil level and add some, if necessary (see Chapter 1).*

18 Crankcase - disassembly and reassembly

1   To examine and repair or replace the crankshaft, connecting rod, balancer shaft, bearings and transmission components, the crankcase must be split into two parts.

Disassembly

2   Remove the engine from the vehicle (see Section 5).

3   Remove the alternator, starter clutch and speed sensor rotor (see Chapter 5).

4   Remove the clutch (see Section 14).

5   Remove the external shift mechanism (see Section 17).

6   Remove the valve cover, cam chain

tensioner, camshaft, cylinder head, cylinder, piston and external oil lines (see Sections 7 through 12 and Chapter 2B).

7   Remove the timing chain and guides (see Section 9).

8   Remove the oil pump (see Section 16).

9   Remove the primary drive gear and balancer gears (see Section 15).

10   Check carefully to make sure there aren't any remaining components that attach the upper and lower halves of the crankcase together.

11   Loosen the crankcase bolts in two or three stages, in a criss-cross pattern **(see illustrations)**. On 660 models, remove the through-bolt and the front engine mount (if you haven't already done so) **(see illustration)**.

12   Place the engine on blocks so the transmission shafts and crankshaft can extend downward. Set up a three-legged puller against the end of the crankshaft so it can pull the upper case half off the crankshaft **(see illustration)**. Note that the puller has to be positioned over the forward portion of the crankcase. This means that you'll need to pay closer attention than usual to how evenly the crankcase halves separate. As you tighten the puller, tap gently on the ends of the transmission shafts and balancer shaft and crankshaft as the case halves are being

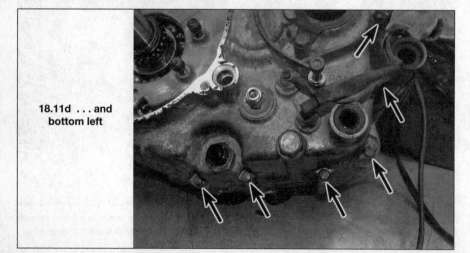

18.11d . . . and bottom left

18.11e Remove the engine mount through-bolt if you haven't already done so (660)

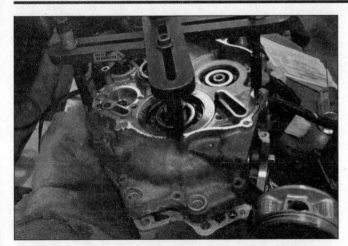

18.12 Position a separator tool on the crankcase, tighten it slowly, and tap on the ends of the balancer shaft and transmission shaft to make sure the halves separate evenly

18.13 The crankshaft, transmission shafts and balancer shaft (both balancer shafts on 700 models) will stay in the left case half as the right half is lifted off

separated. Work slowly and make sure the case halves separate evenly. Carefully pry the crankcase apart at the pry points. Don't pry against the mating surfaces or they'll develop leaks.

13   Lift the right crankcase half off the left half. The crankshaft, balancer shaft(s), transmission shafts and shift drum will remain in the left half **(see illustration)**.

14   Locate the crankcase dowels **(see illustration 18.13)**. If they aren't secure in their holes, remove them and set them aside for safekeeping.

15   Refer to Sections 19 through 21 for information on the internal components of the crankcase.

Reassembly

16   Remove all traces of old gasket and sealant from the crankcase mating surfaces with a sharpening stone or similar tool. Be careful not to let any fall into the case as this is done and be careful not to damage the mating surfaces.

17   Check to make sure the dowel pins are in place in their holes in the mating surface

of the crankcase. Install a new O-ring on the center dowel **(see illustration 18.13)**.

18   Coat both crankcase mating surfaces with Yamaha Quick Gasket (ACC-11001-05-01) or equivalent sealant.

19   Pour some engine oil over the transmission gears, balancer shaft and crankshaft bearing surfaces and the shift drum. Don't get any oil on the crankcase mating surfaces.

20   Carefully place the removed crankcase half onto the other crankcase half. While doing this, make sure the transmission shafts, shift drum and crankshaft fit into their bearings in the upper crankcase half.

21   Install the crankcase half bolts or screws in the correct holes and tighten them so they are just snug. Then tighten them in two or three stages, in a criss-cross pattern, to the torque listed in this Chapter's Specifications.

22   Turn the transmission shafts to make sure they turn freely. Also make sure the crankshaft and balancer shaft turn freely. If they don't, stop and find out why before continuing with assembly.

23   The remainder of installation is the reverse of removal.

19 Crankcase components - inspection and servicing

1   Separate the crankcase and remove the following:
Transmission shafts and gears
Crankshaft and main bearings
Shift drums and forks
Balancer shaft

2   Clean the crankcase halves thoroughly with new solvent and dry them with compressed air. All oil passages should be blown out with compressed air and all traces of old gasket sealant should be removed from the mating surfaces. **Caution:** *DO NOT nick or gouge the crankcase mating surfaces or leaks will result. Check both crankcase sections very carefully for cracks and other damage.*

3   Check the bearings in the case halves **(see illustrations)**. If they don't turn smoothly, replace them, referring to "Tools and Workshop Tips" at the end of this manual.

19.3a Bearing retainers are accessible from inside the case half . . .

19.3b . . . or from the outside

19.4 Remove the screws and remove the oil strainer for inspection (660 shown)

20.2 Lift the balancer (both balancers on 700 models) out of the crankcase

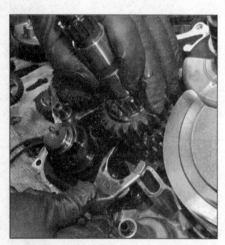

21.2a Pull out the shift shafts and disengage the forks from the gears, noting which way the L, R and C marks face

21.2b On 660 models, there are two forks on one shaft - 700 models have a separate fork for each shaft.

21.2c The forks are marked L (left), C (center) and R (right) to indicate their position

21.2d Install the forks on their shafts so you'll remember how they go

21.2e Lift out the transmission shafts

21.2f The transmission shafts engage like this (660 shown)

21.2g If you need to disassemble the reverse shaft, remove the snap-ring

21.2h Lift the reverse shaft and gear out of their bearing

21.4a Countershaft components (660 models)

21.4b Mainshaft components (660 models)

4 Check the oil strainer screen(s) for clogging or damage. If problems are found, remove the screen(s) for cleaning or replacement. It's a good idea to remove the screen and check its oil passage in the crankcase whenever the crankcase is disassembled **(see illustration)**.

5 If any damage is found that can't be repaired, replace the crankcase halves as a set.

6 Assemble the case halves (see Section 18) and check to make sure the crankshaft and the transmission shafts turn freely.

20 Balancer - removal and installation

1 Disassemble the crankcase (see Section 18).

2 Lift the balancer shaft out of its bearing in the left crankcase half **(see illustration)**. On 700 models, lift the front balancer out of its bearing in the left crankcase.

3 Inspect the balancer shaft bearing and replace it if necessary, referring to "Tools and Workshop Tips" at the end of this manual.

4 Installation is the reverse of removal. Lubricate the balancer bearing with clean engine oil.

21 Transmission shafts and shift drum - removal, inspection and installation

Note: *When disassembling the transmission shafts, place the parts on a long rod or thread a wire through them to keep them in order and facing the proper direction.*

Removal

1 Remove the engine, then separate the case halves (see Sections 5 and 18). The transmission components remain in the left case half when the case is separated.

2 Remove the shift drum, shift forks and transmission shafts from the crankcase **(see illustrations)**.

3 Using snap-ring pliers, remove the snap-rings and take the gears off the shafts.

4 Place the gears in order on a coat hanger or dowel so they won't be mixed up **(see illustrations)**.

21.4c Reverse shaft components (700 models)

1 Snap-ring	3 Bushing	5 Reverse shaft
2 Washer	4 Reverse gear	

21.4d Transmission output shaft components (700 models)

1 Snap-ring
2 Washer
3 Reverse gear
4 Bushing
5 Shift dog
6 Snap-ring
7 Thrust washer
8 Output shaft first gear
9 Spline bushing
10 Output shaft fifth gear
11 Spline washer
12 Spline washer retainer
13 Output shaft third gear
14 Spline bushing
15 Spline washer
16 Snap-ring
17 Output shaft fourth gear
18 Snap-ring
19 Spline washer
20 Output shaft second gear
21 Bushing
22 Output shaft

RIGHT SIDE OF ENGINE

Inspection

5   Wash all of the components in clean solvent and dry them off.

6   Inspect the shift fork grooves in the gears. If a groove is worn or scored, replace the affected part and inspect its corresponding shift fork.

7   Check the shift forks for distortion and wear, especially at the fork ears. If they are discolored or severely worn they are probably bent. Inspect the guide pins for excessive wear and distortion and replace any defective parts with new ones.

8   Check the shift fork guide bars evidence of wear, galling and other damage. Make sure the shift forks move smoothly on the guide bars. If the shafts are worn or bent, replace them with new ones.

9   Check the edges of the grooves in the shift drums for signs of excessive wear.

10   Hold the inner race of the shift drum

bearing with fingers and spin the outer race. Replace the bearing if it's rough, loose or noisy. Replace the shift drum cam if it's worn or damaged (see Section 17).

11   Check the gear teeth for cracking and other obvious damage. Check the bushing surface in the inner diameter of the freewheeling gears for scoring or heat discoloration. Replace damaged parts.

12   Inspect the engagement dogs and dog holes on gears so equipped for excessive wear or rounding off. Replace the paired gears as a set if necessary.

13   Check the transmission shaft bearings in the crankcase for wear or heat discoloration and replace them if necessary (see Section 19).

Installation

14   Installation is the basically the reverse of the removal procedure, but take note of the following points:

a) Use new snap-rings. Install the snap-rings with their rounded edges facing the direction of thrust (toward the component they're securing). Be sure each snap-ring gap is aligned with a spline groove (not with a spline) on the transmission shaft. Refer to "Tools and Workshop Tips" at the end of this manual if necessary.

b) Lubricate the components with engine oil before assembling them.

c) Install the shift forks with their letter/ number marks toward the right side of the engine and their L, C and R marks (left, center and right) toward the left side of the engine (see illustration 21.2c).

d) After assembly, check the gears to make sure they're installed correctly. Move the shift drums through the gear positions and rotate the gears to make sure they mesh and shift correctly.

21.4e Transmission mainshaft components (700 models)

1 Snap-ring
2 Mainshaft second gear
3 Spline lockwasher
4 Lockwasher retainer
5 Mainshaft fourth gear
6 Spline bushing
7 Spline washer
8 Snap-ring
9 Mainshaft third gear
10 Mainshaft fifth gear
11 Mainshaft with integral first gear

Chapter 2 Part B
General engine overhaul procedures

Contents

Degrees of difficulty

Easy, suitable for novice with little experience	**Fairly easy,** suitable for beginner with some experience	**Fairly difficult,** suitable for competent DIY mechanic	**Difficult,** suitable for experienced DIY mechanic	**Very difficult,** suitable for expert DIY or professional

Specifications

660 models

Camshaft

Lobe height (intake)	
Standard	35.69 to 35.79 mm (1.4051 to 1.4091 inches)
Limit	35.59 mm (1.4012 inches)
Lobe height (exhaust)	
Standard	36.5 to 36.6 mm (1.437 to 1.441 inches)
Limit	36.4 mm (1.1.4331 inches)
Camshaft runout limit	0.03 mm (0.0012 inch)
Bearing oil clearance	
Standard	0.020 to 0.054 mm (0.0008 to 0.0021 inch)
Limit	Not specified

Cylinder head, valves and valve springs

Cylinder head warpage limit.. 0.05 mm (0.002 inch)
Valve stem runout limit... 0.01 mm (0.0004 inch)
Valve stem diameter
    Intake
        Standard .... 5.975 to 5.990 mm (0.2352 to 0.2358 inch)
        Limit .... 5.945 mm (0.2341 inch)
    Exhaust
        Standard .... 5.960 to 5.975 mm (0.2346 to 0.2352 inch)
        Limit .... 5.93 mm (0.235 inch)
Valve guide inside diameter (intake and exhaust)
    Standard .... 6.000 to 6.012 mm (0.2362 to 0.2367 inch)
    Limit .... 6.040 mm (0.2378 inch)
Stem-to-guide clearance
    Intake
        Standard .... 0.010 to 0.037 mm (0.0004 to 0.0015 inch)
        Limit .... 0.08 mm (0.0031 inch)
    Exhaust
        Standard .... 0.025 to 0.052 mm (0.0010 to 0.0020 inch)
        Limit .... 0.1 mm (0.0004 inch)
Valve seat width (intake and exhaust)
    Standard .... 0.9 to 1.1 mm (0.0354 to 0.0433 inch)
    Limit .... 1.6 mm (0.063 inch)
Valve margin thickness (intake and exhaust) .... 1.0 mm (0.394 inch)
Valve spring free length (intake)
    Standard .... 35.95 mm (1.42 inches)
    Limit .... 34.15 mm (1.34 inches)
Valve spring free length (exhaust)
    Standard .... 37.75 mm (1.49 inches)
    Limit .... 35.86 mm (1.41 inches)
Valve spring bend limit .... 2.5 degrees at 1.6 mm (0.06 inch)

Cylinder

Bore diameter
    Standard .... 100.005 to 100.045 mm (3.9372 to 3.9388 inches)
    Limit .... 100.1 mm (3.94 inches)
    Measurement point .... At vertical center of the bore, front-to-rear and side-to-side
Out-of-round limit... Not specified
Taper limit.. Not specified

Piston

Diameter... 99.945 to 99.995 mm (3.9348 to 3.9368 inches)
Measuring point.. 10.0 mm (0.394 inch) from bottom of skirt
Piston-to-cylinder clearance
    Standard .... 0.04 to 0.07 mm (0.0020 to 0.0028 inches)
    Limit .... 0.15 mm (0.0059 inch)
Piston pin bore
    Standard .... 22.004 to 22.015 mm (0.8663 to 0.8667 inch)
    Limit .... 22.045 mm (0.8679 inch)
Piston pin outer diameter
    Standard .... 21.991 to 22.000 mm (0.8658 to 0.8661 inch)
    Limit .... 21.971 mm (0.8650 inch)
Piston pin-to-piston clearance .... 0.004 to 0.024 mm (0.0002 to 0.0009 inch)
Ring side clearance
    Top ring
        Standard .... 0.040 to 0.080 mm (0.0016 to 0.0031 inch)
        Limit .... 0.13 mm (0.0051 inch)
    Second ring
        Standard .... 0.030 to 0.070 mm (0.0012 to 0.0028 inch)
        Limit .... 0.13 mm (0.0051 inch)
    Oil ring... Not specified
Ring end gap
    Top ring
        Standard .... 0.30 to 0.45 mm (0.012 to 0.018 inch)
        Limit .... 0.70 mm (0.276 inch)
    Second ring
        Standard .... 0.30 to 0.45 mm (0.012 to 0.018 inch)
        Limit .... 0.88 mm (0.315 inch)

Oil ring
    Standard .... 0.20 to 0.70 mm (0.008 to 0.027 inch)
    Limit .... Not specified

Clutch
Spring free length
    Standard .... 42.8 mm (1.69 inches)
    Limit .... 40.7 mm (1.60 inches)
Metal plate thickness .... 1.1 to 1.3 mm (0.043 to 0.051 inch)
Friction plate thickness
    Six wide plates
        Standard .... 2.74 to 2.86 mm (0.108 to 0.113 inch)
        Limit .... 2.6 mm (0.102 inch)
    Two narrow plates
        Standard .... 2.94 to 3.06 mm (0.116 to 0.120 inch)
        Limit .... 2.8 mm (0.110 inch)
Friction and metal plate warpage limit .... 0.2 mm (0.008 inch)

Oil pump
Outer rotor-to-body clearance .... 0.03 to 0.08 mm (0.001 to 0.003 inch)
Inner-to-outer rotor clearance
    Standard .... 0.12 mm (0.005 inch) or less
    Limit .... 0.20 mm (0.008 inch)

Transmission
Mainshaft and output shaft runout limit .... 0.08 mm (0.003 inch)

Crankshaft and connecting rod
Runout limit .... 0.03 mm (0.0012 inch)
Assembly width .... 74.95 to 75.00 mm (2.9508 to 2.9528 inches)
Connecting rod big-end side clearance
    Standard .... 0.32 to 0.64 mm (0.0126 to 0.0252 inch)
    Limit .... 1.0 mm (0.0394 inch)
Connecting rod big-end freeplay
    Standard .... 0.010 to 0.025 mm (0.0004 to 0.0010 inch)
    Limit .... Not specified
Connecting rod small end freeplay
    Standard .... 0.8 mm (0.0315 inch)
    Limit .... Not specified

700 models

Camshaft
Lobe height (intake)
    Standard .... 43.3 to 43.4 mm (1.7047 to 1.7087 inches)
    Limit .... 43.2 mm (1.7008 inches)
Lobe height (exhaust)
    Standard .... 43.129 to 43.229 mm (1.6980 to 1.7019 inches)
    Limit .... 43.029 mm (1.6941 inches)
Camshaft runout limit .... 0.03 mm (0.0012 inch)

Cylinder head, valves and valve springs
Cylinder head warpage limit .... 0.03 mm (0.0012 inch)
Valve stem runout limit .... 0.01 mm (0.0004 inch)
Valve stem diameter
    Intake
        Standard .... 5.975 to 5.990 mm (0.2352 to 0.2358 inch)
        Limit .... 5.945 mm (0.2341 inch)
    Exhaust
        Standard .... 5.960 to 5.975 mm (0.2346 to 0.2352 inch)
        Limit .... 5.93 mm (0.235 inch)
Valve guide inside diameter (intake and exhaust)
    Standard .... 6.000 to 6.012 mm (0.2362 to 0.2367 inch)
    Limit .... 6.050 mm (0.2382 inch)

700 models (continued)

Cylinder head, valves and valve springs (continued)

Stem-to-guide clearance
  Intake
    Standard .... 0.010 to 0.037 mm (0.0004 to 0.0015 inch)
    Limit .... 0.08 mm (0.0031 inch)
  Exhaust
    Standard .... 0.025 to 0.052 mm (0.0010 to 0.0020 inch)
    Limit .... 0.1 mm (0.0004 inch)
Valve seat width (intake and exhaust)
  Standard .... 1.0 to 1.2 mm (0.0394 to 0.0472 inch)
  Limit .... 1.6 mm (0.063 inch)
Valve margin thickness (intake and exhaust) .... 0.8 to 1.2 mm (0.0315 to 0.0472 inch)
Valve spring free length (intake and exhaust)
  Standard .... 38.79 mm (1.53 inches)
  Limit .... 36.85 mm (1.45 inches)
Valve spring bend limit .... 2.5 degrees at 1.7 mm (0.067 inch)

Cylinder

Bore diameter
  Standard .... 102.000 to 102.010 mm (4.0157 to 4.0161 inches)
  Limit .... 102.080 mm (4.0189 inches)
  Measurement point .... At vertical center of the bore, front-to-rear and side-to-side
Out-of-round limit .... Not specified
Taper limit .... Not specified

Piston

Diameter .... 101.955 to 101.970 mm (4.0140 to 4.0146 inches)
Measuring point .... 10.0 mm (0.394 inch) from bottom of skirt
Piston-to-cylinder clearance
  Standard .... 0.030 to 0.055 mm (0.0012 to 0.0022 inch)
  Limit .... 0.13 mm (0.0051 inch)
Piston pin bore
  Standard .... 23.004 to 23.015 mm (0.9057 to 0.9061 inch)
  Limit .... 23.045 mm (0.9073 inch)
Piston pin outer diameter
  Standard .... 22.991 to 23.000 mm (0.9052 to 0.9055 inch)
  Limit .... 22.971 mm (0.9044 inch)
Piston pin-to-piston clearance
  Standard .... 0.004 to 0.024 mm (0.0002 to 0.0009 inch)
  Limit .... 0.074 mm (0.0029 inch)
Ring side clearance
  Top and second rings
    Standard .... 0.030 to 0.070 mm (0.0016 to 0.0031 inch)
    Limit .... 0.12 mm (0.0047 inch)
  Oil ring .... Not specified
Ring end gap
  Top ring
    Standard .... 0.20 to 0.35 mm (0.008 to 0.014 inch)
    Limit .... 0.60 mm (0.24 inch)
  Second ring
    Standard .... 0.75 to 0.90 mm (0.03 to 0.04 inch)
    Limit .... 1.25 mm (0.0492 inch)
  Oil ring
    Standard .... 0.20 to 0.70 mm (0.008 to 0.027 inch)
    Limit .... Not specified

Clutch

Spring free length
  Standard .... 50.0 mm (1.97 inches)
  Limit .... Not specified
Metal plate thickness .... 1.5 to 1.6 mm (0.059 to 0.063 inch)
Friction plate thickness
  Seven wide plates
    Standard .... 2.92 to 3.08 mm (0.115 to 0.121 inch)
    Limit .... 2.82 mm (0.111 inch)

    One narrow plate

        Standard .... 2.90 to 3.10 mm (0.114 to 0.122 inch)

        Limit .... 2.8 mm (0.110 inch)

Friction and metal plate warpage limit .... 0.2 mm (0.008 inch)

Oil pump

Outer rotor-to-body clearance .... 0.09 to 0.15 mm (0.0035 to 0.0059 inch)

Inner-to-outer rotor clearance

    Standard .... 0.12 mm (0.005 inch) or less

    Limit .... 0.20 mm (0.008 inch)

Transmission

Mainshaft and output shaft runout limit .... 0.08 mm (0.003 inch)

Crankshaft and connecting rod

Runout limit .... 0.03 mm (0.0012 inch)

Assembly width .... 74.95 to 75.00 mm (2.9508 to 2.9528 inches)

Connecting rod big-end side clearance

    Standard .... 0.35 to 0.65 mm (0.0138 to 0.0256 inch)

    Limit .... 1.0 mm (0.0394 inch)

Connecting rod big-end freeplay

    Standard .... 0.010 to 0.025 mm (0.0004 to 0.0010 inch)

    Limit .... Not specified

Connecting rod small end freeplay

    Standard .... 0.16 to 0.40 mm (0.006 to 0.015 inch)

    Limit .... Not specified

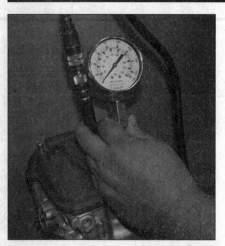

2.5 A compression gauge with a threaded fitting for the spark plug hole is preferred over the type that requires hand pressure to maintain the seal

1 General information

Included in this portion of Chapter 2 are general inspection and overhaul procedures. The information includes advice concerning preparation for an overhaul and the purchase of replacement parts, as well as inspection procedures which will tell you if a part must be reconditioned or replaced.

The Specifications included in this Part are only those necessary for the inspection and overhaul procedures which follow. Refer to Part A of Chapter 2 for additional Specifications and advice.

2 Cylinder compression - check

1   Among other things, poor engine performance may be caused by leaking valves, incorrect valve clearances, a leaking head gasket, or worn piston, rings and/or cylinder wall. A cylinder compression check will help pinpoint these conditions and can also indicate the presence of excessive carbon deposits in the cylinder head.

2   The only tools required are a compression gauge and a spark plug wrench. Depending on the outcome of the initial test, a squirt-type oil can may also be needed.

3   Start the engine and allow it to reach normal operating temperature, then remove the spark plugs (see Chapter 1, if necessary). Work carefully - don't strip the spark plug hole threads and don't burn your hands.

4   Disable the ignition by disconnecting the primary (low tension) wires from the coil (see Chapter 5). Be sure to mark the locations of the wires before detaching them.

5   Install the compression gauge in the spark plug hole **(see illustration)**. Hold or block the throttle wide open.

6   Crank the engine over a minimum of four or five revolutions (or until the gauge reading stops increasing) and observe the initial movement of the compression gauge needle as well as the final total gauge reading. Compare the results to the value listed in this Chapter's Specifications.

7   If the compression built up quickly and evenly to the specified amount, you can assume the engine upper end is in reasonably good mechanical condition. Worn or sticking piston rings and worn cylinders will produce very little initial movement of the gauge needle, but compression will tend to build up gradually as the engine spins over. Valve and valve seat leakage, or head gasket leakage, is indicated by low initial compression which does not tend to build up.

8   To further confirm your findings, add a small amount of engine oil to the cylinder by inserting the nozzle of a squirt-type oil can through the spark plug hole. The oil will tend to seal the piston rings if they are leaking.

9   If the compression increases significantly after the addition of the oil, the piston rings and/or cylinder are definitely worn. If the compression does not increase, the pressure is leaking past the valves or the head gasket. Leakage past the valves may be due to insufficient valve clearances, burned, warped or cracked valves or valve seats or valves that are hanging up in the guides.

10   If compression readings are considerably higher than specified, the combustion chamber is probably coated with excessive carbon deposits. It is possible (but not very likely) for carbon deposits to raise the compression enough to compensate for the effects of leakage past rings or valves. Refer to Section 6, remove the cylinder head and carefully decarbonize the combustion chamber.

3 Camshaft and rocker arms - inspection

Camshaft, chain and guides

Note: *Before replacing the camshaft or the cylinder head because of damage, check with local machine shops specializing in ATV or motorcycle engine work. In the case of the camshaft; it may be possible for cam lobes to be welded, reground and hardened, at a cost far lower than that of a new camshaft. Due to the cost of a new cylinder head it is recommended that all options be explored before condemning it as trash!*

1   Rotate the cam bearings and check for roughness, looseness or noise. Check the sealed side of the outer bearing for signs of leakage. Replace the bearing(s) if problems are found. The bearing that's installed on the 660 camshaft can't be replace separately; the entire camshaft must be replaced if the bearing is bad.

2   Check the camshaft lobes for heat discoloration (blue appearance), score marks, chipped areas, flat spots and spalling. Measure the height of each lobe with a micrometer (refer to "Tools and Workshop Tips" at the end of this manual, if necessary) and compare the results to the minimum lobe height listed in this Chapter's Specifications. If damage is noted or wear is excessive, the camshaft must be replaced. Check the bearing surfaces for scoring or wear. Also, be sure to check the condition of the rocker arms, as described below.

3   Except in cases of oil starvation, the camshaft chain wears very little. If the chain has stretched excessively, which makes it difficult to maintain proper tension, replace it with a new one (see Chapter 2A).

4   Check the sprocket for wear, cracks and other damage, replacing it if necessary. If the sprocket is worn, the chain is also worn, and possibly the sprocket on the crankshaft, If wear this severe is apparent, the entire engine should be disassembled for inspection.

5   Check the chain guides for wear or damage **(see illustration)**. If they are worn or damaged, replace them.

3.5 Check the friction surfaces of the camshaft guides for wear and scoring

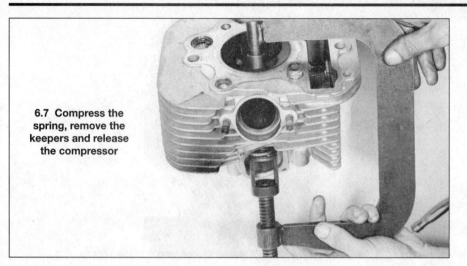

6.7 Compress the spring, remove the keepers and release the compressor

Rocker arms and shafts

6   Check the rocker arms for wear at the cam contact surfaces, inside the shaft bores and at the tips of the valve adjusting screws. Try to twist the rocker arms from side-to-side on the shafts. If they're loose on the shafts or if there's visible wear, measure the rocker arm shaft diameter and bore diameter with a micrometer and hole gauge. If the parts are worn beyond the limits listed in this Chapter's Specifications, replace them. Replace the rocker arm and shaft as a set. On 700 models, spin the rocker rollers and check for rough, loose or noisy movement. Replace the rocker arms if you find problems with the rollers.

4   Cylinder head - inspection

1   Check the cylinder head gasket and the mating surfaces on the cylinder head and cylinder for leakage, which could indicate warpage.
2   Clean all traces of old gasket material from the cylinder head and cylinder. Do not let any of the gasket material fall into the crankcase, the cylinder bore or the bolt holes.
3   Check the flatness of the cylinder head (see Section 6).

5   Valves/valve seats/valve guides - servicing

1   Because of the complex nature of this job and the special tools and equipment required, servicing of the valves, the valve seats and the valve guides (commonly known as a valve job) is best left to a professional.
2   The home mechanic can, however, remove and disassemble the head, do the initial cleaning and inspection, then reassemble and deliver the head to a dealer service

department or properly equipped vehicle repair shop for the actual valve servicing. Refer to Section 6 for those procedures.
3   The dealer service department will remove the valves and springs, recondition or replace the valves and valve seats, replace the valve guides, check and replace the valve springs, spring retainers and keepers (as necessary), replace the valve seals with new ones and reassemble the valve components.
4   After the valve job has been performed, the head will be in like-new condition. When the head is returned, be sure to clean it again very thoroughly before installation on the engine to remove any metal particles or abrasive grit that may still be present from the valve service operations. Use compressed air, if available, to blow out all the holes and passages.

6   Cylinder head and valves - disassembly, inspection and reassembly

1   As mentioned in the previous Section, valve servicing and valve guide replacement should be left to a dealer service department or vehicle repair shop. However, disassembly, cleaning and inspection of the valves and related components can be done (if the necessary special tools are available) by the home mechanic. This way no expense is incurred if the inspection reveals that service work is not required at this time.
2   To properly disassemble the valve components without the risk of damaging them, a valve spring compressor is absolutely necessary. If the special tool is not available, have a dealer service department or vehicle repair shop handle the entire process of disassembly, inspection, service or repair (if required) and reassembly of the valves.

Disassembly

3   Remove the carburetor intake manifold or throttle body intake tube from the cylinder head (see Chapter 4).

4   Before the valves are removed, scrape away any traces of gasket material from the head gasket sealing surface. Work slowly and do not nick or gouge the soft aluminum of the head. Gasket removing solvents, which work very well, are available at most vehicle shops and auto parts stores.
5   Carefully scrape all carbon deposits out of the combustion chamber area. A hand held wire brush or a piece of fine emery cloth can be used once most of the deposits have been scraped away. Do not use a wire brush mounted in a drill motor, or one with extremely stiff bristles, as the head material is soft and may be eroded away or scratched by the wire brush.
6   Before proceeding, arrange to label and store the valves along with their related components so they can be kept separate and reinstalled in the same valve guides they are removed from (again, plastic bags work well for this).
7   Compress the valve spring(s) on the first valve with a spring compressor, then remove the keepers and the retainer from the valve assembly **(see illustration)**. Do not compress the spring(s) any more than is absolutely necessary. Carefully release the valve spring compressor and remove the spring(s), spring seat and valve from the head. If the valve binds in the guide (won't pull through), push it back into the head and deburr the area around the keeper groove with a very fine file or whetstone.
8   Repeat the procedure for the remaining valves. Remember to keep the parts for each valve together so they can be reinstalled in the same location.
9   Once the valves have been removed and labeled, pull off the valve stem seals with pliers and discard them (the old seals should never be reused).
10   Next, clean the cylinder head with solvent and dry it thoroughly. Compressed air will speed the drying process and ensure that all holes and recessed areas are clean.
11   Clean all of the valve springs, keepers, retainers and spring seats with solvent and dry them thoroughly. Do the parts from one valve at a time so that no mixing of parts between valves occurs.
12   Scrape off any deposits that may have formed on the valve, then use a motorized wire brush to remove deposits from the valve heads and stems. Again, make sure the valves do not get mixed up.

Inspection

13   Inspect the head very carefully for cracks and other damage. If cracks are found, a new head will be required. Check the cam bearing surfaces for wear and evidence of seizure. Check the camshaft for wear as well (see Section 3).
14   Using a precision straightedge and a feeler gauge, check the head gasket mating surface for warpage. Lay the straightedge lengthwise, across the head and diagonally

6.17 Check the valve face (A), stem (B) and keeper groove (C) for wear and damage

6.19a Measure the free length of the valve springs

6.19b Check the valve springs for squareness

6.23 Apply the lapping compound very sparingly, in small dabs, to the valve face only

(corner-to-corner), intersecting the head bolt holes, and try to slip a feeler gauge under it, on either side of each combustion chamber (see "Tools and Workshop Tips" at the end of this manual if necessary). The feeler gauge thickness should be the same as the cylinder head warpage limit listed in this Chapter's Specifications. If the feeler gauge can be inserted between the head and the straightedge, the head is warped and must either be machined or, if warpage is excessive, replaced with a new one.

15 Examine the valve seats in each of the combustion chambers. If they are pitted, cracked or burned, the head will require valve service that is beyond the scope of the home mechanic. Measure the valve seat width and compare it to this Chapter's Specifications. If it is not within the specified range, or if it varies around its circumference, valve service work is required.

16 Clean the valve guides to remove any carbon buildup, then measure the inside diameters of the guides (at both ends and the center of the guide) with a small hole

gauge and a micrometer. Record the measurements for future reference. The guides are measured at the ends and at the center to determine if they are worn in a bell-mouth pattern (more wear at the ends). If they are, guide replacement is an absolute must.

17 Carefully inspect each valve face for cracks, pits and burned spots. Check the valve stem and the keeper groove area for cracks (see illustration). Rotate the valve and check for any obvious indication that it is bent. Check the end of the stem for pitting and excessive wear and make sure the bevel is the specified width. The presence of any of the above conditions indicates the need for valve servicing.

18 Measure the valve stem diameter with a micrometer. If the diameter is less than listed in this Chapter's Specifications, the valves will have to be replaced with new ones. Also check the valve stem for bending. Set the valve in a V-block with a dial indicator touching the middle of the stem. Rotate the valve and look for a reading on the gauge (which

indicates a bent stem). If the stem is bent, replace the valve.

19 Check the end of each valve spring for wear and pitting. Measure the free length (see illustration) and compare it to this Chapter's Specifications. Any springs that are shorter than specified have sagged and should not be reused. Stand the spring on a flat surface and check it for squareness (see illustration).

20 Check the spring retainers and keepers for obvious wear and cracks. Any questionable parts should not be reused, as extensive damage will occur in the event of failure during engine operation.

21 If the inspection indicates that no service work is required, the valve components can be reinstalled in the head.

Reassembly

22 If the valve seats have been ground, the valves and seats should be lapped before installing the valves in the head to ensure a positive seal between the valves and seats. This procedure requires coarse and fine valve lapping compound (available at auto parts stores) and a valve lapping tool. If a lapping tool is not available, a piece of rubber or plastic hose can be slipped over the valve stem (after the valve has been installed in the guide) and used to turn the valve.

23 Apply a small amount of coarse lapping compound to the valve face (see illustration), then slip the valve into the guide. Note: Make sure the valve is installed in the correct guide and be careful not to get any lapping compound on the valve stem.

24 Attach the lapping tool (or hose) to the valve and rotate the tool between the palms of your hands. Use a back-and-forth motion rather than a circular motion. Lift the valve off the seat and turn it at regular intervals to distribute the lapping compound properly. Continue the lapping procedure until the valve face and seat contact area is of uniform width and unbroken around the entire circumfer-

6.24 After lapping, the valve face should exhibit a uniform, unbroken contact pattern

6.27 A small dab of grease will help hold the keepers in place on the valve while the spring compressor is released

7.3 Corrosion like this can usually be removed by honing

ence of the valve face and seat **(see illustration)**. Once this is accomplished, lap the valves again with fine lapping compound.

25   Carefully remove the valve from the guide and wipe off all traces of lapping compound. Use solvent to clean the valve and wipe the seat area thoroughly with a solvent soaked cloth. Repeat the procedure for the remaining valves.

26   Lay the spring seat in place in the cylinder head, then install a new valve stem seal on the guide. Use an appropriate size deep socket to push the seal into place until it's properly seated. Don't twist or cock it, or it will not seal properly against the valve stem. Also, don't remove it again or it will be damaged.

27   Coat the valve stems with assembly lube or moly-based grease, then install one of them into its guide. Next, install the spring seat, springs and retainers, compress the springs and install the keepers. **Note:** *Install the springs with the tightly wound coils at the bottom (next to the spring seat).* When compressing the springs with the valve spring compressor, depress them only as far as is absolutely necessary to slip the keepers into place. Apply a small amount of grease to the keepers **(see illustration)** to help hold them in place as the pressure is released from the springs. Make certain that the keepers are securely locked in their retaining grooves.

28   Support the cylinder head on blocks so the valves can't contact the workbench top, then very gently tap each of the valve stems with a soft-faced hammer. This will help seat the keepers in their grooves.

29   Once all of the valves have been installed in the head, check for proper valve sealing by pouring a small amount of solvent into each of the valve ports. If the solvent leaks past the valve(s) into the combustion chamber area, disassemble the valve(s) and repeat the lapping procedure, then reinstall the valve(s) and repeat the check. Repeat the procedure until a satisfactory seal is obtained.

7   Cylinder - inspection

Caution: Don't attempt to separate the liner from the cylinder.

1   Check the top surface of the cylinder for warpage, using the same method as for the cylinder head (see Section 6). Measure along the sides and diagonally across the stud holes.

2   Check the cylinder walls carefully for scratches and score marks.

3   Using the appropriate precision measuring tools, check the cylinder's diameter at the top, center and bottom of the cylinder bore, parallel to the crankshaft axis. Next, measure the cylinder's diameter at the same three locations across the crankshaft axis. Compare the results to this Chapter's Specifications. If the cylinder walls are tapered, out-of-round, worn beyond the specified limits, badly scuffed or scored or corroded **(see illustration)**, have the cylinder rebored and honed by a dealer service department or an ATV repair shop. If a rebore is done, oversize pistons and rings will be required as well. **Note:** *Check to make sure that oversized pistons are available before having the cylinder bored.*

4   As an alternative, if the precision measuring tools are not available, a dealer service department or repair shop will make the measurements and offer advice concerning servicing of the cylinder.

5   If it's in reasonably good condition and not worn to the outside of the limits, and if the piston-to-cylinder clearance can be maintained properly, then the cylinder does not have to be rebored; honing is all that is necessary.

6   To perform the honing operation you will need the proper size flexible hone with fine stones as shown in *Tools and Workshop Tips* at the end of this book, or a bottle brush type hone, plenty of light oil or honing oil, some

shop towels and an electric drill motor. Hold the cylinder block in a vise (cushioned with soft jaws or wood blocks) when performing the honing operation. Mount the hone in the drill motor, compress the stones and slip the hone into the cylinder. Lubricate the cylinder thoroughly, turn on the drill and move the hone up and down in the cylinder at a pace which will produce a fine crosshatch pattern on the cylinder wall with the crosshatch lines intersecting at approximately a 60-degree angle. Be sure to use plenty of lubricant and do not take off any more material than is absolutely necessary to produce the desired effect. Do not withdraw the hone from the cylinder while it is running. Instead, shut off the drill and continue moving the hone up and down in the cylinder until it comes to a complete stop, then compress the stones and withdraw the hone. Wipe the oil out of the cylinder and repeat the procedure on the remaining cylinder. Remember, do not remove too much material from the cylinder wall. If you do not have the tools, or do not desire to perform the honing operation, a dealer service department or vehicle repair shop will generally do it for a reasonable fee.

7   Next, the cylinder must be thoroughly washed with warm soapy water to remove all traces of the abrasive grit produced during the honing operation. Be sure to run a brush through the bolt holes and flush them with running water. After rinsing, dry the cylinder thoroughly and apply a coat of light, rust-preventative oil to all machined surfaces.

8   Piston - removal, inspection and installation

1   The piston is attached to the connecting rod with a piston pin that is a slip fit in the piston and rod.

2   Before removing the piston from the

8.3a The EX (660) or punch (700) mark on the piston goes toward the exhaust side of the engine

8.3b Wear eye protection and pry the circlip out of its groove with a pointed tool

rod, stuff a clean shop towel into the crankcase hole, around the connecting rod. This will prevent the circlips from falling into the crankcase if they are inadvertently dropped.

Removal

3   The 660 piston should have an EX mark that goes toward the front (exhaust) side of the engine **(see illustration)**. The 700 piston should have a punch mark that goes toward the front side of the engine. If this mark is not visible due to carbon buildup, scribe an arrow into the piston crown before removal. Support the piston and pry the circlip out with a pointed tool **(see illustration)**.

4   Push the piston pin out from the opposite end to free the piston from the rod **(see illustration)**. You may have to deburr the area around the groove to enable the pin to slide out (use a triangular file for this procedure). If the pin won't come out, you can fabricate a drawbolt from a long bolt, a nut, a piece of tubing and washers (see "Tools and Workshop Tips" at the end of this manual).

Inspection

5   Before the inspection process can be carried out, the pistons must be cleaned and the old piston rings removed.

6   Using a piston ring removal and installation tool, carefully remove the rings from the pistons **(see illustration)**. Do not nick or gouge the pistons in the process.

7   Scrape all traces of carbon from the tops of the pistons. A hand-held wire brush or a piece of fine emery cloth can be used once the majority of the deposits have been scraped away. Do not, under any circumstances, use a wire brush mounted in a drill motor to remove deposits from the pistons; the piston material is soft and will be eroded away by the wire brush.

8   Use a piston ring groove cleaning tool to remove any carbon deposits from the ring grooves. If a tool is not available, a piece broken off the old ring will do the job. Be very careful to remove only the carbon deposits. Do not remove any metal and do not nick or gouge the sides of the ring grooves.

9   Once the deposits have been removed, clean the piston with solvent and dry it thoroughly. Make sure the oil return holes below the oil ring grooves are clear **(see illustration)**.

10   If the piston is not damaged or worn excessively and if the cylinder is not rebored, a new piston will not be necessary. Normal piston wear appears as even, vertical wear on the thrust surfaces of the piston and slight looseness of the top ring in its groove. New piston rings, on the other hand, should always be used when an engine is rebuilt.

11   Carefully inspect each piston for cracks around the skirt, at the pin bosses and at the ring lands.

12   Look for scoring and scuffing on the thrust faces of the skirt, holes in the piston crown and burned areas at the edge of the crown. If the skirt is scored or scuffed, the engine may have been suffering from overheating and/or abnormal combustion, which caused excessively high operating temperatures. The oil pump should be checked thoroughly. A hole in the piston crown, an

8.4 The piston pin should come out with hand pressure - if it doesn't, this removal tool can be fabricated from readily available parts

8.6 Remove the piston rings with a ring removal and installation tool

8.9 Check the piston pin bore and the piston skirt for wear, and make sure any internal holes are clear

extreme to be sure, is an indication that abnormal combustion (pre-ignition) was occurring. Burned areas at the edge of the piston crown are usually evidence of spark knock (detonation). If any of the above problems exist, the causes must be corrected or the damage will occur again.

13   Measure the piston ring-to-groove clearance (side clearance) by laying a new piston ring in the ring groove and slipping a feeler gauge in beside it. Check the clearance at three or four locations around the groove. Use the correct ring for each groove; they are different. If the clearance is greater then specified, new pistons will have to be used when the engine is reassembled.

14   Check the piston-to-bore clearance by measuring the bore (see Section 7) and the piston diameter (see illustration). Measure the piston across the skirt on the thrust faces at a 90-degree angle to the piston pin, at the specified distance up from the bottom of the skirt. Subtract the piston diameter from the bore diameter to obtain the clearance. If it is greater than specified, the cylinder will have to be rebored and a new oversized piston and rings installed. If the appropriate precision measuring tools are not available, the piston-to-cylinder clearance can be obtained, though not quite as accurately, using feeler gauge stock. Feeler gauge stock comes in 12-inch lengths and various thicknesses and is generally available at auto parts stores. To check the clearance, slip a piece of feeler gauge stock of the same thickness as the specified piston clearance into the cylinder along with appropriate piston. The cylinder should be upside down and the piston must be positioned exactly as it normally would be. Place the feeler gauge between the piston and cylinder on one of the thrust faces (90-degrees to the piston pin bore). The piston should slip through the cylinder (with the feeler gauge in place) with moderate pressure. If it falls through, or slides through easily, the clearance is excessive and a new piston will be required. If the piston binds at the lower end of the cylinder and is loose

8.14 Measure the piston diameter with a micrometer

toward the top, the cylinder is tapered, and if tight spots are encountered as the piston/feeler gauge is rotated in the cylinder, the cylinder is out-of-round. Be sure to have the cylinder and piston checked by a dealer service department or a repair shop to confirm your findings before purchasing new parts.

15   Apply clean engine oil to the pin, insert it partway into the piston and check for free-play by rocking the pin back-and-forth. If the pin is loose, a new piston and possibly new pin must be installed.

16   Repeat Step 15, this time inserting the piston pin into the connecting rod (see illustration). If the pin is loose, measure the pin diameter and the pin bore in the rod (or have this done by a dealer or repair shop). A worn pin can be replaced separately; if the rod bore is worn, the rod and crankshaft must be replaced as an assembly.

17   Refer to Section 9 and install the rings on the pistons.

Installation

18   Install the piston with its mark toward the correct side of the engine (see illustration 8.3a). Lubricate the pin and the rod

8.16 Slip the piston pin into the rod and try to rock it back-and-forth to check for looseness

bore with moly-based grease. Install a new circlips in the groove in one side of the piston (don't reuse the old circlips). Push the pin into position from the opposite side and install another new circlip. Compress the circlips only enough for them to fit in the piston. Make sure the clips are properly seated in the grooves (see illustration).

9   Piston rings - installation

1   Before installing the new piston rings, the ring end gaps must be checked.

2   Insert the top (No. 1) ring into the bottom of the first cylinder and square it up with the cylinder walls by pushing it in with the top of the piston. The ring should be about one-half inch above the bottom edge of the cylinder. To measure the end gap, slip a feeler gauge between the ends of the ring (see illustration) and compare the measurement to the Specifications.

8.18 Make sure both piston pin circlips are securely seated in the piston grooves

9.2 Check the piston ring end gap with a feeler gauge at the bottom of the cylinder

9.4 If the end gap is too small, clamp a file in a vise and file the ring ends (from the outside in only) to enlarge the gap slightly

9.7a Install the oil ring expander - make sure the ends don't overlap

3   If the gap is larger or smaller than specified, double check to make sure that you have the correct rings before proceeding.

4   If the gap is too small, it must be

9.7b Installing an oil ring side rail - don't use a ring installation tool to do this

enlarged or the ring ends may come in contact with each other during engine operation, which can cause serious damage. The end gap can be increased by filing the ring ends very carefully with a fine file **(see illustration)**. When performing this operation, file only from the outside in.

5   Repeat the procedure for the second compression ring (ring gap is not specified for the oil ring rails or spacer).

6   Once the ring end gaps have been checked/corrected, the rings can be installed on the piston.

7   The oil control ring (lowest on the piston) is installed first. It is composed of three separate components. Slip the spacer into the groove, then install the upper side rail **(see illustrations)**. Do not use a piston ring installation tool on the oil ring side rails as they may be damaged. Instead, place one end of the side rail into the groove between the spacer expander and the ring land. Hold it firmly in place and slide a finger around the piston while pushing the rail into the groove (taking care not to cut your fingers on the

sharp edges). Next, install the lower side rail in the same manner.

8   After the three oil ring components have been installed, check to make sure that both the upper and lower side rails can be turned smoothly in the ring groove.

9   Install the no. 2 (middle) ring next **(see illustration)**. It can be readily distinguished from the top ring by its tapered cross-section shape. Do not mix the top and middle rings.

10   To avoid breaking the ring, use a piston ring installation tool and make sure that the identification mark is facing up. Fit the ring into the middle groove on the piston. Do not expand the ring any more than is necessary to slide it into place.

11   Finally, install the no. 1 (top) ring in the same manner. Make sure the identifying mark is facing up. Be very careful not to confuse the top and second rings. Besides the different profiles, the top ring is narrower than the second ring.

12   Once the rings have been properly installed, stagger the end gaps, including those of the oil ring side rails **(see illustration)**.

9.9 Install the middle ring with its identification mark up

9.12 Ring details

10.1 Inspect the clutch housing, clutch center and pressure plate

A   Clutch center bolt posts
B   Clutch center and pressure
    plate friction surfaces
C   Clutch center splines
D   Primary driven gear
E   Clutch housing bushing
F   Clutch housing slot

10.2 Turn the clutch housing over and inspect the gears and the inner part of the bushing

10 Clutch - inspection

1   Check the bolt posts and the friction surface on the pressure plate for damaged threads, scoring or wear (see illustration). Replace the pressure plate if any defects are found. Check the edges of the slots in the clutch housing for indentations made by the friction plate tabs. If the indentations are deep they can prevent clutch release, so the housing should be replaced with a new one. If the indentations can be removed easily with a file, the life of the housing can be prolonged to an extent.
2   Check the bushing surface in the center of the clutch housing for score marks, scratches and excessive wear (see illus-

tration). Also, check the driven gear and oil pump drive gear teeth for cracks, chips and excessive wear. If the bushing or gear is worn or damaged, the clutch housing must be replaced with a new one. If the clutch housing is replaced, the primary drive gear should be replaced as well.
3   Check the splines of the clutch center for indentations made by the tabs on the metal plates. Check the clutch center friction surface for wear or scoring. Replace the clutch center if problems are found.
4   Measure the free length of the clutch springs (see illustration) and compare the results to this Chapter's Specifications. If the springs have sagged, or if cracks are noted, replace them with new ones as a set.
5   If the lining material of the friction plates smells burnt or if it is glazed, new parts are required (see illustration). Note that severe

10.4 Measure the clutch spring free length

10.5a This new clutch was destroyed in a single day because the rider slipped it excessively - fragments of the burnt friction plates (left) got into the engine oil and were trapped by the filter (right)

10.5b Measure the thickness of the friction plates

10.6 Check the metal plates for warpage

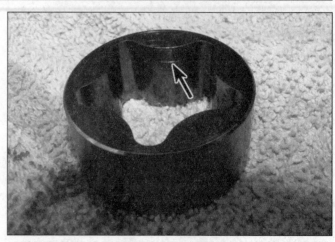

11.2 If the pump rotors are scored like this, the pump should be replaced with a new one

11.3a Use a feeler gauge to measure the inner-to-outer rotor clearance . . .

11.3b . . . and the outer rotor-to-body clearance

11.3c Lay a straightedge across the rotors and pump body and measure the gap with a feeler gauge

damage will cause residue to enter the engine oil, so be sure to change the oil and filter if this type of problem is found. If the metal clutch plates are scored or discolored, they must be replaced with new ones. Measure the thickness of the friction plates (see illustration) and replace with new parts any friction plates that are worn.

6   Lay the metal plates, one at a time, on a perfectly flat surface (such as a piece of plate glass) and check for warpage by trying to slip a feeler gauge between the flat surface and the plate (see illustration). The feeler gauge should be the same thickness as the maximum warp listed in this Chapter's Specifications. Do this at several places around the plate's circumference. If the feeler gauge can be slipped under the plate, it is warped and should be replaced with a new one.

7   Check the tabs on the friction plates for excessive wear and mushroomed edges. They can be cleaned up with a file if the deformation is not severe. Check the friction plates for warpage as described in Step 6.

8   Check the thrust washer for score marks, heat discoloration and evidence of excessive wear.

11 Oil pump - inspection

1   Remove and disassemble the pump, referring to the Part A of this Chapter.
2   Wash all of the pump components in solvent, then dry them off. Check the pump body, the rotors and the cover for scoring and wear (see illustration). If any damage or excessive or uneven wear is evident, replace the pump. If you are rebuilding the engine, it's a good idea to install a new oil pump.
3   Place the rotors in the pump cover. Measure the clearance between the outer rotor and body, and between the inner and outer rotors, with a feeler gauge (see illustrations). Place a straightedge across the pump body and rotors and measure the gap with a feeler gauge (see illustration). If either of the rotor clearances is beyond the limits listed in the Chapter's Specifications, replace the pump. Clearance between the rotors and straightedge isn't specified by Yamaha, but if it's significant, the pump should be replaced.

12 Crankcase bearings - inspection, removal and installation

1   Separate the crankcase and remove the following:
a) Transmission shafts and gears
b) Balancer shaft(s)
c) Crankshaft and main bearings
d) Shift cam and forks
2   Clean the crankcase halves thoroughly with new solvent and dry them with compressed air. All oil passages should be blown out with compressed air and all traces of old gasket sealant should be removed from the mating surfaces.

Caution: Be very careful not to nick or gouge the crankcase mating surfaces or leaks will result. Check both crankcase sections very carefully for cracks and other damage.

3   Check the bearings in the case halves (see Chapter 2A). If they don't turn smoothly, replace them. For bearings that aren't acces-

13.3 Use a tool like this one to push the crankshaft out of the case half

13.4 Check the connecting rod side clearance with a feeler gauge

sible from the outside, a blind hole puller will be needed for removal. Drive the remaining bearings out with a bearing driver or a socket having an outside diameter slightly smaller than that of the bearing outer race. Before installing the bearings, allow them to sit in the freezer overnight, and about fifteen-minutes before installation, place the case half in an oven, set to about 200-degrees F, and allow it to heat up. The bearings are an interference fit, and this will ease installation.

⚠️ *Warning: Before heating the case, wash it thoroughly with soap and water so no explosive fumes are present. Also, don't use a flame to heat the case. Install the bearings with a socket or bearing driver that bears against the bearing outer race.*

4   If any damage is found that can't be repaired, replace the crankcase halves as a set.

5   Assemble the case halves and check to make sure the crankshaft, balancer shaft(s) and transmission shafts turn freely.

13 Crankshaft and connecting rod - removal, inspection and installation

Note: *The procedures in this section require special tools. If you don't have the necessary equipment or suitable substitutes, have the crankshaft removed and installed by a Yamaha dealer.*

Removal

1   Remove the engine and separate the crankcase halves.

2   The transmission shafts and balancer shafts need not be removed.

3   The crankshaft may be loose enough in its bearing that you can lift it out of the crankcase half that it stayed in. If not, push it out with a Yamaha puller or equivalent **(see illustration)**.

Inspection

4   Measure the side clearance between connecting rod and crankshaft with a feeler gauge **(see illustration)**. If it's more than the limit listed in this Chapter's Specifications,

replace the crankshaft and connecting rod as an assembly.

5   Set up the crankshaft in V-blocks with a dial indicator contacting the big end of the connecting rod. Move the connecting rod side-to-side against the indicator pointer and compare the reading to the value listed in this Chapter's Specifications. If it's beyond the limit, the crankshaft can be disassembled and the needle roller bearing replaced. However, this is a specialized job that should be done by a Yamaha dealer or qualified machine shop.

6   Check the crankshaft splines, the cam chain sprocket, the ball bearing at the sprocket end of the crankshaft and the bearing journals for visible wear or damage **(see illustration)**. Yamaha lists the ball bearing end of the crankshaft as a separately available part, but check with your dealer first; it may be more practical to replace the entire crankshaft if the ball bearing or cam sprocket is worn or damaged. Replace the crankshaft if any of the other conditions are found.

7   Set the crankshaft in a lathe or a pair of V-blocks, with a dial indicator contacting each end **(see illustration)**. Rotate the crankshaft and note the runout. If the runout

13.6 Check the crankshaft bearings for rough, loose or noisy movement and check the cam chain sprocket for wear

13.7 Measure runout on each side of the crankshaft (A); if the assembly width (B) is greater than specified, replace the crankshaft

13.9 These tools are used to pull the crankshaft into the left case half

at either end is beyond the limit listed in this Chapter's Specifications, replace the crankshaft and connecting rod as an assembly.

8   Measure the assembly width of the crankshaft **(see illustration 13.7)**. If it exceeds the limit listed in this Chapter's Specifications, replace the crankshaft.

Installation

9   Start the crankshaft into the left case half. If it doesn't go in easily, pull it in the rest of the way with a Yamaha puller or equivalent **(see illustration)**.

10   The remainder of installation is the reverse of removal.

14 Transmission components - inspection

1   Inspect the shift fork grooves in the gears, the middle driven gear holder and the dog clutch. If a groove is worn or scored, replace the affected part and inspect its corresponding shift fork.

2   Check the shift forks for distortion and wear, especially at the fork ears. If they are discolored or severely worn they are probably bent. Inspect the guide pins for excessive wear and distortion and replace any defective parts with new ones.

3   Check the shift fork guide bars evidence of wear, galling and other damage.

Make sure the shift forks move smoothly on the guide bars. If the shafts are worn or bent, replace them with new ones.

4   Check the edges of the grooves in the shift cam(s) for signs of excessive wear.

5   Hold the inner race of the shift cam bearing with fingers and spin the outer race. Replace the bearing if it's rough, loose or noisy.

6   Check the gear teeth for cracking and other obvious damage. Check the bushing surface in the inner diameter of the free-wheeling gears for scoring or heat discoloration. Replace damaged parts.

7   Inspect the engagement dogs and dog holes on gears so equipped for excessive wear or rounding off. Replace the paired gears as a set if necessary.

8   Check the transmission shaft bearings in the crankcase for wear or heat discoloration and replace them if necessary (see Section 12).

15 Initial start-up after overhaul

1   Make sure the engine oil level is correct, then remove the spark plug from the engine. Place the engine kill switch in the Off position and unplug the primary (low tension) wires from the coil.

2   Turn on the key switch and crank the engine over with the starter several times to build up oil pressure. Reinstall the spark

plug, connect the wires and turn the switch to On.

3   Make sure there is fuel in the tank, then operate the choke.

4   Start the engine and allow it to run at a moderately fast idle until it reaches operating temperature.

Caution: If the oil temperature light (if equipped) doesn't go off, or it comes on while the engine is running, stop the engine immediately.

5   Check carefully for oil leaks and make sure the transmission and controls, especially the brakes, function properly before road testing the machine. Refer to Section 16 for the recommended break-in procedure.

6   Upon completion of the road test, and after the engine has cooled down completely, recheck the valve clearances (see Chapter 1).

16 Recommended break-in procedure

1   Any rebuilt engine needs time to break-in, even if parts have been installed in their original locations. For this reason, treat the machine gently for the first few miles to make sure oil has circulated throughout the engine and any new parts installed have started to seat.

2   Even greater care is necessary if the cylinder has been rebored or a new crankshaft has been installed. In the case of a rebore, the engine will have to be broken in as if the machine were new. This means greater use of the transmission and a restraining hand on the throttle for the first few operating days. There's no point in keeping to any set speed limit - the main idea is to vary the engine speed, keep from lugging (laboring) the engine and to avoid full-throttle operation. These recommendations can be lessened to an extent when only a new crankshaft is installed. Experience is the best guide, since it's easy to tell when an engine is running freely.

3   If a lubrication failure is suspected, stop the engine immediately and try to find the cause. If an engine is run without oil, even for a short period of time, irreparable damage will occur.

Chapter 3
Cooling system

Contents

Degrees of difficulty

Easy, suitable for novice with little experience	**Fairly easy,** suitable for beginner with some experience	**Fairly difficult,** suitable for competent DIY mechanic	**Difficult,** suitable for experienced DIY mechanic	**Very difficult,** suitable for expert DIY or professional

Specifications

General
Radiator cap relief pressure
    660 models .... 13.8 to 18.1 psi
    700 models .... 13.3 to 17.4 psi

Torque specifications
Water pump bolts
    660 models .... 10 Nm (86 inch-lbs)
    700 models
        Water pump cover to pump body .... 11 Nm (96 inch-lbs)
        Water pump body to crankcase .... 10 Nm (86 inch-lbs)
Thermostat housing mounting bolt (660 models only) .... 10 Nm (86 inch-lbs)
Thermostat housing cover bolts .... 10 Nm (86 inch-lbs)
Radiator mounting bolts .... 7 Nm (61 inch-lbs)
Coolant reservoir mounting bolts .... 7 Nm (61 inch-lbs)
Coolant temperature sensor
    660 models .... 28 Nm (20 ft-lbs)
    700 models .... 18 Nm (156 inch-lbs)
Coolant hose fitting to cylinder .... 10 Nm (86 inch-lbs)

3.1a On 660 models, the coolant reservoir is located under the left rear fender

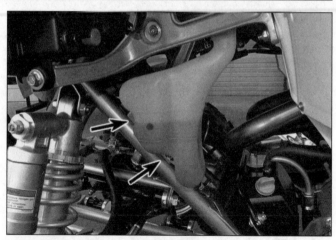

3.1b On 700 models, coolant reservoir is located under the left front fender - disconnect its hoses and remove its bolts (hidden) to remove it

1 General information

The vehicles covered by this manual are equipped with a liquid cooling system which utilizes a water/antifreeze mixture to carry away excess heat produced during combustion. The combustion chamber and cylinder are surrounded by a water jacket, through which the coolant is circulated by the water pump. The pump is mounted to the right side of the crankcase near the front and is driven by a gear. The radiator is mounted at the front of the frame. The coolant is pumped upward through the cylinder water jacket and cylinder head, then flows from the cylinder head to the radiator where it is cooled, then flows through the radiator bottom hose and water pump, then back into the engine.

The cooling system includes a temperature warning light, fan and thermostat. All models have a reservoir tank. As the coolant heats up, it expands and flows into the reservoir tank. As it cools, the coolant is pulled back into the cooling system.

2 Radiator cap - check

If problems such as overheating or loss of coolant occur, check the entire system as described in Chapter 1. The radiator cap opening pressure should be checked by a dealer service department or service station equipped with the special tester required to do the job. If the cap is defective, replace it with a new one.

3 Coolant reservoir - removal and installation

1   On 660 models, the coolant reservoir is located under the left side of the rear fender (see illustration). On 700 models, the coolant reservoir is located forward of the engine on the left side of the vehicle (see illustration).

2   Disconnect the hoses from the tank. Remove the tank mounting bolts and take it off (see illustration 3.1b and the accompanying illustration).

3   Installation is the reverse of removal.

4 Coolant hoses - removal and installation

1   The coolant hoses are all secured by screw-type clamps to fittings on the engine and radiator. On 660 models, the fitting at the left rear corner of the cylinder head is secured by a flange fitting and single bolt, and sealed with an O-ring.

2   On 660 models, the water pump inlet hose connects to the bottom of the radiator (see illustrations). The water pump outlet

3.2 Reservoir mounting bolt locations (660 models)

4.2a On 660 models, the water pump inlet hose runs from the water pump . . .

4.2b ... to the bottom of the radiator

4.2c On 660 models, the water pump outlet hose connects the water pump to a fitting on the cylinder

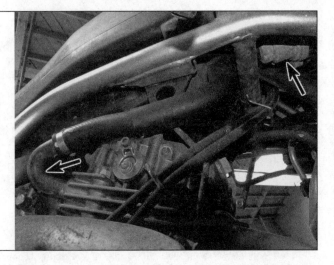

4.2d On 660 models, the engine outlet hose connects a fitting on the cylinder head (left) to the thermostat housing (right) ...

4.2e ... and another hose connects the thermostat housing to the top of the radiator

hose runs from the water pump to a fitting bolted to the front of the cylinder **(see illustration)**. Coolant circulates through the cylinder and cylinder head, then exits through a passage at the top rear of the engine and flows to the thermostat housing **(see illustration)**. When the thermostat is open, the coolant flows through the thermostat and another hose to the top of the radiator **(see illustration)**.

3 On 700 models, the water pump inlet hose connects to the bottom of the radiator **(see illustrations)**. The water pump out-

4.3a On 700 models, the water pump inlet hose runs from the water pump ...

4.3b ... to the bottom of the radiator

4.3c On 700 models, the water pump outlet hose connects the water pump to a fitting on the cylinder

4.3d On 700 models, the engine outlet hose connects the thermostat housing on the cylinder head . . .

let hose runs to a fitting on the front of the cylinder **(see illustration)**. A third hose runs from the thermostat housing at the right rear

4.3e . . . to the top of the radiator (right) near the siphon hose (left)

corner of the cylinder head to the top of the radiator.
4   On 700 models, small-diameter hoses supply engine coolant to the fast idle plunger in the fuel injection throttle body to regulate its operation **(see illustrations)**.
5   To remove a hose, loosen its clamp and carefully pry it off the fitting. To remove the water pump-to-engine hose, unbolt the fitting from the front of the engine, then detach the hose from the water pump body and take the fitting and hose out together. The hose can then be detached from the fitting.
6   If the hose is stuck, pry the edge up slightly with a pointed tool and spray brake or electrical contact cleaner into the gap. Work the tool around the fitting, lifting the edge of the hose and spraying into the gap until the hose comes free of the fitting.
7   In extreme cases, you may have to slit the hose and cut it off the fitting with a knife. Make sure you can get a replacement hose before doing this.

5 Cooling fan and circuit - check and switch replacement

Check

1   If the engine is overheating and the cooling fan isn't coming on, first check the main fuse (all models) and ignition fuse (660 models) (see Chapter 5). If a fuse is blown, check the fan circuit for a short to ground (see the *Wiring diagrams* at the end of this book).
2   If the fuses are good, check the battery, then the main key switch (see Chapter 5).
3   If the fuses, battery and main key switch are good, disconnect the fan motor connector and connect the fan motor directly to a fully charged 12-volt battery using a pair of jumper wires (battery positive to blue; battery negative to black). The fan motor should run. If it doesn't, replace the fan with a new one.
4   On 700 models, check the fan motor

4.4a On 700 models, this small hose supplies coolant to the fast idle plunger . . .

4.4b . . . and this small hose returns the coolant to the engine (throttle body partially removed for clarity)

5.6 On 660 models, the thermoswitch is located in the bottom of the radiator

5.10 On 700 models, the thermoswitch is located in the cylinder head near the thermostat housing

6.3 Disconnect the breather hose from the fan motor (660 shown)

relay. The relay is located under the seat, behind the air filter housing, and can be identified by its wire colors (yellow-red, brown, red-blue and red-white). Pull the relay off its mounting tab and disconnect the wiring harness from it. Connect an ohmmeter and 12-volt battery to the relay terminals as follows:

a) Ohmmeter between the relay terminals that connect to the red-blue and red-white wires. There should be no continuity (infinite resistance).

b) Leave the ohmmeter connected and connect a 12-volt battery between the terminals that connect to the yellow-red and brown wires (positive to brown; negative to yellow-red). The ohmmeter should now show continuity (little or no resistance.

If the relay performs as described, it's good. Connect the wiring harness and reinstall it. If it doesn't perform as described, replace it with a new one.

5   If all of the previously tested components are good, locate the fan circuit breaker.

a) On 660 models, it's in the wiring harness below the handlebars and can be identified by its two red/white wires.

b) On 700 models, it's under the seat near the headlight relay and can be identified by its red and red-white wires.

Disconnect the circuit breaker wires and connect an ohmmeter between them (to the circuit breaker, not to the wiring harness). There be should be continuity (zero ohms). If the ohmmeter indicates resistance, replace the circuit breaker with a new one.

660 models

6   If the fan motor runs when connected directly to the battery, disconnect the electrical connector from the fan thermoswitch mounted in the radiator bottom tank (see

illustration). It can be identified by its wire colors: red-white and blue) **Note:** *Don't mistake the fan thermoswitch for the warning light thermoswitch. The fan thermoswitch is mounted in the bottom tank of the radiator. The warning light thermoswitch is mounted in the thermostat housing.*

7   Connect the positive terminal of a voltmeter to the harness side of the red-white wire (not the switch side of the wire). Connect the negative terminal of the voltmeter to ground (bare metal on the frame).

8   With the main key switch Off, there should be no voltage reading. With the main key switch On, there should 12 volts. If there isn't any voltage, there's a break or bad connection in the wiring, or one of the previously tested components is bad. Check the wiring carefully, looking especially for corrosion at the connectors. If the wiring is good but there's still no voltage, repeat the component tests described earlier.

9   If there is a reading of 12 volts (or more), connect a short jumper wire between the thermoswitch terminals in the wiring harness. If the fan now runs, the thermoswitch is bad and must be replaced (see Steps 14 through 18).

700 models

10   If the fan motor runs when connected directly to the battery, disconnect the electrical connector from the fan thermoswitch mounted in the right rear corner of the cylinder head (see illustration). It can be identified by its wire colors: black-yellow and black-blue).

11   Drain the cooling system (see Chapter 1). Unscrew the thermoswitch from the engine and suspend it in a pan of water with a thermometer so it doesn't touch the sides.

 Warning: Antifreeze is poisonous. DO NOT use a cooking pan for this test.

12   Connect an ohmmeter between the terminals of the switch and heat the water. At room temperature (20-degrees C/68-degrees F), the ohmmeter should indicate 2.32 to 2.59 k-ohms. It should show 0.310 to 0.326 k-ohms when the water is heated to approximately 80-degrees C (176-degrees F).

13   If the switch doesn't perform as specified, replace it (see Steps 14 through 18).

Thermoswitch replacement

14   Drain the cooling system (see Chapter 1).

15   If you haven't already done so, disconnect the electrical connector from the thermoswitch (see illustration 5.6 or 5.10).

16   Unscrew the thermoswitch from the radiator.

17   If the thermoswitch uses a gasket, install a new one. If it doesn't, coat the threads with silicone sealant.

18   Tighten the thermoswitch to the torque listed in this Chapter's Specifications.

6   Radiator and fan - removal and installation

 Warning: The engine must be completely cool before beginning this procedure.

1   Remove the seat, side covers and front fender (see Chapter 8). Drain the cooling system (see Chapter 1).

2   Disconnect the electrical connectors for the fan and warning light switch.

3   Disconnect the breather hose from the fan housing (see illustration).

4   Disconnect the radiator hoses (see Section 3).

6.5a On 660 models, the radiator mounting bolts are accessible from the side (right side shown)

A   *Radiator mounting bolt and grommet*
B   *Fan mounting bolt*

5   Remove the radiator mounting bolts **(see illustrations)**.
6   Lift the radiator away from the frame.

6.7b Upper right radiator fan mounting bolt location (hidden)

7.1a On 660 models, the thermostat housing is a separate unit bolted to the frame

6.5b 700 radiator mounting bolts (upper arrows) and grommet (lower arrow)

Inspect the mounting grommets and replace them if they're worn or deteriorated.
7   Remove the fan mounting bolts and take the fan motor off the radiator **(see illustration 6.5a and the accompanying illustrations)**. The fan and motor are not available separately.
8   Installation is the reverse of removal, with the following additions:
a) *Tighten the mounting bolts securely, but don't overtighten them and distort the grommets.*
b) *Fill the cooling system (see Chapter 1).*
c) *Run the engine and check for coolant leaks.*

7   Thermostat - removal, inspection and installation

1   On 660 models, the thermostat is contained in a separate housing, bolted to the frame and connected to the engine and radiator by hoses **(see illustration)**. On 700 mod-

7.1b On 700 models, the thermostat housing is secured to the cylinder head by two bolts

6.7a Lower left radiator fan mounting bolt location

els, the thermostat is contained in a housing in the cylinder head **(see illustration)**.

Removal

2   Drain the cooling system below the level of the thermostat.
3   Place rags beneath the thermostat housing to catch any residual coolant that drips out, then unbolt the cover from the thermostat housing. Remove the thermostat from the housing.

Inspection

4   Remove any coolant deposits, then visually check the thermostat for corrosion, cracks and other damage. If it was open when it was removed, the thermostat is defective.
5   To check the thermostat operation, submerge it in a container of the specified coolant (50/50 antifreeze and water) along with a thermometer. The thermostat should be suspended so it does not touch the sides of the container.

⚠ *Warning: Antifreeze is poisonous. Do not use a cooking pan to test the thermostat.*

6   Gradually heat the water in the container with a hot plate or stove and check the temperature when the thermostat just starts to open.
7   Compare the opening temperature to the values listed in this Chapter's Specifications.
8   Continue heating the water until the valve is fully open.
9   Measure how far the thermostat valve has opened and compare to the valve listed in this Chapter's Specifications.
10   It these specifications are not met, or if the thermostat doesn't open while the coolant is heated, replace it with a new one.

Installation

11   Install the thermostat in the housing, coil end first. The small bleed hole in the edge of the thermostat goes upward.
12   Install a new O-ring in the thermostat

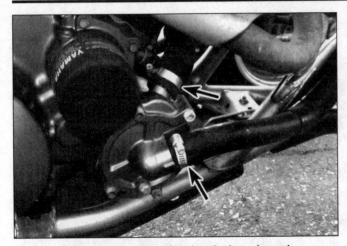

8.2a Inlet hose (lower) and outlet hose (upper) locations (660 models)

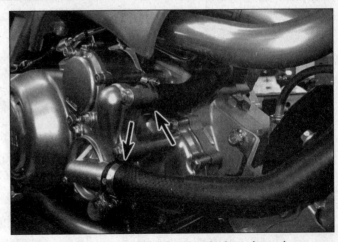

8.2b Inlet hose (lower) and outlet hose (upper) locations (700 models)

housing, install the cover and tighten its bolts securely, but don't overtighten them and strip the threads.

13 Fill and bleed the cooling system (see Chapter 1).

14 The remainder of installation is the reverse of removal.

8 Water pump - removal, inspection and installation

Removal and disassembly

Note: *The following procedure describes removing the water pump completely. If you're only planning to remove the cover so you can inspect the impeller, ignore that steps that don't apply.*

1 Drain the cooling system (see Chapter 1).

2 Disconnect the coolant inlet hose from the water pump **(see illustrations)**. Loosen the clamp on the outlet hose, but don't try to disconnect it yet. It will be easier to disconnect after the water pump body has been

8.3a Water pump bolt locations (660 models)

unbolted from the engine.

3 Remove the pump cover bolts **(see illustrations)**. The bolts are different lengths, so it's a good idea to tag them for reinstallation or to put them in the cover for storage

8.3b Water pump bolt locations (700 models)

once it's been removed **(see illustration)**.

4 Take off the pump cover and O-ring **(see illustration)**.

5 Remove the pump body together with the impeller and drive gear **(see illustration)**.

8.3c It's a good idea to tag the bolts for location or put them back in the cover holes for storage

8.4 Remove the O-ring from the pump cover groove (660 shown)

8.5 With the water pump body detached from the engine, the pump outlet hose can be disconnected

8.6a Remove the snap-ring . . .

8.6b . . . remove the gear and pull the drive pin out of the shaft

8.6c Remove the second snap-ring (660 models only)

8.6d Pull the impeller and shaft out of the pump body

8.6e Water pump components

8.8 Slip the impeller shaft into the bearing and try to move it from side-to-side to check for play

6   The impeller and shaft are one piece (but on 660 models, the impeller and shaft can be separated if necessary). To remove them, remove the snap-ring from the inner end of the shaft and take off the drive gear and its pin **(see illustrations)**. On 660 mod-els, remove the second snap-ring **(see illustration)**. On all models, pull the impeller and shaft out of the pump body **(see illustrations)**.

Inspection

7   Check the impeller seals (conventional and mechanical) for wear or damage. These seals separate the coolant from the engine oil. If the oil is milky or foamy, coolant may have been leaking into it past the seals; replace them (see Section 9).
8   To inspect the bearing, place the impeller shaft in the bearing, wiggle it and check for play **(see illustration)**. If it can be wiggled from side to side, the bearing needs to be replaced. Lift the impeller shaft out of the bearing. Spin the bearing and check it for roughness, looseness or noise and replace it if any problems are found (see Section 9).

Installation

9   Installation is the reverse of removal, with the following additions:

a) *Use a new gasket on the pump body and a new O-ring on the pump cover.*

b) *Install the drive pin for the water pump gear in the impeller shaft after installing the shaft in the pump body.*
c) *Engage the impeller shaft tang with the drive slot.*
d) *Tighten the water pump bolts to the torque listed in this Chapter's Specifications.*
e) *Fill the cooling system and engine oil (see Chapter 1).*
f) *Run the engine and check for coolant leaks.*

9   Water pump seals and bearing - replacement

1   If coolant has been leaking from the weep hole, the water pump seals need to be replaced. There are two seals inside the water pump body. A conventional oil seal is located behind a ball bearing in the inner side of the water pump body **(see illustration)**. A mechanical seal, which is spring-loaded to press against the impeller, is also located in the outer side of the water pump

9.1a Here's the water pump bearing (lower arrow); place a rod against the edge of the mechanical seal (upper arrow) and tap on it to drive the seal out

9.1b Here's the mechanical seal (lower arrow); place a rod against the edge of the water pump bearing (upper arrow) and tap on it to drive the seal out

body **(see illustration)**. The oil seal keeps engine oil out of the coolant; the mechanical seal keeps coolant out of the engine oil. **Note:** *The mechanical seal can't be removed without destroying it. Be sure you have a new one before you remove it from the pump. The conventional seal and bearing will probably also be damaged, so it's a good idea to replace these whenever they're removed.*

 To drive the new seal in, you'll need a tool that bears on the flange of the mechanical seal, and also fits in the recess of the pump body. It should also have a center protrusion that fits inside the seal to keep it from collapsing as it's being installed (see illustration).

2   Remove and disassemble the water pump (see Section 8).
3   Support the water pump body on a work surface, bearing side down, so there's empty space beneath the bearing. Insert a rod through the mechanical seal and rest its tip against the ball bearing **(see illustration 9.1b)**. Tap on the rod with a hammer to drive the ball bearing out. Once this is done, turn the pump body over and pry the conventional seal out of its bore.
4   Place the water pump body on a work surface, mechanical seal side down, so there's empty space beneath the seal. Insert a rod through the bearing bore and rest its tip against the metal portion of the mechanical seal **(see illustration 9.1a)**. Tap on the rod with a hammer to drive the seal out.

9.6a If the edge of the mechanical seal doesn't come with pre-applied sealer, apply Loctite 518 or equivalent to the outer edge

9.6b A tool like this one is necessary to install the mechanical seal without damaging it

5   Tap in a new conventional seal, using a seal driver or a socket the same diameter as the seal. The open side of the seal faces out (toward the bearing). Tap in a new bearing, using the same tool used to install the seal.
6   If the new mechanical seal is not coated with sealant on the outer edge, coat it with Loctite 518 or equivalent **(see illustration)**. Tap it, using a special driver that supports the center of the seal and its outer edge as it's being installed **(see illustration)**. Take care not to let the mechanical seal tilt sideways as it's being installed.

7   Once the mechanical seal is installed, check it to make sure it's straight in the bore, not tilted **(see illustration 8.8)**. The impeller should slide in easily, through the mechanical seal and bearing. If it seems to hang up in the bearing while it's being inserted, the mechanical seal may be cocked sideways. If there's any doubt, measure the tilt of the impeller shaft with a square. If the tilt exceeds the limit listed in this Chapter's Specifications, remove the mechanical seal and install a new one.

Notes

Chapter 4 Part A
Fuel and exhaust systems (660 models)

Contents

Degrees of difficulty

Easy, suitable for novice with little experience	**Fairly easy,** suitable for beginner with some experience	**Fairly difficult,** suitable for competent DIY mechanic	**Difficult,** suitable for experienced DIY mechanic	**Very difficult,** suitable for expert DIY or professional

Specifications

General

Fuel type .... See Chapter 1

Carburetor

Type.. Mikuni BSR33
ID mark 5LP1 00
Main jet
    Left carburetor 140
    Right carburetor 145
Main air jet... 130
Needle/clip position... 5ND1-56-3
Pilot jet... 22.5
Pilot air jet
    Left carburetor 80
    Right carburetor 150
Standard pilot screw setting .... Not specified
Float height... 13 mm (0.51 inch)

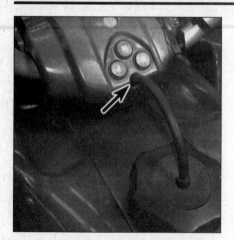

2.1 Pull the vent hose out of the handlebar cover and unscrew the cap from the fuel tank

2.2 Slide the clamp off the carburetor fitting, then pry the hose off the fitting

2.4a Remove the single bolt at the rear of the fuel tank . . .

1 General information

660 models use a pair of Mikuni BSR-33 carburetors with butterfly-type throttle valves. For cold starting on all models, a choke plunger is actuated by a lever on the left handlebar.

The exhaust system consists of twin inlet pipes and a single muffler with a removable spark arrester.

2 Fuel tank - removal and installation

Warning: Gasoline is extremely flammable, so take extra precautions when you work on any part of the fuel system. Don't smoke or allow open flames or bare light bulbs near the work area, and don't work in a garage where a gas-type appliance (such as a water heater or clothes dryer) is present. Since gasoline is carcinogenic, wear fuel-resistant gloves when there's a possibility of being exposed to fuel, and, if you spill any fuel on your skin, rinse it off immediately with soap and water. Mop up any spills immediately and do not store fuel-soaked rags where they could ignite. When you perform any kind of work on the fuel system, wear safety glasses and have a Class B type fire extinguisher on hand.

Removal

1 Pull the fuel tank vent hose out of the handlebar cover and remove the cap from the tank **(see illustration)**.
2 Remove the seat, fuel tank cover and side covers (see Chapter 8).
3 Turn the fuel tap to Off and disconnect the fuel line from the tap **(see illustration)**.
4 Remove one mounting bolt at the rear of the tank and two at the front and lift it off,

2.4b . . . and one at each front corner

together with the fuel tap **(see illustrations)**.
5 If necessary, remove the retainers that secure the front heat shield and the screws that secure the rear heat shield and remove the heat shields **(see illustrations)**.

2.4c Remove the bolts, lockwashers and washers

2.4d Remove the collars that fit inside the grommets

2.5a The front heat shield is secured by two tie wraps . . .

2.5b . . . and the rear heat shield is secured by two screws

generally disassembled completely and the parts are cleaned thoroughly with a carburetor cleaning solvent and dried with filtered, unlubricated compressed air. The fuel and air passages are also blown through with compressed air to force out any dirt that may have been loosened but not removed by the solvent. Once the cleaning process is complete, the carburetor is reassembled using a new top gasket, O-rings and, generally, a new inlet needle valve and seat.

6   Before disassembling the carburetor, make sure you have the necessary gaskets, O-rings and other parts, some carburetor cleaner, a supply of rags, some means of blowing out the carburetor passages and a clean place to work.

Installation

6   Check the condition of the mounting collar at the rear bolt hole, the isolators at the two front bolt holes and the fuel line to the carburetor - if they're hardened, cracked, or show any other signs of deterioration, replace them.

7   Installation is the reverse of removal. Make sure the tank does not pinch any wires. Tighten the tank mounting bolts securely, but don't overtighten them and strip the threads.

3 Carburetor overhaul - general information

1   Poor engine performance, hesitation, hard starting, stalling, flooding and backfiring are all signs that major carburetor maintenance may be required.

2   Keep in mind that many so-called carburetor problems are really not carburetor problems at all, but mechanical problems within the engine or ignition system malfunctions. Try to establish for certain that the carburetor is in need of maintenance before beginning a major overhaul.

3   Check the fuel tap and its strainer screen, the fuel lines, the intake tube clamps, the intake tubes between the carburetors and cylinder head, the O-rings between the intake tubes and cylinder head, the vacuum hoses (including the short stub of hose that covers the vacuum port), the air filter element, the cylinder compression, the spark plug and the ignition timing before assuming that a carburetor overhaul is required. If the vehicle has been unused for more than a month, drain the float chambers and refill the tank with fresh fuel.

4   Most carburetor problems are caused by dirt particles, varnish and other deposits which build up in and block the fuel and air passages. Also, in time, gaskets and O-rings shrink or deteriorate and cause fuel and air leaks which lead to poor performance.

5   When the carburetor is overhauled, it is

4 Carburetors - removal and installation

1   Remove the seat, both side covers and the fuel tank cover (see Chapter 8).

2   Disconnect the vent hoses from the carburetors **(see illustration)**.

3   Disconnect the throttle and choke cables (see Section 7).

4   Loosen the clamping bands at the front and rear of the carburetors **(see illustration 4.2)**.

5   Free the carburetor from the intake tubes and the air cleaner tubes **(see illustration)**.

6   Note how the hoses are routed and free them from the retainer. Remove the carburetor.

7   Installation is the reverse of removal, with the following additions:

a) Adjust the throttle freeplay (see Chapter 1).

b) Adjust the idle speed (see Chapter 1).

4.2 Disconnect the vacuum hoses (A) and loosen the clamping band screws (B)

4.5 Work the carburetors free of the intake tubes

5.3a Remove two screws and the spacer cover

5.3b Remove two long screws that hold the carburetors together

5 Carburetor - disassembly, cleaning and inspection

⚠️ **Warning:** *Gasoline is extremely flammable, so take extra precautions when you work on any part of the fuel system. See the Warning in Section 2.*

Disassembly

1   Remove the carburetors (see Section 4). Don't separate them unless necessary

2   Set the carburetors on a clean working surface. Take note of how the vent hoses are routed, including locations of hose retainers. Don't separate the carburetors from each other unless necessary (for example, if fuel has been leaking from the joint between the carburetors).

3   If you do need to separate the carburetors, remove the plate that covers the connecting tubes **(see illustration)**. Remove the two long screws that hold the carburetors together. Pull the carburetors apart to remove the connecting tube, O-rings, spacers and spring **(see illustrations)**.

5.3c Pull the carburetors apart and remove the spacer (upper arrow) and fuel line inlet T-fitting (lower arrow)

4   To disassemble the carburetors, refer to the **accompanying illustrations**.

Cleaning

Caution: Use only a carburetor cleaning solution that is safe for use with plastic

5.3d Remove the remaining spacer, the fuel connecting tube and its O-rings, and the spring that fits between the carburetors

parts (be sure to read the label on the container).

5   Submerge the metal components in carburetor cleaner for approximately thirty minutes (or longer, if the directions recommend it).

5.4a Remove the float chamber cover screws

5.4b Remove the float chamber cover - replace the O-ring with a new one on assembly

5.4c Remove the float retaining screw . . .

5.4d . . . and lift the float, pulling the needle valve out of its seat

5.4e Work the needle valve seat free of its bore and pull it out

5.4f Unscrew the pilot jet

5.4g Hold the needle jet with a wrench and unscrew the main jet

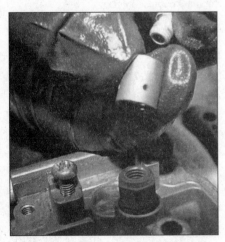

5.4h Lift off the main jet and collar

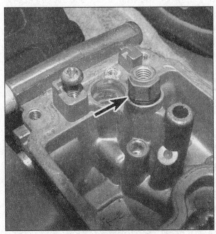

5.4i Unscrew the needle jet . . .

5.4j . . . and lift it out, together with its O-ring

5.4k Bottom the mixture screw and write down the number of turns, then unscrew it and lift it out with its spring, washer and O-ring

5.4l Remove the top cover screws . . .

5.4m . . . lift off the top cover and remove the spring

5.4n Lift the diaphragm and throttle piston out of the carburetor body

5.4o Remove the jet needle retainer . . .

6   After the carburetor has soaked long enough for the cleaner to loosen and dissolve most of the varnish and other deposits, use a brush to remove the stubborn deposits.

5.4p . . . and take the jet needle, washer and clip out of the throttle piston

Rinse it again, then dry it with compressed air. Blow out all of the fuel and air passages in the carburetor body.

Caution: Never clean the jets or passages with a piece of wire or a drill bit, as they will be enlarged, causing the fuel and air metering rates to be upset.

Inspection

7   Check the operation of the choke plunger. If it doesn't move smoothly, replace it. Check the plunger seat for wear or damage (see Chapter 1) and replace it if problems are found. Inspect the hot start valve in the same manner.

8   Check the tapered portion of the pilot screw for wear or damage. Replace the screw if necessary.

9   Check the carburetor body, float chamber and carburetor top for cracks, distorted sealing surfaces and other damage. If any defects are found, replace the faulty component, although replacement of the entire carburetor will probably be necessary (check

with your parts supplier for the availability of separate components).

10   Check the jet needle for straightness by rolling it on a flat surface (such as a piece of glass). Replace it if it's bent or if the tip is worn.

11   Check the tip of the fuel inlet valve needle. If it has grooves or scratches in it, it must be replaced. Push in on the rod in the other end of the needle, then release it - if it doesn't spring back, replace the valve needle.

12   Check the O-rings on the float chamber and the main jet access plug (in the float chamber). Replace them if they're damaged.

13   Check the floats for damage. This will usually be apparent by the presence of fuel inside one of the floats. If the floats are damaged, they must be replaced.

14   Insert the throttle valve in the carburetor body and see that it moves up-and-down smoothly. Check the surface of the throttle valve for wear. If it's worn excessively or doesn't move smoothly in the bore, replace the carburetor.

6.5 Measure float height with a gauge or ruler

6.8 When installing the top cover, align its tab with the boss on the carburetor body

6 Carburetor - reassembly and float height check

Reassembly

Caution: When installing the jets, be careful not to over-tighten them - they're made of soft material and can strip or shear easily.

Note: *When reassembling the carburetor, use new O-rings.*

1   Install the clip on the jet needle if it was removed. Place it in the needle groove listed in this Chapter's Specifications. Install the needle and clip in the throttle valve.
2   Install the air screw along with its spring, washer and O-ring, turning it in until it seats lightly. Now, turn the screw out the number of turns written down during removal.
3   Reverse the disassembly steps to install the jets.

4   Invert the carburetor. Attach the fuel inlet valve needle to the float. Set the float into position in the carburetor, making sure the valve needle seats correctly. Install the float pivot pin.
5   Measure float height as described in Step 8 below before the float chamber is installed **(see illustration)**.
6   Install the float chamber gasket or O-ring. Place the float chamber on the carburetor and install the screws, tightening them securely. Install the main jet access plug in the bottom of the float chamber, using a new O-ring, and tighten it securely.
7   Install the throttle piston, jet needle and top cover. Note how the tab on the cover aligns with the carburetor body **(see illustration)**.

Float check

8   Hold the carburetor so the float hangs down, then tilt it back until the valve needle is just seated **(see illustration 6.5)**. Measure

the distance from the float chamber gasket surface to the top of the float and compare your measurement to the float height listed in this Chapter's Specifications. Bend the float tang as necessary to change the adjustment.

7 Throttle and choke cables - removal and installation

1   These vehicles are equipped with a single accelerator cable that operates the throttle plate in the carburetor.
2   Remove the fuel tank (see Section 2).
3   At the handlebar, loosen the throttle cable adjuster all the way (see Chapter 1).
4   Take the cover off the throttle housing and disconnect the throttle cable from the lever **(see illustrations)**.
5   At the carburetor, remove the throttle

7.4a Unscrew the cable locknut (A) and remove the cover screws (B); if you remove the throttle housing, align the spacer notch with the housing tab (C) during installation

7.4b Push the cable into the housing to create slack, then slip the cable end plug out of the slot - corrosion this severe should be removed completely

7.5a Here are the carburetor throttle housing screws (lower arrows) and choke cable (upper arrow)

7.5b With the cover removed, check for corrosion or foreign material in the throttle housing and clean it up completely

7.6a Slip the cable out of the pulley and take out the end plug

pulley cover **(see illustrations)**.
6   Loosen the cable locknut to create slack in the cable **(see illustration)**. Lift the

7.6b Separate the end plug from the cable

cable out of the groove, turn it to align with the removal slot and slip the cable end plug out of the pulley **(see illustrations)**.
7   Note how the cable is routed and remove it from the vehicle **(see illustration)**.
8   **Note:** *Perform Steps 8 and 9 only if you need to remove the throttle housing from the handlebar. Otherwise, skip to Step 10.* Look for a punch mark on the handlebar next to the split in the throttle housing. If you don't see a mark, make one so the throttle housing can be installed in the correct position.
9   Remove the throttle housing screws and take the throttle housing off the handle-bar **(see illustration)**.
10   Route the cable into place. Make sure it doesn't interfere with any other components and isn't kinked or bent sharply.
11   Lubricate the carburetor end of the cable with multi-purpose grease. Reverse the disconnection steps to connect the throttle cable to the carburetor throttle pulley.
12   Reverse the disconnection steps to connect the cables to the throttle grip.

13   Operate the throttle and make sure it returns to the idle position by itself under spring pressure.

⚠️ **Warning: If the throttle doesn't return by itself, find and solve the problem before continuing with installation. A stuck throttle can lead to loss of control of the vehicle.**

14   Adjust the throttle cable (see Chapter 1).
15   Turn the handlebars back and forth to make sure the cable does not cause the steering to bind.
16   Once you're sure the cable operates properly, install the fuel tank.
17   With the engine idling, turn the handle-bars through their full travel (full left lock to full right lock) and note whether idle speed increases. If it does, the cable is routed incorrectly. Correct this dangerous condition before riding the vehicle.

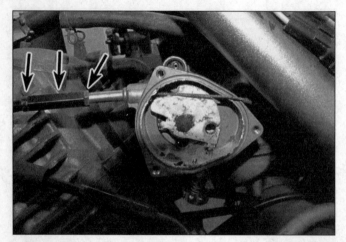

7.6c Loosen the locknut (left) and adjusting nut (center), then unscrew the retaining nut (right) all the way off the fitting and pull the cable out

7.7 The throttle and choke cables are secured by a retainer on the left side of the engine

7.9 Remove the screws and take the throttle housing off the handlebar

7.20 Push the cable housing (left) toward the lever, swing it out of the bracket slot and slide the end plug out of the lever slot (right)

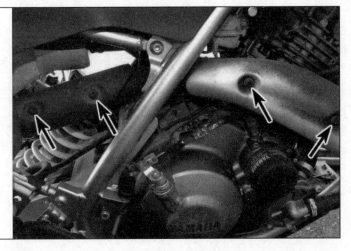

8.2 Remove the heat shield bolts and lift off the heat shields

8.3 Loosen the muffler clamp bolt . . .

Choke cable

18   Locate the choke cable on the left side of the engine (see illustration 7.7).
19   Unscrew the choke plunger from the engine (see illustration 22.3 in Chapter 1).
20   Push the choke cable housing toward the lever (see illustration). Swing the cable housing out of the bracket, then lower the cable end plug out of the lever. Note how the cable is routed and remove it from the machine.
21   Check the rubber seal in the end of the choke plunger for wear and damage and replace it if necessary.
22   Installation is the reverse of removal.

8   Exhaust system - removal and installation

1   Remove the right side cover (see Chapter 8). It will be easier to remove the bolts while the exhaust system is still attached to the engine.

2   If necessary, remove the heat shields (see illustration).
3   Loosen the muffler clamp bolt (see illustration) and unscrew the muffler mounting bolts from the frame. Work the muffler

free of the pipe and remove the gasket.
4   Detach the front pipes from the cylinder head and remove them from the machine (see illustration). Remove the gaskets from the exhaust ports (see illustration).

8.4a . . and detach the pipes from the cylinder head

8.4b Remove the gaskets from the exhaust ports

8.5 Clean any corrosion or carbon from the exhaust ports

9.2 Remove the air filter lid, unscrew the bolts (lower arrows) and disengage the posts from the grommets (upper arrows)

9.3 Loosen the clamps on the outlet tubes

5   Clean any corrosion or carbon from the exhaust ports **(see illustration)**.
6   To replace the spark arrester, refer to Chapter 1.
7   Installation is the reverse of removal. Use new gaskets in the exhaust ports **(see illustration 8.4b)** and at the joint between pipe and muffler.

9 Air cleaner housing - removal and installation

1   Remove the seat (see Chapter 8).
2   Loosen the clamp that secures the housing to the intake duct, release the clips and take off the lid **(see illustration)**.

Unscrew the two bolts that secure the housing to the frame.
3   Loosen the clamps on the air outlet tubes **(see illustration)**. Pull the housing straight back to separate it from the intake duct and to disengage its posts from the grommets in the frame **(see illustration 9.2)**. Lift the housing out of the frame.
4   Installation is the reverse of removal.

Chapter 4 Part B
Fuel, exhaust and emission control systems (700 models)

Contents

Degrees of difficulty

| Easy, suitable for novice with little experience | | Fairly easy, suitable for beginner with some experience | | Fairly difficult, suitable for competent DIY mechanic | | Difficult, suitable for experienced DIY mechanic | | Very difficult, suitable for expert DIY or professional | |

Specifications

Fuel injection system

System type	Single-point throttle body fuel injection
Throttle body	
Model	Mikuni 44EHS/1
ID number	1S3H-10
Idle speed...	1500 to 1700 rpm
Fuel pressure..	46.1 psi (324 kPa)
Intake air pressure sensor output voltage....................................	3.0 to 4.0 volts at sea level
Intake air temperature sensor resistance.....................................	2.21 to 2.69 ohms at 20-degrees C (68-degrees F)
Throttle position sensor	
Maximum resistance..	3.08 to 5.72 k-ohms
Output voltage	0.63 to 0.73 volts
Engine coolant temperature sensor resistance............................	See Chapter 3
Crankshaft position sensor resistance..	192.0 to 288.0 ohms at 68-degrees F (20-degrees C)

Torque specifications

Fuel tank mounting bolts	7 Nm (61 ft-lbs)
Fuel tank top plate nuts	7 Nm (61 ft-lbs)
Air cleaner housing bolts	7 Nm (61 ft-lbs)
Fuel rail screws	5 Nm (43 inch-lbs)
Throttle position sensor screws	3.5 Nm (30 inch-lbs)
Throttle body outlet duct clamp screws	3 Nm (26 inch-lbs)
Air cleaner duct to throttle body clamp screw	4 Nm (35 inch-lbs)
Exhaust pipe to manifold nuts	20 Nm (168 inch-lbs)
Exhaust pipe clamp bolt	
Pipe to muffler	18 Nm (156 inch-lbs)
Pipe to pipe	16 Nm (132 inch-lbs)
Exhaust pipe mounting bolts	34 Nm (24 ft-lbs)
Exhaust system heat shield bolts*	8 Nm (70 inch-lbs)

Use non-hardening thread locking agent on the threads.

1 Fuel Injection system - general information

The fuel injection system is a single-point throttle body system. This means that there is one fuel injector, mounted on a throttle body that attaches to the engine much like a carburetor. The fuel injector injects fuel into the throttle body at the correct point in each engine cycle. The injector is turned on and off by the Engine Control Unit (ECU). When the engine is running, the ECU constantly monitors engine operating conditions with an array of information sensors, calculates the correct amount of fuel, then varies the interval of time during which the injector is open. The fuel injection system provides much better control of the air/fuel mixture than a carburetor, and is therefore able to produce more power, better mileage and lower emissions.

The system uses the ECU and an array of information sensors to determine and deliver the correct air/fuel ratio under all operating conditions. The system consists of three sub-systems: input sensors, the ECU, and output actuators.

Input sensors

Throttle Position (TP) sensor

The TP sensor, mounted on the throttle body, is a potentiometer that monitors the opening angle of the throttle plate and sends a variable voltage signal to the Engine Control Unit (ECU).

Intake Air Pressure (IAP) sensor

The IAP sensor is located on the inlet portion of the air cleaner housing. The IAP sensor measures intake manifold pressure and generates a variable voltage signal that's proportionate to the pressure. The ECU uses this data to calculate the load on the engine.

Intake Air Temperature (IAT) sensor

The IAT sensor, mounted on the air cleaner housing, relays a voltage signal to the ECU that varies in accordance with the temperature of the incoming air in the air cleaner housing. The ECU uses this information to calculate how rich or lean the air/fuel mixture should be.

Crankshaft Position (CKP) sensor

The CKP sensor lets the ECU know where the crankshaft is in the induction cycle. The ECU used this information to control timing of the fuel injector opening.

Engine Coolant Temperature (ECT) sensor

The ECT sensor monitors engine temperature and sends a voltage signal to the ECU. The ECU uses this information to decide whether to enrich the fuel mixture for cold-engine operation.

Lean angle sensor

This is a safety device that signals the ECU to shut off the engine if the vehicle rolls over.

Vehicle Speed Sensor (VSS)

This device, mounted on the top rear of the engine, signals vehicle speed to the ECU.

Engine Control Unit (ECU)

The ECU is a microprocessor, mounted at the rear of the vehicle to the left of the battery. It receives signals from the input sensors, and uses this information to decide exactly when, and for exactly how long, to open the fuel injector. This controls injection timing as well as the amount of fuel injected.

The ECU also control other functions, such as ignition timing, cooling fan operation, and the warning lights.

Output actuators

The output actuators include an electric fuel pump located in the fuel tank, the fuel rail and the fuel injector. The fuel injector delivers fuel into the intake air stream.

Fuel pump

The fuel pump is part of an assembly that includes the filter screen, fuel level sensor and pressure regulator. Pump components are not available separately. The fuel pressure regulator maintains fuel pressure at a constant 46.1 psi (324 kPa).

Fuel rail and injector

The fuel rail is mounted on the throttle body, with a fuel injector between the throttle body and fuel rail. Fuel flows from the pump into the fuel rail, and as the injector opens, into the throttle body and then into the engine. A fuel pulsation damper is built into the fuel rail.

Throttle body

The throttle body controls the amount of air entering the engine. It's activated by a cable, which is controlled by the rider through a thumb lever on the right handlebar.

2 Fuel injection system - check

1 Check all electrical connectors that are related to the system. Check the ground wire connections for tightness. Loose connectors and poor grounds can cause many problems that resemble more serious malfunctions.
2 Verify that the battery is fully charged. The Engine Control Unit (ECU), information sensors and output actuators (the fuel injector is an output actuator) depend on a stable voltage supply in order to meter fuel correctly.
3 Inspect the air filter element (see Chapter 1). A dirty or partially blocked filter will

severely impede performance and economy.
4 Check all fuses related to the fuel system (see Chapter 5). If you find a blown fuse, replace it and see if it blows again. If it does, look for a wire shorted to ground in the circuit(s) protected by that fuse. Also check the main relay (see Chapter 5).
5 Check the air induction system between the throttle body and the intake manifold for air leaks, which will cause a lean air/fuel mixture ratio (when the mixture ratio becomes excessively lean, the engine will begin misfiring). Also inspect the condition of all vacuum hoses connected to the intake manifold and to the throttle body. A loose or broken vacuum hose will allow unmetered air into the intake manifold. Unmetered air, especially at idle and during other high-intake-manifold-vacuum conditions, will cause the engine to misfire.
6 Remove the air cleaner housing and check the throttle body for dirt, carbon, varnish, or other residue in the throttle body, particularly around the throttle plate. If it's dirty, clean it with a clean shop towel and a petroleum-based solvent. Do not use caustic carburetor cleaners.
7 With the engine running, place an automotive stethoscope against the injector and listen for a clicking sound that indicates operation. If you don't have a stethoscope, touch the tip of a long screwdriver against the injector and listen through the handle.
8 If you can hear the injector operating, but the engine is misfiring, the electrical circuits are functioning correctly, but the injector might be dirty or clogged. Try a commercial injector cleaning product (available at auto parts stores). If cleaning the injector doesn't help, the injector probably needs to be cleaned professionally, or replaced.
9 If the injector is not operating (it makes no sound), disconnect the injector electrical connector and measure the resistance across the injector terminals with an ohmmeter. If there's an open circuit (infinite resistance) or short circuit (no resistance), replace the injector.
10 If the injector is not operating, but the resistance reading is not infinite or zero, the ECM or the circuit between the ECM and the injector might be faulty.

3 Self-diagnosis system and trouble codes

Scan tool information

1 Analyzing the engine management system used on these vehicles can be done by flashing the Malfunction Indicator Light (MIL) on the instrument cluster.

Self-diagnosis system general description

2 All models are equipped with an onboard self-diagnosis system. This system

consists of an on-board computer known as the Engine Control Unit (ECU), and information sensors, which monitor various functions of the engine and send data to the ECU. This system incorporates a series of diagnostic monitors that detect and identify fuel injection system faults and store the information in the computer memory. This system also tests sensors and output actuators, diagnoses drive cycles, freezes data and clears codes.

3   In some cases of component failure, the ECU will substitute a fixed value for the variable voltage that the component would normally send to the ECU. This allows the engine to operate in fail-safe mode until the problem can be fixed.

4   This powerful diagnostic computer can be accessed using the multi-function display.

5   It isn't a good idea to attempt diagnosis or replacement of the ECU or emission control components at home while the vehicle is under warranty. Because of the vehicle warranty and because any owner-induced damage to the ECU, sensors and/or control devices might void this warranty, take the vehicle to a dealer service department if the ECU or a system component malfunctions.

Diagnostic Trouble Codes (DTCs)

6   All 700 models are equipped with on-board diagnostics. When the ECU recognizes a malfunction in a monitored fuel injection system component or circuit, it turns on the Malfunction Indicator Light (MIL) on the instrument cluster. The MIL normally illuminates for a few seconds after the main key switch is turned On. If a trouble code is set, the MIL will either flash while the starter is cranking, indicating that the engine can't be started, or glow steadily after the engine starts. A steady glow indicates that the engine is running in fail-safe mode. If the engine is turned off while the light is glowing, the diagnostic code number for the affected circuit will appear on the multi-function display's screen (if there's more than one code stored, the lowest-numbered code will be displayed). The ECU will continue to display the MIL until the problem is fixed and the Diagnostic Trouble Code (DTC) is cleared from the ECU's memory. **Note:** *If the MIL doesn't come on at all, possible causes are the throttle position sensor, ignition coil or fuel injector. Refer to procedures later in this Chapter to test these components.*

Accessing the DTCs

7   The DTC number will display automatically when the engine is shut off. If more than one code is stored, only the lowest-numbered code will be displayed. To read any higher-numbered code, the problem indicated by the first code must be repaired, then the code must be cleared.

Clearing the DTCs

8   To clear a DTC, the problem that caused it to display must be repaired. After this is done, perform the ECU reinstatement action listed in the table below. In any additional codes are stored, the next higher numbered code will be displayed. Repair the code, perform the reinstatement action, and check for additional codes. Do this until all codes have been cleared.

Diagnostic Trouble Codes

9   The accompanying table is a list of the Diagnostic Trouble Codes (DTCs). If the problem persists after you have checked the component and repaired the related connectors, wire harness and vacuum hoses (if applicable), have the vehicle checked by a dealer service department or other qualified repair shop.

Code	Problem area	Causes	Symptom(s)	ECU reinstatement action (after repairing the problem)
12	Crankshaft position sensor	Defective sensor, circuit problem	Engine will not start	Crank the engine
13	Intake air pressure sensor	Open or short circuit	Engine will run	Turn the main key switch to On
14	Intake air pressure sensor	Hose loose or obstructed	Engine will run	Run the engine at idle
15	Throttle position sensor	Open or short circuit	Engine will run	Turn the main key switch to On
16	Throttle position sensor	Sensor jammed	Engine will run	Let the engine idle, then rev it
21	Coolant temperature sensor	Open or short circuit	Engine will run	Turn the main key switch to On
22	Intake air temperature sensor	Open or short circuit	Engine will run	Turn the main key switch to On
30	Lean angle sensor	Overturned vehicle or loose sensor	Engine will not start	Turn the main key switch Off, then On
33	Ignition coil	Bad primary circuit in coil	Engine will not run	Run the engine at idle
41	Lean angle sensor	Open or short circuit	Engine will not run	Turn the main key switch to On
42*	Speed sensor	No signals from sensor	Engine will run	Ride the vehicle at 20 to 30 kph (15 to 22 mph)

Code	Problem area	Causes	Symptom(s)	ECU reinstatement action (after repairing the problem)
42*	Neutral switch	Open circuit	Engine will run	Ride the vehicle at 20 to 30 kph (15 to 22 mph)
43	System voltage	Open or short circuit in ECU voltage line	Engine will run	Run the engine at idle
44	Error in writing CO adjustment to EEPROM	Possible defective ECU	Engine will run	Turn the main key switch to On
46	Abnormal fuel injection system voltage	Open or shirt circuit, bad battery or regulator/rectifier	Engine will run	Run the engine at idle
50	ECU memory check error	Bad ECU memory	Engine will not run	Turn the main key switch to On
Er-1, Er-2, Er-3, Er-4	ECU signal error	Bad ECU	Engine will not run	Replace ECU

Code 42 is shared by the speed sensor and neutral switch.

Diagnosing individual components

10 After you've read a code as described above, you can use the multi-function display like a scan tool to check individual components as described below.
11 Turn the engine kill switch and main key switch to Off (if they aren't already).
12 Disconnect the wiring harness from the fuel pump (see Section 6).
13 Hold down the Select and Reset buttons on the multi-function display (at the same time). While holding the buttons down, turn the main key switch to ON and keep holding the buttons down for at least 8 more seconds.
14 The display will go blank and the word "dIAG" will appear on the display. Release the buttons, then press and hold them again for two seconds, then release them.
15 A code number with a lower-case "d" followed by two digits will appear in the display. Code numbers range from d01 to d70. Refer to the following table to select the code number that applies to the component you want to check. To select a higher code number, press and hold the Select button for one full second or more. To select a lower code number, press and hold the Reset button for one full second or more.
16 When you select a code, the performance values of the selected component will be displayed on the screen. Refer to the following table for the displayed values and the action to take. Some of the components can be tested using an ohmmeter or voltmeter; refer to other Sections in this Chapter.

Diagnostic code	Component	Display value	Action
d01	Throttle angle	Throttle closed: 15-20 Throttle wide open: 95-100	Move throttle by hand to open and closed positions. Test the throttle position sensor and check its wiring.
d03	Intake air pressure sensor	Intake air pressure (variable)	With the kill switch On, crank the engine and move the throttle switch. The reading should vary; if not, test the sensor.
d05	Intake air temperature sensor	Intake air temperature (variable)	Measure actual temperature with a thermometer and compare to the displayed temperature. If they're different, test the sensor and check its wiring.
d06	Coolant temperature sensor	Coolant temperature (variable)	Measure actual temperature with a thermometer and compare to the displayed temperature. If they're different, test the sensor and check its wiring.
d07	Vehicle speed pulse	Zero through 999	Spin the rear wheels. The number should increase. If not, test the sensor.

Diagnostic code	Component	Display value	Action
d08	Lean angle sensor	Upright: 0.4 to 1.4 Tilted more than 65-degrees: 3.7 to 4.4	If displayed values are incorrect, test the lean angle sensor.
d09	Fuel system voltage	Approximately 12.0	With the kill switch set to Run, measure voltage across the battery terminals. If it's lower, charge the battery.
d21	Neutral switch	Transmission in Neutral: On Transmission in Neutral: Off	Shift gears and check the reading. If it's incorrect, test the switch and check its wiring.
d30	Ignition coil	MIL flashes five times for one second each; ignition coil activates once for each flash	Check spark (Chapter 5). There should be one spark for each MIL flash.
d36	Fuel injector	MIL flashes five times for one second each; fuel injector activates once for each flash	Listen to the fuel injector. There should be one click for each flash.
d50	Fuel pump relay and pump	MIL flashes five times for one second each; fuel pump relay activates once for each flash	Listen to the fuel pump relay. There should be one click for each flash.
d51	Cooling fan relay	MIL flashes five times for one second each; cooling fan relay activates once for each flash	Listen to the cooling fan relay. There should be one click for each flash.
d60	EEPROM trouble code display	No codes stored: 00 Codes stored: 01	Not applicable
d61	Diagnostic trouble code display	No codes stored: 00 Codes stored: 01	Not applicable
d62	Diagnostic trouble code erasure history	No codes erased: 00 Codes erased: Maximum of 15	To erase history, set engine kill switch to Stop, then to Run.
d70	Control number	00 through 255	Not applicable

4 Fuel pressure relief procedure

Warning: Gasoline is extremely flammable, so take extra precautions when you work on any part of the fuel system. Don't smoke or allow open flames or bare light bulbs near the work area, and don't work in a garage where a gas-type appliance (such as a water heater or clothes dryer) is present. Since gasoline is carcinogenic, wear fuel-resistant gloves when there's a possibility of being exposed to fuel, and, if you spill any fuel on your skin, rinse it off immediately with soap and water. Mop up any spills immediately and do not store fuel-soaked rags where they could ignite. When you perform any kind of work on the fuel system, wear safety glasses and have a Class B type fire extinguisher on hand.

Warning: Be sure to disconnect the battery (see Chapter 5) before disconnecting any fuel lines.

Yamaha does not specify a procedure for relieving residual fuel pressure when disconnecting fuel lines, only that you have shop rags handy to catch any spilled fuel. Observe the precautions described in the **Warnings** above. In addition, wear eye protection and catch any spilled fuel in an approved gasoline container.

5 Fuel pump/fuel pressure - check

Warning: Gasoline is extremely flammable, so take extra precautions when you work on any part of the fuel system. See the Warning in Section 4.

General checks

1 Verify that there is fuel in the fuel tank.
2 Verify that the fuel pump actually runs. Turn the ignition switch to ON - you should hear a brief whirring noise for a few seconds as the pump comes on and pressurizes the

6.2 Release the latch on the electrical connector and disconnect it from the fuel pump

6.3a Lift the retainer off its post, then pry the ends of the clip apart . . .

system. **Note:** *If you can't hear the pump, open the fuel filler cap, then have an assistant turn the ignition switch to ON while you listen to the pump through the fuel filler neck.*

Fuel pump/fuel pressure test

3   To measure the fuel pressure, you'll need a fuel pressure gauge capable of reading pressures up to 50 psi (343 kPa). You will also need some fuel hose.

4   Before disconnecting any fuel line fittings, relieve the fuel system pressure (see Section 4).

5   Remove the fuel tank cover (see Chapter 8).

6   Disconnect the fuel line from the fuel pump mounting plate on top of the tank **(see illustrations 6.3a, 6.3b and 6.3c)**. Connect the fuel pressure gauge between the tank fitting and the disconnected end of the hose, using a T-fitting.

7   Start the engine and let it run.

8   Note the indicated fuel pressure reading on the gauge and compare it with the value listed in this Chapter's Specifications.

9   If the indicated pressure is as specified, the system is operating correctly.

10   If the indicated pressure is lower than the specified range, the fuel intake might be clogged or the fuel pump or fuel pressure regulator might be defective. There are no individually replaceable parts on the pump unit, installed in the fuel tank; if it won't supply the specified pressure, and the problem can't be solved by cleaning the pump intake, the pump must be replaced as an assembly.

11   After the test is complete, relieve the system fuel pressure (see Section 4).

12   Disconnect the cable from the negative battery terminal.

13   Remove your fuel pressure testing rig, then reconnect the fuel line to the tank fitting.

14   Reconnect the cable to the negative battery terminal (see Chapter 5). Start the engine and check for fuel leaks.

15   Reinstall the fuel tank cover.

---

6 Fuel pump - removal and installation

> **Warning: Gasoline is extremely flammable, so take extra precautions when you work on any part of the fuel system. See the Warning in Section 4.**

1   Remove the seat and fuel tank cover (see Chapter 8).

2   Disconnect the wiring connector from the fuel pump **(see illustration)**.

3   Disconnect the fuel line from the tank fitting **(see illustrations)**. Cap the fitting and plug the line.

6.3b . . . slide the clip off the hose end . . .

6.3c . . . and carefully pull the hose off the pump fitting

6.4a Note the location of the alignment notches and remove the retainer nuts

A Retainer to pump alignment notches
B Retainer to tank alignment notch
C Retainer nuts

6.4b Lift off the retainer

4   Remove the nuts and lift off the fuel pump retainer **(see illustrations)**. Lift the fuel pump out of the tank **(see illustration)**.
5   Remove the sealing ring from the opening **(see illustration 6.4c)**.

6.4c Lift the pump out of the tank and inspect the sealing ring

6   Installation is the reverse of removal, with the following additions:
   a) *Use a new sealing ring if the old one is compressed, brittle or deteriorated.*
   b) *Note that the fuel hose is directional - if you disconnected both ends of it, it must be installed so the end with the red clip goes on the fuel pump and the end with the orange clip goes on the fuel rail.*
   c) *Push the hose onto the fitting and slide the clip over the fitting until it clicks into place* **(see illustration 6.3a)**.

7   Fuel tank - removal and installation

> ⚠ *Warning: Gasoline is extremely flammable, so take extra precautions when you work on any part of the fuel system. See the Warning in Section 4.*

1   The fuel tank is held in place by four bolts.
2   Remove the seat, front panel, fuel tank cover and front fender (see Chapter 8).
3   Unplug the electrical connector and disconnect the fuel line from the tank top plate (see Section 6).
4   Remove the screws that secure the rubber cover at the rear of the tank **(see illustration)**.
5   Remove the four mounting bolts and washers from the four corners of the tank **(see illustration 7.4 and the accompanying illustration)**. Lift off the tank.
6   If necessary, remove the shield that fits under the tank **(see illustrations)**.
7   Before installing the tank, check the condition of the rubber mounting dampers - if they're hardened, cracked, or show any other signs of deterioration, replace them. The front mounting dampers each has a metal collar that fits inside it. The rear mounting dampers have flanged metal collars. The flanges go on the undersides of the bushings.

7.4 Remove the cover screws (lower arrows) and tank rear retaining bolts (upper arrows)

7.5 Remove the tank front retaining bolts

7.6a Note how the tank pads engage the frame and heat shield . . .

7.6b . . . then remove the heat shield and disconnect the hose from its underside

8   Installation is the reverse of removal. Make sure the tank seats properly and does not pinch any control cables or wires. Make sure the foam insulators are in position (see illustration).

8 Fuel tank - cleaning and repair

⚠ **Warning: Gasoline is extremely flammable, so take extra precautions when you work on any part of the fuel system. See the Warning in Section 4.**

1   All repairs to the fuel tank should be carried out by a professional who has experience in this critical and potentially dangerous work. Even after cleaning and flushing of the fuel system, explosive fumes can remain and ignite during repair of the tank.

2   If the fuel tank is removed from the vehicle, it should not be placed in an area where sparks or open flames could ignite the fumes coming out of the tank. Be especially careful inside garages where a gas-type appliance is located.

9 Air filter housing - removal and installation

1   Remove the air filter element cover (see Chapter 1).
2   If you're planning to remove the duct as well as the air cleaner housing, disconnect the electrical connector from the intake air temperature sensor and disconnect the hose that runs from the left side of the duct to the throttle body (see illustration). Loosen the clamp that secures the front end of the duct to the throttle body and detach the duct (see illustration).

7.8 Make sure the tank insulators are in position

3   Loosen the clamp that secures the front end of the air cleaner housing to the duct.
4   Remove the housing mounting bolts

9.2a Disconnect the wiring harness for the IAT sensor (lower arrow) and the vent hose (upper arrow)

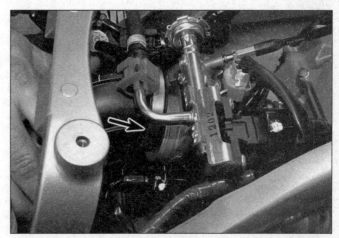

9.2b Loosen the clamp and disconnect the duct from the throttle body

9.4 Air filter housing bolt locations

10.1 TP sensor screw locations (throttle body partially removed for clarity)

11.1 Throttle body components

1 Intake air pressure sensor
2 Fuel injector electrical connector
3 Clamps on throttle body outlet duct
4 Clamp on air filter housing outlet duct
5 Fuel injector
6 Fuel rail

and collars (see illustration).

5 Disconnect the hose at the left front lower corner of the housing. If necessary, lift the housing partway out for access to the hose.

6 Separate the air cleaner housing from the duct and lift it out of the frame. If you're also removing the duct, lift it out.

7 Installation is the reverse of removal.

10 Throttle Position (TP) sensor - check, adjustment and replacement

Check

1 Locate the TP sensor on the throttle body (see illustration).

2 Connect the positive probe of a voltmeter (0-20 volt scale) to the yellow wire's terminal in the connector. Connect the voltmeter negative terminal to the black/blue wire's connector. Note: The wiring connector must be connected during this check. If your voltmeter's terminals are too thick to fit into the connector terminals, insert short pieces of stiff wire into the connector to act as contacts for the voltmeter terminals.

3 Turn the ignition switch to On (but don't start the engine). The voltmeter should indicate 0.63 to 0.73 volts (this is the sensor output voltage). If it doesn't, adjust the sensor (see Steps 4 through 6).

Adjustment

4 Loosen the mounting screws (see illustration 10.1). Carefully rotate the sensor back and forth to get the correct output voltage, then tighten the screw.

5 If the correct voltage can't be obtained, turn the main key switch to Off and disconnect the wiring connector from the TP sensor. Remove its mounting screws and take if off the engine.

6 Connect the positive probe of an ohmmeter to the sensor terminal that connects to the blue wire. Connect the negative ohmmeter terminal to the sensor terminal that connects to the black/blue wire. Rotate the sensor to obtain the maximum ohmmeter reading. If it's not between 3.08 and 5.72 ohms, replace the sensor with a new one.

Replacement

7 Disconnect the electrical connector. Remove the mounting screws and take the sensor off.

8 Install the sensor and tighten the mounting screws, leaving them loose enough so the sensor can be rotated.

9 Adjust the sensor output voltage (see Steps 4 through 6).

10 Once the correct reading is obtained, mark the sensor position on the throttle body with a felt pen.

11 Tighten the mounting screws, making sure that the felt pen marks stay aligned.

12 Remove the voltmeter and probes.

11 Intake Air Pressure (IAP) sensor - check and replacement

1 The IAP sensor is mounted on top of the throttle body (see illustration).

Check

2 Remove the seat (see Chapter 8).

3 Connect the positive probe of a voltmeter (0-20 volt scale) to the pink/blue wire's terminal in the connector. Connect the voltmeter negative terminal to the black/blue wire's connector. Note: The wiring connector must be connected during this check. If your voltmeter's terminals are too thick to fit into the connector terminals, insert short pieces of stiff wire into the connector to act as contacts for the voltmeter terminals.

4 Turn the ignition switch to On (but don't start the engine). The voltmeter should indicate 3.00 to 4.00 volts with the vehicle at sea level (this is the sensor output voltage). If it doesn't, replace the sensor (see Steps 5 and 6).

Replacement

5 Disconnect the electrical connector and disconnect the hose (see illustration

11.6 Disconnect the IAP sensor hose

12.4 Remove these screws to detach the fuel rail from the throttle body

11.1 and the accompanying illustration). Remove the mounting screws and remove the sensor.

6 Installation is the reverse of removal.

12 Fuel rail and injector - removal and installation

1 Remove the fuel tank and the heat shield beneath it (see Section 7).
2 Release the latch on the fuel line and disconnect it from the fuel rail **(see illustration 11.1)**.
3 Disconnect the electrical connectors from the intake air pressure sensor and fuel injector **(see illustration 11.1)**.
4 Remove the fuel rail mounting screws, using a no. 3 Phillips screwdriver or bit **(see illustration)**.
5 Pull the fuel up and back to separate it from the throttle body. If the injector comes with it, pull the injector out of the fuel rail; if the injector stays in the throttle body, pull it out of the throttle body.

6 Remove the throttle body O-rings.
7 Clean all debris from the area around the injector with spray cleaner or compressed air.
8 Installation is the reverse of removal. Use new O-rings on the injector; lubricate the O-rings with clean engine oil.

13 Throttle cable - removal and installation

1 Loosen the cable adjuster at the handlebar all the way (see Chapter 1).
2 Remove the cover from the throttle housing and check the gasket **(see illustration)**.
3 Disconnect the cable end from the throttle pulley inside the cover. Unscrew the cable housing nut from the throttle housing and pull the cable out.
4 Remove the cover from the throttle body pulley **(see illustration)**. Pull the rubber cover off the adjuster locknut, then loosen

the locknut and adjuster. Inside the cover, disconnect the cable from the throttle body pulley and remove the end plug from the cable. Pull the cable out of the housing.
5 Note how the cable is routed and remove it from its retainers.
6 Route the cable into place. Make sure it doesn't interfere with any other components and isn't kinked or bent sharply.
7 Lubricate the ends of the cable with multi-purpose grease and connect them to the pulleys at the throttle body and at the throttle grip.
8 If it's necessary to remove the throttle cable housing from the handlebar, check for an alignment mark next to the seam in the throttle housing clamp. If there isn't one, make your own. Remove the throttle housing clamp screws and take the throttle housing off the handlebar **(see illustration)**.
9 Adjust the throttle cable (see Chapter 1).
10 Turn the handlebars back and forth to make sure the cable doesn't cause the steering to bind. With the engine idling, turn the handlebars back and forth and make sure

13.2 Remove the screws, lift off the cover and check the gasket

13.4 Remove the screws from the throttle pulley cover on the throttle body

13.8 Remove the screws to detach the throttle housing from the handlebar

14.6 Work the throttle body out of the outlet duct

17.1 The VSS is located on top of the engine behind the cylinder

idle speed doesn't change. If it does, find and fix the cause before riding the vehicle.
11   Install components removed for access.

14 Throttle body - removal and installation

1.   Remove the fuel tank and the heat shield beneath it (see Section 7).
2   Disconnect the handlebar end of the throttle cable, then the throttle body end (see Section 13). Unless the cable needs to be replaced, it can be left in the vehicle to ease installation.
3   Disconnect the wiring connectors from the Intake Air Temperature (IAT) sensor and fuel injector (see illustration 11.1). Disconnect the wiring connector from the Throttle Position (TP) sensor (see Section 10).
4   Release the latch on the fuel line and disconnect it from the throttle body (see illustration 11.1).
5   Disconnect the coolant hoses from the fast idle plunger (see Chapter 3).
6   Loosen the clamps at the front throttle body (see illustration 11.1). Loosen the clamp at the rear and disconnect the air cleaner duct (see illustration 9.2). Work the throttle body out of the intake manifold (see illustration).
7   Lift the throttle body out and remove the duct that attaches it to the engine. Cover the opening in the cylinder head with clean rags to keep out dirt, small parts, etc.
8   The fuel injector and TP sensor can be replaced separately. The fast idle plunger is a permanent part of the throttle body; if it has failed, the entire throttle body must be replaced.
9   If the throttle body needs to be cleaned, use a petroleum-based solvent only. Do not use caustic carburetor cleaning solutions.
10   Installation is the reverse of removal.

15 Intake Air Temperature (IAT) sensor - check, removal and installation

Caution: The IAT sensor is delicate. Don't strike it with tools or drop it. If it's dropped, it should be replaced with a new one.

Check

1   Remove the seat (see Chapter 8).
2   Unplug the connector from the IAT sensor (see illustration 9.2a). Connect an ohmmeter between the wire terminals in the sensor (positive to the brown-white wire's terminal; negative to the black-white wire's terminal).
3   Sensor resistance should be 2.21 to 2.69 ohms at 20-degrees C (68-degrees F). If resistance is not within the specified range, replace the sensor with a new one.

Removal and installation

4   Remove the seat (see Chapter 8).
5   Work the sensor free from the air cleaner duct and lift it out (see illustration 9.2a).
6   Installation is the reverse of removal. Use a new O-ring.

16 Crankshaft Position (CKP) sensor - check, removal and installation

1   The CKP sensor is attached to the inside of the left crankcase cover.

Check

2   Follow the wiring harness from the left crankcase cover to the connector and disconnect it. The CKP sensor harness has two wires, one blue-yellow and one green-white.
3   Connect an ohmmeter between the terminals in the sensor side of the harness (not the wiring harness side). Connect the

positive probe to the blue-yellow wire's terminal. Connect the negative probe to the green-white wire's terminal. Compare the measured resistance with the values listed in this Chapter's Specifications. If it's not within the specified range, replace it (see Steps 4 through 6).

Replacement

4   Remove the left crankcase cover (see Chapter 2).
5   Remove the sensor screws, remove the sensor and install a new one. Use non-permanent thread locking agent on the threads of the sensor screws.
6   Install the left crankcase cover (see Chapter 2).

17 Vehicle Speed Sensor (VSS) - check, removal and installation

1   The VSS is located on top of the engine behind the cylinder (see illustration).

Check

2   Follow the wiring harness from the sensor to its connector and disconnect it. Connect a voltmeter (0-20 volt setting) between the wires in the sensor side of the connector, positive to the white wire and negative to the black/blue wire.
3   With the engine off, jack up the rear of the vehicle so the tires are off the ground and support it securely.
4   Slowly rotate one of the rear tires and watch the voltmeter. It should cycle back and forth between 0.6 volts and 4.8 volts as the tire is rotated. If it doesn't, replace the sensor.

Removal and installation

5   If you haven't already done so, disconnect the electrical connector from the sensor.

18.1 The lean angle sensor is located forward of the battery

19.2 The ECU is located to the left of the air filter housing

Free the wiring harness from any retainers.
6   Unbolt the VSS from the engine and pull it out (see illustration 17.1). Remove the sensor O-ring.
7   Installation is the reverse of removal. Use a new O-ring, coated with clean engine oil. Tighten the bolt securely, but don't overtighten it and strip the threads.

18 Lean angle sensor - check and replacement

1   The lean angle sensor is located under the seat just forward of the battery (see illustration). It can be identified by its wires, one blue and one yellow-green.
2   Remove the seat and taillight assembly (see Chapters 8 and 5).
3   Unbolt the lean angle sensor, but leave its wiring connector attached.
4   Connect the positive probe of a volt-

meter (0-20 volt scale) to the yellow/green wire's terminal in the connector. Connect the voltmeter negative terminal to the black/blue wire's terminal. Note: *The wiring connector must be connected during this check. If your voltmeter's terminals are too thick to fit into the connector terminals, insert short pieces of stiff wire into the connector to act as contacts for the voltmeter terminals.*
5   Turn the main key switch to On, but don't start the engine.
6   Hold the sensor in its installed position and check the voltage reading. It should be within the range listed in this Chapter's Specifications. Tilt the sensor so its connector is downward. As it passes 65-degrees from it installed position, the voltage reading should increase to the higher range listed in this Chapter's Specifications.
7   If the sensor performs as specified, it's good. If not, disconnect its connector and replace it with a new one.
8   Installation is the reverse of removal. Make sure the word UP, molded on the sensor case, is facing upward.

19 Engine Control Unit (ECU) - removal and installation

1   Remove the seat and taillight assembly (see Chapters 8 and 5).
2   Pull the ECU up for access to the connector (see illustration).
3   Squeeze the connector latch to release and pull the connector out of the ECU.
4   Installation is the reverse of removal.

20 Exhaust system - removal and installation

1   Remove the right side cover (see Chapter 8).
2   If necessary, remove the mounting bolts from the main heat shield and take it off the pipes (see illustrations).
3   Loosen the muffler clamp bolt and

20.2a Remove the upper heat shield bolts (left arrows) and loosen the pipe clamp (right arrow)

20.2b Two more bolts secure the underside of the main heat shield

20.3 Loosen the clamp at the front of the muffler and remove the mounting bolts

20.4 Unscrew the nuts that secure the pipe flanges to the cylinder head

unscrew the mounting bolts **(see illustration)**. Work the muffler free of the pipe and remove the gasket.

4   Loosen the clamp that secures the left front pipe to the right front pipe **(see illustration 20.2a)**. Remove the nuts that secure the pipes to the cylinder head **(see illustration)**. Detach the left front pipe from the cyl-inder head and from the right front pipe, then detach the left front pipe from the cylinder head. Remove the pipes from the machine.

5   To replace the muffler core, refer to Chapter 1.

6   Installation is the reverse of removal. Install the right pipe in the cylinder head first, then install the left pipe and secure it to the right pipe with the clamp. Use new gasket in the exhaust ports and at the pipe joints. The gaskets have a rounded chamfer on the outer circumference at one end, the an angled chamfer at the inner circumference on the other end. The rounded chamfer faces into the pipe and the angled chamfer faces out.

Chapter 5
Ignition and electrical systems

Contents

Degrees of difficulty

Easy, suitable for novice with little experience	**Fairly easy,** suitable for beginner with some experience	**Fairly difficult,** suitable for competent DIY mechanic	**Difficult,** suitable for experienced DIY mechanic	**Very difficult,** suitable for expert DIY or professional 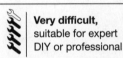

Specifications

Ignition coil resistance
660
    Primary... 0.1 to 0.28 ohms
    Secondary... 6.32 to 9.48 k-ohms
700
    Primary... 3.4 to 4.6 ohms
    Secondary... 10.4 to 5.6 k-ohms

Spark plug cap resistance
All models... 10 k-ohms

Alternator stator coil resistance
660... 0.43 to 0.65 ohms
700... 0.0.248 to 0.372 ohms to 0.48 ohms

Regulator/rectifier
Output voltage... 14.1 to 14.9 volts

Alternator pulse generator resistance
660... 445 to 545 ohms
700... Not applicable

Fuel sender (700)
Ammeter reading (see text)................................. 60 to 135 milliamps

Fuse rating

660 (main and spare)..	20 amps
700	
Main and spare	20 amps
Headlight...	15 amps
Signaling system, ignition, fuel injection.............................	10 amps
Spares (in fuse box)	15 and 10 amps

Bulb ratings

Headlight (all models)	30/30 watts
Tail/brake light	
660	21/5 watts
700	LED

Torque specifications

Alternator rotor nut	
660	150 Nm (110 ft-lbs)
700	60 Nm (43 ft-lbs) (1)
Alternator stator coil bolts	7 Nm (61 inch-lbs)
Ignition pulse generator bolts (660)...	7 Nm (61 inch-lbs)
Wiring harness retainer bolts (inside left crankcase cover)	
660	10 Nm (86 inch-lbs)
700	7 Nm (61 inch-lbs)
Starter clutch bolts	
660	16 Nm (144 inch-lbs) (2)
700	30 Nm (22 ft-lbs) (2)
Starter mounting bolts..	10 Nm (86 inch-lbs)

1 Lubricate the threads with clean engine oil
2 Use non-permanent thread locking agent on the bolt threads.

3.3a On 660 models, disconnect the negative cable (lower right), positive cable (lower left) and remove the retainer bolts (upper arrows)

3.3b On 700 models, unbolt the battery retainer and cover and lift the cover for access to the battery

1 General information

The electrical system on all models includes a battery and charging system, lighting system (including warning lights) and an electric starter.

The ignition system on 660 models consists of an alternator that generates the current, a capacitive discharge ignition (CDI) unit that receives and stores it, and a pulse generator that triggers the CDI unit to discharge its current into the ignition coil, where it is stepped up to a voltage high enough to jump the spark plug gap. To aid in locating a problem in the ignition circuit, wiring diagrams are included at the end of this manual.

The CDI ignition system functions on the same principle as a breaker point ignition system with the pulse generator and CDI unit performing the tasks previously associated with the breaker points and mechanical advance system. As a result, adjustment and maintenance of breakerless ignition components is eliminated (with the exception of spark plug replacement).

The 700 ignition system is a transistor controlled ignition (TCI) type. This system is similar to the CDI system used on 660 models, but ignition timing is controlled by the electronic control unit, which also controls the fuel injection system. Ignition system components that are also part of the fuel injection system (the ECU and crankshaft position sensor) are covered in Chapter 4B.
Note: *Keep in mind that electrical parts, once purchased, can't be returned. To avoid unnecessary expense, make very sure the faulty component has been positively identified before buying a replacement part.*

2 Electrical troubleshooting

Electrical problems often stem from simple causes, such as loose or corroded connections. Prior to any electrical troubleshooting, always visually check the condition of the wires and connections in the circuit.

If testing instruments are going to be utilized, use the diagrams to plan where you will make the necessary connections in order to accurately pinpoint the trouble spot.

The basic tools needed for electrical troubleshooting include a test light or voltmeter, an ohmmeter or a continuity tester (which includes a bulb, battery and set of test leads) and a jumper wire, preferably with a circuit breaker incorporated, which can be used to bypass electrical components.

A continuity check is performed to see if a circuit, section of circuit or individual component is capable of passing electricity through it. Connect one lead of a self-powered test light or ohmmeter to one end of the circuit being tested and the other lead to the other end of the circuit. If the bulb lights (or the ohmmeter indicates little or no resistance), there is continuity, which means the circuit is passing electricity through it properly. The kill switch can be checked in the same way.

Remember that the electrical circuit on these motorcycles is designed to conduct electricity through the wires, kill switch, etc. to the electrical component (CDI unit, etc.). From there it is directed to the frame (ground) where it is passed back to the alternator. Electrical problems are basically an interruption in the flow of electricity.

Because of their nature, the individual ignition system components can be checked but not repaired. If ignition system troubles

occur, and the faulty component can be isolated, the only cure for the problem is to replace the part with a new one. Keep in mind that most electrical parts, once purchased, can't be returned. To avoid unnecessary expense, make very sure the faulty component has been positively identified before buying a replacement part.

Most battery damage is caused by heat, vibration, and/or low electrolyte levels, so keep the battery securely mounted, inspect it at regular intervals and make sure the charging system is functioning properly.

3 Battery - inspection and maintenance

1   The battery is a maintenance free type.
2   Remove the seat (see Chapter 8). Check around the base inside of the battery for sediment, which is the result of sulfation caused by low electrolyte levels. These deposits will cause internal short circuits, which can quickly discharge the battery. Look for cracks in the case and replace the battery if either of these conditions is found.

 Warning: Always disconnect the negative cable first and reconnect it last to prevent sparks that could cause the battery to explode.

3   Check the battery terminals and cable ends for tightness and corrosion. If corrosion is evident, remove the cables from the battery and clean the terminals and cable ends with a wire brush or knife and emery paper. If you need to remove the battery, remove the retainer and lift it out of the carrier **(see illustrations)**. Reconnect the cables and apply a thin coat of petroleum jelly to the connections to slow further corrosion.

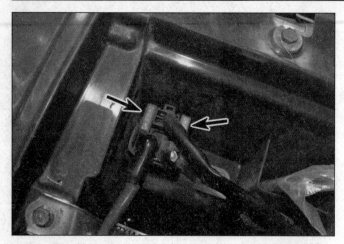

5.1a The 600 main fuse and spare fuse (arrows) are located under the seat, behind the battery

5.1b The 700 main fuse and spare fuse (arrows) are located under the seat on the left side of the vehicle

4   The battery case should be kept clean to prevent current leakage, which can discharge the battery over a period of time (especially when it sits unused). Wash the outside of the case with a solution of baking soda and water. Do not get any baking soda solution in the battery cells. Rinse the battery thoroughly, then dry it.
5   If acid has been spilled on the frame or battery box, neutralize it with the baking soda and water solution, dry it thoroughly, then touch up any damaged paint.
6   If the motorcycle sits unused for long periods of time, disconnect the cables from the battery terminals. Refer to Section 4 and charge the battery approximately once every month.

4   Battery - charging

1   If the machine sits idle for extended periods or if the charging system malfunctions, the battery can be charged from an external source.
2   Charging the maintenance-free battery requires a variable-voltage charger, digital voltmeter and ammeter. If the charger doesn't have an ammeter built in, you can hook up an external ammeter. **Caution:** *Never connect an ammeter between the battery terminals. The ammeter's fuse will blow, or if it doesn't have a fuse, the ammeter will be ruined.*
3   When charging the battery, always remove it from the machine. If the battery case is translucent, check the electrolyte level by looking through the case before hooking up the charger. If the electrolyte level is low, the battery must be discarded; never remove the sealing plug to add water.
4   Disconnect the battery cables (negative cable first), then connect a digital voltmeter

between the battery terminals and measure the voltage (open circuit voltage).
5   If open circuit voltage is 12.8 volts or higher, the battery is fully charged. If it's lower, recharge the battery. Refer to the battery manufacturer's instructions for charging rate and time.
6   A quick charge can be used in an emergency, provided the maximum charge rates and times are not exceeded (exceeding the maximum rate or time may ruin the battery). A quick charge should always be followed as soon as possible by a charge at the standard rate and time.
7   Hook up the battery charger leads (positive lead to battery positive terminal and negative lead to battery negative terminal, then, and only then, plug in the battery charger.

 Warning: The gas escaping from a charging battery is explosive, so keep open flames and sparks well away from the area. Also, the electrolyte is extremely corrosive and will damage anything it comes in contact with.

8   Start charging at a high voltage setting (20 to 25 volts, but no more than 25 volts) and watch the ammeter for about 5 minutes. The charging amperage should exceed the maximum charging amperage listed on the battery. If it doesn't, replace the battery with a new one.
9   When the charging current increases beyond the specified maximum, reduce the charging voltage to reduce the charging current to the rate listed on the battery. Do this periodically as the battery charges (at least every five hours).
10   Allow the battery to charge for the specified time listed in this Chapter's Specifications. If the battery overheats or gases excessively, the charging rate is too high. Either disconnect the charger or lower the charging rate to prevent damage to the battery.
11   After the specified time, unplug the

5.1c The auxiliary fuses on 700 models are in this fuse box under the seat (see text for functions)

charger first, then disconnect the leads from the battery.
12   Wait 30 minutes, then measure voltage between the battery terminals. If it's 12.8 volts or higher, the battery is fully charged. If it's between 12.0 and 12.7 volts, charge the battery again (refer to the battery manufacturer's instructions for charging rate and time).

5   Fuses - check and replacement

1   All models have a single main fuse of the bayonet type, located near the battery (see illustrations). A spare fuse is located near the main fuse. 700 models also have fuses for the signaling system, headlights, ignition system and fuel injection system, located in a fuse holder under the seat (see

6.6 Pull the cap off the spark plug, unscrew it from the wire and check its resistance with an ohmmeter

6.12 A simple spark gap testing fixture can be made from a block of wood, two nails, a large alligator clip, a screw and a piece of wire

illustration). Looking at the fuses from the front of the vehicle, their functions are, left to right: Signaling system, headlights, ignition and fuel injection system. The two fuses forward of these four fuses are spares.

2   The fuse can be checked visually without removing it from its holder; just look through the plastic to see if the metal element inside is broken. If so, pull the fuse out and push a new one in.

3   If the fuse blows, be sure to check the wiring harnesses very carefully for evidence of a short circuit. Look for bare wires and chafed, melted or burned insulation. If a fuse is replaced before the cause is located, the new fuse will blow immediately.

4   Never, under any circumstances, use a higher rated fuse or bridge the fuse terminals, as damage to the electrical system - or even a fire - could result.

5   Occasionally a fuse will blow or cause an open circuit for no obvious reason. Corrosion of the fuse ends and fuse holder terminals may occur and cause poor fuse contact. If this happens, remove the corrosion with a wire brush or emery paper, then spray the fuse end and terminals with electrical contact cleaner.

6 Ignition system - check

![warning] **Warning: Because of the very high voltage generated by the ignition system, extreme care should be taken when these checks are performed.**

1   If the ignition system is the suspected cause of poor engine performance or failure to start, a number of checks can be made to isolate the problem.

2   Check the main fuse (see Section 5). If you're working on a 700, also check the ignition system fuse.

3   Make sure the battery is fully changed (see Section 4).

Engine will not start

4   Refer to Chapter 1 and disconnect the spark plug wire. Connect the wire to a spare spark plug and lay the plug on the engine with the threads contacting the engine. If necessary, hold the spark plug with an insulated tool. Crank the engine over and make sure a well-defined, blue spark occurs between the spark plug electrodes.

![warning] **Warning: Don't remove the spark plug from the engine to perform this check - atomized fuel being pumped out of the open spark plug hole could ignite, causing severe injury!**

5   If no spark occurs, the following checks should be made:

6   Unscrew the spark plug cap from the plug wire and check its resistance with an ohmmeter **(see illustration)**. If it's not as listed in this Chapter's Specifications, replace the cap.

7   Refer to Section 7 and check the ignition coil primary and secondary resistance.

8   If you're working on a 660, check the ignition pick-up coil (see Section 9). If you're working on a 700, check the crankshaft position sensor and the lean angle sensor (see Chapter 4B).

9   Make sure all electrical connectors are clean and tight. Check all wires for shorts, opens and correct installation.

10   If the preceding checks produce positive results but there is still no spark at the plug, refer to Section 8 and check the CDI unit (660) or refer to Chapter 4B and check the ECU (700).

Engine starts but misfires

11   If the engine starts but misfires, make the following checks before deciding that the ignition system is at fault.

12   The ignition system must be able to produce a spark across a six-millimeter (1/4-inch) gap (minimum). A simple test fixture **(see illustration)** can be constructed to make sure the minimum spark gap can be jumped. Make sure the fixture electrodes are positioned seven millimeters apart.

13   Connect the spark plug wire to the protruding test fixture electrode, then attach the fixture's alligator clip to a good engine ground.

14   Crank the engine over with the starter and see if well-defined, blue sparks occur between the test fixture electrodes. If the minimum spark gap test is positive, the ignition coil is functioning properly. If the spark will not jump the gap, or if it is weak (orange colored), refer to Steps 4 through 10 of this Section and perform the component checks described.

7 Ignition coil - check, removal and installation

1   The primary and secondary coil resistances can be measured with an ohmmeter. If the coil is undamaged, and if the resistances are as specified, it is probably capable of proper operation.

2   Remove the coil as described below and check it visually for cracks and other damage.

Removal

3   The 660 ignition coil is located at the left front of the vehicle, on the frame above the

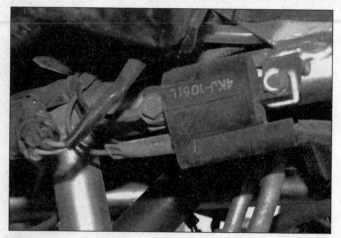

7.3a Here's the 600 ignition coil - Disconnect the primary positive wire and unscrew the bolts to remove it

7.3b Disconnect the primary positive wire from the 700 ignition coil . . .

7.3c . . . and unscrew its bolts, working from inside the frame

oil tank (see illustration). The 700 ignition coil is located at the right front of the vehicle, below the regulator-rectifier (see illustrations). To remove the coil, disconnect the spark plug wire from the plug. Label the coil primary circuit electrical wires, then disconnect them.
4   Remove the coil mounting bolts, then lift the coil out.

Check

5   Unscrew the spark plug cap from the plug wire.
6   Connect an ohmmeter between the primary (small) terminals (see illustration). Set the ohmmeter selector switch in the Rx1 position and compare the measured resistance to the primary resistance values listed in this Chapter's Specifications. If the resistance is not as specified, the coil is probably defective and should be replaced with a new one.
7   Connect the ohmmeter between the coil primary positive terminal and the spark plug wire (see illustration 7.6). Place the ohmmeter selector switch in the Rx100 position and compare the measured resistance to the secondary resistance values listed in this Chapter's Specifications. If the resistance is not as specified, the coil is probably defective and should be replaced with a new one.
8   Connect the ohmmeter to the ends of the spark plug cap and check the resistance (see illustration 7.6). If the resistance is not as specified, the spark plug cap is bad.

Installation

9   Installation is the reverse of removal.

8   CDI unit (660) - check, removal and installation

Check

1   The CDI unit is tested by process of elimination (when all other possible causes of ignition problems have been checked and eliminated, the CDI unit is at fault).
2   Check the ignition coil, alternator exciter coil, pulse generator and kill switch as described elsewhere in this Chapter.
3   Carefully check the wiring harnesses for breaks or bad connections.
4   If the harness and all other system components tested good, the CDI unit may be defective. Before buying a new one, it's a good idea to substitute a known good CDI unit.

Removal and installation

5   Remove the seat (see Chapter 8).
6   Locate the CDI unit under the seat. Unplug its connector, remove the mounting screws and lift the CDI unit out (see illustration).
7   Installation is the reverse of the removal steps.

7.6 Ignition coil test

1   Measure primary winding resistance
2   Measure secondary winding resistance

IGNITION COIL

2662-5A-4.5 HAYNES

8.6 Remove the CDI unit mounting screws (arrows), lift it up and unplug its electrical connectors

9.4a Follow the alternator wiring harness (arrow) to its connector and unplug it - this is the 600 . . .

9.4b . . . and this is the 700

9 Alternator and regulator/rectifier - check and replacement

Note: *The 700 uses a crankshaft position sensor instead of a pickup coil. Refer to Chapter 4B for checking and replacement procedures.*

Check

1   Remove the seat (see Chapter 8). Connect a voltmeter between the battery terminals (refer to Section 3 if necessary). Connect the voltmeter positive lead to the battery positive terminal and the voltmeter negative lead to the battery negative terminal.

2   Connect an induction-pickup tachometer to the spark plug wire, following the manufacturer's instructions.

3   Make sure the transmission is in neutral and start the engine. Operate the throttle to raise engine speed to 5000 rpm. If charging voltage is at or above the level listed in this Chapter's Specifications, the alternator and regulator-rectifier are good. If it's below the specified level perform the following checks to isolate the cause.

4   Locate the alternator wiring harness on the left side of the engine and follow it to its connectors **(see illustrations)**.

660

5   To check the ignition system pickup coil, disconnect the connector for the white-red and white-green wires.

6   Connect an ohmmeter to the wires in the alternator side of the connector (not the wiring harness side), positive probe to white-red and negative probe to white-green. If the readings are much outside the value listed in this Chapter's Specifications, replace the pickup coil as described below.

7   To check the charging coil, disconnect the connector for the three white wires. Connect an ohmmeter between two wires at a time (in the alternator side of the connector,

not the wiring harness side). If the reading between any two wires is outside the value listed in this Chapter's Specifications, replace the charging coil as described below.

700

8   To check the stator coils, disconnect the coil connector (three white wires). Connect an ohmmeter between two wires at a time and measure the resistance between each pair. Compare the reading to the value listed in this Chapter's Specifications. If it's not within the specified range, replace the stator coil as described below.

All models

9   Locate the regulator-rectifier on the left side of the vehicle (660) or the right side of the vehicle (700) **(see illustrations)**. Without disconnecting the regulator connector, connect a voltmeter to the terminals for the red and black wires. Connect the voltmeter positive lead to the red wire's terminal and the voltmeter negative lead to the back wire's terminal. If necessary, insert short pieces of stiff wire into the terminals from the back side

to serve as contact points for the voltmeter.

10   Make sure the transmission is in neutral and start the engine. Operate the throttle to raise engine speed to 5000 rpm. If charging voltage is at or above the level listed in this Chapter's Specifications, the alternator and regulator-rectifier are good. If it's below the specified level perform the following checks to isolate the cause.

11   If the problem still hasn't been located, carefully check all of the wires in the charging system for breaks or bad connections. Make any necessary repairs and repeat Step 10.

12   If the charging voltage is still too low, the regulator-rectifier is probably at fault. Since this is an expensive component that can't be returned once purchased, it's a good idea to have the test double-checked by a dealer service department or other qualified shop.

Rotor removal

Note: *To remove the alternator rotor, a puller will be required, either a three-legged puller for 660 models or a special Yamaha puller*

9.9a The 600 regulator-rectifier (arrow) is attached to the left side of the frame forward of the coolant reservoir

9.9b The 700 regulator-rectifier (arrow) is at the right front of the vehicle, behind the headlight

9.14 Unscrew the rotor nut and remove the washer

9.15a On 660 models, thread the rotor nut on backwards to protect the end of the crankshaft . . .

9.15b . . . install a three-legged puller like this one and tighten it to push the rotor off the crankshaft

9.16 On 700 models, thread the puller onto the rotor and tighten the puller screw against the crankshaft, then hold the puller body with a wrench and tighten the puller screw to push the rotor off

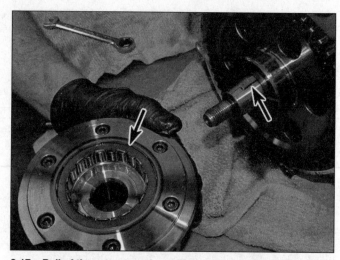

9.17a Pull of the rotor, together with the starter clutch (left arrow) and remove the Woodruff key (right arrow)

9.17b Be sure there aren't any small metal objects stuck to the rotor magnets; an inconspicuous item like this Woodruff key (arrow) can ruin the rotor and stator if the engine is run

or its aftermarket equivalent for 700 models. Don't try to remove the rotor without the proper puller, as it's almost sure to be damaged. Pullers are readily available from motorcycle dealers and aftermarket tool suppliers.

13   Remove the left crankcase cover (see Chapter 2A).

14   Hold the alternator rotor with a universal holder. You can also use a strap wrench. If you don't have one of these tools and the engine is in the frame, the rotor can be locked by placing the transmission in gear and holding the rear brake on. Unscrew the rotor nut and remove the washer (see illustration).

660 models

15   Turn the rotor nut around from its normal installed position and thread it partway onto the crankshaft (see illustration). This forms a pushing surface for the puller to keep the crankshaft from being damaged. Attach a three-legged puller to the rotor

using three bolts (see illustration). Tighten the puller until the rotor pops loose from the crankshaft.

700 models

16   Thread an alternator puller into the center of the rotor and use it to remove the rotor (see illustration). If the rotor doesn't come off easily, tap sharply on the end of the puller to release the rotor's grip on the tapered crankshaft end.

All models

17   Pull the rotor off (see illustration). Check the Woodruff key; if it's not secure in its slot, pull it out and set it aside for safekeeping. A convenient method is to stick the Woodruff key to the magnets inside the rotor (see illustration), but be certain not to forget it's there, as serious damage to the rotor and stator coils will occur if the engine is run with anything stuck to the magnets.

9.26 Unbolt the stator coils, ignition pulse generator or crankshaft position sensor and the wiring harness retainer

10.5a Handlebar switch housing screws (660)

Rotor installation

18 Take a look to make sure there isn't anything stuck to the inside of the rotor (see illustration 9.17b).

19 Degrease the center of the rotor and the end of the crankshaft.

20 Make sure the Woodruff key is positioned securely in its slot (see illustration 9.17a).

21 Align the rotor slot with the Woodruff key. Place the rotor on the crankshaft.

22 Install the rotor washer and nut. Hold the rotor from turning with one of the methods described in Step 14 and tighten the nut to the torque listed in this Chapter's Specifications.

23 The remainder of installation is the reverse of the removal steps.

Stator coils and pulse generator/CKP sensor replacement

24 The stator coils and pulse generator (660) or crankshaft position sensor (700) are replaced as a unit.

25 Remove the left engine cover and alternator rotor as described above.

26 Remove three screws that secure the stator coils (all models), two screws that secure the ignition pulse generator (660) or crankshaft position sensor (700) and two screws that secure the wiring harness retainer to the inside of the crankcase cover (all models) (see illustration). Remove them from the inside of the left crankcase cover.

27 Installation is the reverse of the removal steps. Apply non-permanent thread locking agent to the threads of the stator coil screws and tighten to the torque listed in this Chapter's Specifications.

Regulator/rectifier replacement

28 The regulator/rectifier is located on the left side of the vehicle (660) or under the right front fender (see illustration 9.9a or 9.9b).

29 Disconnect the electrical connector from the regulator/rectifier. Remove its mounting nuts or bolts and lift it off.

30 Installation is the reverse of the removal steps.

10 Kill switch - check, removal and installation

1 The kill switch, mounted in the switch housing on the left handlebar, shorts the ignition circuit to ground when it's set to the Off position.

Check

2 Follow the wires from the switch to their connectors and unplug them.

3 Connect an ohmmeter between the wire terminals in the switch side of the connectors (not the side that leads back to the wiring harness). With the switch in the Off position, the ohmmeter should show no continuity (infinite resistance); with the switch in the On position, the ohmmeter should show continuity (little or no resistance).

4 Repeat the test several times. The ohmmeter should move from continuity to no continuity each time the switch is moved. If it shows no continuity in the Off position, or continuity in the Run position, replace the switch.

Removal and installation

5 To remove the switch, remove the screws (see illustrations) separate the upper and lower halves of the switch housing and

10.5b Handlebar switch housing screws (700)

take it off the handlebar. The kill switch isn't available separately; it and the and headlight switch are both part of the switch housing, which is available only as a complete unit.

6 Installation is the reverse of removal.

11 Starter circuit - component check and replacement

1 The electric starter used on these models includes a safety circuit that prevents the starter from operating unless the transmission is in neutral or the clutch lever is pulled in.

Starter relay

2 Remove the seat (see Chapter 8). If you're working on a 700, remove the battery retainer strap (see Section 3).

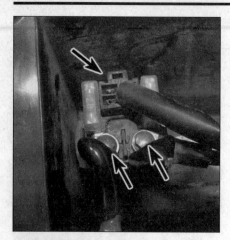

11.3a The 660 starter relay is under the seat behind the battery - unplug its connector and unscrew the mounting bolts to remove it

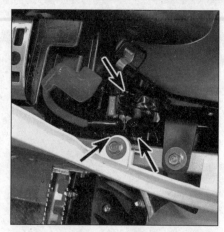

11.3b The 700 starter relay is under the seat to the left of the air filter housing - unplug its connector and unscrew the mounting bolts to remove it

11.7 Several major 700 electrical components are located in this area behind the battery

A   Cooling fan relay
B   Headlight relay
C   Fuse box
D   Relay unit

3   Disconnect the battery cables from the relay, negative cable first, then disconnect the wiring connector from the starter relay **(see illustrations)**.

4   Connect an ohmmeter between the battery terminals on the relay. The ohmmeter should indicate infinite resistance (no continuity).

5   Connect a fully charged battery (the vehicle's battery will work) to the relay terminals, using lengths of wire. The ohmmeter between the relay's battery terminals should now indicate continuity (little or no resistance).

6   If the relay doesn't perform as described, remove it from its mount and install a new one.

Starting circuit cut-off relay (700)

7   Remove the seat (see Chapter 8). The starting circuit cut-off relay is contained within the relay unit behind the air filter housing **(see illustration)**.

8   Remove the relay unit from its mount and disconnect the wiring connector.

9   Connect an ohmmeter positive terminal to the relay terminal that connects to the blue-white wire. Connect the ohmmeter negative terminal to the relay terminal that connects to the black-yellow wire. There should be no continuity (the ohmmeter should show infinite resistance.

10   With the ohmmeter still connected as described in Step 9, connect the positive terminal of a fully charged battery (the vehicle's battery will work) to the relay terminal that connects to the light blue wire, using a length of wire. Connect the battery negative terminal to the relay terminal that connects to the black-yellow wire. The ohmmeter between the relay's battery terminals should now indicate continuity (little or no resistance).

11   If the relay doesn't perform as described, replace the relay unit with a new one.

---

12 Starter motor - check and replacement

Check

 Warning: This check may cause sparks. Make sure there is no leaking gasoline or anything else flammable in the vicinity.

 Warning: Make sure the transmission is in Neutral or the vehicle will jump forward during Step 2.

 Warning: The jumper cable used for this procedure must be of a gauge at least as heavy as the battery cable or it may overheat, causing its insulation to melt and possibly catch fire.

1   Locate the starter motor and disconnect its cable **(see illustrations)**.

2   Connect a jumper cable from the battery positive terminal directly to the starter motor terminal. Connect the cable to the battery first, then to the starter motor terminal. The starter should crank the engine.

3   If the starter doesn't crank at all, replace it. If it turns but doesn't crank the engine, remove and inspect the starter reduction gears and slipper clutch (see Sections 13 and 15).

Replacement

4   If you haven't already done so, disconnect the starter cable.

5   Remove the starter mounting bolts and lift it out of the engine **(see illustration 12.1)**.

6   Installation is the reverse of the removal steps. Use a new O-ring and tighten the bolts to the torque listed in this Chapter's Specifications.

12.1 Disconnect the cable and remove the mounting bolts (arrows), then pull the starter out of the engine

---

13 Starter reduction gears - removal and installation

1   The starter reduction gears transfer torque from the starter pinion to the starter clutch drive gear, which is mounted on the back of the alternator rotor. The starter clutch turns the crankshaft. On 660 models, the starter pinion turns an idler gear, which turns a second idler gear, which turns the starter clutch drive gear. On 700 models, the starter pinion turns a torque-limiting slipper clutch, which turns an idler gear, which turns the starter clutch drive gear.

2   This section describes removal of the idler gears. To remove the 700 slipper clutch, see Section 15.

13.3a Unbolt the idler gear cover and take it off . . .

13.3b . . . and remove the idler gear . . .

13.3c Pull the idler gear off its shaft and inspect the bearings

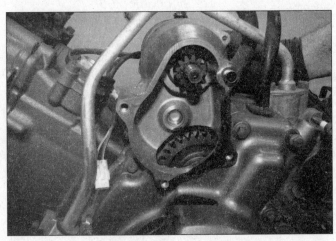

13.3d Rotate the lower idler gear to check the gear and starter clutch for wear or damage

13.4 Take the idler gear off its shaft and pull the shaft out of the crankcase

Idler gear removal

3   The first idler gear on 660 models can be removed without removing the left crankcase cover. Remove the idler gear cover, then slip the gear off the shaft (see illustrations). Inspect the starter pinion gear and second idler gear, inside the cover (see illustration). The starter pinion gear isn't available separately, so the starter will need to be replaced if the pinion gear is worn or damaged. If the second idler gear is worn or damaged, remove it as described below.

4   To remove the second idler gear (660) or only idler gear (700), remove the left crankcase cover (see Chapter 2A). Pull the gear off its shaft (see illustration). Pull the shaft out of the crankcase.

Starter clutch drive gear removal

5   Remove the left crankcase cover and alternator rotor (see Chapter 2A and Section 9).
6   If you haven't already done so, remove the rotor Woodruff key (see illustration).

13.6a Remove the Woodruff key (left arrow) if not already done and pull the starter clutch drive gear (right arrow) off the crankshaft . . .

Slip the drive gear off the crankshaft, noting which direction it faces. Remove the thrust washer behind the starter drive gear (see illustration).

13.6b . . . and remove the washer from behind the gear

Inspection

7   Check the gears for wear or damage such as chipped teeth. Check the shafts for scoring or heat damage that might indicate

lack of lubrication. Replace the gear if problems are found.

8   On the inside of the starter clutch gear, check the bearing (660) or bushing (700) for wear or damage.

9   Since needle roller bearing wear is difficult to see, the idler gear bearing on 660 models should be replaced if its condition is in doubt. On 700 models, replace the gear if problems are found.

Installation

10   Installation is the reverse of the removal steps.

14 Starter clutch - removal and installation

1   If the starter motor spins but doesn't crank the engine, you can check the starter clutch without removing it from the engine.
2   If you're working on a 660, remove the first idler gear (see Section 13). Reach into the slipper clutch recess and spin the starter idler gear with a finger **(see illustration 13.3d)**. It should spin freely and smoothly in one direction and not at all in the other direction. If it spins both ways, the starter clutch is probably damaged. If the movement of the gear is rough or uneven, the starter clutch or one of the reduction gears may be damaged. Remove the starter clutch for further inspection as described below.
3   If you're working on a 700, remove the slipper clutch (see Section 15). Spin the idler gear with a finger and check for damage as described in Step 2.

Removal

4   Remove the alternator rotor (see Section 9). The starter clutch is mounted in the back of the rotor **(see illustration 13.6a)**.
5   Mark the starter clutch so you can reinstall it facing the correct direction. Remove the bolts that secure the starter clutch to the alternator rotor and take the starter clutch off. **Note:** *If the starter clutch is installed facing the wrong way, the starter will spin without cranking the engine.*

Inspection

6   Check all parts for visible wear and damage and replace any parts that show problems.
7   Test the starter clutch. Place it in position on the back of the alternator rotor. Place the starter clutch drive gear in the starter clutch. Hold the rotor steady, with the gear toward you, and try to twist the clutch. It should twist freely in a counterclockwise direction, but not at all in the clockwise direction.
8   If the gear will turn both ways or neither way, the starter clutch is bad. If the gear will turn freely clockwise, but not at all coun-

17.1 Pull on the rubber tab to separate the cover from the headlight housing

terclockwise, the starter clutch rollers are installed upside down.

Installation

9   Installation is the reverse of the removal steps. Tighten the starter clutch bolts to the torque listed in this Chapter's Specifications and use non-permanent thread locking agent on the bolt threads. Be sure to check the starter clutch function as described in Step 7 before completing final installation.

15 Slipper clutch (700) - removal, inspection and installation

1   These vehicles use a torque limiting slipper clutch between the starter pinion and the idler gear. The slipper clutch is mounted behind of the cylinder, inside the left crankcase cover.

Removal

2   Remove the left crankcase cover (see Chapter 2A). Take the slipper clutch off the engine.

Inspection

3   The slipper clutch components aren't available separately, so if there's wear or damage, replace the slipper clutch as a unit.

Installation

4   Installation is the reverse of the removal steps.

16 Lighting circuit - check

System check

1   If the headlight or taillight doesn't work on a 660, check the bulb (see Section 17). If

it's good, check the socket for corrosion and the wiring for breaks or bad connections. The taillight on 700 models is a light-emitting diode (LED) assembly that's replaced as a unit.
2   If neither light works, check switch continuity with an ohmmeter, referring to continuity diagrams in the wiring diagrams at the end of this manual. Disconnect its wiring connector and connect an ohmmeter to the switch terminals.
3   If the brake light doesn't work, check it in the same manner as the headlight and taillight (se Steps 1 and 2). If none of the lights work and the switch is good, check the lighting system wiring for breaks or bad connections. If you're working on a 700, check the headlight relay.

Relay check (700)

4   You'll need a fully charged 12-volt battery and an ohmmeter for this test (the vehicle's battery will work).
5   The headlight relay is under the seat behind the air filter housing **(see illustration 11.7)**. Remove the seat (see Chapter 8) for access to the relay.
6   Detach the relay from its rubber holder and disconnect it from the wiring harness.
7   Connect the positive terminal of an ohmmeter to the relay terminal that connects to the blue wire. Connect the ohmmeter negative terminal to the relay terminal that connects to the green wire, then move the negative probe to the terminal that connects to the yellow wire (the one in the center of the relay). The ohmmeter should indicate no continuity (infinite resistance) in both cases.
8   Connect the positive terminal of a fully charged 12-volt battery (the vehicle's battery will work) to the relay terminal that connects to the other yellow wire (the one at the side of the relay, not the one in the center). Connect the battery negative terminal to the terminal that connects to the blue wire.
9   With the battery connected as described in Step 8, connect the ohmmeter as described in Step 7. This time, the ohmmeter should show continuity (little or no resistance) in both cases.
10   If the relay doesn't perform as described, replace it.

17 Bulb replacement

Headlights

1   Working beneath the fender, pull the removal tab to pull the rubber cap off of the headlight assembly **(see illustration)**.
2   Press the wiring connector into its socket and turn it counterclockwise, then

17.2a Twist the socket counterclockwise . . .

17.2b . . . to disengage its tabs (arrows), then pull it out of the housing

17.3 Pull the bulb out; don't touch the glass on a new bulb with your fingers

remove it from the headlight (see illustrations).

3 Pull the bulb out, holding it by the metal base (see illustration).

4 Installation is the reverse of the removal steps. Hold the bulb by its base (see illustration 17.3). Be sure not to touch the bulb glass with your fingers - oil from your skin will cause the bulb to overheat and fail prematurely. If you do touch the bulb, wipe it off with a clean rag dampened with rubbing alcohol.

5 Reinstall the rubber cap, making sure the TOP mark on the cap is upward (see illustration). If you removed both rubber caps at the same time, refer to the L (left) and R (right) marks to make sure they're reinstalled on the correct sides of the vehicle.

Tail/brake light

Conventional bulb (660)

6 660 models use a conventional bulb for the brake/taillight. To replace it, remove the lens securing screws and take off the

lens (see illustration). Press the bulb into its socket and turn it counterclockwise to remove. Install in the reverse order.

Light-emitting diode (LED) (700)

7 700 models use a light-emitting diode (LED) unit. If it fails, the entire assembly must be replaced.

8 Remove the seat and rear fender (see Chapter 8).

9 Disconnect the wiring harness from the taillight. Remove the taillight mounting screws and take the assembly out of the cover (see illustration).

10 Installation is the reverse of the removal steps.

Warning lights

11 If you're working on a 660, remove the instrument light socket from the bracket, then pull the bulb out, push a new one in and reinstall the socket.

12 The warning lights on 700 models are part of the multi-function display. If one of them fails, the entire unit must be replaced

17.5 Make sure the Top mark is upward; the R and L marks indicate right and left sides of the vehicle

as an assembly. Refer to Section 24 for multi-function display test procedures.

17.6 On 660 models, remove the lens screws (arrows) for access to the bulb

17.9 On 700 models, remove the screws (arrows) and take off the taillight unit

18.1 Turn the adjuster (arrow) to adjust the headlight

19.1 The clutch switch is located in the lever pivot - press its release prong (arrow) and pull the switch out

18 Headlight adjustment

The headlight can be adjusted vertically by turning the adjuster wheel located under the fender **(see illustration)**.

19 Clutch switch - check and replacement

1   The clutch switch is mounted in the clutch lever pivot **(see illustration)**.
2   Follow the wiring harness from the switch to its connector and disconnect it.
3   Connect an ohmmeter between the terminals in the switch side of the connector. With the clutch lever pulled in, there should be no resistance (zero ohms). With the lever released, there should be infinite resistance.
4   If the switch doesn't perform as described, slide back the lever pivot cover,

press the switch retainer prong and pull the switch out of the clutch lever pivot. Push a new switch in until the retainer prong engages, then connect the wiring harness and reposition the cover.

20 Neutral and Reverse switches and diodes - check and replacement

Neutral and Reverse switches

1   Disconnect the electrical connector from the switch **(see illustrations)**.
2   Connect one lead of an ohmmeter to a good ground and the other lead to the terminal post on the switch.
3   There should be no resistance between the switch and ground when the transmission is in Neutral or Reverse. In any other gear, there should be infinite resistance.
4   If the switch doesn't perform as described, unscrew it and screw in a new one, using a new gasket.

Diodes

5   The diodes are located in the relay unit, under the seat behind the air filter housing **(see illustration 11.7)**. Remove the seat (see Chapter 8), remove the relay unit from its mounting tab and disconnect the electrical connector.
6   Connect the positive terminal of an ohmmeter to the relay terminal that connects to the light blue wire. Connect the ohmmeter negative terminal to the relay terminal that connects to the red-black wire. The ohmmeter should indicate continuity (little or no resistance). If not, replace the relay unit with a new one.
7   Connect the positive terminal of an ohmmeter to the relay terminal that connects to the red-black wire. Connect the ohmmeter negative terminal to the relay terminal that connects to the light blue wire. The ohmmeter should indicate no continuity (infinite resistance). If not, replace the relay unit with a new one.
8   Connect the positive terminal of an ohmmeter to the relay terminal that connects to the light blue wire. Connect the ohmmeter negative terminal to the relay terminal that connects to the light green wire. The ohm-

20.1a The 660 neutral switch (upper arrow) and reverse switch (lower arrow) are located near the shift pedal

20.1b The 700 neutral switch (upper arrow) and reverse switch (lower arrow) are located near the shift pedal

21.1a The 660 front brake switch is located in the lever pivot - press its release prong (arrow) and pull the switch out

21.1b The 700 front brake switch (arrow) is secured to the lever pivot by a single screw

21.1c The 660 rear brake light switch is located above the brake pedal - unhook its spring (lower arrow) and turn its nut (upper arrow) all the way off the switch body to remove it

meter should indicate continuity (little or no resistance). If not, replace the relay unit with a new one.

9   Connect the positive terminal of an ohmmeter to the relay terminal that connects to the light green wire. Connect the ohmmeter negative terminal to the relay terminal that connects to the light blue wire. The ohmmeter should indicate no continuity (infinite resistance). If not, replace the relay unit with a new one.

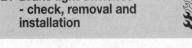

21   Brake light switches - check, removal and installation

1   Locate the switch **(see illustrations)**. Follow the wiring harness from the switch to its connector and disconnect it.
2   Connect an ohmmeter between the terminals in the switch side of the connector. Operate the brake lever or pedal. With the lever pulled in or the pedal pressed, there should be no resistance (zero ohms). With the lever or pedal released, there should be infinite resistance.
3   If the front brake light switch doesn't perform as described, replace it. The switch is not adjustable. To replace it, press the switch retainer prong and pull the switch out of the brake lever pivot. Push a new switch in until the retainer prong engages, then connect the wiring harness.
4   The rear brake light switch can be adjusted. Hold the switch body so it won't turn and turn the adjusting nut to raise or lower the switch in the bracket **(see illustration 21.1c or 21.1d)**.
5   If adjustment of the rear brake light switch doesn't help, replace the switch with a new one. Unhook the switch from the brake pedal, unscrew the nut off the switch body

and take it out of the bracket. Reverse the removal procedure to install the new switch, then adjust it as described in Step 4.

22   Main key switch - check and replacement

1   The main key switch (ignition switch) is located in the front cover **(see illustrations)**.

Check

2   To check the switch, follow its wiring harness to the connector and disconnect it (remove the front fender, referring to Chapter 8, if necessary for access).
3   Connect an ohmmeter between the red and brown wires in the switch side of the wiring harness. The ohmmeter should indicate continuity (zero ohms) with the switch in the On position. If it doesn't, replace it.

21.1d The 700 rear brake light switch is located above the brake pedal - unhook its spring (lower arrow) and turn its nut (upper arrow) all the way off the switch body to remove it

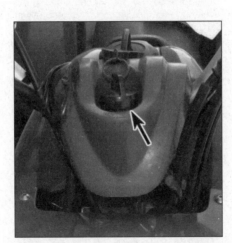

22.1a Here's the 660 main key switch

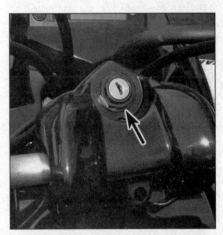

22.1b Here's the 700 main key switch

24.17 Remove the front cover for access to the multi-function display connector

Replacement

4   Disconnect the switch wiring connector as described above.

5   Unscrew the switch nut and lift the switch out of the fender.

6   Installation is the reverse of the removal steps.

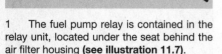

23 Fuel pump relay (700) - check and replacement

1   The fuel pump relay is contained in the relay unit, located under the seat behind the air filter housing **(see illustration 11.7)**.

2   Remove the seat. Lift the relay unit off its mounting tab and disconnect the wiring connector.

3   Remove the relay unit from its mount and disconnect the wiring connector.

4   Connect an ohmmeter positive terminal to the relay terminal that connects to the brown-green wire. Connect the ohmmeter negative terminal to the relay terminal that connects to the light green wire. There should be no continuity (the ohmmeter should show infinite resistance).

5   With the ohmmeter still connected as described in Step 5, connect the positive terminal of a fully charged battery (the vehicle's battery will work) to the relay terminal that connects to the light blue wire, using a length of wire. Connect the battery negative terminal to the relay terminal that connects to the blue-red wire. The ohmmeter between the relay's battery terminals should now indicate continuity (little or no resistance).

6   If the relay doesn't perform as described, replace the relay unit with a new one.

24 Multi-function display (700) - check and replacement

Check

1   The multi-function display, mounted in the front panel, contains a speedometer, odometer, two trip meters, a clock, an engine hour meter, warning lights and indicator lights.

2   If any of the functions does not work, check the fuses (main fuse, ignition system fuse and signaling system fuse) (see Section 5). Replace any blown fuses.

3   Check the battery condition (see Section 3).

4   Check the main key switch (see Section 22).

5   Check the wiring for the affected circuit, referring to the wiring diagram at the end of this manual.

6   If the neutral light doesn't come on, check the neutral switch (see Section 20).

7   If the switch is good, check the diodes (see Section 20). Replace the relay unit if the diodes are bad.

8   If the switch and diodes are good, check the circuit wiring for breaks or bad connections. If the wiring is good, the display unit is probably at fault. Since this is an expensive component that can't be returned once purchased, it's a good idea to have it checked by a dealer service department or other qualified shop.

9   If the reverse light doesn't come on, check the reverse switch (see Section 20).

10   If the switch is good, check the circuit wiring for breaks or bad connections. If the wiring is good, the display unit is probably at fault. Since this is an expensive component that can't be returned once purchased, it's a good idea to have it checked by a dealer service department or other qualified shop.

11   If the coolant temperature warning light doesn't come on, check the coolant temperature sender (see Chapter 3).

12   If the sender is good, check the circuit wiring for breaks or bad connections. If the wiring is good, the display unit is probably at fault. Since this is an expensive component that can't be returned once purchased, it's a good idea to have it checked by a dealer service department or other qualified shop.

13   If the fuel level warning light doesn't come on, check the fuel sender (see Section 25).

14   If the sender is good, check the circuit wiring for breaks or bad connections. If the wiring is good, the display unit is probably at fault. Since this is an expensive component that can't be returned once purchased, it's

a good idea to have it checked by a dealer service department or other qualified shop.

15   If the speedometer doesn't work, check the vehicle speed sensor (see Chapter 4B).

16   If the speed sensor is good, check the circuit wiring for breaks or bad connections. If the wiring is good, the display unit or engine control unit (ECU) is probably at fault. Since these are expensive components that can't be returned once purchased, it's a good idea to have them checked by a dealer service department or other qualified shop.

Replacement

17   Remove the front cover for access to the electrical connector, then disconnect it **(see illustration)**.

18   Detach the unit from the front panel and lift it out.

19   Installation is the reverse of the removal steps.

25 Fuel sender - check

1   The fuel sender is part of the fuel pump unit, which is mounted inside the fuel tank.

2   Remove the fuel pump (see Chapter 4B).

⚠ *Warning: Blow the fuel pump dry with compressed air (or a hair dryer set on Cold) to make sure that a spark from the battery does not ignite any residual gasoline on the pump.*

3   Connect the positive probe of an ammeter (set to measure milliamps) to the positive terminal of a 12-volt battery (the vehicle's battery will do). Connect the ammeter negative probe to the terminal in the fuel pump electrical connector that connects to the orange-green wire (the fuel pump side of the connector, not the wiring harness side). This is the terminal farthest to the left when looking into the open end of the connector.

4   Connect one end of a length of wire to the fuel pump terminal that connects to the black-white wire. Connect the other end of the wire to the negative terminal of the battery.

5   The ammeter should now indicate a current reading. Position the float on the fuel pump so the distance from the fuel pump mounting flange to halfway down the float is 79.5 mm (3.13 inches). The current reading on the ammeter should be within the range listed in this Chapter's Specifications. If it isn't, replace the fuel pump as an assembly.

Chapter 6
Steering, suspension and final drive

Contents

Degrees of difficulty

Easy, suitable for novice with little experience		**Fairly easy,** suitable for beginner with some experience		**Fairly difficult,** suitable for competent DIY mechanic		**Difficult,** suitable for experienced DIY mechanic		**Very difficult,** suitable for expert DIY or professional	

Specifications

Front spring preload (groove position)
  660
      Standard... 3
      Minimum (hardest setting).. 1
      Maximum (softest setting).. 5
  700 (installed length)
      Standard... 260.0 mm (10.24 inches)
      Minimum (hardest setting).. 251.0 mm (9.88 inches)
      Maximum (softest setting).. 263.0 mm (10.35 inches)

Front shock absorber compression damping (700 only; clicks out from fully turned in)
  Slow compression damping
    Standard 10
    Minimum (hardest setting) 20
    Maximum (softest setting) 1
  Fast compression damping (turns out from fully turned in)
    Standard 2
    Minimum (hardest setting) 4
    Maximum (softest setting) .... Fully turned in
Front shock absorber rebound damping (700 only; clicks out from fully turned in)
  Standard 12
  Minimum (hardest setting) 20
  Maximum (softest setting) 3
Rear spring preload (installed length)
  660
    Standard .... 253 mm (9.96 inches)
    Minimum (hardest setting) .... 245 mm (9.65 inches)
    Maximum (softest setting) .... 260 mm (10.24 inches)
  700
    Standard .... 233.0 mm (9.17 inches)
    Minimum (hardest setting) .... 228.0 mm (8.98 inches)
    Maximum (softest setting) .... 243.0 mm (9.57 inches)
Rear spring compression damping
  660 (clicks in, from fully turned out)
    Standard 7
    Minimum (softest setting) 1
    Maximum (hardest setting) 12
  700
    Slow compression damping (clicks out, from fully turned in)
      Standard 10
      Minimum (hardest setting) 20
      Maximum (softest setting) 1
    Fast compression damping (clicks out, from fully turned in)
      Standard 2
      Minimum (softest setting) 4
      Maximum (hardest setting) .... Fully turned in
Rear axle runout limit .... 1.5 mm (0.06 inch)
Minimum distance between axle nut lines (660) .... 0.15 mm (0.59 inch)

Torque specifications

Steering

Handlebar bracket bolts .... 23 Nm (17 ft-lbs)
Steering shaft nut .... 110 Nm (80 ft-lbs)
Steering shaft bearing bolts .... 23 Nm (17 ft-lbs)
Tie-rod nuts .... 25 Nm (18 ft-lbs)
Tie-rod locknuts .... 15 Nm (132 inch-lbs)

Front suspension

Front shock absorber bolts and nuts
  660 .... 45 Nm (32 ft-lbs)
  700 .... 48 Nm (35 ft-lbs)
Balljoint castle nuts .... 25 Nm (18 ft-lbs)
Front suspension arm pivot bolts and nuts
  660
    Upper .... 38 Nm (27 ft-lbs)
    Lower .... 32 Nm (23 ft-lbs)
  700
    Upper .... 55 Nm (40 ft-lbs)
    Lower .... 38 Nm (27 ft-lbs)

Rear suspension

Rear shock absorber bolts
  660 (upper and lower) .... 32 Nm (23 ft-lbs)
  700 (upper) .... 55 Nm (40 ft-lbs)
  700 (lower) .... 43 Nm (31 ft-lbs)
Rear suspension linkage pivot bolts
  660 .... 32 Nm (23 ft-lbs)

700
        Connecting arm to frame .... 55 Nm (40 ft-lbs)
        Connecting arm to connecting link .... 43 Nm (31 ft-lbs)
        Connecting link to swingarm .... 43 Nm (31 ft-lbs)
Swingarm pivot bolt and nut
    660 .... 95 Nm (68 ft-lbs)
    700 .... 100 Nm (72 ft-lbs)
Rear axle nut(s)*
    660 .... See text
    700 .... 240 Nm (170 ft-lbs)
Rear axle nut lockbolts*
    660 .... Not specified
    700 .... 7 Nm (61 inch-lbs)

Final drive

Front sprocket nut
    660 .... 70 Nm (50 ft-lbs)
    700 .... 85 Nm (61 ft-lbs)
Rear sprocket nuts
    660 .... 24 Nm (17 ft-lbs)
    700 .... 72 Nm (52 ft-lbs)
*Apply non-permanent thread locking agent to the threads.

1 General information

The front suspension consists of upper and lower control arms on each side of the vehicle, supported by a shock absorber with a concentric coil spring.

The steering system consists of knuckles mounted at the outer ends of the front suspension and connected to a steering shaft by tie-rods. The steering shaft is turned by a one-piece handlebar.

The rear suspension on all models consists of a single shock absorber with concentric coil spring, progressive linkage and a swingarm. Final drive is by a chain and sprockets.

2 Handlebar - removal and installation

Removing the handlebar to service other components

1 If you're removing the handlebar simply to gain access to the steering shaft, it's not necessary to remove the clutch lever bracket, the left switch housing, the throttle cable housing or the front brake master cylinder.

2 Pull the fuel tank breather hose out of the hole in the handlebar trim cover.

3 Pull the handlebar cover off.

4 Look for a punch mark on the front of each handlebar bracket **(see illustration)**. If you can't find the factory punch marks, make your own marks to ensure that the brackets are correctly oriented when they're reinstalled.

5 Remove the handlebar bracket bolts, remove the upper bracket halves, then lift the handlebar off the lower bracket halves **(see illustration)**.

2.4 Look for a mark indicating handlebar position (arrow) and make your own mark if you can't see one

Caution: Support the handlebar assembly with a piece of wire or rope; allowing it to hang free will damage the cables, hoses and wiring.

6 Installation is the reverse of removal. Make sure that the factory punch marks (or the ones you made prior to disassembly) face to the front. Tighten the handlebar bracket bolts to the torque listed in this Chapter's Specifications.

Caution: Tighten the front bracket bolts first, then the rear bracket bolts. This will leave a gap between the upper and lower bracket halves at the rear of each bracket (see illustration). Don't try to close the gap by overtightening or you'll break the brackets.

Replacing the handlebar

7 If you're replacing the handlebar, remove all cable ties, then remove the clutch lever bracket, the left switch housing, the throttle cable housing (see Chapter 4), and the front brake master cylinder (see Chapter 7).

2.5 Mark the front side of each bracket, then remove the bracket bolts (arrows) and lift off the brackets and handlebar

8 Follow Steps 2 through 5 above.

9 Installation is the reverse of removal. Tighten the handlebar bracket bolts to the torque listed in this Chapter's Specifications, observing the **Caution** in Step 6.

3 Steering shaft - removal, inspection and installation

Removal

1 Remove the handlebar and brackets (see Section 2).

2 Remove the front fender (see Chapter 8).

3 Remove the fuel tank (see Chapter 4).

4 Straighten the lockwasher tabs and remove the two nuts, the lockwasher, the washer and the steering shaft bearing halves **(see illustration)**.

5 Disconnect the inner ends of the tie-rods from the steering shaft (see Section 5).

6 Remove the cotter pin and nut from the

2.6 There should be a small gap (arrows) at the back of each bracket after the bolts are tightened

3.4 Bend back the lockwasher tabs, remove the bolts (arrows), separate the bracket halves and remove the upper and lower bearings

3.6a To detach the lower end of the steering shaft from the frame, remove this cotter pin and nut (arrow); this is a 660 . . .

3.6b . . . and this is a 700

bottom of the steering shaft **(see illustrations)**.

7   Remove the steering shaft from the vehicle.

8   Pry out the seals from the steering shaft's lower pivot in the frame, unscrew the retainer with a hex bit and remove the lower bearing from the frame.

Inspection

9   Clean all the parts with solvent and dry them thoroughly, using compressed air, if available.

10   Inspect the steering shaft bearings and seals for wear, deterioration or damage. Replace them if there's any doubt about their condition.

11   Inspect the steering shaft and its integral steering arm for bending or other signs of damage. Do not attempt to repair any steering components. Replace them with new parts if defects are found.

Installation

12   Installation is the reverse of removal, with the following additions:

a) *Lubricate the steering shaft upper bearing and seals with grease.*
b) *Use a new lockwasher and cotter pins and tighten all fasteners to the torque values listed in this Chapter's Specifications.*

---

4   Shock absorbers - removal, installation and adjustment

Removal and installation

⚠ **Warning: Do not attempt to disassemble these shock absorbers. They are nitrogen-charged under high pressure. Replace the shocks and springs as a unit.**

Front shock absorbers

Note: *This procedure applies to either front shock absorber.*

1   Support the front of the vehicle securely on jackstands and remove the front wheels.

2   Support the outer ends of the front lower arms with jackstands so they won't drop when the shock absorbers are removed.

3   Remove the nuts and bolts that attach the upper end of the shock to the frame bracket and the lower end to the bracket on the lower control arm **(see illustration)**. Separate the shock from the frame bracket and from the control arm bracket and lift it out.

4   Inspect the shock absorber for signs of wear or damage such as oil leaks, bending, a weak spring and worn bushings. Replace both shock absorbers as a pair if any problems are found.

5   Installation is the reverse of the removal steps. Tighten the nuts and bolts to the torque listed in this Chapter's Specifications.

Rear shock absorber

6   Remove the seat (see Chapter 8).

7   Jack up the rear end of the vehicle and support it securely on jackstands. Slip a rag beneath the shock so the swingarm and shock body won't be scratched.

8   Remove the mounting bolt, washer, nut

4.3a Here are the upper and lower shock absorber bolts on a 660

4.3b Here are the upper and lower shock absorber bolts on a 700

4.8a On a 660, remove the nut (arrow) from the shock absorber upper bolt . . .

4.8b . . . then remove the bolt (A) and washer (B) - remove the bushings (C) if necessary

4.8c Here are the 700 shock absorber upper locknut (A), spring preload adjuster (B) and compression damping adjusters (C)

4.9a Here are the 660 shock absorber lower nut and bolt (lower arrows) and rebound damping adjuster (upper arrow)

and bushing at the top of the shock **(see illustrations)**.

9   At the lower end of the shock, remove the nut, washer, lower shock mounting bolt (and the washer under the bolt head on 660 models) **(see illustrations)**. To ensure that the various washers, spacers, bushings, etc. are installed in the correct sequence and relationship to one another, it's a good idea to immediately install all parts on the lower shock mounting bolt in the order in which they were removed. Separate the shock from the upper mounting bracket and from the suspension linkage connecting link and lift it out of the vehicle.

10   Installation is the reverse of the removal steps, with the following additions:

a) *Make sure that you install all parts, in order, when reattaching the lower end of the shock to the relay arm.*
b) *Tighten the nut and bolt to the torque listed in this Chapter's Specifications.*
c) *Install a thrust washer on each side of the pivot pin.*
d) *Use a new cotter pin in the pivot pin.*

Adjustment

Front shock absorbers (660)

11   Front shock absorber spring preload is adjusted by turning the adjuster ring at the bottom of the shock with a spanner wrench

(see illustration). (The spanner should be in your machine's toolkit; if not, you can obtain one at any Yamaha dealer.)

Front shock absorbers (700)

12   Front shock absorber spring preload is adjusted by turning the adjuster ring at the top of the shock with a spanner wrench **(see illustration 4.8c)**. (The spanner should be in your machine's toolkit; if not, you can obtain one at any Yamaha dealer.)

13   Loosen the locknut (the lower nut), turn the adjuster ring to obtain the desired preload, then tighten the locknut.

14   Front shock absorber rebound damping is adjusted by turning the screw on the bottom inner side of the shock absorber. Turning the adjuster clockwise increases the rebound damping force (slower rebound); turning the adjuster counterclockwise decreases the rebound damping force (faster rebound). To set the rebound damping adjuster to its standard position, turn it all the way in, then back it out the number of clicks listed in this Chapter's Specifications.

4.9b The lower end of the 700 rear shock absorber (arrow) is attached to the middle of the connecting link by a nut and bolt

4.11 Front spring preload on 660 models is adjusted by changing the position of the adjusting cam (arrow) in the ring

4.20 To adjust rear spring preload on 660 models, loosen the locknut (upper arrow) and turn the adjuster (lower arrow)

4.21 Here's the rebound damping adjuster on 700 models (arrow)

5.3 Remove the cotter pin (arrow) and unscrew the locknut to detach the outer tie-rod end from the steering knuckle

Caution: Do NOT attempt to turn the rebound adjuster beyond the maximum or minimum setting.

15 700 models have two compression damping adjustments: slow compression damping and fast compression damping.

16 Slow compression damping is adjusted by turning the adjuster screw. Fast compression damping is adjusted by turning the nut that surrounds the screw.

17 To set the slow adjuster to its standard position, turn it all the way in, then back it out the number of clicks listed in this Chapter's Specifications.

Caution: Do NOT attempt to turn the compression damping adjuster beyond the maximum or minimum setting.

18 To set the fast adjuster to its standard position, turn the nut in all the way, then back it out the number of clicks listed in this Chapter's Specifications.

Caution: Do NOT attempt to turn the compression damping adjuster beyond the maximum or minimum setting.

Rear shock absorber

19 The rear shock absorber is fully adjustable for spring preload, compression damping and rebound damping.

20 Spring preload is adjusted by changing the length of the spring. Loosen the preload adjuster locknut at the top of the shock, then turn the adjuster nut with a spanner wrench **(see illustration 4.8c or the accompanying illustration)**. The spanner should be in your machine's toolkit; if not, you can obtain one at any Yamaha dealer. Turn the adjuster clockwise to reduce spring length or counterclockwise to increase spring length. Measure the spring length and compare your measurement to the values listed in this Chapter's Specifications.

Caution: Do NOT attempt to turn the spring preload adjuster beyond the maximum or minimum setting. Tighten the locknut when you're done.

21 Rebound damping force is adjusted by turning the adjuster at the bottom of the shock **(see illustration 4.9a or the accompanying illustration)**. Turning the adjuster clockwise increases the rebound damping force (slower rebound); turning the adjuster counterclockwise decreases the rebound damping force (faster rebound). To set the rebound damping adjuster to its standard position, turn it all the way in, then back it out the number of clicks listed in this Chapter's Specifications.

Caution: Do NOT attempt to turn the rebound adjuster beyond the maximum or minimum setting.

22 Rear shock absorber compression damping on 660 models is adjusted by turning the screw on the shock reservoir **(see illustration 4.20)**. Turning the adjuster clockwise increases the compression damping force (slower rebound); turning the adjuster counterclockwise decreases the compression damping force (faster rebound). To set the adjuster to its standard position, turn it all the way in, then back it out the number of clicks listed in this Chapter's Specifications.

Caution: Do NOT attempt to turn the compression damping adjuster beyond the maximum or minimum setting.

23 700 models have two compression damping adjustments: slow compression damping and fast compression damping.

24 Slow compression damping is adjusted by turning the adjuster screw **(see illustration 4.8c)**. Fast compression damping is adjusted by turning the nut that surrounds the screw.

25 To set the slow adjuster to its standard position, turn it all the way in, then back it out the number of clicks listed in this Chapter's Specifications.

Caution: Do NOT attempt to turn the compression damping adjuster beyond the maximum or minimum setting.

26 To set the fast adjuster to its standard position, turn the nut in all the way, then back it out the number of clicks listed in this Chapter's Specifications.

5.4 Tie-rod puller

Caution: Do NOT attempt to turn the compression damping adjuster beyond the maximum or minimum setting.

5 Tie-rods - removal, inspection and installation

Removal

1 Place the steering in the straight-ahead position.

2 If both of the tie-rods are to be removed, mark them "Left" and "Right" so they're not accidentally switched during reassembly.

3 Remove the cotter pin from the nut at the outer end of the tie-rod and undo the nut **(see illustration)**.

4 Separate the tie-rod stud from the knuckle with a tie-rod puller or pickle fork balljoint separator **(see illustration)**.

Caution: It's very easy to damage the rubber boot on the tie-rod with a pickle fork separator. If you're going to use the tie-rod again, it's best to use another type of tool.

5.5a The inner tie-rod ends on 660 models (arrows) face upward

5.5b The inner tie-rod ends on 700 models (arrows) face downward

5   Repeat Steps 1 and 2 to disconnect the inner end of the tie rod from the steering shaft (see illustration).

Inspection

6   Check the tie-rod shaft for bending or other damage and replace it if any problems are found. Don't try to straighten the shaft.

7   Check the tie-rod balljoint boots for cracks or deterioration. Twist and rotate the threaded studs. They should move easily, without roughness or looseness. If a boot or stud show any problems, unscrew the tie-rod end from the tie-rod and install a new one.

Installation

8   Thread the tie-rod ends onto the tie-rods. The length of exposed threads on each end of the tie-rod must be even. The flat on the tie-rod that's used to adjust toe-in goes at the outer end of the tie-rod.

9   The remainder of installation is the reverse of the removal steps, with the following additions:

a)   Use new cotter pins and bend them to hold the nuts securely.
b)   Check front wheel toe-in and adjust as necessary (see Chapter 1).

6   Steering knuckles - removal, inspection, and installation

Removal

1   Jack up the front end of the vehicle and support it securely on jackstands. Remove the front wheels.

2   Disconnect the outer end of the tie-rod from the steering knuckle (see Section 5).

3   Remove the outer disc cover, the front brake caliper, the wheel hub and the inner disc cover (see Chapter 7).

4   Remove the front shock absorber (see Section 4).

5   Remove the cotter pin and nut from the upper and lower balljoint studs (see illustrations).

6   Separating the balljoints from the steering knuckle requires a separator tool. Automotive tie-rod separator tools are suitable (try it for fit before you buy it, if possible) and can be rented from tool yards or purchased inexpensively (see illustration 5.4).

7   If balljoint separation proves difficult, the knuckle and suspension arms can be removed as a single assembly, then taken to a Yamaha dealer for balljoint removal.

Inspection

8   Inspect the knuckle carefully for cracks, bending or other damage. Replace it if any problems are found. If the vehicle has been in a collision or has been bottomed hard, it's a good idea to have the knuckle magnafluxed by a machine shop to check for hidden cracks.

Installation

9   Installation is the reverse of removal, with the following addition: Use new cotter pins and tighten the nuts to the torque listed in this Chapter's Specifications.

6.5a Remove the cotter pins and nuts (arrows) to detach the suspension arms from the steering knuckle - this is a 660 ...

6.5b ... and this is a 700

7.3a On 660 models, remove the nuts and bolts to detach the inner ends of the suspension arms - the upper and lower front bolt heads (left arrows) face forward, and the head of the lower rear bolt (right arrow) faces rearward

7.3b On 700 models, all three of the suspension arm pivot bolts (arrows) face forward . . .

7 Suspension arms and balljoints - removal, inspection and installation

Suspension arms

Removal

1   Securely block both rear wheels so the vehicle won't roll. Loosen the front wheel nuts with the tires still on the ground, then jack up the front end, support it securely on jackstands and remove the front wheels.
2   Remove the steering knuckle (see Section 6). If you're removing an upper arm, remove the brake hose shield and disengage the brake hose from the arm (see Chapter 7).
3   Remove the pivot bolts and nuts and remove the suspension arm **(see illustrations)**.

Inspection

4   Inspect the suspension arm(s) for bending, cracks or corrosion. Replace damaged parts. Don't attempt to straighten them.
5   Inspect all rubber bushings for cracks or deterioration. Check the inner collars on the lower suspension arms for damage or corrosion. Inspect the pivot bolts for wear as well. Replace the bushings and pivot bolts if they're worn or deteriorated.
6   Check the balljoint boot for cracks or deterioration. Twist and rotate the threaded stud. It should move easily, without roughness or looseness. On 660 models, the balljoints can't be replaced separately from the suspension arms. If the boot or stud show any problems, replace the suspension arm together with the balljoint. On 700 models, see Step 9.

Installation

7   Installation is the reverse of removal, but don't torque the suspension fasteners while

7.3c . . . remove the nuts and lockwasher (arrows) to remove the bolts

the vehicle is off the ground. Tighten the nuts and bolts *slightly* while the vehicle is jacked up, then tighten them to the torque listed in this Chapter's Specifications after the vehicle is resting on its wheels.

Balljoints

8   On 660 models, the balljoints are an integral part of the suspension arms; they cannot be separated. If the balljoint or the suspension arm is damaged or worn, they must be replaced as a single assembly.
9   On 700 models, the balljoints can be removed from the suspension arms and replaced separately. With the suspension arm disconnected from the knuckle, remove the snap-ring **(see illustration)** and press the balljoint out of the suspension arm. If you don't have a press, have the ball-joint pressed out by a dealer service department or other qualified shop.

7.9 This snap-ring secures the lower balljoint on 700 models

8 Rear axle - removal, inspection and installation

⚠ *Warning: The axle nuts are secured with thread locking agent and tightened to a very high torque. When tightening or loosening them with the vehicle jacked up, be sure the vehicle is securely supported so it can't fall.*

Note: *This procedure is reasonably easy if the vehicle is clean and free of corrosion. If not, it can be very difficult. If you're working on a vehicle that has been ridden in water or in salt air (such as in sand dunes near the ocean), read through the procedure before starting so you can plan for the special measures that may be necessary.*

8.4a Remove the two Allen bolts (arrow, one bolt shown) from the outer axle nut

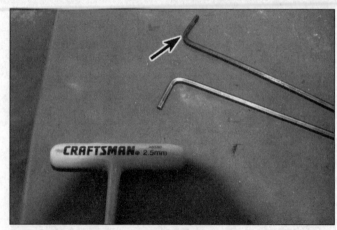

8.4b You'll need a good-quality 2.5 mm Allen wrench - the force needed to undo the Allen bolts may twist an ordinary Allen wrench (arrow)

660 models

Removal

1 Block the front wheels so the vehicle won't roll.
2 Jack up the rear end of the vehicle and

8.5a This special tool or an aftermarket equivalent is needed to loosen the axle nuts

support it securely, positioning the jackstands so they won't obstruct removal of the axle. The supports must be secure enough so the vehicle won't be knocked off of them while the axle is removed. Remove the rear wheels.
3 Remove the rear wheel hubs (see Chapter 7).
4 Remove the axle nut lockbolts (see illustration). There are two lockbolts, one on each side of the outer axle nut.

 TOOL TiP *The lockbolts are secured with Loctite, so they may be difficult to remove. You'll need a 2.5mm Allen wrench of good quality. The force required may be enough to twist an ordinary Allen wrench (see illustration).*

5 Set the parking brake to keep the axle from turning, then unscrew the outer axle nut.

 TOOL TiP *You'll need a special 50 mm wrench to unscrew the nut (Yamaha part no. YM-37132 or equivalent) (see illustration). This tool, or an aftermarket*

equivalent, is available from Yamaha dealers or other suppliers. You'll also need a breaker bar, and probably a long pipe to slip over the breaker bar for extra leverage.

Note: *If there is significant corrosion, setting the parking brake may not be enough to keep the axle from turning. We held the inner nut with a chain wrench, with its handle resting against a strong support* (see illustration).
6 Once the outer nut axle nut is loose, unscrew the inner nut (see illustration). Release the parking brake so the rear caliper can be removed.
7 Loosen the drive chain (see Chapter 1). Disengage the chain from the rear sprocket.
8 Remove the brake caliper (see Chapter 7). The brake hose and cable can be left connected. Secure the caliper out of the way. If you plan to replace the brake disc, this is a convenient time to remove it. Otherwise, it can remain bolted to the hub.
9 Unscrew the two hub nuts, working through holes in the brake disc (see illustrations).

8.5b If the nut is hard to remove, you'll need a way to hold the inner nut securely - we used a chain wrench, resting on a strong support and strapped down with a heavy-duty cargo strap

8.6 Once the outer nut is loose, unscrew the inner nut with the same special tool used on the outer nut

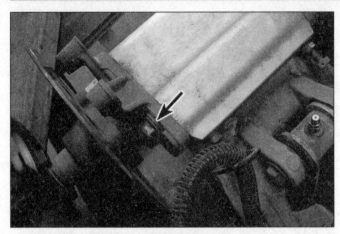

8.9a Unscrew the upper hub nut (arrow) . . .

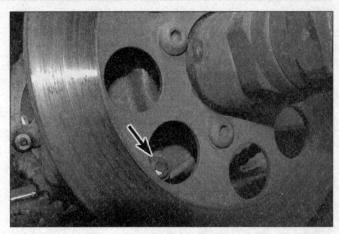

8.9b . . . and the lower hub nut (arrow)

8.10a Tape a socket over the nut and tap on it to free the axle

8.10b If the axle can't be tapped out due to corrosion, remove the swingarm and axle together and press the axle out

8.11a Check the splines (arrow) for corrosion and mechanical damage . . .

10   Thread the hub nut back onto the right-hand end of the axle to protect the threads. Tape a socket over the nut **(see illustration)**, then tap on the nut to free the axle from the hub and remove it from the left side of the vehicle. **Note:** *The axle should come out*

with a few firm taps. If the axle splines inside the hub are corroded, you may need to use a hydraulic press. In this case, remove the swingarm together with the axle and place it in the press with the brake disc up **(see illustration)**.

Inspection

11   Check the axle for obvious damage, such as step wear of the splines or bending, and replace it as necessary **(see illustration)**. Check the hub bolts and inside of the hub for corrosion or other foreign material **(see illustrations)**.

8.11b . . . and if there are any problems, check the splines inside the brake disc hub (arrow)

8.11c Corrosion can also affect the hub bolts

8.11d Check the inside of the swingarm for corrosion and dirt

8.16 Seat the hub bolt heads in their recesses before tightening the nuts

8.22 Draw a line across the two nuts

8.23 After tightening, measure the distance between the lines

12   Inspect the brake disc and replace it if necessary (see Chapter 7).

13   Place the axle in V-blocks and set up a dial indicator to contact each of the outer ends in turn (see "Tools and Workshop Tips" at the end of this manual for information on dial indicators). Rotate the axle and compare runout to the value listed in this Chapter's Specifications. If runout is excessive, replace the axle.

14   Inspect the hub seals and bearings and replace them if necessary (see Chapter 7).

15   Inspect the sprockets and drive chain (see Sections 12 and 13).

Installation

16   Before tightening the hub nuts, fit the heads of the hub bolts into their recesses **(see illustration)**. Once this is done, tighten the hub nuts to the torque listed in this Chapter's Specifications.

17   Insert the axle from the left side of the hub. Install the brake disc and its hub onto the axle.

18   Apply non-permanent thread locking agent to the nut threads on the axle. Tighten the axle nuts with a torque wrench adapter (Yamaha tool 09890-01498/YM37134 or an

equivalent 50 mm crow's foot wrench). Be sure to install the adapter at right angles to the torque wrench centerline. If the adapter is installed in a direct line with the torque wrench centerline, it will amplify the torque and the nut will be overtightened. Tighten the nuts in the following sequence.

19   Install the inner nut and tighten it with fingers only. Spin the axle and make sure it rotates freely. If it doesn't, stop and find out why before continuing.

20   Tighten the inner nut to 55 Nm (40 ft-lbs).

21   Hold the inner nut so it can't turn and tighten the outer nut against it to 190 mm (140 ft-lbs).

22   Draw a line across the two nuts **(see illustration)**.

23   Hold the outer nut so it can't turn and tighten the inner nut against it to the final torque 240 Nm (170 ft-lbs). The line on the inner nut should have moved so that there's a gap of at least 15 mm (0.59 inch) between the two lines **(see illustration)**. If the gap is too small, tighten the inner nut against the outer nut some more until the gap is as specified.

24   The remainder of installation is the reverse of the removal steps. After installation, adjust the drive chain as described in Chapter 1.

700 models

Removal

25   Block the front wheels so the vehicle won't roll.

26   Jack up the rear end of the vehicle and support it securely, positioning the jackstands so they won't obstruct removal of the axle. The supports must be secure enough so the vehicle won't be knocked off of them while the axle is removed. Remove the rear wheels.

27   Remove the rear wheel hubs (see Chapter 7).

28   Remove the axle nut lockbolts **(see illustration)**. There are two lockbolts, one on each side of the outer axle nut.

TOOL TiP *The lockbolts are secured with Loctite, so they may be difficult to remove. You'll need a 2.5mm Allen wrench of good quality. The force required may be enough to twist an ordinary Allen wrench (see illustration 8.4b).*

29   Set the parking brake to keep the axle from turning, then unscrew the axle nut, using a 46 mm wrench (Yamaha tool YM37134 or equivalent) **(see illustration 8.5a)**. Slip the nut and its washer off the end of the axle **(see illustration)**.

8.28 Unscrew the Allen bolt from the axle nut with a high-quality Allen wrench

8.29 Remove the axle nut and the washer behind it (arrow) - the concave side of the washer faces the swingarm on installation

8.30 Remove the hub pinch bolts (arrows)

10.7a Remove the nut (arrow) from the bolt at the forward end of the connecting arm . . .

30   Remove the hub pinch bolts **(see illustration)**.
31   Remove the rear brake caliper (see Chapter 7). Remove the brake disc, together with its hub, and take off the O-ring that's on the axle behind the brake disc hub.
32   Thread the hub nut back onto the right-hand end of the axle to protect the threads. Tape a socket over the nut **(see illustration 8.10a)**, then tap on the nut to free the axle from the hub and remove it from the left side of the vehicle.

Inspection

33   Axle inspection is the same as for 660 models, described earlier in this Section.

Installation

34   Installation is the reverse of the removal steps. Use non-permanent thread locking on the threads of the axle nut and its lock-bolts.

10.7b . . . and remove the bolt (arrow) . . .

9 Swingarm bearings - check

1   Remove the rear wheels (see Chapter 7), then remove the rear shock absorber (see Section 4).
2   Grasp the rear of the swingarm with one hand and place your other hand at the junction of the swingarm and the frame. Try to move the rear of the swingarm from side-to-side. If the bearings are worn, they will allow some freeplay, which produces movement between the swingarm and the frame at the front (the swingarm will move forward and backward at the front, not from side-to-side). If any play is noted, the bearings should be replaced with new ones (see Sections 10 and 11).
3   Next, move the swingarm up and down through its full travel. It should move freely, without any binding or rough spots. If it does not move freely, remove the swingarm (see Section 10) and inspect the bearings (see Section 11).

10 Shock linkage and swingarm - removal and installation

1   If the swingarm is being removed just for pivot bearing replacement, the brake caliper, rear hub and rear axle need not be removed from the swingarm.

Removal

2   Raise the rear end of the vehicle and support it securely on jackstands.
3   Remove the rear wheels, the rear wheel hubs and the brake caliper (see Chapter 7).
4   Unbolt the swingarm protector from the underside of the swingarm. Take the drive chain off the engine sprocket (see Section 12).
5   If you're replacing the swingarm with a new one, remove the rear axle (see Section 8).
6   Support the swingarm so it won't drop, then detach the lower end of the shock absorber from the relay arm (see Section 4).
7   Remove the pivot bolt that connects the front end of the connecting arm to the frame **(see illustrations)**.

10.7c . . . here's how the bolt fits in the frame - pump some grease into the nipple to make sure the grease passage (arrow) is clear

10.8a Unscrew the swingarm pivot bolt nut (arrow) . . .

10.8b . . . and remove the washer . . .

10.8c . . . then pull out the bolt

10.10 The suspension linkage connecting link is attached to the connecting arm at the front (left arrow), to the shock absorber in the center (center arrow) and to the swingarm at the rear (right arrow)

10.12 Fit the head of the swingarm pivot bolt (arrow) into its recess before tightening the nut

11.3 Remove the dust covers, seals and collars for access to the swingarm bearings and linkage bushings

8   Remove the locknut and washer, then pull the pivot bolt out of the swingarm **(see illustrations)**.
9   Pull the swingarm back and away from the vehicle.
10   Remove the relay arm and the connecting arm **(see illustration)**.
11   Inspect the pivot bearings in the swingarm for dryness or deterioration (see Section 11).

Installation

12   Lift the swingarm into position in the frame. Install the pivot bolt and locknut to hold the swingarm in the frame, but don't tighten them yet. Make sure the oval bolt head fits into the recess in the frame **(see illustration)**.
13   Raise and lower the swingarm several times, moving it through its full travel to seat the bearings and pivot bolt.

14   Tighten the pivot bolt locknut to the torque listed in this Chapter's Specifications.
15   The remainder of installation is the reverse of the removal steps.

11 Swingarm bearings - replacement

1   The swingarm pivot bolt rides on two needle roller bearings.
2   Remove the swingarm (see Section 10).
3   Remove the collar and pry the seal from each side of the swingarm **(see illustration)**.
4   Inspect the swingarm pivot bearing in each end of the swingarm. If either bearing is rough or loose, or has excessive play, replace the bearings as a set.
5   Remove the bearings with a blind hole puller and slide hammer. If you don't have

12.2a Unbolt the 660 engine sprocket cover and take it off (lower bolt hidden)

12.2b The 700 sprocket cover bolts (arrows) also secure a chain guide inside the cover

the proper tools, have the bearings replaced by a Yamaha dealer or machine shop.

6   While the bearings are removed, remove the collar, clean it thoroughly, inspect it for burrs, scoring and other damage. If the collar is damaged or worn, replace it. Lubricate the collar with grease and insert it back into the swingarm (make sure that the pivot bore is clean).

7   Tap new bearings into position with a bearing driver or socket just slightly smaller than the diameter of the outer race.

8   Pack the bearings with waterproof lithium-based wheel bearing grease.

9   Tap new seals into position with a seal driver or a socket just slightly smaller than the outside diameter of the seal.

13.4a Bend back the lockwasher tab (arrow) . . .

13.4b . . . unscrew the nut, noting which side faces the engine, and pull the sprocket off the transmission shaft

| 12 | Drive chain - removal, cleaning, inspection and installation | |

Removal

1   Remove the swingarm (see Section 10).
2   Remove the front sprocket cover from the engine **(see illustrations)**.
3   Loosen the chain adjusters as needed to create slack so you can disengage the chain from the rear sprocket (see Chapter 1).
4   Lift the chain off the sprockets and remove it from the vehicle.
5   Check the chain guide and rollers on the swingarm and frame for wear or damage and replace them as necessary (see Chapter 1).

Cleaning and inspection

6   The drive chain has small rubber O-rings between the chain plates. Soak the chain in kerosene and use a brush to work the solvent into the spaces between the links and plates.

Caution: Do NOT use steam, high-pressure washes or solvents, all of which can damage the O-rings, to clean the chain. Use only kerosene.

7   Wipe the chain dry, then inspect it carefully for worn or damaged links. Replace the chain if wear or damage is found at any point.

8   If the chain is worn or damaged, inspect the sprockets. If they're worn or damaged, replace them also.

Caution: Do NOT install a new chain on worn sprockets; it will wear out quickly.

9   Lubricate the chain (Yamaha recommends engine oil or chain lube suitable for O-ring chains).

Installation

10   Installation is the reverse of removal.
11   Adjust the chain when you're done (see Chapter 1).

13 Sprockets - check and replacement

1   Whenever the sprockets are inspected, the chain should be inspected and replaced if it's worn. Installing a worn chain on new sprockets will cause them to wear quickly.
2   Check the teeth on the engine sprocket and rear sprocket for wear. The engine sprocket is visible through the cover slots **(see illustration 12.2a or 12.2b)**.
3   If the sprockets are worn, remove the chain (see Section 12) and the left rear wheel and hub (see Chapter 7).
4   To remove the engine sprocket, bend back the lockwasher tab **(see illustration)**. Remove the nut and pull the sprocket off the transmission shaft, together with the chain **(see illustration)**.
5   Inspect the seal behind the engine

13.5 Pull out the collar (arrow) and
carefully pry the seal
out of its bore

13.6 Bend back the tabs on the three
double lockwashers (arrows) and
unscrew the nuts

13.7 Hold the Allen bolts (arrows, lower
bolt hidden) and unscrew the self-locking
nuts from the other side of the sprocket

sprocket **(see illustration)**. If it has been leaking, pull out the collar and pry it out (take care not to scratch the seal bore) and tap in a new seal with a socket the same diameter as the seal.

6   To remove the rear sprocket on a 660, bend back the lockwasher tabs and unscrew the nuts **(see illustration)**. Take the lock-

washers off the sprocket and slip the sprocket over the end of the axle.

7   To remove the rear sprocket on a 700, hold the Allen bolts with a wrench and unscrew the nuts **(see illustration)**. Slip the sprocket over the end of the axle.

8   Installation is the reverse of the removal steps. Be sure to use new a drive sprocket

lockwasher. Tighten the drive sprocket nut and driven sprocket nuts to the torque listed in this Chapter's Specifications.

9   Install the chain (see Section 12).

10   Adjust the chain when you're done (see Chapter 1).

Chapter 7
Brakes, wheels and tires

Contents

Degrees of difficulty

Easy, suitable for novice with little experience	**Fairly easy,** suitable for beginner with some experience	**Fairly difficult,** suitable for competent DIY mechanic	**Difficult,** suitable for experienced DIY mechanic	**Very difficult,** suitable for expert DIY or professional

Specifications

Brakes

Brake pedal height	See Chapter 1
Brake pad thickness (limit)	
Front	1.0 mm (0.04 inch)
Rear	1.0 mm (0.04 inch)
Brake disc	
Standard thickness	
660 (front and rear)	3.5 mm (0.14 inch)
700	
Front	3.5 mm (0.14 inch)
Rear	4.0 mm (0.16 inch)
Maximum runout	0.10 mm (0.004 inch)
Minimum allowable thickness	
660 (front and rear)	3.0 mm (0.12 inch) (1)
700	
Front	3.0 mm (0.12 inch) (1)
Rear	3.5 mm (0.14 inch)
Parking brake cable adjustment length	See Chapter 1

Wheels and tires

Tire pressures	See "Daily (pre-ride) checks" at the beginning of this manual
Tire tread depth	See "Daily (pre-ride) checks" at the beginning of this manual

Torque specifications

Wheel lug nuts	45 Nm (32 ft-lbs)
Front hub nuts	70 Nm (50 ft-lbs) (2)
Rear hub nuts	
660	120 Nm (85 ft-lbs) (2)
700	200 Nm (145 ft-lbs) (2)
Front brake calipers and disc	
Mounting bolts	
660	28 Nm (20 ft-lbs)
700	27 Nm (19 ft-lbs)
Brake pad retaining bolts	
660	18 Nm (156 in-lbs) (4)
700	17 Nm (144 inch-lbs) (4)
Brake hose-to-caliper banjo bolts	27 Nm (19 ft-lbs) (3)
Brake disc retaining bolts	28 Nm (20 ft-lbs) (4)
Rear brake caliper and disc	
Mounting bolts	
660	28 Nm (20 ft-lbs)
700	34 Nm (24 ft-lbs)
Brake pad retaining bolts	18 Nm (156 in-lbs) (4)
Brake hose-to-caliper banjo bolt	30 Nm (22 ft-lbs) (3)
Brake disc retaining bolts	
660	28 Nm (20 ft-lbs) (4)
700	33 Nm (24 ft-lbs)
Parking brake case/bracket bolts	
660	25 Nm (18 ft-lbs) (4)
700	22 Nm (16 ft-lbs) (4)
Parking brake adjusting bolt locknut	
660	16 Nm (132 inch-lbs)
700	9 Nm (78 inch-lbs)
Front master cylinder	
Brake hose banjo bolt	27 Nm (19 ft-lbs) (3)
Handlebar clamp bolts	7 Nm (61 inch-lbs)
Rear master cylinder	
Brake hose banjo bolt	30 Nm (22 ft-lbs) (3)
Rear hub nuts and through-bolts (660 only)	90 Nm (65 ft-lbs)
Rear axle nut	
660	See text
700	240 Nm (170 ft-lbs) (4)
Rear axle nut lockbolts	7 Nm (61 inch-lbs) (3)

1 *Refer to marks stamped into the disc (they supersede information printed here).*

2 *If the cotter pin holes don't line up, tighten the nut just enough to align them. Don't loosen the nut to align the cotter pin holes.*

3 *Use new sealing washers.*

4 *Apply non-permanent thread locking agent to the threads.*

2.7 It's easy to install a wheel wrong side out, like this one - but the axle (right) indicates that the tire valve and rotational arrow (center and left) are in the wrong position

4.2 Remove the outer disc shield from the hub

1 General information

The vehicles covered by this manual are equipped with three hydraulically-operated disc brakes: a disc at each front wheel and a single disc on the rear axle. The front brakes are operated by a lever-actuated master cylinder on the right end of the handlebar; the rear brake is operated by a pedal-actuated master cylinder on the right side of the vehicle, right behind the right footrest. The rear brake caliper is equipped with a parking brake system, which is actuated by a lever on the left end of the handlebar.

The front calipers on 660 models have single pistons. The front calipers on 700 models have dual pistons. The rear caliper on all models has a single piston. All models are equipped with wheels which require very little maintenance and allow tubeless tires to be used.

Caution: Brake components rarely require disassembly. Do not disassemble components unless absolutely necessary.

2 Wheels - inspection, removal and installation

Inspection

1   Clean the wheels thoroughly to remove mud and dirt that may interfere with the inspection procedure or mask defects. Make a general check of the wheels and tires as described in Chapter 1.
2   The wheels should be visually inspected for cracks, flat spots on the rim and other damage. Since tubeless tires are involved, look very closely for dents in the area where the tire bead contacts the rim. Dents in this area may prevent complete sealing of the tire against the rim, which leads to deflation of the tire over a period of time.
3   If damage is evident, the wheel will have to be replaced with a new one. Never attempt to repair a damaged wheel.

Removal

4   Securely block the wheels at the opposite end of the vehicle from the wheel being removed, so it can't roll.
5   Loosen the lug nuts on the wheel being removed. Jack up one end of the vehicle and support it securely on jackstands.
6   Remove the lug nuts and pull the wheel off.

Installation

7   Position the wheel on the studs. Make sure the directional arrow on the tire points in the forward rotating direction of the wheel.

⚠️ *Warning: It's easily possible to install the wheels on these vehicles inside out, and the wheels will still look like they're installed correctly. However, the tire valve will be on the inside of the wheel instead of on the outside, where it's supposed to be (see illustration). If the tire is installed correctly on the wheel and the wheel is installed inside out, the tread pattern will face the wrong direction, which could cause a loss of traction or vehicle control.*

8   Snug the wheel nuts evenly in a criss-cross pattern.
9   Remove the jackstands, lower the vehicle and tighten the wheel nuts, again in a criss-cross pattern, to the torque listed in this Chapter's Specifications.

3 Tires - general information

1   Tubeless tires are used as standard equipment on this vehicle. Unlike motorcycle tires, they run at very low air pressures and are completely unsuited for use on pavement. Inflating ATV tires to excessive pressures will rupture them, making replacement of the tire necessary.
2   The force required to break the seal between the rim and the bead of the tire is substantial, much more than required for motorcycle tires, and is beyond the capabilities of an individual working with normal tire irons or even a normal bead breaker. A special bead breaker is required for ATV tires; it produces a great deal of force and concentrates it in a relatively small area.
3   Also, repair of the punctured tire and replacement on the wheel rim requires special tools, skills and experience that the average do-it-yourselfer lacks.
4   For these reasons, if a puncture or flat occurs with an ATV tire, the wheel should be removed from the vehicle and taken to a dealer service department or a repair shop for repair or replacement of the tire. The accompanying illustrations can be used as a guide to tire replacement in an emergency, provided the necessary bead breaker is available.

4 Front wheel hub and bearing - removal and installation

Removal

Note: This procedure applies to either front hub.
1   Remove the front wheel (see (Section 2).
2   Remove the disc outer cover **(see illustration)**, if equipped.
3   Bend back the cotter pin and pull it out of the hub nut **(see illustration)**.

4.3 Bend back the cotter pin and pull it out

4.4 Have someone firmly apply the front brakes while you crack the hub nut loose

4.6 You may need a slide hammer and adapter to pull the hub off the spindle

5.2 Pull on the caliper body to press the pistons in and provide removal clearance for the pads

5.3 Loosen - but don't remove - the brake pad retaining bolts while the caliper is still bolted to the steering knuckle

5.4 Unscrew the brake hose banjo fitting (left arrow); on installation, be sure the tab on the brake hose fits against the stop on the caliper (left arrow)

4   Have an assistant apply the front brake while you loosen the hub nut (see illustration). Remove the hub nut and the washer.

5   Remove the front brake caliper and inner disc cover (see Section 6). The inner cover itself doesn't interfere with hub removal, but the caliper can't be removed without detaching the inner cover from the steering knuckle. It's not necessary to disconnect the brake hose from the caliper; set the caliper aside and hang it from the suspension with a coat hanger.

6   Pull the hub off the spindle. If the hub is stuck, remove it with a puller (see illustration).

Bearing inspection and replacement

7   Wipe off the spindle and hub.

Caution: Do NOT immerse the hub in any kind of cleaning solvent. The sealed hub bearings, which cannot be disassembled and repacked, could be damaged if any solvent enters them.

8   Insert your fingers into each hub bearing and turn the bearing. If the bearing feels rough or dry, replace it.

9   Pry out the old seals and discard them.

10   To drive each bearing from the hub, lay the hub on a workbench, with the outer side of the hub facing down, then insert a soft metal (brass) drift into the hub from the inner side of the hub, push the floating spacer to the side and tap gently against the inner face of the outer bearing. Then flip over the hub, inner side facing down, insert the drift from the outer side of the hub, and drive out the inner bearing the same way.

11   To install the new bearings, drive them into place with an old socket. The socket must have an outside diameter that's the same, or slightly smaller than, the outer diameter of the bearings.

Caution: Do NOT strike the center race or the ball bearings.

12   Tap new inner and outer seals into place with a block of wood. Do NOT use the old seals.

Installation

13   Installation is the reverse of removal. Lubricate the spindle with wheel bearing grease. Tighten the hub nut to the torque listed in this Chapter's Specifications. If necessary, tighten it an additional amount to

align the cotter pin slots. Don't loosen the nut to align the slots. Install a new cotter pin and bend it to secure the nut.

5   Front brake pads - replacement

Note: Always replace both pairs of brake pads at the same time.

1   Remove the front wheel (see Section 2). Remove the outer disc cover.

660 models

2   Slide the caliper to compress the pistons into the bore, providing removal clearance for the pads (see illustration).

3   Loosen the brake pad retaining bolts (see illustration). The pad retaining bolts are easier to loosen while the caliper is still bolted to the steering knuckle.

4   If you're removing the caliper to overhaul it, remove the brake hose-to-caliper banjo bolt (see illustration) and disconnect the brake hose from the caliper now. If you're only remov-

5.5 Unscrew the caliper mounting bolts (arrows)

5.7 Remove the caliper, then remove the pad retaining bolts

ing the caliper to replace the brake pads, or to remove the steering knuckle, do NOT disconnect the brake hose from the caliper.

5   Unbolt the caliper from the steering knuckle (see illustration).

6   Remove the caliper. If you're only removing the caliper to replace the brake pads, hang the caliper from the suspension with a coat hanger.

Caution: Do NOT allow the caliper to hang from its brake hose.

7   Remove the brake pad retaining bolts (see illustration).

8   Remove the brake pads (see illustrations).

9   Inspect the pad spring (see illustration). If it's damaged or distorted, replace it.

10   If the inner brake pad has a shim, remove it and install it on the new inner pad.

11   Check the area around the piston for fluid leakage (see illustration 5.9). If fluid has been leaking past the pistons, overhaul the caliper as described in Section 6.

12   Installation is the reverse of removal. Using a C-clamp, depress the pistons back into the caliper bores to provide enough

5.8a Remove the outer brake pad . . .

5.8b . . . and the inner pad

room for the new pads to clear the disc. Be sure to tighten the caliper bolts to the torque listed in this Chapter's Specifications. Apply non-permanent thread locking agent to the threads of the brake pad bolts and tighten them to the torque listed in this Chapter's Specifications (see illustration 5.3).

13   Replace the brake pads on the other front caliper as described above.

700 models

14   Slide the caliper to compress the pistons into the bore, providing removal clearance for the pads (see illustration).

5.9 Check the pad spring (lower arrow) and replace it if it's worn or damaged; check the area around the pistons (arrows) for fluid leaks

5.14 Squeeze the pad against the disc to press the piston into the caliper

5.15 Loosen the pad retaining bolts with an Allen wrench while the caliper is still bolted to the steering knuckle

5.16 Unscrew the brake hose union bolt if you're removing the caliper for overhaul, and on installation, place the hose tab against the stop (center arrow); remove the caliper mounting bolts (upper and lower arrows) . . .

5.19 . . . and take the caliper off, then remove the pad retaining bolts

5.20a Remove the outer brake pad, noting how the notched end fits against the pin (arrow) . . .

5.20b . . . then remove the inner pad

15   Loosen the brake pad retaining bolts **(see illustration)**. The pad retaining bolts are easier to loosen while the caliper is still bolted to the steering knuckle.
16   If you're removing the caliper to over-

haul it, remove the brake hose-to-caliper banjo bolt **(see illustration)** and disconnect the brake hose from the caliper now. If you're only removing the caliper to replace the brake pads, or to remove the steering knuckle, do

NOT disconnect the brake hose from the caliper.
17   Unbolt the caliper from the steering knuckle **(see illustration 5.16)**.
18   Remove the caliper. If you're only removing the caliper to replace the brake pads, hang the caliper from the suspension with wire or rope.

Caution: Do NOT allow the caliper to hang from its brake hose.

19   Remove the brake pad retaining bolts **(see illustration)**.
20   Remove the brake pads **(see illustrations)**.
21   Inspect the pad spring **(see illustration)**. If it's damaged or distorted, replace it.
22   If the inner brake pad has a shim, remove it and install it on the new inner pad.
23   Check the area around the pistons for fluid leakage **(see illustration)**. If fluid has been leaking past the pistons, overhaul the caliper as described in Section 6.
24   Installation is the reverse of removal. Using a C-clamp, depress the pistons back into the caliper bores to provide enough

5.21 Check the pad spring and replace it if it's worn, corroded or damaged

5.23 Check the area around the pistons (arrows) for fluid leakage

5.24 Apply non-permanent thread locking agent to the threads of the pad retaining pins and tighten them to the torque listed in this Chapter's Specifications

6.7 Remove the old piston seal from its groove in the bore with a wood or plastic tool (if you use a metal tool, don't scratch the bore)

7.3 To measure front disc runout, position a dial indicator so that its probe is about half an inch from the outer edge of the disc

room for the new pads to clear the disc. Be sure to tighten the caliper bolts to the torque listed in this Chapter's Specifications. Apply non-permanent thread locking agent to the threads of the brake pad bolts and tighten them to the torque listed in this Chapter's Specifications **(see illustration)**.

25   Replace the brake pads on the other front caliper as described above.

6   Front brake caliper - removal, overhaul and installation

Warning: The dust created by the brake system is harmful to your health. Never blow it out with compressed air and don't inhale any of it. An approved filtering mask should be worn when working on the brakes. Do not, under any circumstances, use petroleum-based solvents to clean brake parts. Use brake cleaner only!

Note: *This procedure applies to both front calipers.*

Removal

1   Disconnect the brake hose from the caliper, remove the caliper from the steering knuckle and remove the brake pads, shim (if equipped) and pad spring (see Section 5).

Overhaul

2   Clean the exterior of the caliper with denatured alcohol or brake system cleaner.

3   Place a few rags between the piston and the caliper frame to act as a cushion, lay the caliper on the work bench so that the piston is facing down, toward the work bench surface, then use compressed air, directed into the fluid inlet, to remove the piston(s). Use only small quick blasts of air to ease the piston out of the bore. If a piston is blown out with too much force, it might be damaged

 Warning: Never place your fingers in front of the piston in an attempt to catch or protect it when applying compressed air. Doing so could result in serious injury.

4   If compressed air isn't available, reconnect the caliper to the brake hose and pump the brake lever until the piston is free. You'll have to put brake fluid in the master cylinder reservoir and get most of the air out of the hose to use this method.

5   Once the piston is protruding from the caliper, remove it.

6   Remove the old dust seal from the caliper bore.

7   Using a wood or plastic tool, remove the piston seal **(see illustration)**.

8   Clean the piston and piston bore with denatured alcohol, fresh brake fluid or brake system cleaner and dry them off with filtered, unlubricated compressed air. Inspect the surfaces of the piston and the piston bores for rust, corrosion, nicks, burrs and loss of plating. If you find defects on the surface of either piston or piston bore, replace the piston and caliper assembly (the piston is matched to the caliper). If the caliper is in bad shape, inspect the master cylinder too.

9   Lubricate the new piston seal with clean brake fluid and install it in its groove in the caliper bore. Make sure it's not twisted and is fully and correctly seated.

10   Lubricate the piston with clean brake fluid and install it into its bore in the caliper. Using your thumbs, push the piston all the way in; make sure it doesn't become cocked in the bore.

11   Install the new dust seal. Make sure that the inner lip of the seal is seated in its groove in the piston and the outer circumference of the seal is seated in its groove in the caliper bore.

Installation

12   Install the caliper and brake pads (see Section 5).

13   Install the brake hose-to-caliper banjo bolt **(see illustration 5.4 or 5.16)**. Be sure to use new sealing washers. Tighten the banjo bolt to the torque listed in this Chapter's Specifications.

14   Remove and overhaul the other front brake caliper.

15   Bleed the front brake system (see Section 15).

7   Front brake disc - inspection, removal and installation

Note: *This procedure applies to both front discs.*

1   Remove the front wheels (see Section 2).

Inspection

2   Visually inspect the surface of the disc for score marks and other damage. Light scratches are normal after use and won't affect brake operation, but deep grooves and heavy score marks will reduce braking efficiency and accelerate pad wear. If the disc is badly grooved it must be machined or replaced.

3   To check disc runout, mount a dial indicator with the plunger on the indicator touching the surface of the disc about 1/2-inch from the outer edge **(see illustration)**. Slowly turn the wheel hub and watch the indicator needle, comparing your reading with the disc runout limit listed in this Chapter's Specifications. If the runout is greater than allowed, replace the disc.

4   The disc must not be machined or allowed to wear to a thickness less than the minimum listed in this Chapter's Specifications. The thickness of the disc can be checked with a micrometer. If the thickness of the disc is less than the minimum, it must be replaced.

8.1a Rear brake caliper details (660)

1   *Locknut*
2   *Parking brake adjusting bolt*
3   *Brake hose banjo fitting*
4   *Caliper mounting bolts*

8.1b Rear brake caliper details (700)

1   *Locknut*
2   *Parking brake adjusting bolt*
3   *Brake hose banjo bolt*
4   *Caliper mounting bolts*

Removal and installation

5   Remove the front wheel hub (see Section 4).

6   To detach the brake disc from the hub, remove the four disc retaining bolts.

7   Installation is the reverse of removal. Tighten the disc retaining bolts to the torque listed in this Chapter's Specifications.

---

8   Rear brake pads - replacement

⚠️ **Warning: The dust created by the brake system is harmful to your health. Never blow it out with compressed air and don't inhale any of it. An approved filtering mask should be worn when working on the brakes. Do not, under**

any circumstances, use petroleum-based solvents to clean brake parts. Use brake cleaner only!

1   Loosen the parking brake adjusting locknut and back off the bolt, then pull the caliper body toward the bracket to press the piston in slightly **(see illustrations)**. This will free the pads so they will be easier to remove.

2   Loosen the brake pad retaining bolts **(see illustrations)**. (The brake pad retaining bolts are secured with thread locking agent and will be easier to loosen while the caliper is still bolted onto the caliper bracket.)

3   If you're planning to overhaul the caliper, remove the brake hose-to-caliper banjo bolt **(see illustration 8.1a or 8.1b)**, disconnect the brake hose from the caliper and discard the old sealing washers. If you're simply replacing the brake pads, or if you're only removing the caliper to remove other components, such as the axle, do NOT disconnect the brake hose.

4   Remove the brake caliper bolts **(see illustration 8.1a or 8.1b)** and take the caliper off. While the caliper is off the disc, tie it up out of the way.

5   Remove the brake pad retaining bolts (and lockplate on 660 models) **(see illustration 8.2a or 8.2b)**, then remove the brake pads **(see illustrations)**.

6   Check the area around the piston for brake fluid leakage **(see illustration)**. If fluid has been leaking, overhaul the caliper (see Section 9).

7   If you're working on a 660, remove the shim from the inner pad (the pad closest to the piston) and install it on the new inner pad. Be sure to install the shim so that its arrow mark points in the same direction that the disc rotates when the vehicle is moving forward. The pads on 700 models each have a shim. Install the shim next to the piston so its dowel fits into the groove in the piston face.

8.2a On 660 models, bend back the lockplate tabs (arrows) and loosen the pad retaining bolts

8.2b On 700 models, loosen the pad retaining bolts (left arrows) with an Allen wrench and note how the outer pad engages the caliper pin (right arrow)

8.5a Lift the caliper off, unscrew the pad retaining bolts and remove the outer pad . . .

8.5b . . . then remove the inner pad

8.6 Check the area around the piston (arrow) for fluid leakage

8   Installation is otherwise the reverse of removal. If you disconnected the brake fluid hose from the caliper, reinstall it with its anti-twist stopper against the boss on the caliper **(see illustration 8.1a or 8.1b and the accompanying illustration)**. use new sealing washers on the banjo fitting and tighten the bolt to the torque listed in this Chapter's Specifications. Be sure to tighten the caliper retaining bolts and the pad retaining bolts to the torque listed in this Chapter's Specifications. Use a new lockplate on 660 models. On 700 models, apply non-permanent thread locking agent to the threads of the pad retaining bolts.

9 Rear brake caliper - removal, overhaul and installation

⚠ *Warning: The dust created by the brake system is harmful to your health. Never blow it out with compressed air and don't inhale any of it. An approved filtering mask*

should be worn when working on the brakes. Do not, under any circumstances, use petroleum-based solvents to clean brake parts. Use brake cleaner only!

Removal

1   Disconnect the parking brake cable (see Section 17).
2   Disconnect the brake hose from the caliper, remove the caliper and remove the brake pads (see Section 8).

Overhaul

3   Clean the exterior of the caliper with denatured alcohol or brake system cleaner.
4   Loosen the parking brake adjuster lock-nut and unscrew the bolt **(see illustration 8.1a or 8.1b)**. remove the parking brake lever and return spring.
5   Remove the parking brake case bolts, detach the case/bracket assembly from the caliper body and remove the gasket **(see illustrations)**. Set the parking brake case aside for now.
6   Separate the caliper bracket from the caliper.

8.8 The neck of the 660 brake hose should rest against this stop (arrow) after the banjo bolt is tightened

7   Place a few rags between the piston and the caliper frame to act as a cushion, lay the caliper on the work bench so that the piston is facing down, toward the work bench

9.5a Here's the 660 parking brake case (right arrow) and rubber cap (left arrow)

9.5b Here's the 700 parking brake case (upper arrow) and rubber cap (lower arrow)

9.9a Typical rear caliper details

1   Pin boot
2   Caliper body
3   Pad spring
4   Piston seal
5   Dust seal
6   Piston

surface, then use compressed air, directed into the fluid inlet, to remove the piston. Use only small quick blasts of air to ease the piston out of the bore. If a piston is blown out with too much force, it might be damaged.

⚠️ **Warning: Never place your fingers in front of the piston in an attempt to catch or protect it when applying compressed air. Doing so could result in serious injury.**

8   If compressed air isn't available, reconnect the caliper to the brake hose and pump the brake lever until the piston is free. You'll have to put brake fluid in the master cylinder reservoir and get most of the air out of the hose to use this method.

9   Once the piston is protruding from the caliper, remove it **(see illustration)** and remove the old dust seal **(see illustration)**.

10   Using a wood or plastic tool, remove the piston seal **(see illustration 9.9b)**.

11   Clean the piston and piston bore with denatured alcohol, fresh brake fluid or brake system cleaner and dry them off with filtered, unlubricated compressed air. Inspect the surfaces of the piston and the piston bores for rust, corrosion, nicks, burrs and loss of

plating. If you find defects on the surface of either piston or piston bore, replace the piston and caliper assembly (the piston is matched to the caliper). If the caliper is in bad shape, inspect the master cylinder too. Check the pin boot(s) **(see illustration)** for damage or deterioration and replace it if problems are found.

12   Lubricate the new piston seal with clean brake fluid and install it in its groove in the caliper bore. Make sure it's not twisted and is fully and correctly seated.

13   Lubricate the piston with clean brake fluid and install it into its bore in the caliper. Using your thumbs, push the piston all the way in; make sure it doesn't become cocked in the bore.

14   Install the new dust seal. Make sure that the inner lip of the seal is seated in its groove in the piston and the outer circumference of the seal is seated in its groove in the caliper bore.

15   If you're working on a 660, remove the spring, adjuster nut and bearing from the parking brake case **(see illustration 9.5a)**. The bearing consists of three parts: a bearing race without a tab on its outer edge, three

balls, and another bearing race with a tab on its outer edge.

16   If you're working on a 700, remove the case cover from the case **(see illustration 9.5b)**. Unscrew the parking brake shaft from the parking brake case.

660

17   Reassembly of the parking brake case is essentially the reverse of disassembly. Make sure that the tab on the bearing race is aligned with the slit in the parking brake case, the bearing race grooves face toward the balls, and be sure to grease the bearing balls and races. Tighten the parking brake case bolts to the torque listed in this Chapter's Specifications. When installing the parking brake lever, make sure it's positioned as shown in the parking brake adjustment procedure in Chapter 1.

700 models

18   Lubricate the parking brake shaft with grease and install it in the case. The notch in the hex end of the parking brake shaft is installed between the two notches on the case next to the shaft bore.

19   When installing the parking brake lever, make sure it's positioned as shown in the parking brake adjustment procedure in Chapter 1.

Installation

20   Install the caliper and brake pads (see Sections 8 and 9).

21   Connect the brake hose-to-caliper banjo bolt, making sure its stop is against the boss on the caliper **(see illustration 8.8 or 13.8c)**. Be sure to use new sealing washers. Tighten the banjo bolt to the torque listed in this Chapter's Specifications.

22   Bleed the front brake system (see Section 15).

23   Adjust the parking brake (see Chapter 1).

9.9b Remove the dust seal (lower arrow) and piston seal (upper arrow) with a wood or plastic tool

9.11 Check the pin boot for deterioration or damage

10.2 Remove the cotter pin, then unscrew the nut . . .

10.3 . . . and remove the washer

10 Rear wheel hubs - removal and installation

1   Remove the rear wheels (see Section 2).
2   Bend back the cotter pin and pull it out of the hub nut **(see illustration)**.
3   Apply the parking brake to lock the rear axle. Unscrew the hub nut and remove the washer **(see illustration)**.
4   Pull the hub off the axle shaft (or tap it off with a soft-faced mallet if it's difficult to remove) **(see illustration)**. Clean the hub and the axle splines.
5   Installation is the reverse of removal.

11 Rear brake disc - inspection, removal and installation

Inspection

1   Visually inspect the surface of the disc for score marks and other damage. Light scratches are normal after use and won't affect brake operation, but deep grooves and heavy score marks will reduce braking efficiency and accelerate pad wear. If the disc is badly grooved it must be machined or replaced.
2   To check disc runout, mount a dial indicator with the plunger on the indicator touching the surface of the disc about 1/2-inch from the outer edge **(see illustration 7.3)**. Slowly turn the wheel hub and watch the indicator needle, comparing your reading with the disc runout limit listed in this Chapter's Specifications. If the runout is greater than allowed, replace the disc.
3   The disc must not be machined or allowed to wear to a thickness less than the minimum listed in this Chapter's Specifications. The thickness of the disc can be

10.4 If the hub is difficult to remove, tap it off with a soft-faced mallet and clean the splines

checked with a micrometer. If the thickness of the disc is less than the minimum, it must be replaced.

Removal and installation

4   Remove the right rear wheel hub (see Section 10).

5   Remove the rear caliper (see Section 9).
6   Remove the disc retaining bolts **(see illustrations)** and remove the disc.
7   Installation is the reverse of removal. Be sure to tighten the disc retaining bolts to the torque listed in this Chapter's Specifications.

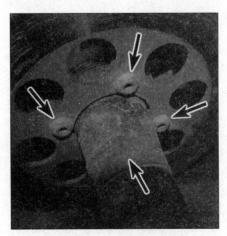

11.6a Brake disc bolts (660) (lower bolt hidden)

11.6b Brake disc bolts (700) (lower bolt hidden)

12.4a Here's the 660 banjo bolt (arrow); use new sealing washers on assembly and align the neck of the hose as shown

12.4b Here's the 700 banjo bolt (arrow); use new sealing washers on assembly and position the neck of the hose against its stop

12.5a Remove the 660 master cylinder clamp bolts (arrows); the arrow on the clamp must point up when installed

12.5b Remove the 700 master cylinder clamp bolts (arrows); the arrow on the clamp must point up when installed

12.6a Brake lever pivot bolt nut (660)

12 Front brake master cylinder - removal, overhaul and installation

1   If the front brake master cylinder is leaking fluid, or if the lever does not produce a firm feel when the brake lever is applied, and bleeding the brakes does not help, master cylinder overhaul is recommended.

2   Before disassembling the master cylinder, read through the entire procedure and make sure that you have the correct rebuild kit. Also, you will need some new, clean brake fluid of the recommended type, some clean rags and internal snap-ring pliers. **Note:** *To prevent damage to the paint from spilled brake fluid, always cover the top cover or upper fuel tank when working on the master cylinder.*

Caution: Disassembly, overhaul and reassembly of the brake master cylinder must be done in a spotlessly clean work area to avoid contamination and possible failure of the brake hydraulic system components.

Removal

3   Remove the reservoir cover retaining screw. Remove the reservoir and the rubber diaphragm. Siphon as much brake fluid from the reservoir as you can to avoid spilling it on the bike.

4   Pull back the rubber dust boot and loosen the brake hose banjo bolt **(see illustrations)** and separate the brake hose from the master cylinder. Wrap the end of the hose in a clean rag and suspend the hose in an upright position or bend it down carefully and place the open end in a clean container. The objective is to prevent excessive loss of brake fluid, fluid spills and system contamination.

5   Remove the master cylinder mounting bolts **(see illustrations)** and separate the master cylinder from the handlebar.

Caution: Do not tip the master cylinder upside down or any brake fluid still in the reservoir will run out.

Overhaul

6   Remove the brake lever pivot bolt nut, unscrew the pivot bolt and remove the lever **(see illustrations)**.

12.6b Here are the 700 front brake lever position adjuster bolt (lower arrow) and pivot bolt (upper arrow)

7   Carefully remove the rubber dust boot from the end of the piston **(see illustration)**. Using snap-ring pliers, remove the snap-ring and slide out the piston assembly and the spring **(see illustration)**.

12.7a Remove the rubber boot . . .

12.7b . . . compress the piston and remove the snap-ring . . .

8   Lay the parts out in the order in which they're removed to prevent confusion during reassembly.

9   Clean all of the parts with brake system cleaner (available at motorcycle dealerships and auto parts stores), isopropyl alcohol or clean brake fluid. Make sure the delivery port at the bottom of the master cylinder reservoir is clear **(see illustration)**.

Caution: Do not, under any circumstances, use a petroleum-based solvent to clean brake parts. If compressed air is available, use it to dry the parts thoroughly (make sure it's filtered and unlubricated). Check the master cylinder bore for corrosion, scratches, nicks and score marks. If damage is evident, the master cylinder must be replaced with a new one. If the master cylinder is in poor condition, then the calipers should be checked as well.

10   The dust seal, piston assembly and spring are included in the rebuild kit. Use all of the new parts, regardless of the apparent condition of the old ones.

11   Before reassembling the master cylinder, soak the piston and the rubber cup seals in clean brake fluid for ten or fifteen minutes. Lubricate the master cylinder bore with clean brake fluid, then carefully insert the piston and related parts in the reverse order of disassembly. Make sure the lips on the cup seals do not turn inside out when they are slipped into the bore.

12   Depress the piston, then install the snap-ring (make sure the snap-ring is properly seated in the groove). Install the rubber dust boot (make sure the lip is seated properly in the piston groove).

13   Lubricate the brake lever pivot bolt and the friction surface on the lever that pushes against the piston assembly.

Installation

14   Attach the master cylinder to the handlebar. Make sure that the arrow on the clamp is pointing up **(see illustration 12.5a or 12.5b)**. Tighten the bolts to the torque

12.7c . . . and remove the piston and spring from the bore

listed in this Chapter's Specifications.

15   Connect the brake hose to the master cylinder, using new sealing washers. Tighten the banjo bolt to the torque listed in this Chapter's Specifications.

16   Fill the master cylinder with the recommended brake fluid (see Chapter 1), then bleed the front brake system (see Section 15).

13 Rear brake master cylinder - removal, overhaul and installation

1   If the rear brake master cylinder is leaking fluid, or if the lever does not produce a firm feel when the brake pedal is applied, and bleeding the brakes does not help, master cylinder overhaul is recommended.

2   Before disassembling the master cylinder, read through the entire procedure and make sure that you have the correct rebuild kit. Also, you will need some new, clean brake fluid of the recommended type, some clean rags and internal snap-ring pliers.

Caution: To prevent damage to the paint from spilled brake fluid, always cover the top cover or upper fuel tank when working on the master cylinder.

 Warning: Disassembly, overhaul and reassembly of the brake master cylinder must be done in a spotlessly clean work area to avoid contamination and possible failure of the brake hydraulic system components.

12.9 Make sure the fluid port in the bottom of the reservoir is clear - if there's a baffle plate, make sure it's securely installed

13.3a Remove the bolts (arrows) and take the protective cover off (660)

13.3b Here are the 700 hose protector bolts (left arrows) and master cylinder mounting bolts (right arrows)

13.6a Slide the hose clamp (arrow) down the reservoir hose and disconnect the hose from the reservoir (660 shown)

13.6b Another way to disconnect the hose on 700 models is to remove the screw (upper arrow) and detach the hose fitting from the master cylinder - remove the cotter pin (lower arrow) and pull out the clevis pin

Removal

3   If you're working on a 660, remove the protective cover from the master cylinder reservoir **(see illustration)**. If you're working on a 700, remove the seat and right side cover (see Chapter 8). Unbolt the protective cover form the reservoir hose **(see illustration)**.

4   Unscrew the reservoir cap and siphon as much brake fluid from the reservoir as you can to avoid spilling it on the vehicle.

5   If you're working on a 660, remove the right rear footpeg bracket (see Chapter 8).

6   Squeeze the reservoir hose clamp **(see illustrations)**, and slide it along the hose. Detach the brake hose coming from the master cylinder reservoir and put the end in a container while the brake fluid drains. After the fluid has drained, slip a plastic bag over the end of the hose and secure it with rubber bands. Try to prevent fluid spills and system contamination. **Note:** *If you're working on a 700, you may find it easier to remove the screw that secures the reservoir hose fitting to the master cylinder body and separate the fitting from the master*

cylinder **(see illustration)**.

7   Remove the cotter pin and clevis pin, then disconnect the pushrod clevis from the rear brake pedal **(see illustration 13.6b or the accompanying illustration)**.

8   Remove the master cylinder mounting bolts **(see illustration 13.3b or the accompanying illustration)**, and detach the master cylinder from the frame. Remove the banjo bolt to disconnect the brake hose (the hose that runs to the rear caliper) from the master cylinder **(see illustrations)**. Discard the old sealing washers.

9   If necessary, unbolt the reservoir and remove it from the vehicle.

Overhaul

10   Back off the pushrod clevis locknut, mark the position of the clevis by marking the threads with a large felt pen or some other suitable marking agent, then unscrew the clevis from the pushrod. Unscrew and remove the locknut from the pushrod. Carefully remove the rubber dust boot from the pushrod. Using snap-ring pliers, remove the snap-ring and slide out the piston assembly and the spring **(see illustrations)**.

11   Lay the parts out in the order in which they're removed to prevent confusion during reassembly.

12   Clean all of the parts with brake system cleaner (available at motorcycle dealerships and auto parts stores), isopropyl alcohol or clean brake fluid.

Caution: Do not, under any circumstances, use a petroleum-based solvent to clean brake parts. If compressed air is available, use it to dry the parts thoroughly (make sure it's filtered and unlubricated). Check the master cylinder bore for corrosion, scratches, nicks and score marks. If damage is evident, the master cylinder must be replaced with a new one. If the master cylinder is in poor condition, then the calipers should be checked as well.

13.7 Remove the cotter pin (arrow) and pull out the clevis pin

13.8a Master cylinder mounting bolts (660)

13.8b When you connect the brake hose, position the hose neck against the stop (660) . . .

13.8c . . . on 700 models, rest the hose tab against the stop

13.10a Remove the snap-ring (660, shown) or screw (700) to detach the reservoir hose fitting from the master cylinder

13.10b Lift the fitting out and remove its O-ring

13.10c Measure the length of the pushrod and write it down for later installation

13.10d Loosen the locknut (arrow) and unscrew the pushrod clevis from the pushrod

13.10e Take the dust boot off, then compress the piston, remove its snap-ring and remove the piston from the bore

13.10f Rear master cylinder details (700 models use a screw instead of a snap-ring to retain the reservoir hose fitting)

13.15 Seat the snap-ring securely in its groove

13   The dust seal, piston assembly and spring are included in the rebuild kit. Use all of the new parts, regardless of the apparent condition of the old ones.

14   Before reassembling the master cylinder, soak the piston and the rubber cup seals in clean brake fluid for ten or fifteen minutes. Lubricate the master cylinder bore with clean brake fluid, then carefully insert the piston and related parts in the reverse order of disassembly. Make sure the lips on the cup seals do not turn inside out when they are slipped into the bore.

15   Depress the piston, then install the snap-ring (make sure the snap-ring is properly seated in the groove) **(see illustration)**.

16   Install the rubber dust boot onto the pushrod, push it all the way on and make sure the lip is seated correctly over the ridge on the end of the master cylinder. Install the locknut on the pushrod. Screw it on beyond the mark you made for the clevis prior to disassembly. Screw the clevis onto the pushrod. Make sure that it's aligned with the mark

you made before disassembly. Tighten the locknut securely.

Installation

17   Connect the rear caliper brake hose to the master cylinder, using new sealing washers. Tighten the banjo bolt to the torque listed in this Chapter's Specifications.

18   Install the master cylinder on the frame and install - but don't tighten - the master cylinder retaining bolts.

19   Reattach the pushrod clevis to the rear brake pedal.

20   Tighten the rear brake master cylinder retaining bolts to the torque listed in this Chapter's Specifications.

21   Reattach the reservoir hose to the master cylinder. Use a new hose clamp.

22   Fill the master cylinder with the recommended brake fluid (see Chapter 1), then bleed the rear brake system (see Section 15).

23   Refer to Chapter 1 and adjust the brake pedal position.

---

14 Brake hoses and lines - inspection and replacement

Inspection

1   Once a week or, if the motorcycle is used less frequently, before every ride, check the condition of the brake hoses.

2   Twist and flex the rubber hoses while looking for cracks, bulges and seeping fluid **(see illustrations)**. Check extra carefully around the areas where the hoses connect with the metal fittings, as these are common areas for hose failure.

3   Inspect the metal banjo fittings connected to the brake hoses. If the fittings are rusted, scratched or cracked, replace them.

Replacement

4   Cover the surrounding area with plenty of rags, then disconnect the ends of the hose. If you're replacing a brake hose, remove the banjo bolt from the caliper and disconnect the hose. Discard the old sealing washers.

5   To disconnect a front brake hose from a metal line, pull off the metal clip with a pair of pliers **(see illustration 14.2b)**, then unscrew the fitting with a flare nut wrench.

6   All rear brake hoses are attached to the rear master cylinder and to the rear caliper by banjo bolts.

7   Position the new hose, making sure it isn't twisted or otherwise strained, between the two components. Where a hose is attached by a banjo bolt, use new sealing washers on both sides of the fitting, and tighten banjo bolts to the torque listed in this Chapter's Specifications. On non-banjo fittings, tighten the fitting securely.

8   Flush the old brake fluid from the system, refill the system with the recommended fluid (see Chapter 1) and bleed the air from the system (see Section 15). Check the operation of the brakes carefully before riding the motorcycle.

---

15 Brake system - bleeding

1   Bleeding the brake system removes all the air bubbles from the brake fluid reservoirs, the lines and the brake calipers. Bleeding is necessary whenever a brake system hydraulic connection is loosened, when a component or hose is replaced, or when the master cylinder or caliper is overhauled. Leaks in the system may also allow air to enter, but leaking brake fluid will reveal their presence and warn you of the need for repair.

2   To bleed the brakes, you will need some new, clean brake fluid of the recommended

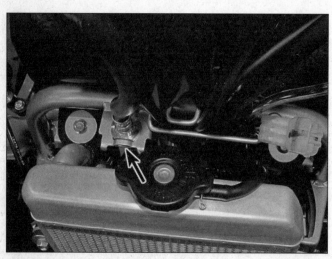

14.2a This clip (arrow) secures the front master cylinder hose to the metal line (700 shown) . . .

14.2b . . . the metal line is secured to a T-fitting by a flare nut - the front brake hoses (arrows) run along the upper suspension arms to the front calipers

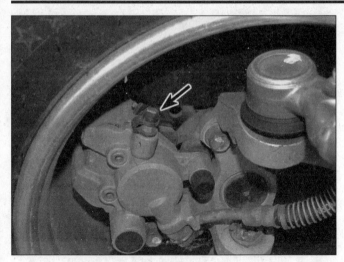

15.5a Here's a 660 front caliper bleed valve

15.5b Here's a 700 front caliper bleed valve

type (see Chapter 1), a length of clear vinyl or plastic tubing, a small container partially filled with clean brake fluid, some rags and a wrench to fit the brake caliper bleeder valves.

3   Cover the fuel tank and any other painted surfaces near the reservoir to prevent damage in the event that brake fluid is spilled.

4   Remove the front reservoir cover screws and remove the cover and diaphragm (or, on rear brakes, simply unscrew the reservoir cover). Slowly pump the brake lever (or brake pedal) a few times, until no air bubbles can be seen floating up from the holes at the bottom of the reservoir. Doing this bleeds the air from the master cylinder end of the line. Top up the reservoir with new fluid, then install the reservoir diaphragm and cover, but don't tighten the screws (or cover); you may have to remove the cover and diaphragm several times during the procedure.

5   Remove the rubber dust cover from the bleeder valve on the caliper (see illus-

trations) and slip a box wrench over the bleeder. Attach one end of the clear vinyl or plastic tubing to the bleed valve and submerge the other end in the brake fluid in the container.

6   Carefully pump the brake lever or brake pedal three or four times and hold it while opening the caliper bleeder valve. When the valve is opened, brake fluid will flow out of the caliper into the clear tubing and the lever will move toward the handlebar (or the pedal will move down). Retighten the bleeder valve, then release the brake lever or pedal.

7   Repeat this procedure until no air bubbles are visible in the brake fluid leaving the caliper and the lever or pedal is firm when applied. **Note:** *Remember to add fluid to the reservoir as the level drops. Use only new, clean brake fluid of the recommended type. Never re-use the fluid lost during bleeding.*

8   Keep an eye on the fluid level in the reservoir, especially if there's a lot of air in the system. Every time you crack open the bleeder valve, the fluid level in the reservoir

drops a little. Do not allow the fluid level to drop below the lower mark during the bleeding process. If the level looks low, remove the reservoir cover and add some fluid.

9   When you're done, inspect the fluid level in the reservoir one more time, add some fluid if necessary, then install the diaphragm and reservoir cover and tighten the screws securely. Wipe up any spilled brake fluid and check the entire system for leaks. **Note:** *If bleeding is difficult, it may be necessary to let the brake fluid in the system stabilize for a few hours (it may be aerated). Repeat the bleeding procedure when the tiny bubbles in the system have settled out.*

16 Brake pedal - removal and installation

1   Remove the right footpeg (see Chapter 8).

15.5c Here's the rear caliper bleed valve on a 660

15.5d Here's the rear caliper bleed valve on a 700

16.2a On a 660, unhook the brake light switch spring (top right) and pedal return spring (top left), remove the cotter pin and pull out the clevis pin (bottom left), then remove the circlip (bottom right) and pull the pedal off

16.2b On a 700, unhook the brake light switch spring (right), remove the cotter pin and pull out the clevis pin (left), then remove the pedal pivot bolt (center) . . .

16.3 . . . unhook the pedal return spring (arrow, viewed from under the right side of the vehicle) and remove the pedal

2   Remove the cotter pin and clevis pin to disconnect the master cylinder from the pedal (see illustrations).

3   Unhook the brake switch spring and pedal return spring (see illustration 16.2a or 16.2b and the accompanying illustration).

4   Remove the circlip (660) or pedal pivot bolt (700). Take the pedal off.

5   Installation is the reverse of the removal steps. If you're working on a 660, use a new circlip. If you're working on a 700, tighten the pedal bolt to the torque listed in this Chapter's Specifications.

17 Parking brake cable and lever - removal and installation

1   Loosen the parking brake cable adjuster (see Chapter 1) to create maximum slack in the cable. Pull the cable housing out of the lever slot, then slip the cable out of the slot in the bracket (see illustrations).

2   At the rear caliper, loosen the parking brake cable adjuster locknut and back off the bolt (see illustrations). Disconnect the return spring from the lever.

3   Remove the Allen bolts that secure the cable bracket to the parking brake case/lever bracket (see illustration).

4   Turn the cable bracket over and remove two screws that secure the guide plate (see illustration). Take the guide plate off, noting how its pin engages the hole in the parking brake lever (see illustration). Rotate the cable to align with the slot in the lever, lift the cable end plug out of the lever.

5   Take the lever off of the bracket, noting how the lever hole fits over the collar (see illustration).

6   Remove the collar from the bracket (see illustration).

17.1a Pull the cable housing out of the bracket and rotate the cable (arrow) out of the slot, this is a 660 . . .

17.1b . . . and this is a 700

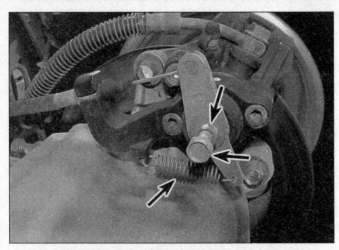

17.2a At the caliper, loosen the locknut (top), back off the adjusting bolt (center) and unhook the return spring (bottom). This is a 660 . . .

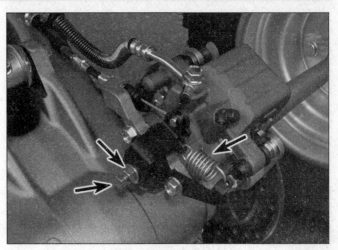

17.2b . . . and this is a 700

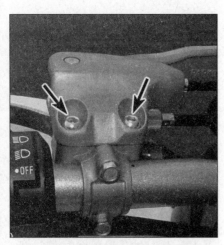

17.3 Remove the Allen bolts that secure the cable bracket to the clutch lever bracket (arrows, 700 shown)

17.4a Take the cable bracket off, turn it over, remove two screws and take off the cable guide (arrow) . . .

17.4b . . . noting how its pin aligns with the hole in the lever (arrows)

17.5 Lift off the lever, noting how its pin fits into the collar (arrows) . . .

17.6 . . . and pull the collar out, noting how it fits into the bracket hole (arrows)

17.7a Rotate the cable to align it with the lever slot (lower arrow) and slip the end plug (upper arrow) out of the lever

17.7b Pull the cable housing (left arrow) forward out of the bracket, then slip the cable sideways out of the slot (right arrow)

17.8 The parking brake cable is secured to the swingarm and engine by several retainers (arrows, 700 shown)

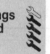

18.5 On 700 models, this snap-ring (arrow) secures the caliper bracket to the hub

the lever (see illustration).
8   Free the cable from its retainers on the swingarm (see illustration).
9   Follow the cable from the swingarm up to the handlebar, freeing it from its remaining retainers. Note how the cable is routed and remove it from the vehicle.
10   Installation is the reverse of the removal steps.

18 Rear axle hub and bearings - removal, inspection and installation

Removal

1   Jack up the rear end of the vehicle and support it securely on jackstands.
2   Remove the rear wheels (see Section 2).
3   Remove the drive chain and rear axle (see Chapter 6).
4   If you're working on a 660, remove the

7   At the caliper, rotate the cable so it aligns with the slot in the lever on the caliper, then slip it sideways to remove the cable end

plug from the lever (see illustration). Pull the cable housing forward out of the bracket, then slip the cable sideways out of the slot in

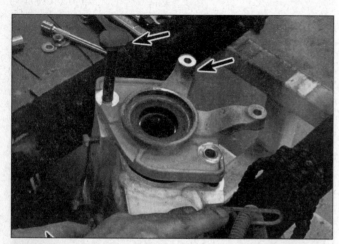

18.6a Take the caliper bracket (right arrow) off the swingarm - if corrosion makes a hub bolt hard to remove on a 660, insert the other bolt (left arrow) or a suitable punch into the hole and tap on it to remove the corroded bolt

18.6b Here are the 660 swingarm (top), caliper bracket (right) and hub (left) - the 700 hub is similar, but has four O-rings

hub bolts (see Chapter 6).

5   If you're working on a 700, remove the large snap-ring that secures the brake caliper bracket **(see illustration)**.

6   Remove the caliper bracket from the right side of the swingarm and remove the hub from the left side **(see illustrations)**.

Inspection and bearing replacement

7   Pry out the seal from each side of the hub **(see illustration)**.

8   Spin the bearing(s) inside each end of the hub and check for roughness, looseness or noise.

9   Insert a metal drift or punch into the hub and tilt it so it pushes the spacer aside and catches the edge of the bearing on the far side. Tap gently against the bearing, on opposite sides of the bearing, to drive it from the hub. Insert the drift from the other side and drive the other bearing out in the same way (700 models have two bearings on each side of the hub). Remove the spacer.

10   The new bearings should be sealed on both sides. Place one of the new bearings in the hub. Tap the bearing into position with a bearing driver or socket the same diameter as the bearing outer race.

11   Install the spacer.

12   Install the remaining bearing(s) in the same manner.

13   Install a new seal in each side of the hub with its lip facing into the hub. Coat the seal lips with multi-purpose grease.

Installation

14   Installation is the reverse of removal. If you're working on a 700, install new O-rings on the hub. Be sure to tighten the hub nuts and bolts to the torque listed in this Chapter's Specifications.

15   Adjust the drive chain when you're done (see Chapter 1).

18.7 Pry the seal out of each end of the hub and check the bearings for roughness, looseness or noise - if problems are found, remove them and the spacer (see text)

Deflate the tire and remove the valve core. Release the bead on the side opposite the tire valve with an ATV bead breaker, following the manufacturer's instructions. Make sure you have the correct blades for the tire size (using the wrong size blade may damage the wheel, the tire or the blade). Lubricate the bead with water before removal (don't use soap or any type of lubricant).

If one side of the wheel has a smaller flange, remove and install the tire from that side. Use two tire levers to work the bead over the edge of the rim.

Use tire levers to start the second bead over the rim flange.

TIRE CHANGING SEQUENCE

Turn the tire over and release the other bead.

Before installing, ensure that tire is suitable for wheel. Take note of any sidewall markings such as direction of rotation arrows, then work the first bead over the rim flange.

Hold the bead while you work the last section of it over the rim flange. Install the valve core and inflate the tire, making sure not to overinflate it.

Chapter 8
Bodywork and frame

Contents

Degrees of difficulty

Easy, suitable for novice with little experience | **Fairly easy,** suitable for beginner with some experience | **Fairly difficult,** suitable for competent DIY mechanic | **Difficult,** suitable for experienced DIY mechanic | **Very difficult,** suitable for expert DIY or professional

---

1 General information

This Chapter covers the procedures necessary to remove and install the body panels and other body parts. Since many service and repair operations on these vehicles require removal of the panels and/or other body parts, the procedures are grouped here and referred to from other Chapters.

In the case of damage to the panels or other body parts, it is usually necessary to remove the broken component and replace it with a new (or used) one. The material that the plastic body parts is composed of doesn't lend itself to conventional repair techniques. There are, however, some shops that specialize in plastic welding, so it would be advantageous to check around first before throwing the damaged part away.

Note: *When attempting to remove any body panel, first study the panel closely, noting any fasteners and associated fittings, to be sure of returning everything to its correct place on installation. In some cases, the aid of an assistant will be required when removing panels, to help avoid damaging the surface. Once the visible fasteners have been removed, try to lift off the panel as described but DO NOT FORCE the panel - if it will not release, check that all fasteners have been removed and try again. Where a panel engages another by means of tabs and slots, be careful not to break the tabs or to damage the bodywork. Remember that a few moments of patience at this stage will save you a lot of money in replacing broken panels!*

2.1 To release the seat, pull the latch and lift the rear of the seat

2.2a The seat is also secured by hooks at the front and center (arrows, 660 shown)

2.2b The posts at the rear corners of the seat fit into holes in the fender (700 shown)

and the locating posts at the rear of the seat into their holes.

3 Front bumper - removal and installation

1   Remove the bumper mounting bolts **(see illustrations)** and separate the bumper from the vehicle.
2   Installation is the reverse of removal. Tighten the bumper bolts securely.

4 Fuel tank cover - removal and installation

660

1   Unscrew the fuel tank filler cap.
2   Remove a trim clip from each corner of

2 Seat - removal and installation

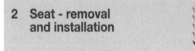

1   Lift the latch at the rear of the seat **(see illustration)** and lift the back end of the seat.

2   Disengage the lobes at the front end of the seat from their corresponding receptacles in the frame and lift the seat off the vehicle **(see illustrations)**.
3   Installation is the reverse of removal. Insert the hooks at the front of the seat into the corresponding receptacle(s) in the frame

3.1a Front bumper mounting bolts (660)

3.1b Front bumper mounting bolts (700)

4.2a Remove a trim clip from each corner of the 660 fuel tank cover (arrows) . . .

4.2b . . . and disengage the cover tabs from the slots in the fender (arrows)

the cover and disengage the tabs **(see illustrations)**. Lift the cover off the tank.
3   Installation is the reverse of the removal steps. Engage the tabs on the cover with the slots in the front fender.

700

4   Remove the seat (see Section 2). Unscrew the cap from the fuel tank.
5   Remove two bolts at the rear corners of the cover **(see illustration)**.
6   Remove the two screws that secure the rear corners of the front panel and the front corners of the fuel tank cover **(see illustration)**. Carefully pull the cover rearward.
7   Installation is the reverse of removal.

4.5 Remove the bolts (arrows) that secure the rear corners of the 700 fuel tank cover . . .

4.6 . . . and the two screws that secure the front corners (arrows) - disengage the front of the cover from the front panel and lift the cover off

5 Front panel - removal and installation	

1   Remove two screws that secure the front panel to the front fender **(see illus-**

trations)**. Disengage the tabs along the sides and bottom of the panel and lift it off **(see illustration)**.

2   Installation is the reverse of the removal steps.

5.1a Remove two screws that secure the upper edge of the front panel (this is a 660) . . .

5.1b . . . and this is a 700 . . .

5.1c . . . then disengage the tabs from the slots and lift the front panel off

6.2 Remove the bolts that secure the rear corners of the 660 front fender (arrows) . . .

6.3 . . . the screw at the lower front (arrow) . . .

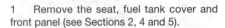

6 Front fender - removal and installation

1   Remove the seat, fuel tank cover and front panel (see Sections 2, 4 and 5).

660

2   Remove two bolts that secure the rear edge of the fender **(see illustration)**.
3   Remove the screw that secures the bottom front of the fender **(see illustration)**.
4   Working under the fender, remove the fasteners that secure the fender stay to the fender (on both sides of the vehicle) **(see illustrations)**.
5   Working from the front of the vehicle, grasp the sides of the fender, spread it carefully and lift it off **(see illustration)**.
6   Installation is the reverse of the removal steps.

6.4a . . . a bolt and nut above the headlight on each side . . .

6.4b . . . a bolt at the inner rear corner on each side . . .

6.4c . . . and the stamped nut that secures the bolt

6.5 Carefully spread the fender and lift it off

6.7 Remove the bolts that secure the rear corners of the 700 front fender (arrows) . . .

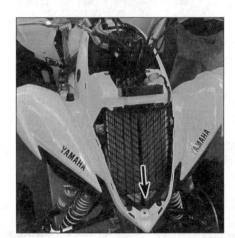

6.8 . . . the screw at the lower front (arrow) . . .

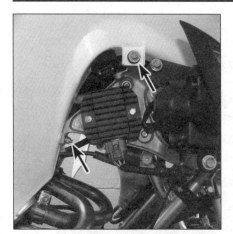

6.9a ... a nut and bolt from under the fender on the right side (arrows) ...

6.9b ... and on the left side (arrows)

6.11 Carefully spread the fender and lift it off

700

7   Remove two bolts that secure the rear edge of the fender **(see illustration)**.

8   Remove the screw that secures the bottom front of the fender **(see illustration)**.

9   Working under the fender, remove the fasteners that secure the fender stay to the fender (on both sides of the vehicle) **(see illustrations)**.

10   Disconnect the electrical connector for the multi-function display just forward of the handlebars (see Chapter 5 if necessary).

11   Working from the front of the vehicle, grasp the sides of the fender, spread it carefully and lift it off **(see illustration)**.

12   Installation is the reverse of the removal steps.

7	Rear fender - removal and installation

660

1   Remove the seat, front panel and front fender (see Sections 2, 5 and 6).

2   Remove the battery, starter relay and CDI unit (see Chapter 5). The battery retainer bolts also secure the top of the fender.

3   On each side of the vehicle, remove the nuts and screw that secure the fender to the footrest and frame bracket **(see illustration)**.

4   Carefully spread the fender and lift it off the vehicle.

7.3 Remove the fasteners that secure the underside of the 660 rear fender to the frame

700

5   Remove the bolts that secure the rear edge of the front fender and the front edge of the rear fender.

6   On each side of the vehicle, remove the bolt that secures the bottom front corner of the fender to the footrest **(see illustration)**.

7   Under the fender on each side of the vehicle, remove the bolt that secures the fender to the frame **(see illustration)**.

7.6 Footrest bolts (700) - the upper one secures a corner of the rear fender

7.7 Under the rear fender, unbolt the fender from the frame bracket (arrow)

7.8 Remove one bolt that secures the rear of the fender

8.1 Footrest bolts (660) - the upper one secures a corner
of the rear fender

8   Remove one bolt that secures the top rear of the fender **(see illustration)**.
9   Lift the fender off.
10   Installation is the reverse of removal.

8   Footrests and footpegs - removal and installation

1   To detach a footrest, remove the fasteners that attach it to the rear fender, foot plate and footpeg, then lift it out **(700 models, see illustration 7.6; 660 models, see the accompanying illustration)**.
2   To detach a footpeg, unbolt it from the frame. If you're removing the left footpeg from a 660, detach the shift pedal from it after you remove it (see Chapter 2A). If you're removing the right footpeg form a 700, refer to Chapter 7 and remove the brake pedal.
3   Installation is the reverse of removal.

9   Skid plates - removal and installation

1   Skid plates are secured to the underside of the frame beneath the engine and to the underside of the swingarm. To remove a skid plate, unbolt it and lower it away from the vehicle.
2   Installation is the reverse of removal.

10 Frame - general information, inspection and repair

1   660 models use a frame made of round-section steel tubing. 700 models use an aluminum frame. The 660 frame is made in one piece, with a detachable rear extension made of steel tubing. The 700 frame is made in sections, bolted together with safety Torx bolts (except for the rear sub-frame, which is secured by Allen bolts). The frame, except for the rear sub-frame, is available only as a complete unit.

The sub-frame is available separately.
2   The frame shouldn't require attention unless accident damage has occurred. In most cases, frame replacement is the only satisfactory remedy for such damage. A few frame specialists have the jigs and other equipment necessary for straightening the frame to the required standard of accuracy, but even then there is no simple way of assessing to what extent the frame may have been over-stressed.
3   After the machine has accumulated a lot of miles, the frame should be examined closely for signs of cracking or splitting at the welded joints. Corrosion can also cause weakness at these joints. Loose engine mount bolts can cause elongation of the bolt holes and can fracture the engine mounting points. Minor damage can often be repaired by welding, depending on the nature and extent of the damage.
4   Remember that a frame that is out of alignment will cause handling problems. If misalignment is suspected as the result of an accident, it will be necessary to strip the machine completely so the frame can be thoroughly checked.

Wiring diagram - 660 models

Wiring diagram - 700 models

Dimensions and weights

General Specifications

660

Wheelbase	1245 mm (49.0 inches)
Width	1100 mm (43.3 inches)
Length	1830 mm (72.0 inches)
Overall height	1150 mm (45.3 inches)
Ground clearance	265 mm (10.4 inches)
Seat height	860 mm (33.9 inches)
Weight (with oil and full fuel tank)	193 kg (426 lbs)

700

Wheelbase	1280 mm (50.4 inches)
Width	1170 mm (46.1 inches)
Length	2310 mm (90.9 inches)
Overall height	1130 mm (44.5 inches)
Ground clearance	240 mm (9.4 inches)
Seat height	815 mm (32.1 inches)
Weight (with oil and full fuel tank)	192 kg (423 lbs)

Notes

Buying tools

A good set of tools is a fundamental requirement for servicing and repairing a motorcycle. Although there will be an initial expense in building up enough tools for servicing, this will soon be offset by the savings made by doing the job yourself. As experience and confidence grow, additional tools can be added to enable the repair and overhaul of the motorcycle. Many of the special tools are expensive and not often used so it may be preferable to rent them, or for a group of friends or motorcycle club to join in the purchase.

As a rule, it is better to buy more expensive, good quality tools. Cheaper tools are likely to wear out faster and need to be replaced more often, nullifying the original savings.

> ⚠️ **Warning: To avoid the risk of a poor quality tool breaking in use, causing injury or damage to the component being worked on, always aim to purchase tools which meet the relevant national safety standards.**

The following lists of tools do not represent the manufacturer's service tools, but serve as a guide to help the owner decide which tools are needed for this level of work. In addition, items such as an electric drill, hacksaw, files, soldering iron and a workbench equipped with a vise, may be needed. Although not classed as tools, a selection of bolts, screws, nuts, washers and pieces of tubing always come in useful.

For more information about tools, refer to the Haynes *Motorcycle Workshop Practice Techbook* (Bk. No. 3470).

Manufacturer's service tools

Inevitably certain tasks require the use of a service tool. Where possible an alternative tool or method of approach is recommended, but sometimes there is no option if personal injury or damage to the component is to be avoided. Where required, service tools are referred to in the relevant procedure.

Service tools can usually only be purchased from a motorcycle dealer and are identified by a part number. Some of the commonly-used tools, such as rotor pullers, are available in aftermarket form from mail-order motorcycle tool and accessory suppliers.

Maintenance and minor repair tools

1 *Set of flat-bladed screwdrivers*
2 *Set of Phillips head screwdrivers*
3 *Combination open-end and box wrenches*
4 *Socket set (3/8 inch or 1/2 inch drive)*
5 *Set of Allen keys or bits*
6 *Set of Torx keys or bits*
7 *Pliers, cutters and self-locking grips (vise grips)*
8 *Adjustable wrenches*
9 *C-spanners*
10 *Tread depth gauge and tire pressure gauge*
11 *Cable oiler clamp*
12 *Feeler gauges*
13 *Spark plug gap measuring tool*
14 *Spark plug wrench or deep plug sockets*
15 *Wire brush and emery paper*
16 *Calibrated syringe, measuring cup and funnel*
17 *Oil filter adapters*
18 *Oil drainer can or tray*
19 *Pump type oil can*
20 *Grease gun*
21 *Straight-edge and steel rule*
22 *Continuity tester*
23 *Battery charger*
24 *Hydrometer (for battery specific gravity check)*
25 *Antifreeze tester (for liquid-cooled engines)*

Repair and overhaul tools

1 Torque wrench
   (small and mid-ranges)
2 Conventional, plastic or
   soft-faced hammers
3 Impact driver set

4 Vernier caliper
5 Snap-ring pliers
   (internal and external, or
   combination)
6 Set of cold chisels
   and punches

7 Selection of pullers
8 Breaker bars
9 Chain breaking/
   riveting tool set
10 Wire stripper and
   crimper tool

11 Multimeter (measures
   amps, volts and ohms)
12 Stroboscope (for
   dynamic timing checks)
13 Hose clamp
   (wingnut type shown)

14 Clutch holding tool
15 One-man brake/clutch
   bleeder kit

Special tools

1 Micrometers
   (external type)
2 Telescoping gauges
3 Dial gauge

4 Cylinder
   compression gauge
5 Vacuum gauges (left) or
   manometer (right)
6 Oil pressure gauge

7 Plastigage kit
8 Valve spring compressor
   (4-stroke engines)
9 Piston pin drawbolt tool

10 Piston ring removal and
   installation tool
11 Piston ring clamp
12 Cylinder bore hone
   (stone type shown)

13 Stud extractor
14 Screw extractor set
15 Bearing driver set

1 Workshop equipment and facilities

The workbench

● Work is made much easier by raising the bike up on a ramp - components are much more accessible if raised to waist level. The hydraulic or pneumatic types seen in the dealer's workshop are a sound investment if you undertake a lot of repairs or overhauls **(see illustration 1.1)**.

1.1 Hydraulic motorcycle ramp

● If raised off ground level, the bike must be supported on the ramp to avoid it falling. Most ramps incorporate a front wheel locating clamp which can be adjusted to suit different diameter wheels. When tightening the clamp, take care not to mark the wheel rim or damage the tire - use wood blocks on each side to prevent this.
● Secure the bike to the ramp using tie-downs **(see illustration 1.2)**. If the bike has only a sidestand, and hence leans at a dangerous angle when raised, support the bike on an auxiliary stand.

1.2 Tie-downs are used around the passenger footrests to secure the bike

● Auxiliary (paddock) stands are widely available from mail order companies or motorcycle dealers and attach either to the wheel axle or swingarm pivot **(see illustration 1.3)**. If the motorcycle has a centerstand, you can support it under the crankcase to prevent it toppling while either wheel is removed **(see illustration 1.4)**.

1.3 This auxiliary stand attaches to the swingarm pivot

1.4 Always use a block of wood between the engine and jack head when supporting the engine in this way

Fumes and fire

● Refer to the *Safety first!* page at the beginning of the manual for full details. Make sure your workshop is equipped with a fire extinguisher suitable for fuel-related fires (Class B fire - flammable liquids) - it is not sufficient to have a water-filled extinguisher.
● Always ensure adequate ventilation is available. Unless an exhaust gas extraction system is available for use, ensure that the engine is run outside of the workshop.
● If working on the fuel system, make sure the workshop is ventilated to avoid a build-up of fumes. This applies equally to fume build-up when charging a battery. Do not smoke or allow anyone else to smoke in the workshop.

Fluids

● If you need to drain fuel from the tank, store it in an approved container marked as suitable for the storage of gasoline **(see illustration 1.5)**. Do not store fuel in glass jars

1.5 Use an approved can only for storing gasoline

or bottles.
● Use proprietary engine degreasers or solvents which have a high flash-point, such as kerosene, for cleaning off oil, grease and dirt - never use gasoline for cleaning. Wear rubber gloves when handling solvent and engine degreaser. The fumes from certain solvents can be dangerous - always work in a well-ventilated area.

Dust, eye and hand protection

● Protect your lungs from inhalation of dust particles by wearing a filtering mask over the nose and mouth. Many frictional materials still contain asbestos which is dangerous to your health. Protect your eyes from spouts of liquid and sprung components by wearing a pair of protective

1.6 A fire extinguisher, goggles, mask and protective gloves should be at hand in the workshop

goggles **(see illustration 1.6)**.
● Protect your hands from contact with solvents, fuel and oils by wearing rubber gloves. Alternatively apply a barrier cream to your hands before starting work. If handling hot components or fluids, wear suitable gloves to protect your hands from scalding and burns.

What to do with old fluids

● Old cleaning solvent, fuel, coolant and oils should not be poured down domestic drains or onto the ground. Package the fluid up in old oil containers, label it accordingly, and take it to a garage or disposal facility. Contact your local disposal company for location of such sites.

Note: It is illegal to dump oil down the drain. Check with your local auto parts store, disposal facility or environmental agency to see if they accept the oil for recycling.

2 Fasteners - screws, bolts and nuts

Fastener types and applications

Bolts and screws

● Fastener head types are either of hexagonal, Torx or splined design, with internal and external versions of each type **(see illustrations 2.1 and 2.2)**; splined head fasteners are not in common use on motorcycles. The conventional slotted or Phillips head design is used for certain screws. Bolt or screw length is always measured from the underside of the head to the end of the item **(see illustration 2.11)**.

2.1 Internal hexagon/Allen (A), Torx (B) and splined (C) fasteners, with corresponding bits

2.2 External Torx (A), splined (B) and hexagon (C) fasteners, with corresponding sockets

● Certain fasteners on the motorcycle have a tensile marking on their heads, the higher the marking the stronger the fastener. High tensile fasteners generally carry a 10 or higher marking. Never replace a high tensile fastener with one of a lower tensile strength.

Washers (see illustration 2.3)

● Plain washers are used between a fastener head and a component to prevent damage to the component or to spread the load when torque is applied. Plain washers can also be used as spacers or shims in certain assemblies. Copper or aluminum plain washers are often used as sealing washers on drain plugs.

2.3 Plain washer (A), penny washer (B), spring washer (C) and serrated washer (D)

● The split-ring spring washer works by applying axial tension between the fastener head and component. If flattened, it is fatigued and must be replaced. If a plain (flat) washer is used on the fastener, position the spring washer between the fastener and the plain washer.

● Serrated star type washers dig into the fastener and component faces, preventing loosening. They are often used on electrical ground connections to the frame.

● Cone type washers (sometimes called Belleville) are conical and when tightened apply axial tension between the fastener head and component. They must be installed with the dished side against the component and often carry an OUTSIDE marking on their outer face. If flattened, they are fatigued and must be replaced.

● Tab washers are used to lock plain nuts or bolts on a shaft. A portion of the tab washer is bent up hard against one flat of the nut or bolt to prevent it loosening. Due to the tab washer being deformed in use, a new tab washer should be used every time it is removed.

● Wave washers are used to take up endfloat on a shaft. They provide light springing and prevent excessive side-to-side play of a component. Can be found on rocker arm shafts.

Nuts and cotter pins

● Conventional plain nuts are usually six-sided **(see illustration 2.4)**. They are sized by thread diameter and pitch. High tensile nuts carry a number on one end to denote their tensile strength.

2.4 Plain nut (A), shouldered locknut (B), nylon insert nut (C) and castellated nut (D)

● Self-locking nuts either have a nylon insert, or two spring metal tabs, or a shoulder which is staked into a groove in the shaft - their advantage over conventional plain nuts is a resistance to loosening due to vibration. The nylon insert type can be used a number of times, but must be replaced when the friction of the nylon insert is reduced, i.e. when the nut spins freely on the shaft. The spring tab type can be reused unless the tabs are damaged. The shouldered type must be replaced every time it is removed.

● Cotter pins are used to lock a castellated nut to a shaft or to prevent loosening of a plain nut. Common applications are wheel axles and brake torque arms. Because the cotter pin arms are deformed to lock around the nut a new cotter pin must always be used on installation - always use the correct size cotter pin which will fit snugly in the shaft hole. Make sure the cotter pin arms are correctly located around the nut **(see illustrations 2.5 and 2.6)**.

2.5 Bend cotter pin arms as shown (arrows) to secure a castellated nut

2.6 Bend cotter pin arms as shown to secure a plain nut

Caution: If the castellated nut slots do not align with the shaft hole after tightening to the torque setting, tighten the nut until the next slot aligns with the hole - never loosen the nut to align its slot.

● R-pins (shaped like the letter R), or slip pins as they are sometimes called, are sprung and can be reused if they are otherwise in good condition. Always install R-pins with their closed end facing forwards **(see illustration 2.7)**.

2.7 Correct fitting of R-pin. Arrow indicates forward direction

Snap-rings (see illustration 2.8)

● Snap-rings (sometimes called circlips) are used to retain components on a shaft or in a housing and have corresponding external or internal ears to permit removal. Parallel-sided (machined) snap-rings can be installed either way round in their groove, whereas stamped snap-rings (which have a chamfered edge on one face) must be installed with the chamfer facing the thrust load (see illustration 2.9).

2.8 External stamped snap-ring (A), internal stamped snap-ring (B), machined snap-ring (C) and wire snap-ring (D)

● Always use snap-ring pliers to remove and install snap-rings; expand or compress them just enough to remove them. After installation, rotate the snap-ring in its groove to ensure it is securely seated. If installing a snap-ring on a splined shaft, always align its opening with a shaft channel to ensure the snap-ring ends are well supported and unlikely to catch (see illustration 2.10).

2.9 Correct fitting of a stamped snap-ring

THRUST LOAD

THRUST WASHER

SHARP EDGE

CHAMFERED EDGE

0650H

2.10 Align snap-ring opening with shaft channel

● Snap-rings can wear due to the thrust of components and become loose in their grooves, with the subsequent danger of becoming dislodged in operation. For this reason, replacement is advised every time a snap-ring is disturbed.

● Wire snap-rings are commonly used as piston pin retaining clips. If a removal tang is provided, long-nosed pliers can be used to dislodge them, otherwise careful use of a small flat-bladed screwdriver is necessary. Wire snap-rings should be replaced every time they are disturbed.

Thread diameter and pitch

● Diameter of a male thread (screw, bolt or stud) is the outside diameter of the threaded portion (see illustration 2.11). Most motorcycle manufacturers use the ISO (International Standards Organization) metric system expressed in millimeters. For example, M6 refers to a 6 mm diameter thread. Sizing is the same for nuts, except that the thread diameter is measured across the valleys of the nut.

● Pitch is the distance between the peaks of the thread (see illustration 2.11). It is expressed in millimeters, thus a common bolt size may be expressed as 6.0 x 1.0 mm (6 mm thread diameter and 1 mm pitch). Generally pitch increases in proportion to thread diameter, although there are always exceptions.

● Thread diameter and pitch are related for conventional fastener applications and the accompanying table can be used as a guide. Additionally, the AF (Across Flats), wrench or socket size dimension of the bolt or nut (see illustration 2.11) is linked to thread and pitch specification. Thread pitch can be measured with a thread gauge (see illustration 2.12).

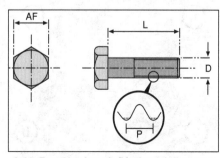

AF

L

D

P

2.11 Fastener length (L), thread diameter (D), thread pitch (P) and head size (AF)

2.12 Using a thread gauge to measure pitch

AF size	Thread diameter x pitch (mm)
8 mm	M5 x 0.8
8 mm	M6 x 1.0
10 mm	M6 x 1.0
12 mm	M8 x 1.25
14 mm	M10 x 1.25
17 mm	M12 x 1.25

● The threads of most fasteners are of the right-hand type, ie they are turned clockwise to tighten and counterclockwise to loosen. The reverse situation applies to left-hand thread fasteners, which are turned counterclockwise to tighten and clockwise to loosen. Left-hand threads are used where rotation of a component might loosen a conventional right-hand thread fastener.

Seized fasteners

● Corrosion of external fasteners due to water or reaction between two dissimilar metals can occur over a period of time. It will build up sooner in wet conditions or in countries where salt is used on the roads during the winter. If a fastener is severely corroded it is likely that normal methods of removal will fail and result in its head being ruined. When you attempt removal, the fastener thread should be heard to crack free and unscrew easily - if it doesn't, stop there before damaging something.

● A smart tap on the head of the fastener will often succeed in breaking free corrosion which has occurred in the threads (see illustration 2.13).

● An aerosol penetrating fluid (such as WD-40) applied the night beforehand may work its way down into the thread and ease removal. Depending on the location, you may be able to make up a modeling-clay well around the fastener head and fill it with penetrating fluid.

2.13 A sharp tap on the head of a fastener will often break free a corroded thread

● If you are working on an engine internal component, corrosion will most likely not be a problem due to the well lubricated environment. However, components can be very tight and an impact driver is a useful tool in freeing them (see illustration 2.14).

2.14 Using an impact driver to free a fastener

● Where corrosion has occurred between dissimilar metals (e.g. steel and aluminum alloy), the application of heat to the fastener head will create a disproportionate expansion rate between the two metals and break the seizure caused by the corrosion. Whether heat can be applied depends on the location of the fastener - any surrounding components likely to be damaged must first be removed (see illustration 2.15). Heat can be applied using a paint stripper heat gun or clothes iron, or by immersing the component in boiling water - wear protective gloves to prevent scalding or burns to the hands.

2.15 Using heat to free a seized fastener

● As a last resort, it is possible to use a hammer and cold chisel to work the fastener head unscrewed (see illustration 2.16). This will damage the fastener, but more importantly extreme care must be taken not to damage the surrounding component.

Caution: Remember that the component being secured is generally of more value than the bolt, nut or screw - when the fastener is freed, do not unscrew it with force, instead work the fastener back and forth when resistance is felt to prevent thread damage.

2.16 Using a hammer and chisel to free a seized fastener

Broken fasteners and damaged heads

● If the shank of a broken bolt or screw is accessible you can grip it with self-locking grips. The knurled wheel type stud extractor tool or self-gripping stud puller tool is particularly useful for removing the long studs which screw into the cylinder mouth surface of the crankcase or bolts and screws from which the head has broken off (see illustration 2.17). Studs can also be removed by locking two nuts together on the threaded end of the stud and using a wrench on the lower nut (see illustration 2.18).

2.17 Using a stud extractor tool to remove a broken crankcase stud

2.18 Two nuts can be locked together to unscrew a stud from a component

● A bolt or screw which has broken off below or level with the casing must be extracted using a screw extractor set. Centerpunch the fastener to centralize the drill bit, then drill a hole in the fastener (see illustration 2.19). Select a drill bit which is approximately half to three-quarters the diameter of the fastener

2.19 When using a screw extractor, first drill a hole in the fastener . . .

and drill to a depth which will accommodate the extractor. Use the largest size extractor possible, but avoid leaving too small a wall thickness otherwise the extractor will merely force the fastener walls outwards wedging it in the casing thread.

● If a spiral type extractor is used, thread it counterclockwise into the fastener. As it is screwed in, it will grip the fastener and unscrew it from the casing (see illustration 2.20).

2.20 . . . then thread the extractor counterclockwise into the fastener

● If a taper type extractor is used, tap it into the fastener so that it is firmly wedged in place. Unscrew the extractor (counter-clockwise) to draw the fastener out.

● Alternatively, the broken bolt/screw can

Warning: Stud extractors are very hard and may break off in the fastener if care is not taken - ask a machine shop about spark erosion if this happens.

be drilled out and the hole retapped for an oversize bolt/screw or a diamond-section thread insert. It is essential that the drilling is carried out squarely and to the correct depth, otherwise the casing may be ruined - if in doubt, entrust the work to a machine shop.

● Bolts and nuts with rounded corners cause the correct size wrench or socket to slip when force is applied. Of the types of wrench/socket available always use a six-point type rather than an eight or twelve-point type - better grip

2.21 Comparison of surface drive box wrench (left) with 12-point type (right)

is obtained. Surface drive wrenches grip the middle of the hex flats, rather than the corners, and are thus good in cases of damaged heads **(see illustration 2.21).**

● Slotted-head or Phillips-head screws are often damaged by the use of the wrong size screwdriver. Allen-head and Torx-head screws are much less likely to sustain damage. If enough of the screw head is exposed you can use a hacksaw to cut a slot in its head and then use a conventional flat-bladed screwdriver to remove it. Alternatively use a hammer and cold chisel to tap the head of the fastener around to loosen it. Always replace damaged fasteners with new ones, preferably Torx or Allen-head type.

HAYNES HiNT

A dab of valve grinding compound between the screw head and screwdriver tip will often give a good grip.

Thread repair

● Threads (particularly those in aluminum alloy components) can be damaged by overtightening, being assembled with dirt in the threads, or from a component working loose and vibrating. Eventually the thread will fail completely, and it will be impossible to tighten the fastener.

● If a thread is damaged or clogged with old locking compound it can be renovated with a thread repair tool (thread chaser) **(see illustrations 2.22 and 2.23);** special thread

2.22 A thread repair tool being used to correct an internal thread

chasers are available for spark plug hole threads. The tool will not cut a new thread, but clean and true the original thread. Make sure that you use the correct diameter and pitch tool. Similarly, external threads can be cleaned up with a die or a thread restorer file **(see illustration 2.24).**

2.24 Using a thread restorer file

● It is possible to drill out the old thread and retap the component to the next thread size. This will work where there is enough surrounding material and a new bolt or screw can be obtained. Sometimes, however, this is not possible - such as where the bolt/screw passes through another component which must also be suitably modified, also in cases where a spark plug or oil drain plug cannot be obtained in a larger diameter thread size.

● The diamond-section thread insert (often known by its popular trade name of Heli-Coil) is a simple and effective method of replacing the thread and retaining the original size. A kit can be purchased which contains the tap, insert and installing tool **(see illustration 2.25).** Drill out the damaged thread with the size drill specified **(see illustration 2.26).** Carefully retap the thread **(see illustration 2.27).** Install the

2.23 A thread repair tool being used to correct an external thread

2.25 Obtain a thread insert kit to suit the thread diameter and pitch required

2.26 To install a thread insert, first drill out the original thread . . .

2.27 . . . tap a new thread . . .

2.28 . . . fit insert on the installing tool . . .

2.29 . . . and thread into the component . . .

2.30 . . . break off the tang when complete

insert on the installing tool and thread it slowly into place using a light downward pressure **(see illustrations 2.28 and 2.29).** When positioned between a 1/4 and 1/2 turn below the surface withdraw the installing tool and use the break-off tool to press down on the tang, breaking it off **(see illustration 2.30).**

● There are epoxy thread repair kits on the market which can rebuild stripped internal threads, although this repair should not be used on high load-bearing components.

Thread locking and sealing compounds

● Locking compounds are used in locations where the fastener is prone to loosening due to vibration or on important safety-related items which might cause loss of control of the motorcycle if they fail. It is also used where important fasteners cannot be secured by other means such as lockwashers or cotter pins.

● Before applying locking compound, make sure that the threads (internal and external) are clean and dry with all old compound removed. Select a compound to suit the component being secured - a non-permanent general locking and sealing type is suitable for most applications, but a high strength type is needed for permanent fixing of studs in castings. Apply a drop or two of the compound to the first few threads of the fastener, then thread it into place and tighten to the specified torque. Do not apply excessive thread locking compound otherwise the thread may be damaged on subsequent removal.

● Certain fasteners are impregnated with a dry film type coating of locking compound on their threads. Always replace this type of fastener if disturbed.

● Anti-seize compounds, such as copper-based greases, can be applied to protect threads from seizure due to extreme heat and corrosion. A common instance is spark plug threads and exhaust system fasteners.

3 Measuring tools and gauges

Feeler gauges

● Feeler gauges (or blades) are used for measuring small gaps and clearances **(see illustration 3.1)**. They can also be used to measure endfloat (sideplay) of a component on a shaft where access is not possible with a dial gauge.

● Feeler gauge sets should be treated with care and not bent or damaged. They are etched with their size on one face. Keep them clean and very lightly oiled to prevent corrosion build-up.

3.1 Feeler gauges are used for measuring small gaps and clearances - thickness is marked on one face of gauge

● When measuring a clearance, select a gauge which is a light sliding fit between the two components. You may need to use two gauges together to measure the clearance accurately.

Micrometers

● A micrometer is a precision tool capable of measuring to 0.01 or 0.001 of a millimeter. It should always be stored in its case and not in the general toolbox. It must be kept clean and never dropped, otherwise its frame or measuring anvils could be distorted resulting in inaccurate readings.

● External micrometers are used for measuring outside diameters of components and have many more applications than internal micrometers. Micrometers are available in different size ranges, typically 0 to 25 mm, 25 to 50 mm, and upwards in 25 mm steps; some large micrometers have interchangeable anvils to allow a range of measurements to be taken. Generally the largest precision measurement you are likely to take on a motorcycle is the piston diameter.

● Internal micrometers (or bore micrometers) are used for measuring inside diameters, such as valve guides and cylinder bores. Telescoping gauges and small hole gauges are used in conjunction with an external micrometer, whereas the more expensive internal micrometers have their own measuring device.

External micrometer

Note: *The conventional analogue type instrument is described. Although much easier to read, digital micrometers are considerably more expensive.*

● Always check the calibration of the micrometer before use. With the anvils closed (0 to 25 mm type) or set over a test gauge

3.2 Check micrometer calibration before use

(for the larger types) the scale should read zero **(see illustration 3.2)**; make sure that the anvils (and test piece) are clean first. Any discrepancy can be adjusted by referring to the instructions supplied with the tool. Remember that the micrometer is a precision measuring tool - don't force the anvils closed, use the ratchet (4) on the end of the micrometer to close it. In this way, a measured force is always applied.

● To use, first make sure that the item being measured is clean. Place the anvil of the micrometer (1) against the item and use the thimble (2) to bring the spindle (3) lightly into contact with the other side of the item **(see illustration 3.3)**. Don't tighten the thimble down because this will damage the micrometer - instead use the ratchet (4) on the end of the micrometer. The ratchet mechanism applies a measured force preventing damage to the instrument.

● The micrometer is read by referring to the linear scale on the sleeve and the annular scale on the thimble. Read off the sleeve first to obtain the base measurement, then add the fine measurement from the thimble to obtain the overall reading. The linear scale on the sleeve represents the measuring range of the micrometer (eg 0 to 25 mm). The annular scale

3.3 Micrometer component parts

1 Anvil	3 Spindle	5 Frame
2 Thimble	4 Ratchet	6 Locking lever

on the thimble will be in graduations of 0.01 mm (or as marked on the frame) - one full revolution of the thimble will move 0.5 mm on the linear scale. Take the reading where the datum line on the sleeve intersects the thimble's scale. Always position the eye directly above the scale otherwise an inaccurate reading will result.

In the example shown the item measures 2.95 mm **(see illustration 3.4)**:

Linear scale	2.00 mm
Linear scale	0.50 mm
Annular scale	0.45 mm
Total figure	**2.95 mm**

3.4 Micrometer reading of 2.95 mm

3.5 Micrometer reading of 46.99 mm on linear and annular scales . . .

3.6 . . . and 0.004 mm on vernier scale

3.7 Expand the telescoping gauge in the bore, lock its position . . .

3.8 . . . then measure the gauge with a micrometer

Most micrometers have a locking lever (6) on the frame to hold the setting in place, allowing the item to be removed from the micrometer.
● Some micrometers have a vernier scale on their sleeve, providing an even finer measurement to be taken, in 0.001 increments of a millimeter. Take the sleeve and thimble measurement as described above, then check which graduation on the vernier scale aligns with that of the annular scale on the thimble **Note:** *The eye must be perpendicular to the scale when taking the vernier reading - if necessary rotate the body of the micrometer to ensure this.* Multiply the vernier scale figure by 0.001 and add it to the base and fine measurement figures.

In the example shown the item measures 46.994 mm **(see illustrations 3.5 and 3.6)**:

Linear scale (base)	46.000 mm
Linear scale (base)	00.500 mm
Annular scale (fine)	00.490 mm
Vernier scale	00.004 mm
Total figure	**46.994 mm**

Internal micrometer

● Internal micrometers are available for measuring bore diameters, but are expensive and unlikely to be available for home use. It is suggested that a set of telescoping gauges and small hole gauges, both of which must be used with an external micrometer, will suffice for taking internal measurements on a motorcycle.
● Telescoping gauges can be used to measure internal diameters of components. Select a gauge with the correct size range, make sure its ends are clean and insert it into the bore. Expand the gauge, then lock its position and withdraw it from the bore **(see illustration 3.7)**. Measure across the gauge ends with a micrometer **(see illustration 3.8)**.
● Very small diameter bores (such as valve guides) are measured with a small hole gauge. Once adjusted to a slip-fit inside the component, its position is locked and the gauge withdrawn for measurement with a micrometer **(see illustrations 3.9 and 3.10)**.

Vernier caliper

Note: *The conventional linear and dial gauge type instruments are described. Digital types are easier to read, but are far more expensive.*
● The vernier caliper does not provide the precision of a micrometer, but is versatile in being able to measure internal and external diameters. Some types also incorporate a depth gauge. It is ideal for measuring clutch plate friction material and spring free lengths.
● To use the conventional linear scale vernier, loosen off the vernier clamp screws (1) and set its jaws over (2), or inside (3), the item to be measured **(see illustration 3.11)**. Slide the jaw into contact, using the thumb-wheel (4) for fine movement of the sliding scale (5) then tighten the clamp screws (1). Read off the main scale (6) where the zero on the sliding scale (5) intersects it, taking the whole number to the left of the zero; this provides the base measurement. View along the sliding scale and select the division which lines up exactly

3.9 Expand the small hole gauge in the bore, lock its position . . .

3.10 . . . then measure the gauge with a micrometer

with any of the divisions on the main scale, noting that the divisions usually represents 0.02 of a millimeter. Add this fine measurement to the base measurement to obtain the total reading.

3.11 Vernier component parts (linear gauge)

1 Clamp screws
2 External jaws
3 Internal jaws
4 Thumbwheel
5 Sliding scale
6 Main scale
7 Depth gauge

In the example shown the item measures 55.92 mm **(see illustration 3.12)**:

Base measurement	55.00 mm
Fine measurement	00.92 mm
Total figure	**55.92 mm**

3.12 Vernier gauge reading of 55.92 mm

3.13 Vernier component parts (dial gauge)

1 Clamp screw
2 External jaws
3 Internal jaws
4 Thumbwheel
5 Main scale
6 Sliding scale
7 Dial gauge

● Some vernier calipers are equipped with a dial gauge for fine measurement. Before use, check that the jaws are clean, then close them fully and check that the dial gauge reads zero. If necessary adjust the gauge ring accordingly. Slacken the vernier clamp screw (1) and set its jaws over (2), or inside (3), the item to be measured **(see illustration 3.13)**. Slide the jaws into contact, using the thumbwheel (4) for fine movement. Read off the main scale (5) where the edge of the sliding scale (6) intersects it, taking the whole number to the left of the zero; this provides the base measurement. Read off the needle position on the dial gauge (7) scale to provide the fine measurement; each division represents 0.05 of a millimeter. Add this fine measurement to the base measurement to obtain the total reading.

In the example shown the item measures 55.95 mm **(see illustration 3.14)**:

Base measurement	55.00 mm
Fine measurement	00.95 mm
Total figure	**55.95 mm**

3.14 Vernier gauge reading of 55.95 mm

Plastigage

● Plastigage is a plastic material which can be compressed between two surfaces to measure the oil clearance between them. The width of the compressed Plastigage is measured against a calibrated scale to determine the clearance.

● Common uses of Plastigage are for measuring the clearance between crankshaft journal and main bearing inserts, between crankshaft journal and big-end bearing inserts, and between camshaft and bearing surfaces. The following example describes big-end oil clearance measurement.

● Handle the Plastigage material carefully to prevent distortion. Using a sharp knife, cut a length which corresponds with the width of the bearing being measured and place it carefully across the journal so that it is parallel with the shaft **(see illustration 3.15)**. Carefully install both bearing shells and the connecting rod. Without rotating the rod on the journal tighten its bolts or nuts (as applicable) to the specified torque. The connecting rod and bearings are then disassembled and the crushed Plastigage examined.

3.15 Plastigage placed across shaft journal

● Using the scale provided in the Plastigage kit, measure the width of the material to determine the oil clearance **(see illustration 3.16)**. Always remove all traces of Plastigage after use using your fingernails.

Caution: Arriving at the correct clearance demands that the assembly is torqued correctly, according to the settings and sequence (where applicable) provided by the motorcycle manufacturer.

3.16 Measuring the width of the crushed Plastigage

Dial gauge or DTI (Dial Test Indicator)

● A dial gauge can be used to accurately measure small amounts of movement. Typical uses are measuring shaft runout or shaft endfloat (sideplay) and setting piston position for ignition timing on two-strokes. A dial gauge set usually comes with a range of different probes and adapters and mounting equipment.
● The gauge needle must point to zero when at rest. Rotate the ring around its periphery to zero the gauge.
● Check that the gauge is capable of reading the extent of movement in the work. Most gauges have a small dial set in the face which records whole millimeters of movement as well as the fine scale around the face periphery which is calibrated in 0.01 mm divisions. Read off the small dial first to obtain the base measurement, then add the measurement from the fine scale to obtain the total reading.

Base measurement	1.00 mm
Fine measurement	0.48 mm
Total figure	**1.48 mm**

3.17 Dial gauge reading of 1.48 mm

In the example shown the gauge reads 1.48 mm (see illustration 3.17):
● If measuring shaft runout, the shaft must be supported in vee-blocks and the gauge mounted on a stand perpendicular to the shaft. Rest the tip of the gauge against the center of the shaft and rotate the shaft slowly while watching the gauge reading (see illustration 3.18). Take several measurements along the length of the shaft and record the

3.18 Using a dial gauge to measure shaft runout

maximum gauge reading as the amount of runout in the shaft. **Note:** *The reading obtained will be total runout at that point - some manufacturers specify that the runout figure is halved to compare with their specified runout limit.*
● Endfloat (sideplay) measurement requires that the gauge is mounted securely to the surrounding component with its probe touching the end of the shaft. Using hand pressure, push and pull on the shaft noting the maximum endfloat recorded on the gauge (see illustration 3.19).

3.19 Using a dial gauge to measure shaft endfloat

● A dial gauge with suitable adapters can be used to determine piston position BTDC on two-stroke engines for the purposes of ignition timing. The gauge, adapter and suitable length probe are installed in the place of the spark plug and the gauge zeroed at TDC. If the piston position is specified as 1.14 mm BTDC, rotate the engine back to 2.00 mm BTDC, then slowly forwards to 1.14 mm BTDC.

Cylinder compression gauges

● A compression gauge is used for measuring cylinder compression. Either the rubber-cone type or the threaded adapter type can be used. The latter is preferred to ensure a perfect seal against the cylinder head. A 0 to 300 psi (0 to 20 Bar) type gauge (for gasoline engines) will be suitable for motorcycles.
● The spark plug is removed and the gauge either held hard against the cylinder head (cone type) or the gauge adapter screwed into the cylinder head (threaded type) (see illustration 3.20). Cylinder compression is measured with the engine turning over, but not running - carry out the compression test as described in

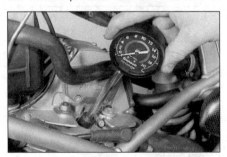

3.20 Using a rubber-cone type cylinder compression gauge

Troubleshooting Equipment. The gauge will hold the reading until manually released.

Oil pressure gauge

● An oil pressure gauge is used for measuring engine oil pressure. Most gauges come with a set of adapters to fit the thread of the take-off point (see illustration 3.21). If the take-off point specified by the motorcycle manufacturer is an external oil pipe union, make sure that the specified replacement union is used to prevent oil starvation.

3.21 Oil pressure gauge and take-off point adapter (arrow)

● Oil pressure is measured with the engine running (at a specific rpm) and often the manufacturer will specify pressure limits for a cold and hot engine.

Straight-edge and surface plate

● If checking the gasket face of a component for warpage, place a steel rule or precision straight-edge across the gasket face and measure any gap between the straight-edge and component with feeler gauges (see illustration 3.22). Check diagonally across the component and between mounting holes (see illustration 3.23).

3.22 Use a straight-edge and feeler gauges to check for warpage

3.23 Check for warpage in these directions

● Checking individual components for warpage, such as clutch plain (metal) plates, requires a perfectly flat plate or piece of plate glass and feeler gauges.

4   Torque and leverage

What is torque?

● Torque describes the twisting force around a shaft. The amount of torque applied is determined by the distance from the center of the shaft to the end of the lever and the amount of force being applied to the end of the lever; distance multiplied by force equals torque.

● The manufacturer applies a measured torque to a bolt or nut to ensure that it will not loosen in use and to hold two components securely together without movement in the joint. The actual torque setting depends on the thread size, bolt or nut material and the composition of the components being held.

● Too little torque may cause the fastener to loosen due to vibration, whereas too much torque will distort the joint faces of the component or cause the fastener to shear off. Always stick to the specified torque setting.

Using a torque wrench

● Check the calibration of the torque wrench and make sure it has a suitable range for the job. Torque wrenches are available in Nm (Newton-meters), kgf m (kilograms-force meter), lbf ft (pounds-feet), lbf in (inch-pounds). Do not confuse lbf ft with lbf in.

● Adjust the tool to the desired torque on the scale (see illustration 4.1). If your torque wrench is not calibrated in the units specified, carefully convert the figure (see *Conversion Factors*). A manufacturer sometimes gives a torque setting as a range (8 to 10 Nm) rather than a single figure - in this case set the tool midway between the two settings. The same torque may be expressed as 9 Nm ± 1 Nm. Some torque wrenches have a method of locking the setting so that it isn't inadvertently altered during use.

4.1 Set the torque wrench index mark to the setting required, in this case 12 Nm

● Install the bolts/nuts in their correct location and secure them lightly. Their threads must be clean and free of any old locking compound. Unless specified the threads and flange should be dry - oiled threads are necessary in certain circumstances and the manufacturer will take this into account in the specified torque figure. Similarly, the manufacturer may also specify the application of thread-locking compound.

● Tighten the fasteners in the specified sequence until the torque wrench clicks, indicating that the torque setting has been reached. Apply the torque again to double-check the setting. Where different thread diameter fasteners secure the component, as a rule tighten the larger diameter ones first.

● When the torque wrench has been finished with, release the lock (where applicable) and fully back off its setting to zero - do not leave the torque wrench tensioned. Also, do not use a torque wrench for loosening a fastener.

Angle-tightening

● Manufacturers often specify a figure in degrees for final tightening of a fastener. This usually follows tightening to a specific torque setting.

● A degree disc can be set and attached to the socket (see illustration 4.2) or a protractor can be used to mark the angle of movement on the bolt/nut head and the surrounding casting (see illustration 4.3).

4.2 Angle tightening can be accomplished with a torque-angle gauge . . .

4.3 . . . or by marking the angle on the surrounding component

Loosening sequences

● Where more than one bolt/nut secures a component, loosen each fastener evenly a little at a time. In this way, not all the stress of the joint is held by one fastener and the components are not likely to distort.

● If a tightening sequence is provided, work in the REVERSE of this, but if not, work from the outside in, in a criss-cross sequence (see illustration 4.4).

4.4 When loosening, work from the outside inwards

Tightening sequences

● If a component is held by more than one fastener it is important that the retaining bolts/nuts are tightened evenly to prevent uneven stress build-up and distortion of sealing faces. This is especially important on high-compression joints such as the cylinder head.

● A sequence is usually provided by the manufacturer, either in a diagram or actually marked in the casting. If not, always start in the center and work outwards in a criss-cross pattern (see illustration 4.5). Start off by securing all bolts/nuts finger-tight, then set the torque wrench and tighten each fastener by a small amount in sequence until the final torque is reached. By following this practice,

4.5 When tightening, work from the inside outwards

the joint will be held evenly and will not be distorted. Important joints, such as the cylinder head and big-end fasteners often have two- or three-stage torque settings.

Applying leverage

● Use tools at the correct angle. Position a socket or wrench on the bolt/nut so that you pull it towards you when loosening. If this can't be done, push the wrench without curling your fingers around it (see illustration 4.6) - the wrench may slip or the fastener loosen suddenly, resulting in your fingers being crushed against a component.

4.6 If you can't pull on the wrench to loosen a fastener, push with your hand open

● Additional leverage is gained by extending the length of the lever. The best way to do this is to use a breaker bar instead of the regular length tool, or to slip a length of tubing over the end of the wrench or socket.
● If additional leverage will not work, the fastener head is either damaged or firmly corroded in place (see Fasteners).

5 Bearings

Bearing removal and installation

Drivers and sockets

● Before removing a bearing, always inspect the casing to see which way it must be driven out - some casings will have retaining plates or a cast step. Also check for any identifying markings on the bearing and, if installed to a certain depth, measure this at this stage. Some roller bearings are sealed on one side - take note of the original installed position.
● Bearings can be driven out of a casing using a bearing driver tool (with the correct size head) or a socket of the correct diameter. Select the driver head or socket so that it contacts the outer race of the bearing, not the balls/rollers or inner race. Always support the casing around the bearing housing with wood blocks, otherwise there is a risk of fracture. The bearing is driven out with a few blows on the driver or socket from a heavy mallet. Unless access is severely restricted (as with wheel bearings), a pin-punch is not recommended unless it is moved around the bearing to keep it square in its housing.

● The same equipment can be used to install bearings. Make sure the bearing housing is supported on wood blocks and line up the bearing in its housing. Install the bearing as noted on removal - generally they are installed with their marked side facing outwards. Tap the bearing squarely into its housing using a driver or socket which bears only on the bearing's outer race - contact with the bearing balls/rollers or inner race will destroy it (see illustrations 5.1 and 5.2).
● Check that the bearing inner race and balls/rollers rotate freely.

5.1 Using a bearing driver against the bearing's outer race

5.2 Using a large socket against the bearing's outer race

Pullers and slide-hammers

● Where a bearing is pressed on a shaft a puller will be required to extract it (see illustration 5.3). Make sure that the puller clamp or legs fit securely behind the bearing and are unlikely to slip out. If pulling a bearing

5.3 This bearing puller clamps behind the bearing and pressure is applied to the shaft end to draw the bearing off

off a gear shaft for example, you may have to locate the puller behind a gear pinion if there is no access to the race and draw the gear pinion off the shaft as well (see illustration 5.4).

> **Caution: Ensure that the puller's center bolt locates securely against the end of the shaft and will not slip when pressure is applied. Also ensure that puller does not damage the shaft end.**

5.4 Where no access is available to the rear of the bearing, it is sometimes possible to draw off the adjacent component

● Operate the puller so that its center bolt exerts pressure on the shaft end and draws the bearing off the shaft.
● When installing the bearing on the shaft, tap only on the bearing's inner race - contact with the balls/rollers or outer race will destroy the bearing. Use a socket or length of tubing as a drift which fits over the shaft end (see illustration 5.5).

5.5 When installing a bearing on a shaft use a piece of tubing which bears only on the bearing's inner race

● Where a bearing locates in a blind hole in a casing, it cannot be driven or pulled out as described above. A slide-hammer with knife-edged bearing puller attachment will be required. The puller attachment passes through the bearing and when tightened expands to fit firmly behind the bearing (see illustration 5.6). By operating the slide-hammer part of the tool the bearing is jarred out of its housing (see illustration 5.7).
● It is possible, if the bearing is of reasonable weight, for it to drop out of its housing if the casing is heated as described opposite. If

5.6 Expand the bearing puller so that it locks behind the bearing . . .

5.7 . . . attach the slide hammer to the bearing puller

this method is attempted, first prepare a work surface which will enable the casing to be tapped face down to help dislodge the bearing - a wood surface is ideal since it will not damage the casing's gasket surface. Wearing protective gloves, tap the heated casing several times against the work surface to dislodge the bearing under its own weight **(see illustration 5.8)**.

5.8 Tapping a casing face down on wood blocks can often dislodge a bearing

● Bearings can be installed in blind holes using the driver or socket method described above.

Drawbolts

● Where a bearing or bushing is set in the eye of a component, such as a suspension linkage arm or connecting rod small-end, removal by drift may damage the component. Furthermore, a rubber bushing in a shock absorber eye cannot successfully be driven out of position. If access is available to a hydraulic press, the task is straightforward. If not, a drawbolt can be fabricated to extract the bearing or bushing.

5.9 Drawbolt component parts assembled on a suspension arm

1 *Bolt or length of threaded bar*
2 *Nuts*
3 *Washer (external diameter greater than tubing internal diameter)*
4 *Tubing (internal diameter sufficient to accommodate bearing)*
5 *Suspension arm with bearing*
6 *Tubing (external diameter slightly smaller than bearing)*
7 *Washer (external diameter slightly smaller than bearing)*

5.10 Drawing the bearing out of the suspension arm

● To extract the bearing/bushing you will need a long bolt with nut (or piece of threaded bar with two nuts), a piece of tubing which has an internal diameter larger than the bearing/ bushing, another piece of tubing which has an external diameter slightly smaller than the bearing/bushing, and a selection of washers **(see illustrations 5.9 and 5.10)**. Note that the pieces of tubing must be of the same length, or longer, than the bearing/bushing.
● The same kit (without the pieces of tubing) can be used to draw the new bearing/bushing back into place **(see illustration 5.11)**.

5.11 Installing a new bearing (1) in the suspension arm

Temperature change

● If the bearing's outer race is a tight fit in the casing, the aluminum casing can be heated to release its grip on the bearing. Aluminum will expand at a greater rate than the steel bearing outer race. There are several ways to do this, but avoid any localized extreme heat (such as a blow torch) - aluminum alloy has a low melting point.
● Approved methods of heating a casing are using a domestic oven (heated to 100°C/200°F) or immersing the casing in boiling water **(see illustration 5.12)**. Low temperature range localized heat sources such as a paint stripper heat gun or clothes iron can also be used **(see illustration 5.13)**. Alternatively, soak a rag in boiling water, wring it out and wrap it around the bearing housing.

> ⚠️ **Warning: All of these methods require care in use to prevent scalding and burns to the hands. Wear protective gloves when handling hot components.**

5.12 A casing can be immersed in a sink of boiling water to aid bearing removal

5.13 Using a localized heat source to aid bearing removal

● If heating the whole casing note that plastic components, such as the neutral switch, may suffer - remove them beforehand.
● After heating, remove the bearing as described above. You may find that the expansion is sufficient for the bearing to fall out of the casing under its own weight or with a light tap on the driver or socket.
● If necessary, the casing can be heated to aid bearing installation, and this is sometimes the recommended procedure if the motorcycle manufacturer has designed the housing and bearing fit with this intention.

● Installation of bearings can be eased by placing them in a freezer the night before installation. The steel bearing will contract slightly, allowing easy insertion in its housing. This is often useful when installing steering head outer races in the frame.

Bearing types and markings

● Plain shell bearings, ball bearings, needle roller bearings and tapered roller bearings will all be found on motorcycles **(see illustrations 5.14 and 5.15)**. The ball and roller types are usually caged between an inner and outer race, but uncaged variations may be found.

5.14 Shell bearings are either plain or grooved. They are usually identified by color code (arrow)

5.15 Tapered roller bearing (A), needle roller bearing (B) and ball journal bearing (C)

● Shell bearings (often called inserts) are usually found at the crankshaft main and connecting rod big-end where they are good at coping with high loads. They are made of a phosphor-bronze material and are impregnated with self-lubricating properties.
● Ball bearings and needle roller bearings consist of a steel inner and outer race with the balls or rollers between the races. They require constant lubrication by oil or grease and are good at coping with axial loads. Taper roller bearings consist of rollers set in a tapered cage set on the inner race; the outer race is separate. They are good at coping with axial loads and prevent movement along the shaft - a typical application is in the steering head.
● Bearing manufacturers produce bearings to ISO size standards and stamp one face of the bearing to indicate its internal and external diameter, load capacity and type **(see illustration 5.16)**.
● Metal bushings are usually of phosphor-bronze material. Rubber bushings are used in suspension mounting eyes. Fiber bushings have also been used in suspension pivots.

5.16 Typical bearing marking

Bearing troubleshooting

● If a bearing outer race has spun in its housing, the housing material will be damaged. You can use a bearing locking compound to bond the outer race in place if damage is not too severe.
● Shell bearings will fail due to damage of their working surface, as a result of lack of lubrication, corrosion or abrasive particles in the oil **(see illustration 5.17)**. Small particles of dirt in the oil may embed in the bearing material whereas larger particles will score the bearing and shaft journal. If a number of short journeys are made, insufficient heat will be generated to drive off condensation which has built up on the bearings.

5.17 Typical bearing failures

● Ball and roller bearings will fail due to lack of lubrication or damage to the balls or rollers. Tapered-roller bearings can be damaged by overloading them. Unless the bearing is sealed on both sides, wash it in kerosene to remove all old grease then allow it to dry. Make a visual inspection looking to dented balls or rollers, damaged cages and worn or pitted races **(see illustration 5.18)**.
● A ball bearing can be checked for wear by listening to it when spun. Apply a film of light oil to the bearing and hold it close to the ear - hold the outer race with one hand and spin the

5.18 Example of ball journal bearing with damaged balls and cages

5.19 Hold outer race and listen to inner race when spun

inner race with the other hand **(see illustration 5.19)**. The bearing should be almost silent when spun; if it grates or rattles it is worn.

6 Oil seals

Oil seal removal and installation

● Oil seals should be replaced every time a component is dismantled. This is because the seal lips will become set to the sealing surface and will not necessarily reseal.
● Oil seals can be pried out of position using a large flat-bladed screwdriver **(see illustration 6.1)**. In the case of crankcase seals, check first that the seal is not lipped on the inside, preventing its removal with the crankcases joined.

6.1 Pry out oil seals with a large flat-bladed screwdriver

● New seals are usually installed with their marked face (containing the seal reference code) outwards and the spring side towards the fluid being retained. In certain cases, such as a two-stroke engine crankshaft seal, a double lipped seal may be used due to there being fluid or gas on each side of the joint.

- Use a bearing driver or socket which bears only on the outer hard edge of the seal to install it in the casing - tapping on the inner edge will damage the sealing lip.

Oil seal types and markings

- Oil seals are usually of the single-lipped type. Double-lipped seals are found where a liquid or gas is on both sides of the joint.
- Oil seals can harden and lose their sealing ability if the motorcycle has been in storage for a long period - replacement is the only solution.
- Oil seal manufacturers also conform to the ISO markings for seal size - these are molded into the outer face of the seal (see illustration 6.2).

6.2 These oil seal markings indicate inside diameter, outside diameter and seal thickness

---

7 Gaskets and sealants

Types of gasket and sealant

- Gaskets are used to seal the mating surfaces between components and keep lubricants, fluids, vacuum or pressure contained within the assembly. Aluminum gaskets are sometimes found at the cylinder joints, but most gaskets are paper-based. If the mating surfaces of the components being joined are undamaged the gasket can be installed dry, although a dab of sealant or grease will be useful to hold it in place during assembly.
- RTV (Room Temperature Vulcanizing) silicone rubber sealants cure when exposed to moisture in the atmosphere. These sealants are good at filling pits or irregular gasket faces, but will tend to be forced out of the joint under very high torque. They can be used to replace a paper gasket, but first make sure that the width of the paper gasket is not essential to the shimming of internal components. RTV sealants should not be used on components containing gasoline.
- Non-hardening, semi-hardening and hard setting liquid gasket compounds can be used with a gasket or between a metal-to-metal joint. Select the sealant to suit the application: universal non-hardening sealant can be used on virtually all joints; semi-hardening on joint faces which are rough or damaged; hard setting sealant on joints which require a permanent bond and are subjected to high temperature and pressure. **Note:** *Check first if the paper gasket has a bead of sealant*

impregnated in its surface before applying additional sealant.

- When choosing a sealant, make sure it is suitable for the application, particularly if being applied in a high-temperature area or in the vicinity of fuel. Certain manufacturers produce sealants in either clear, silver or black colors to match the finish of the engine. This has a particular application on motorcycles where much of the engine is exposed.
- Do not over-apply sealant. That which is squeezed out on the outside of the joint can be wiped off, whereas an excess of sealant on the inside can break off and clog oilways.

Breaking a sealed joint

- Age, heat, pressure and the use of hard setting sealant can cause two components to stick together so tightly that they are difficult to separate using finger pressure alone. Do not resort to using levers unless there is a pry point provided for this purpose (see illustration 7.1) or else the gasket surfaces will be damaged.
- Use a soft-faced hammer (see illustration 7.2) or a wood block and conventional hammer to strike the component near the mating surface. Avoid hammering against cast extremities since they may break off. If this method fails, try using a wood wedge between the two components.

Caution: If the joint will not separate, double-check that you have removed all the fasteners.

7.1 If a pry point is provided, apply gentle pressure with a flat-bladed screwdriver

7.2 Tap around the joint with a soft-faced mallet if necessary - don't strike cooling fins

Removal of old gasket and sealant

- Paper gaskets will most likely come away complete, leaving only a few traces stuck

Most components have one or two hollow locating dowels between the two gasket faces. If a dowel cannot be removed, do not resort to gripping it with pliers - it will almost certainly be distorted. Install a close-fitting socket or Phillips screwdriver into the dowel and then grip the outer edge of the dowel to free it.

on the sealing faces of the components. It is imperative that all traces are removed to ensure correct sealing of the new gasket.
- Very carefully scrape all traces of gasket away making sure that the sealing surfaces are not gouged or scored by the scraper (see illustrations 7.3, 7.4 and 7.5). Stubborn deposits can be removed by spraying with an aerosol gasket remover. Final preparation of

7.3 Paper gaskets can be scraped off with a gasket scraper tool . . .

7.4 . . . a knife blade . . .

7.5 . . . or a household scraper

7.6 Fine abrasive paper is wrapped around a flat file to clean up the gasket face

7.7 A kitchen scourer can be used on stubborn deposits

the gasket surface can be made with very fine abrasive paper or a plastic kitchen scourer **(see illustrations 7.6 and 7.7)**.

● Old sealant can be scraped or peeled off components, depending on the type originally used. Note that gasket removal compounds are available to avoid scraping the components clean; make sure the gasket remover suits the type of sealant used.

8 Chains

Breaking and joining final drive chains

● Drive chains for all but small bikes are continuous and do not have a clip-type connecting link. The chain must be broken using a chain breaker tool and the new chain securely riveted together using a new soft rivet-type link. Never use a clip-type connecting link instead of a rivet-type link, except in an emergency. Various chain breaking and riveting tools are available, either as separate tools or combined as illustrated in the accompanying photographs - read the instructions supplied with the tool carefully.

⚠ **Warning: The need to rivet the new link pins correctly cannot be overstressed - loss of control of the motorcycle is very likely to result if the chain breaks in use.**

● Rotate the chain and look for the soft link. The soft link pins look like they have been

8.1 Tighten the chain breaker to push the pin out of the link . . .

8.2 . . . withdraw the pin, remove the tool . . .

8.3 . . . and separate the chain link

deeply center-punched instead of peened over like all the other pins **(see illustration 8.9)** and its sideplate may be a different color. Position the soft link midway between the sprockets and assemble the chain breaker tool over one of the soft link pins **(see illustration 8.1)**. Operate the tool to push the pin out through the chain **(see illustration 8.2)**. On an O-ring chain, remove the O-rings **(see illustration 8.3)**. Carry out the same procedure on the other soft link pin.

Caution: Certain soft link pins (particularly on the larger chains) may require their ends to be filed or ground off before they can be pressed out using the tool.

● Check that you have the correct size and strength (standard or heavy duty) new soft link - do not reuse the old link. Look for the size marking on the chain sideplates **(see illustration 8.10)**.
● Position the chain ends so that they are

8.4 Insert the new soft link, with O-rings, through the chain ends . . .

8.5 . . . install the O-rings over the pin ends . . .

8.6 . . . followed by the sideplate

engaged over the rear sprocket. On an O-ring chain, install a new O-ring over each pin of the link and insert the link through the two chain ends **(see illustration 8.4)**. Install a new O-ring over the end of each pin, followed by the sideplate (with the chain manufacturer's marking facing outwards) **(see illustrations 8.5 and 8.6)**. On an unsealed chain, insert the link through the two chain ends, then install the sideplate with the chain manufacturer's marking facing outwards.
● Note that it may not be possible to install the sideplate using finger pressure alone. If using a joining tool, assemble it so that the plates of the tool clamp the link and press the sideplate over the pins **(see illustration 8.7)**. Otherwise, use two small sockets placed over

8.7 Push the sideplate into position using a clamp

8.8 Assemble the chain riveting tool over one pin at a time and tighten it fully

8.9 Pin end correctly riveted (A), pin end unriveted (B)

the rivet ends and two pieces of the wood between a C-clamp. Operate the clamp to press the sideplate over the pins.

● Assemble the joining tool over one pin (following the manufacturer's instructions) and tighten the tool down to spread the pin end securely **(see illustrations 8.8 and 8.9)**. Do the same on the other pin.

> ⚠️ **Warning: Check that the pin ends are secure and that there is no danger of the sideplate coming loose. If the pin ends are cracked the soft link must be replaced.**

Final drive chain sizing

● Chains are sized using a three digit number, followed by a suffix to denote the chain type **(see illustration 8.10)**. Chain type is either standard or heavy duty (thicker sideplates), and also unsealed or O-ring/X-ring type.

● The first digit of the number relates to the pitch of the chain, ie the distance from the center of one pin to the center of the next pin **(see illustration 8.11)**. Pitch is expressed in eighths of an inch, as follows:

8.10 Typical chain size and type marking

8.11 Chain dimensions

Sizes commencing with a 4 (for example 428) have a pitch of 1/2 inch (12.7 mm)
Sizes commencing with a 5 (for example 520) have a pitch of 5/8 inch (15.9 mm)
Sizes commencing with a 6 (for example 630) have a pitch of 3/4 inch (19.1 mm)

● The second and third digits of the chain size relate to the width of the rollers, for example the 525 shown has 5/16 inch (7.94 mm) rollers **(see illustration 8.11)**.

9 Hoses

Clamping to prevent flow

● Small-bore flexible hoses can be clamped to prevent fluid flow while a component is worked on. Whichever method is used, ensure that the hose material is not permanently distorted or damaged by the clamp.
  a) A brake hose clamp available from auto parts stores **(see illustration 9.1)**.
  b) A wingnut type hose clamp **(see illustration 9.2)**.

9.1 Hoses can be clamped with an automotive brake hose clamp . . .

9.2 . . . a wingnut type hose clamp . . .

  c) Two sockets placed on each side of the hose and held with straight-jawed self-locking pliers **(see illustration 9.3)**.
  d) Thick card stock on each side of the hose held between straight-jawed self-locking pliers **(see illustration 9.4)**.

9.3 . . . two sockets and a pair of self-locking grips . . .

9.4 . . . or thick card and self-locking grips

Freeing and fitting hoses

● Always make sure the hose clamp is moved well clear of the hose end. Grip the hose with your hand and rotate it while pulling it off the union. If the hose has hardened due to age and will not move, slit it with a sharp knife and peel its ends off the union **(see illustration 9.5)**.

● Resist the temptation to use grease or soap on the unions to aid installation; although it helps the hose slip over the union it will equally aid the escape of fluid from the joint. It is preferable to soften the hose ends in hot water and wet the inside surface of the hose with water or a fluid which will evaporate.

9.5 Cutting a coolant hose free with a sharp knife

Length (distance)

Inches (in)	X	25.4	= Millimeters (mm)	X 0.0394	= Inches (in)
Feet (ft)	X	0.305	= Meters (m)	X 3.281	= Feet (ft)
Miles	X	1.609	= Kilometers (km)	X 0.621	= Miles

Volume (capacity)

Cubic inches (cu in; in³)	X	16.387	= Cubic centimeters (cc; cm³)	X 0.061	= Cubic inches (cu in; in³)
Imperial pints (Imp pt)	X	0.568	= Liters (l)	X 1.76	= Imperial pints (Imp pt)
Imperial quarts (Imp qt)	X	1.137	= Liters (l)	X 0.88	= Imperial quarts (Imp qt)
Imperial quarts (Imp qt)	X	1.201	= US quarts (US qt)	X 0.833	= Imperial quarts (Imp qt)
US quarts (US qt)	X	0.946	= Liters (l)	X 1.057	= US quarts (US qt)
Imperial gallons (Imp gal)	X	4.546	= Liters (l)	X 0.22	= Imperial gallons (Imp gal)
Imperial gallons (Imp gal)	X	1.201	= US gallons (US gal)	X 0.833	= Imperial gallons (Imp gal)
US gallons (US gal)	X	3.785	= Liters (l)	X 0.264	= US gallons (US gal)

Mass (weight)

Ounces (oz)	X	28.35	= Grams (g)	X 0.035	= Ounces (oz)
Pounds (lb)	X	0.454	= Kilograms (kg)	X 2.205	= Pounds (lb)

Force

Ounces-force (ozf; oz)	X	0.278	= Newtons (N)	X 3.6	= Ounces-force (ozf; oz)
Pounds-force (lbf; lb)	X	4.448	= Newtons (N)	X 0.225	= Pounds-force (lbf; lb)
Newtons (N)	X	0.1	= Kilograms-force (kgf; kg)	X 9.81	= Newtons (N)

Pressure

Pounds-force per square inch (psi; lbf/in²; lb/in²)	X	0.070	= Kilograms-force per square centimeter (kgf/cm²; kg/cm²)	X 14.223	= Pounds-force per square inch (psi; lbf/in²; lb/in²)
Pounds-force per square inch (psi; lbf/in²; lb/in²)	X	0.068	= Atmospheres (atm)	X 14.696	= Pounds-force per square inch (psi; lbf/in²; lb/in²)
Pounds-force per square inch (psi; lbf/in²; lb/in²)	X	0.069	= Bars	X 14.5	= Pounds-force per square inch (psi; lbf/in²; lb/in²)
Pounds-force per square inch (psi; lbf/in²; lb/in²)	X	6.895	= Kilopascals (kPa)	X 0.145	= Pounds-force per square inch (psi; lbf/in²; lb/in²)
Kilopascals (kPa)	X	0.01	= Kilograms-force per square centimeter (kgf/cm²; kg/cm²)	X 98.1	= Kilopascals (kPa)

Torque (moment of force)

Pounds-force inches (lbf in; lb in)	X	1.152	= Kilograms-force centimeter (kgf cm; kg cm)	X 0.868	= Pounds-force inches (lbf in; lb in)
Pounds-force inches (lbf in; lb in)	X	0.113	= Newton meters (Nm)	X 8.85	= Pounds-force inches (lbf in; lb in)
Pounds-force inches (lbf in; lb in)	X	0.083	= Pounds-force feet (lbf ft; lb ft)	X 12	= Pounds-force inches (lbf in; lb in)
Pounds-force feet (lbf ft; lb ft)	X	0.138	= Kilograms-force meters (kgf m; kg m)	X 7.233	= Pounds-force feet (lbf ft; lb ft)
Pounds-force feet (lbf ft; lb ft)	X	1.356	= Newton meters (Nm)	X 0.738	= Pounds-force feet (lbf ft; lb ft)
Newton meters (Nm)	X	0.102	= Kilograms-force meters (kgf m; kg m)	X 9.804	= Newton meters (Nm)

Vacuum

Inches mercury (in. Hg)	X	3.377	= Kilopascals (kPa)	X 0.2961	= Inches mercury
Inches mercury (in. Hg)	X	25.4	= Millimeters mercury (mm Hg)	X 0.0394	= Inches mercury

Power

Horsepower (hp)	X	745.7	= Watts (W)	X 0.0013	= Horsepower (hp)

Velocity (speed)

Miles per hour (miles/hr; mph)	X	1.609	= Kilometers per hour (km/hr; kph)	X 0.621	= Miles per hour (miles/hr; mph)

Fuel consumption*

Miles per gallon, Imperial (mpg)	X	0.354	= Kilometers per liter (km/l)	X 2.825	= Miles per gallon, Imperial (mpg)
Miles per gallon, US (mpg)	X	0.425	= Kilometers per liter (km/l)	X 2.352	= Miles per gallon, US (mpg)

Temperature

Degrees Fahrenheit = (°C x 1.8) + 32   Degrees Celsius (Degrees Centigrade; °C) = (°F - 32) x 0.56

It is common practice to convert from miles per gallon (mpg) to liters/100 kilometers (l/100km), where mpg (Imperial) x l/100 km = 282 and mpg (US) x l/100 km = 235

Fraction/decimal/millimeter equivalents

DECIMALS to MILLIMETERS

Decimal	mm	Decimal	mm
0.001	0.0254	0.500	12.7000
0.002	0.0508	0.510	12.9540
0.003	0.0762	0.520	13.2080
0.004	0.1016	0.530	13.4620
0.005	0.1270	0.540	13.7160
0.006	0.1524	0.550	13.9700
0.007	0.1778	0.560	14.2240
0.008	0.2032	0.570	14.4780
0.009	0.2286	0.580	14.7320
0.010	0.2540	0.590	14.9860
0.020	0.5080		
0.030	0.7620		
0.040	1.0160	0.600	15.2400
0.050	1.2700	0.610	15.4940
0.060	1.5240	0.620	15.7480
0.070	1.7780	0.630	16.0020
0.080	2.0320	0.640	16.2560
0.090	2.2860	0.650	16.5100
0.100	2.5400	0.660	16.7640
0.110	2.7940	0.670	17.0180
0.120	3.0480	0.680	17.2720
0.130	3.3020	0.690	17.5260
0.140	3.5560		
0.150	3.8100	0.700	17.7800
0.160	4.0640	0.710	18.0340
0.170	4.3180	0.720	18.2880
0.180	4.5720	0.730	18.5420
0.190	4.8260	0.740	18.7960
0.200	5.0800	0.750	19.0500
0.210	5.3340	0.760	19.3040
0.220	5.5880	0.770	19.5580
0.230	5.8420	0.780	19.8120
0.240	6.0960	0.790	20.0660
0.250	6.3500		
0.260	6.6040	0.800	20.3200
0.270	6.8580	0.810	20.5740
0.280	7.1120	0.820	21.8280
0.290	7.3660	0.830	21.0820
0.300	7.6200	0.840	21.3360
0.310	7.8740	0.850	21.5900
0.320	8.1280	0.860	21.8440
0.330	8.3820	0.870	22.0980
0.340	8.6360	0.880	22.3520
0.350	8.8900	0.890	22.6060
0.360	9.1440		
0.370	9.3980		
0.380	9.6520	0.900	22.8600
0.390	9.9060	0.910	23.1140
0.400	10.1600	0.920	23.3680
0.410	10.4140	0.930	23.6220
0.420	10.6680	0.940	23.8760
0.430	10.9220	0.950	24.1300
0.440	11.1760	0.960	24.3840
0.450	11.4300	0.970	24.6380
0.460	11.6840	0.980	24.8920
0.470	11.9380	0.990	25.1460
0.480	12.1920	1.000	25.4000
0.490	12.4460		

FRACTIONS to DECIMALS to MILLIMETERS

Fraction	Decimal	mm	Fraction	Decimal	mm
1/64	0.0156	0.3969	33/64	0.5156	13.0969
1/32	0.0312	0.7938	17/32	0.5312	13.4938
3/64	0.0469	1.1906	35/64	0.5469	13.8906
1/16	0.0625	1.5875	9/16	0.5625	14.2875
5/64	0.0781	1.9844	37/64	0.5781	14.6844
3/32	0.0938	2.3812	19/32	0.5938	15.0812
7/64	0.1094	2.7781	39/64	0.6094	15.4781
1/8	0.1250	3.1750	5/8	0.6250	15.8750
9/64	0.1406	3.5719	41/64	0.6406	16.2719
5/32	0.1562	3.9688	21/32	0.6562	16.6688
11/64	0.1719	4.3656	43/64	0.6719	17.0656
3/16	0.1875	4.7625	11/16	0.6875	17.4625
13/64	0.2031	5.1594	45/64	0.7031	17.8594
7/32	0.2188	5.5562	23/32	0.7188	18.2562
15/64	0.2344	5.9531	47/64	0.7344	18.6531
1/4	0.2500	6.3500	3/4	0.7500	19.0500
17/64	0.2656	6.7469	49/64	0.7656	19.4469
9/32	0.2812	7.1438	25/32	0.7812	19.8438
19/64	0.2969	7.5406	51/64	0.7969	20.2406
5/16	0.3125	7.9375	13/16	0.8125	20.6375
21/64	0.3281	8.3344	53/64	0.8281	21.0344
11/32	0.3438	8.7312	27/32	0.8438	21.4312
23/64	0.3594	9.1281	55/64	0.8594	21.8281
3/8	0.3750	9.5250	7/8	0.8750	22.2250
25/64	0.3906	9.9219	57/64	0.8906	22.6219
13/32	0.4062	10.3188	29/32	0.9062	23.0188
27/64	0.4219	10.7156	59/64	0.9219	23.4156
7/16	0.4375	11.1125	15/16	0.9375	23.8125
29/64	0.4531	11.5094	61/64	0.9531	24.2094
15/32	0.4688	11.9062	31/32	0.9688	24.6062
31/64	0.4844	12.3031	63/64	0.9844	25.0031
1/2	0.5000	12.7000	1	1.0000	25.4000

Preparing for storage

Before you start

If repairs or an overhaul is needed, see that this is carried out now rather than left until you want to ride the vehicle again.

Give the vehicle a good wash and scrub all dirt from its underside. Make sure the vehicle dries completely before preparing for storage.

Engine

● Remove the spark plug and lubricate the cylinder bore with approximately a teaspoon of motor oil using a spout-type oil can (see illustration 1). Reinstall the spark plug. Crank the engine over a couple of times to coat the piston rings and bores with oil. If the machine has a recoil starter, use this to turn the engine over. If not, flick the kill switch to the OFF position and crank the engine over on the starter (see illustration 2). If the nature of the ignition system prevents the starter operating with the kill switch in the OFF position, remove the spark plug and fit it back in its cap; ensure

that the plug is grounded against the cylinder head when the starter is operated (see illustration 3).

> ⚠️ **Warning: It is important that the plug is grounded away from the spark plug hole otherwise there is a risk of atomized fuel from the cylinder igniting.**

> **HAYNES HINT**
> On a single cylinder four-stroke engine, you can seal the combustion chamber completely by positioning the piston at TDC on the compression stroke.

● Drain the carburetor otherwise there is a risk of jets becoming blocked by gum deposits from the fuel (see illustration 4).

● If the machine is going into long-term storage, consider adding a fuel stabilizer to the fuel in the tank. If the tank is drained completely, and it's a metal tank, corrosion of its internal surfaces may occur if left unprotected for a long period. The tank can be treated with a rust preventative especially for this purpose. Alternatively, remove the tank and pour half a liter of motor oil into it, install the filler cap and shake the tank to coat its internals with oil before draining off the excess. The same effect can also be achieved by spraying WD40 or a similar water-dispersant around the inside of the tank via its flexible nozzle.

● Make sure the cooling system contains the correct mix of antifreeze. Antifreeze also contains important corrosion inhibitors.

● The air intakes and exhaust can be sealed off by covering or plugging the openings. Ensure that you do not seal in any condensation; run the engine until it is

Squirt a drop of motor oil into each cylinder

Flick the kill switch to OFF . . .

. . . and ensure that the metal bodies of the plugs (arrows) are grounded against the cylinder head

Connect a hose to the carburetor float chamber drain stub (arrow) and unscrew the drain screw

Exhausts can be sealed off with a plastic bag

Disconnect the negative lead (A) first, followed by the positive lead (B)

hot, then switch off and allow to cool. Tape a piece of thick plastic over the silencer end **(see illustration 5)**. Note that some advocate pouring a tablespoon of motor oil into the silencer before sealing them off.

Battery

● Remove it from the machine - in extreme cases of cold the battery may freeze and crack its case **(see illustration 6)**.
● Check the electrolyte level and top up if necessary (conventional refillable batteries). Clean the terminals.
● Store the battery off the vehicle and away from any sources of fire. Position a wooden block under the battery if it is to sit on the ground.
● Give the battery a trickle charge for a few hours every month or keep it on a maintenance charger **(see illustration 7)**.

Tires

● Place the machine on jackstands; not only will this protect the tires, but will also ensure that no load is placed on the suspension bushings or wheel bearings.

Pivots and controls

● Lubricate all lever, pedal, stand and footrest pivot points. If grease nipples are fitted to the suspension components, apply lubricant to the pivots.
● Lubricate all control cables.

Other components

● Apply a wax protectant to all painted and plastic components. Wipe off any excess, but don't polish to a shine. Where fitted, clean the screen with soap and water.
● Coat metal parts with Vaseline (petroleum jelly).
● Apply a vinyl cleaner to the seat.

Storage conditions

● Aim to store the machine in a shed or garage which does not leak and is free from damp.

Use a suitable battery charger - this kit also assesses battery condition

● Drape an old blanket or bedspread over the vehicle to protect it from dust and direct contact with sunlight (which will fade paint).

Getting back on the road

Engine and transmission

● Change the oil and replace the oil filter. If this was done prior to storage, check that the oil hasn't emulsified - a thick whitish substance which occurs through condensation.
● Remove the spark plug. Using a spout-type oil can, squirt a few drops of oil into the cylinder. This will provide initial lubrication as the piston rings and bore come back into contact. Service the spark plug, or buy a new one, and install it in the engine.

● Check that the clutch isn't stuck on. The plates can stick together if left standing for some time, preventing clutch operation. Engage a gear and try rocking the machine back and forth with the clutch lever held against the handlebar. If this doesn't work on cable-operated clutches, hold the clutch lever back against the handlebar with a strong rubber band or cable tie for a couple of hours **(see illustration 8)**.
● If the air intakes or silencer end(s) were blocked off, remove the plug or cover used.

Hold the clutch lever back against the handlebar with rubber bands or a cable tie

REF•26 Storage

● If the fuel tank was coated with a rust preventative, oil or a stabilizer added to the fuel, drain and flush the tank and dispose of the fuel sensibly. If no action was taken with the fuel tank prior to storage, it is advised that the old fuel is disposed of since it will go bad over a period of time. Refill the fuel tank with fresh fuel.

Frame and running gear
● Oil all pivot points and cables.
● Check the tire pressures.
● Lubricate the final drive chain (where applicable).
● Check that the brakes operate correctly. Apply each brake hard and check that it's not possible to move the vehicle forwards, then check that the brake frees off again once released. Brake caliper pistons can stick due to corrosion around the piston head, or on the sliding caliper types, due to corrosion of the slider pins. If the brake doesn't free after repeated operation, take the caliper off for examination. Similarly drum brakes can stick due to a seized operating cam, cable or rod linkage.
● If the vehicle has been in long-term storage, replace the brake fluid and clutch fluid (where applicable).
● Depending on where the vehicle has been stored, the wiring, cables and hoses may have been nibbled by rodents. Make a visual check and investigate disturbed wiring loom tape.

Battery
● If the battery has been previously removed and given top up charges it can simply be reconnected. Remember to connect the positive cable first and the negative cable last.
● On conventional refillable batteries, if the battery has not received any attention, remove it from the vehicle and check its electrolyte level. Top up if necessary then charge the battery. If the battery fails to hold a charge and a visual check show heavy white sulfation of the plates, the battery is probably defective and must be replaced. This is particularly likely if the battery is old. Confirm battery condition with a specific gravity check.
● On sealed (MF) batteries, if the battery has not received any attention, remove it from the machine and charge it according to the information on the battery case - if the battery fails to hold a charge it must be replaced.

Starting procedure
● If a recoil starter is fitted, turn the engine over a couple of times with the ignition OFF to distribute oil around the engine. If no recoil starter is fitted, flick the engine kill switch OFF and the ignition ON and crank the engine over a couple of times to work oil around the upper cylinder components. If the nature of the ignition system is such that the starter won't work with the kill switch OFF, remove the

spark plug, fit it back into its cap and ground its body on the cylinder head. Reinstall the spark plug afterwards.

 Warning: It is important that the plug is grounded away from the spark plug hole otherwise there is a risk of atomized fuel from the cylinder igniting.

● Switch the kill switch to RUN, operate the choke and start the engine. If the engine won't start don't continue cranking the engine - not only will this flatten the battery, but the starter motor will overheat. Switch the ignition off and try again later. If the engine refuses to start, go through the troubleshooting procedures in this manual. **Note:** *If the machine has been in storage for a long time, old fuel or a carburetor blockage may be the problem. Gum deposits in carburetors can block jets - if a carburetor cleaner doesn't prove successful the carburetors must be dismantled for cleaning.*
● Once the engine has started, check that the lights and horn work properly.
● Treat the machine gently for the first ride and check all fluid levels on completion. Settle the machine back into the maintenance schedule.

This Section provides an easy reference-guide to the more common faults that are likely to afflict your machine. Obviously, the opportunities are almost limitless for faults to occur as a result of obscure failures, and to try and cover all eventualities would require a book. Indeed, a number have been written on the subject.

Successful troubleshooting is not a mysterious art but the application of a bit of knowledge combined with a systematic and logical approach to the problem. Approach any troubleshooting by first accurately identifying the symptom and then checking through the list of possible causes, starting with the simplest or most obvious and progressing in stages to the most complex. Take nothing for granted, but above all apply liberal quantities of common sense.

The main symptom of a fault is given in the text as a major heading below which are listed the various systems or areas which may contain the fault. Details of each possible cause for a fault and the remedial action to be taken are given. Further information should be sought in the relevant Chapter.

1 Engine doesn't start or is difficult to start

- ☐ Starter motor doesn't rotate
- ☐ Starter motor rotates but engine does not turn over
- ☐ Starter works but engine won't turn over (seized)
- ☐ No fuel flow
- ☐ Engine flooded
- ☐ No spark or weak spark
- ☐ Compression low
- ☐ Stalls after starting
- ☐ Rough idle

2 Poor running at low speed

- ☐ Spark weak
- ☐ Fuel/air mixture incorrect
- ☐ Compression low
- ☐ Poor acceleration

3 Poor running or no power at high speed

- ☐ Firing incorrect
- ☐ Fuel/air mixture incorrect
- ☐ Compression low
- ☐ Knocking or pinging
- ☐ Miscellaneous causes

4 Overheating

- ☐ Engine overheats
- ☐ Firing incorrect
- ☐ Fuel/air mixture incorrect
- ☐ Compression too high
- ☐ Engine load excessive
- ☐ Lubrication inadequate
- ☐ Miscellaneous causes

5 Clutch problems

- ☐ Clutch slipping
- ☐ Clutch not disengaging completely

6 Gear shifting problems

- ☐ Doesn't go into gear, or lever doesn't return
- ☐ Jumps out of gear
- ☐ Overshifts

7 Abnormal engine noise

- ☐ Knocking or pinging
- ☐ Piston slap or rattling
- ☐ Valve noise
- ☐ Other noise

8 Abnormal driveline noise

- ☐ Clutch noise
- ☐ Transmission noise
- ☐ Final drive noise

9 Abnormal chassis noise

- ☐ Suspension noise
- ☐ Driveaxle noise (4WD models)
- ☐ Brake noise

10 Oil temperature indicator light comes on

- ☐ Engine lubrication system
- ☐ Electrical system

11 Excessive exhaust smoke

- ☐ White smoke
- ☐ Black smoke
- ☐ Brown smoke

12 Poor handling or stability

- ☐ Handlebar hard to turn
- ☐ Handlebar shakes or vibrates excessively
- ☐ Handlebar pulls to one side
- ☐ Poor shock absorbing qualities

13 Braking problems

- ☐ Front brakes are spongy, don't hold
- ☐ Brake lever pulsates
- ☐ Brakes drag

14 Electrical problems

- ☐ Battery dead or weak
- ☐ Battery overcharged

1 Engine doesn't start or is difficult to start

Starter motor does not rotate

- [ ] Engine kill switch Off.
- [ ] Fuse blown. Check fuse (Chapter 5).
- [ ] Battery voltage low. Check and recharge battery (Chapter 5).
- [ ] Starter motor defective. Make sure the wiring to the starter is secure. Test starter relay (Chapter 5). If the relay is good, then the fault is in the wiring or motor.
- [ ] Starter relay faulty. Check it according to the procedure in Chapter 5.
- [ ] Starter switch not contacting. The contacts could be wet, corroded or dirty. Disassemble and clean the switch (Chapter 5).
- [ ] Wiring open or shorted. Check all wiring connections and harnesses to make sure that they are dry, tight and not corroded. Also check for broken or frayed wires that can cause a short to ground (see Wiring Diagrams at the end of this manual).
- [ ] Ignition (main key) switch defective. Check the switch according to the procedure in Chapter 5. Replace the switch with a new one if it is defective.
- [ ] Engine kill switch defective. Check for wet, dirty or corroded contacts. Clean or replace the switch as necessary (Chapter 5).
- [ ] Starting circuit cut-off relay (700), neutral switch or reverse switch defective. Check the switches according to the procedure in Chapter 5. Replace the switch with a new one if it is defective.

Starter motor rotates but engine does not turn over

- [ ] Starter motor clutch defective. Inspect and repair or replace (Chapter 5).
- [ ] Damaged starter reduction gears. Inspect and replace the damaged parts (Chapter 5).

Starter works but engine won't turn over (seized)

- [ ] Seized engine caused by one or more internally damaged components. Failure due to wear, abuse or lack of lubrication. Damage can include seized valves, valve lifters, camshaft, piston, crankshaft, connecting rod bearings, or transmission gears or bearings. Refer to Chapter 2 for engine disassembly.

No fuel flow

- [ ] No fuel in tank.
- [ ] Tank cap air vent or breather hose obstructed. Usually caused by dirt or water. Remove it and clean the cap vent hole.
- [ ] Clogged strainer in fuel tap (carbureted models). Remove and clean the strainer (Chapter 1).
- [ ] Fuel line clogged. Disconnect the fuel line and carefully blow through it.
- [ ] Inlet needle valve clogged (carbureted models). A very bad batch of fuel with an unusual additive may have been used, or some other foreign material has entered the tank. Many times after a machine has been stored for many months without running, the fuel turns to a varnish-like liquid and forms deposits on the inlet needle valve and jets. The carburetors should be removed and overhauled if draining the float chamber doesn't solve the problem.
- [ ] Fuel pump or pressure regulator defective or fuel filter clogged (fuel injected models). See Chapter 4B.

Engine flooded

- [ ] Float level too high (carbureted models). Check as described in Chapter 4A and replace the float if necessary.
- [ ] Inlet needle valve worn or stuck open (carbureted models). A piece of dirt, rust or other debris can cause the inlet needle to seat improperly, causing excess fuel to be admitted to the float bowl. In this case, the float chamber should be cleaned and the needle and seat inspected. If the needle and seat are worn, then the leaking will persist and the parts should be replaced with new ones (Chapter 4A).
- [ ] Starting technique incorrect (carbureted models). Under normal circumstances (if all the carburetor functions are sound) the machine should start with little or no throttle. When the engine is cold, the choke should be operated and the engine started without opening the throttle. When the engine is at operating temperature, only a very slight amount of throttle should be necessary. If the engine is flooded, turn the fuel tap off and hold the throttle open while cranking the engine. This will allow additional air to reach the cylinder. Remember to turn the fuel tap back on after the engine starts.
- [ ] Injector needle valve worn or stuck open (fuel injected models). A piece of dirt, rust or other debris can cause the needle to seat improperly, causing excess fuel to be admitted to the throttle body. If the engine is hard to start after sitting overnight, the injector may be slowly leaking fuel into the engine. The injector should be cleaned and the needle and seat inspected (see Chapter 4B). If the needle and seat are worn, the injector should be replaced.
- [ ] Starting technique incorrect (fuel injected models). Under normal circumstances (if all the components of the fuel injection system are good), the engine should start with the throttle closed.

1 Engine doesn't start or is difficult to start (continued)

No spark or weak spark

☐ Ignition switch Off.

☐ Engine kill switch turned to the Off position.

☐ Battery voltage low. Check and recharge battery as necessary (Chapter 5).

☐ Spark plug dirty, defective or worn out. Locate reason for fouled plug using spark plug condition chart and follow the plug maintenance procedures in Chapter 1.

☐ Spark plug cap or plug wire faulty. Check condition. Replace either or both components if cracks or deterioration are evident (see Chapter 5).

☐ Spark plug cap not making good contact. Make sure the cap is securely attached to the plug wire and fits securely over the top of the spark plug.

☐ CDI pulse generator (carbureted models) or crankshaft position sensor (fuel injected models) defective. Check the unit, referring to Chapter 5 (carbureted models) or Chapter 4B (fuel injected models).

☐ CDI unit (carbureted models) or ECU (fuel injected models) defective. Check the unit, referring to Chapter 5 (carbureted models) or Chapter 4B (fuel injected models).

☐ Ignition coil defective. Check the coil, referring to Chapter 5.

☐ Main key switch or kill switch shorted. This is usually caused by water, corrosion, damage or excessive wear. The kill switch can be disassembled and cleaned with electric contact cleaner. If cleaning doesn't help, replace the switches (see Chapter 5).

☐ Wiring shorted or broken between:

    a) *Main key switch or engine kill switch*

    b) *CDI unit (carbureted models) or ECU (fuel injected models) and engine kill switch*

    c) *CDI unit (carbureted models) or ECU (fuel injected models) and ignition coil*

    d) *Ignition coil and spark plug*

    e) *CDI unit and pick-up coil (carbureted models) or crankshaft position sensor and ECU (fuel injected models)*

Compression low

☐ Spark plug loose. Remove the plug and inspect the threads. Reinstall and tighten to the specified torque (Chapter 1).

☐ Cylinder head not sufficiently tightened down. If the cylinder head is suspected of being loose, then there's a chance that the gasket or head is damaged if the problem has persisted for any length of time. The head nuts and bolts should be tightened to the proper torque in the correct sequence (Chapter 2).

☐ Improper valve clearance. This means that the valve is not closing completely and compression pressure is leaking past the valve. Check and adjust the valve clearances (Chapter 1).

☐ Cylinder and/or piston worn. Excessive wear will cause compression pressure to leak past the rings. This is usually accompanied by worn rings as well. A top end overhaul is necessary (Chapter 2).

☐ Piston rings worn, weak, broken, or sticking. Broken or sticking piston rings usually indicate a lubrication or carburetion problem that causes excess carbon deposits or seizures to form on the pistons and rings. Top end overhaul is necessary (Chapter 2).

☐ Piston ring-to-groove clearance excessive. This is caused by excessive wear of the piston ring lands. Piston replacement is necessary (Chapter 2).

☐ Cylinder head gasket damaged. If the head is allowed to become loose, or if excessive carbon build-up on a piston crown and combustion chamber causes extremely high compression, the head gasket may leak. Retorquing the head is not always sufficient to restore the seal, so gasket replacement is necessary (Chapter 2).

☐ Cylinder head warped. This is caused by overheating or improperly tightened head nuts and bolts. Machine shop resurfacing or head replacement is necessary (Chapter 2).

☐ Valve spring broken or weak. Caused by component failure or wear; the spring(s) must be replaced (Chapter 2).

☐ Valve not seating properly. This is caused by a bent valve (from over-revving or improper valve adjustment), burned valve or seat (improper carburetion) or an accumulation of carbon deposits on the seat (from carburetion or lubrication problems). The valves must be cleaned and/or replaced and the seats serviced if possible (Chapter 2).

Stalls after starting

☐ Improper choke action (carbureted models). Make sure the choke lever is getting a full stroke and staying in the out position.

☐ Ignition malfunction. See Chapter 5.

☐ Carburetor malfunction (carbureted models). See Chapter 4A.

☐ Fuel contaminated. The fuel can be contaminated with either dirt or water, or can change chemically if the machine is allowed to sit for several months or more. Drain the tank and float bowl and refill with fresh fuel (Chapter 4).

☐ Intake air leak. Check for a loose joint between the carburetor or throttle body and intake manifold. On a carbureted model, check for a loose carburetor top. On a fuel injected model, check the intake air pressure sensor hose for cracks or a loose fit.

☐ Engine idle speed incorrect. Refer to Chapter 1 and adjust the idle speed.

Rough idle

☐ Ignition malfunction. See Chapter 5.

☐ Idle speed incorrect. See Chapter 1.

☐ Carburetor or fuel injection system malfunction. See Chapter 4.

☐ Idle fuel/air mixture incorrect. See Chapter 4.

☐ Fuel contaminated. The fuel can be contaminated with either dirt or water, or can change chemically if the machine is allowed to sit for several months or more. Drain the tank and fuel system (Chapter 4).

☐ Intake air leak. Check for a loose joint between the carburetor or throttle body and intake manifold. On a carbureted model, check for a loose carburetor top. On a fuel injected model, check the intake air pressure sensor hose for cracks or a loose fit.

☐ Air filter clogged. Service or replace the air filter element (Chapter 1).

2 Poor running at low speed

Spark weak

☐ Battery voltage low. Check and recharge battery (Chapter 5).
☐ Spark plug fouled, defective or worn out. Refer to Chapter 1 for spark plug maintenance.
☐ Spark plug cap or plug wire defective. Refer to Chapters 1 and 5 for details on the ignition system.
☐ Spark plug cap not making contact.
☐ Incorrect spark plug. Wrong type, heat range or cap configuration. Check and install correct plug listed in Chapter 1. A cold plug or one with a recessed firing electrode will not operate at low speeds without fouling.
☐ CDI unit or ECU defective. See Chapter 4A or 5.
☐ CDI pick-up coil or crankshaft position sensor defective. See Chapter 4A or 5.
☐ Ignition coil defective. See Chapter 5.

Fuel/air mixture incorrect

☐ Pilot screw out of adjustment (carbureted models) (Chapter 4).
☐ Pilot jet or air passage clogged (carbureted models). Remove and overhaul the carburetor (Chapter 4).
☐ Air bleed holes clogged (carbureted models). Remove carburetor and blow out all passages (Chapter 4).
☐ Air cleaner clogged, poorly sealed or missing.
☐ Air cleaner-to-carburetor boot poorly sealed (carbureted models). Look for cracks, holes or loose clamps and replace or repair defective parts.
☐ Float level too high or too low (carbureted models). Check and replace the float if necessary (Chapter 4).
☐ Fuel tank air vent obstructed. Make sure that the air vent passage in the filler cap is open.
☐ Carburetor or throttle body intake joint loose. Check for cracks, breaks, tears or loose clamps or bolts. Repair or replace the rubber boot and its O-ring (if equipped).

Compression low

☐ Spark plug loose. Remove the plug and inspect the threads. Reinstall and tighten to the specified torque (Chapter 1).
☐ Cylinder head not sufficiently tightened down. If the cylinder head is suspected of being loose, then there's a chance that the gasket and head are damaged if the problem has persisted for any length of time. The head nuts and bolts should be tightened to the proper torque in the correct sequence (Chapter 2).
☐ Improper valve clearance. This means that the valve is not closing completely and compression pressure is leaking past the valve. Check and adjust the valve clearances (Chapter 1).
☐ Cylinder and/or piston worn. Excessive wear will cause compression pressure to leak past the rings. This is usually accompanied by worn rings as well. A top end overhaul is necessary (Chapter 2).
☐ Piston rings worn, weak, broken, or sticking. Broken or sticking piston rings usually indicate a lubrication or carburetion problem that causes excess carbon deposits or seizures to form on the pistons and rings. Top end overhaul is necessary (Chapter 2).
☐ Piston ring-to-groove clearance excessive. This is caused by excessive wear of the piston ring lands. Piston replacement is necessary (Chapter 2).
☐ Cylinder head gasket damaged. If the head is allowed to become loose, or if excessive carbon build-up on the piston crown and combustion chamber causes extremely high compression, the head gasket may leak. Retorquing the head is not always sufficient to restore the seal, so gasket replacement is necessary (Chapter 2).
☐ Cylinder head warped. This is caused by overheating or improperly tightened head nuts and bolts. Machine shop resurfacing or head replacement is necessary (Chapter 2).
☐ Valve spring broken or weak. Caused by component failure or wear; the spring(s) must be replaced (Chapter 2).
☐ Valve not seating properly. This is caused by a bent valve (from over-revving or improper valve adjustment), burned valve or seat (improper carburetion) or an accumulation of carbon deposits on the seat (from carburetion, lubrication problems). The valves must be cleaned and/or replaced and the seats serviced if possible (Chapter 2).

Poor acceleration

☐ Carburetor leaking or dirty (carbureted models). Overhaul the carburetor (Chapter 4A).
☐ Timing not advancing. The CDI magneto or the CDI unit may be defective. If so, they must be replaced with new ones, as they can't be repaired.
☐ Engine oil viscosity too high. Using a heavier oil than that recommended in Chapter 1 can damage the oil pump or lubrication system and cause drag on the engine.
☐ Brakes dragging. Usually caused by debris which has entered the brake piston sealing boots, corroded wheel calipers or from a warped disc or bent axle. Repair as necessary (Chapter 7).
☐ Timing not advancing (fuel injected models). The crankshaft position sensor or ECU may be at fault (see Chapter 4B).

3 Poor running or no power at high speed

Firing incorrect

☐ Air cleaner restricted. Clean or replace element (Chapter 1).
☐ Spark plug fouled, defective or worn out. See Chapter 1 for spark plug maintenance.
☐ Spark plug cap or secondary (HT) wiring defective. See Chapters 1 and 5 for details of the ignition system.
☐ Spark plug cap not in good contact. See Chapter 5.
☐ Incorrect spark plug. Wrong type, heat range or cap configuration. Check and install correct plugs listed in Chapter 1. A cold plug or one with a recessed firing electrode will not operate at low speeds without fouling.
☐ CDI unit or CDI magneto defective. See Chapter 5.
☐ Ignition coil defective. See Chapter 5.

Fuel/air mixture incorrect (carbureted models)

☐ Pilot screw out of adjustment. See Chapter 4A for adjustment procedures.
☐ Main jet clogged. Dirt, water or other contaminants can clog the main jets. Clean the fuel tap strainer and in-tank strainer, the float bowl area, and the jets and carburetor orifices (Chapter 4A).
☐ Main jet wrong size. The standard jetting is for sea level atmospheric pressure and oxygen content. See Chapter 4A for high altitude adjustments.
☐ Throttle shaft-to-carburetor body clearance excessive. Refer to Chapter 4A for inspection and part replacement procedures.
☐ Air bleed holes clogged. Remove and overhaul carburetor (Chapter 4A).
☐ Air cleaner clogged, poorly sealed, or missing.
☐ Air cleaner-to-carburetor boot poorly sealed. Look for cracks, holes or loose clamps, and replace or repair defective parts.
☐ Float level too high or too low. Check float level and replace the float if necessary (Chapter 4A).
☐ Fuel tank air vent obstructed. Make sure the air vent passage in the filler cap is open.
☐ Carburetor intake joint loose. Check for cracks, breaks, tears or loose clamps or bolts. Repair or replace the rubber boots (Chapter 4A).
☐ Fuel tap clogged. Remove the tap and clean it (Chapter 1).
☐ Fuel line clogged. Pull the fuel line loose and carefully blow through it.

Fuel/air mixture incorrect (fuel injected models)

☐ Fuel tank vent hose or fitting obstructed.
☐ Fuel pump or pressure regulator faulty, or the fuel filter is blocked (see Chapter 4B).
☐ Fuel hose clogged. Remove the fuel hose (see Chapter 4B) and blow air through it.
☐ Fuel rail or injector clogged. Check the fuel pump. If the machine has been unused for several months, the fuel turns to a varnish-like liquid that can cause an injector needle to stick to its seat. Drain the tank and fuel system (see Chapter 4B).
☐ Intake air leak. Check for a loose connection between the throttle body and intake manifold, and check the intake air pressure sensor hose for leaks or a loose fit.
☐ Air filter clogged. Clean the air filter element or replace it with a new one (see Chapter 1).

Compression low

☐ Spark plug loose. Remove the plug and inspect the threads. Reinstall and tighten to the specified torque (Chapter 1).
☐ Cylinder head not sufficiently tightened down. If the cylinder head is suspected of being loose, then there's a chance that the gasket and head are damaged if the problem has persisted for any length of time. The head nuts and bolts should be tightened to the proper torque in the correct sequence (Chapter 2).
☐ Improper valve clearance. This means that the valve is not closing completely and compression pressure is leaking past the valve. Check and adjust the valve clearances (Chapter 1).
☐ Cylinder and/or piston worn. Excessive wear will cause compression pressure to leak past the rings. This is usually accompanied by worn rings as well. A top end overhaul is necessary (Chapter 2).
☐ Piston rings worn, weak, broken, or sticking. Broken or sticking piston rings usually indicate a lubrication or carburetion problem that causes excess carbon deposits or seizures to form on the pistons and rings. Top end overhaul is necessary (Chapter 2).
☐ Piston ring-to-groove clearance excessive. This is caused by excessive wear of the piston ring lands. Piston replacement is necessary (Chapter 2).
☐ Cylinder head gasket damaged. If a head is allowed to become loose, or if excessive carbon build-up on the piston crown and combustion chamber causes extremely high compression, the head gasket may leak. Retorquing the head is not always sufficient to restore the seal, so gasket replacement is necessary (Chapter 2).
☐ Cylinder head warped. This is caused by overheating or improperly tightened head nuts and bolts. Machine shop resurfacing or head replacement is necessary (Chapter 2).
☐ Valve spring broken or weak. Caused by component failure or wear; the spring(s) must be replaced (Chapter 2).
☐ Valve not seating properly. This is caused by a bent valve (from over-revving or improper valve adjustment), burned valve or seat (improper carburetion) or an accumulation of carbon deposits on the seat (from carburetion or lubrication problems). The valves must be cleaned and/or replaced and the seats serviced if possible (Chapter 2).

Knocking or pinging

☐ Carbon build-up in combustion chamber. Use of a fuel additive that will dissolve the adhesive bonding the carbon particles to the crown and chamber is the easiest way to remove the build-up. Otherwise, the cylinder head will have to be removed and decarbonized (Chapter 2).
☐ Incorrect or poor quality fuel. Old or improper grades of fuel can cause detonation. This causes the piston to rattle, thus the knocking or pinging sound. Drain old fuel and always use the recommended fuel grade.
☐ Spark plug heat range incorrect. Uncontrolled detonation indicates the plug heat range is too hot. The plug in effect becomes a glow plug, raising cylinder temperatures. Install the proper heat range plug (Chapter 1).
☐ Improper air/fuel mixture. This will cause the cylinder to run hot, which leads to detonation. Clogged jets or an air leak can cause this imbalance. See Chapter 4.

Miscellaneous causes

☐ Throttle valve doesn't open fully. Adjust the cable slack (Chapter 1).
☐ Clutch slipping. May be caused by improper adjustment or loose or worn clutch components. Refer to Chapter 1 for adjustment or Chapter 2 for clutch overhaul procedures.
☐ Timing not advancing.
☐ Engine oil viscosity too high. Using a heavier oil than the one recommended in Chapter 1 can damage the oil pump or lubrication system and cause drag on the engine.
☐ Brakes dragging. Usually caused by debris which has entered the brake piston sealing boot, or from a warped disc or bent axle. Repair as necessary.

4 Overheating

Engine overheats

☐ Coolant level low. Check and add coolant (see *Daily (pre-ride) checks* at the beginning of this manual)

☐ Leak in cooling system. Check cooling system hoses and radiator for leaks and other damage. Replace or repair parts as necessary (see Chapter 3).

☐ Defective thermostat. Check and replace if necessary (see Chapter 3).

☐ Bad radiator cap. Remove the cap and have it pressure tested.

☐ Coolant passages clogged. Drain, clean the passages and refill with fresh coolant (see Chapter 3).

☐ Water pump defective. Remove the pump and check the components (see Chapter 3).

☐ Clogged or damaged radiator fins (see Chapter 3).

☐ Faulty cooling fan, fan relay or fan switch (see Chapter 3).

☐ Engine oil level low. Check and add oil (Chapter 1).

☐ Wrong type of oil. If you're not sure what type of oil is in the engine, drain it and fill with the correct type (Chapter 1).

☐ Air leak at intake joint. Check and tighten or replace as necessary (Chapter 4).

☐ Fuel level low. Check and adjust if necessary (Chapter 4).

☐ Worn oil pump or clogged oil passages. Replace pump or clean passages as necessary.

☐ Clogged external oil line. Remove and check for foreign material (see Chapter 2).

☐ Carbon build-up in combustion chambers. Use of a fuel additive that will dissolve the adhesive bonding the carbon particles to the piston crown and chambers is the easiest way to remove the build-up. Otherwise, the cylinder head will have to be removed and decarbonized (Chapter 2).

☐ Operation in high ambient temperatures.

Firing incorrect

☐ Spark plug fouled, defective or worn out. See Chapter 1 for spark plug maintenance.

☐ Incorrect spark plug (see Chapter 1).

☐ Faulty ignition coil (Chapter 4).

Fuel/air mixture incorrect (carbureted models)

☐ Pilot screw out of adjustment (Chapter 4A).

☐ Main jet clogged. Dirt, water and other contaminants can clog the main jet. Clean the fuel tap strainer, the float bowl area and the jets and carburetor orifices (Chapter 4A).

☐ Main jet wrong size. The standard jetting is for sea level atmospheric pressure and oxygen content.

☐ Air cleaner poorly sealed or missing.

☐ Air cleaner-to-carburetor boot poorly sealed. Look for cracks, holes or loose clamps and replace or repair.

☐ Fuel level too low. Check fuel level and float level and adjust or replace the float if necessary (Chapter 4A).

☐ Fuel tank air vent obstructed. Make sure that the air vent passage in the filler cap is open.

☐ Carburetor intake manifold loose. Check for cracks or loose clamps or bolts. Check the carburetor-to-manifold gasket and the manifold-to-cylinder head O-ring (Chapter 4A).

Fuel/air mixture incorrect (fuel injected models)

☐ Fuel tank vent hose or fitting obstructed.

☐ Fuel pump or pressure regulator faulty, or the fuel filter is blocked (see Chapter 4B).

☐ Fuel hose clogged. Remove the fuel hose (see Chapter 4B) and blow air through it.

☐ Fuel rail or injector clogged. Check the fuel pump. If the machine has been unused for several months, the fuel turns to a varnish-like liquid that can cause an injector needle to stick to its seat. Drain the tank and fuel system (see Chapter 4B).

☐ Intake air leak. Check for a loose connection between the throttle body and intake manifold, and check the intake air pressure sensor hose for leaks or a loose fit.

☐ Air filter clogged. Clean the air filter element or replace it with a new one (see Chapter 1).

Compression too high

☐ Carbon build-up in combustion chamber. Use of a fuel additive that will dissolve the adhesive bonding the carbon particles to the piston crown and chamber is the easiest way to remove the build-up. Otherwise, the cylinder head will have to be removed and decarbonized (Chapter 2).

☐ Improperly machined head surface or installation of incorrect gasket during engine assembly.

Engine load excessive

☐ Clutch slipping. Can be caused by damaged, loose or worn clutch components. Refer to Chapter 2 for overhaul procedures.

☐ Engine oil level too high. The addition of too much oil will cause pressurization of the crankcase and inefficient engine operation. Check Specifications and drain to proper level (Chapter 1).

☐ Engine oil viscosity too high. Using a heavier oil than the one recommended in Chapter 1 can damage the oil pump or lubrication system as well as cause drag on the engine.

☐ Brakes dragging. Usually caused by debris which has entered the brake piston sealing boots (hydraulic front brakes), corroded wheel cylinders or calipers (hydraulic front brakes), sticking brake cam (mechanical front or all rear brakes) or from a warped drum, warped disc or bent axle. Repair as necessary (Chapter 7).

Lubrication inadequate

☐ Engine oil level too low. Friction caused by intermittent lack of lubrication or from oil that is overworked can cause overheating. The oil provides a definite cooling function in the engine. Check the oil level (Chapter 1).

☐ Poor quality engine oil or incorrect viscosity or type. Oil is rated not only according to viscosity but also according to type. Some oils are not rated high enough for use in this engine. Check the Specifications section and change to the correct oil (Chapter 1).

☐ Camshaft or journals worn. Excessive wear causing drop in oil pressure. Replace cam or cylinder head. Abnormal wear could be caused by oil starvation at high rpm from low oil level or improper viscosity or type of oil (Chapter 1).

☐ Crankshaft and/or bearings worn. Same problems as paragraph above. Check and replace crankshaft assembly if necessary (Chapter 2).

Miscellaneous causes

☐ Modification to exhaust system. Most aftermarket exhaust systems cause the engine to run leaner, which makes it run hotter. When installing an aftermarket exhaust system, always rejet the carburetor (if equipped).

5 Clutch problems

Clutch slipping

☐ Clutch friction plates worn or warped. Overhaul the clutch (Chapter 2).

☐ Clutch metal plates worn or warped (Chapter 2).

☐ Clutch spring(s) broken or weak. Old or heat-damaged spring(s) (from slipping clutch) should be replaced with new ones (Chapter 2).

☐ Clutch release mechanism defective. Replace any defective parts (Chapter 2).

☐ Clutch center or housing unevenly worn. This causes improper engagement of the plates. Replace the damaged or worn parts (Chapter 2).

☐ Wrong type of engine oil. The friction modifiers in automotive engine oils can sometimes caused the clutch to slip. Use oil that meets JASO standard MA or MA2.

Clutch not disengaging completely

☐ Clutch improperly adjusted (see Chapter 1).

☐ Clutch plates warped or damaged. This will cause clutch drag, which in turn will cause the machine to creep. Overhaul the clutch (Chapter 2).

☐ Sagged or broken clutch spring(s). Check and replace the spring(s) (Chapter 2).

☐ Engine oil deteriorated. Old, thin, worn out oil will not provide proper lubrication for the discs, causing the secondary clutch to drag. Replace the oil and filter (Chapter 1).

☐ Engine oil viscosity too high. Using a thicker oil than recommended in Chapter 1 can cause the secondary clutch plates to stick together, putting a drag on the engine. Change to the correct viscosity oil (Chapter 1).

☐ Clutch housing seized on shaft. Lack of lubrication, severe wear or damage can cause the housing to seize on the shaft. Overhaul of the clutch, and perhaps transmission, may be necessary to repair the damage (Chapter 2).

☐ Clutch release mechanism defective. Worn or damaged release mechanism parts can stick and fail to apply force to the pressure plate. Overhaul the release mechanism (Chapter 2).

☐ Clutch center nut. Causes housing and center misalignment putting a drag on the engine. Engagement adjustment continually varies. Overhaul the clutch (Chapter 2).

6 Gear shifting problems

Doesn't go into gear or lever doesn't return

☐ Clutch not disengaging. See Section 5.

☐ Shift fork(s) bent or seized. May be caused by lack of lubrication. Overhaul the transmission (Chapter 2).

☐ Gear(s) stuck on shaft. Most often caused by a lack of lubrication or excessive wear in transmission bearings and bushings. Overhaul the transmission (Chapter 2).

☐ Shift drum binding. Caused by lubrication failure or excessive wear. Replace the drum and bearing (Chapter 2).

☐ Shift lever return spring weak or broken (Chapter 2).

☐ Shift lever broken. Splines stripped out of lever or shaft, caused by allowing the lever to get loose. Replace necessary parts (Chapter 2).

☐ Shift mechanism pawl broken or worn. Full engagement and rotary movement of shift drum results. Inspect shift mechanism and replace broken or worn parts (Chapter 2).

☐ Pawl spring broken. Allows pawl to float, causing sporadic shift operation. Replace spring (Chapter 2).

Jumps out of gear

☐ Shift fork(s) worn. Overhaul the transmission (Chapter 2).

☐ Gear groove(s) worn. Overhaul the transmission (Chapter 2).

☐ Gear dogs or dog slots worn or damaged. The gears should be inspected and replaced. No attempt should be made to service the worn parts.

Overshifts

☐ Pawl spring weak or broken (Chapter 2).

☐ Shift drum stopper lever not functioning (Chapter 2).

7 Abnormal engine noise

Knocking or pinging

☐ Carbon build-up in combustion chamber. Use of a fuel additive that will dissolve the adhesive bonding the carbon particles to the piston crown and chamber is the easiest way to remove the build-up. Otherwise, the cylinder head will have to be removed and decarbonized (Chapter 2).

☐ Incorrect or poor quality fuel. Old or improper fuel can cause detonation. This causes the pistons to rattle, thus the knocking or pinging sound. Drain the old fuel (Chapter 4) and always use the recommended grade fuel (Chapter 1).

☐ Spark plug heat range incorrect. Uncontrolled detonation indicates that the plug heat range is too hot. The plug in effect becomes a glow plug, raising cylinder temperatures. Install the proper heat range plug (Chapter 1).

☐ Improper air/fuel mixture. This will cause the cylinder to run hot and lead to detonation. Clogged jets or an air leak can cause this imbalance. See Chapter 4A.

Piston slap or rattling

☐ Cylinder-to-piston clearance excessive. Caused by improper assembly. Inspect and overhaul top end parts (Chapter 2).

☐ Connecting rod bent. Caused by over-revving, trying to start a badly flooded engine or from ingesting a foreign object into the combustion chamber. Replace the damaged parts (Chapter 2).

☐ Piston pin or piston pin bore worn or seized from wear or lack of lubrication. Replace damaged parts (Chapter 2).

☐ Piston ring(s) worn, broken or sticking. Overhaul the top end (Chapter 2).

☐ Piston seizure damage. Usually from lack of lubrication or overheating. Replace the pistons and bore the cylinder, as necessary (Chapter 2).

☐ Connecting rod upper or lower end clearance excessive. Caused by excessive wear or lack of lubrication. Replace worn parts.

Valve noise

☐ Incorrect valve clearances. Adjust the clearances by referring to Chapter 1.

☐ Valve spring broken or weak. Check and replace weak valve springs (Chapter 2).

☐ Camshaft or cylinder head worn or damaged. Lack of lubrication at high rpm is usually the cause of damage. Insufficient oil or failure to change the oil at the recommended intervals are the chief causes.

Other noise

☐ Cylinder head gasket leaking.

☐ Exhaust pipe leaking at cylinder head connection. Caused by improper fit of pipe, damaged gasket or loose exhaust flange. All exhaust fasteners should be tightened evenly and carefully. Failure to do this will lead to a leak.

☐ Crankshaft runout excessive. Caused by a bent crankshaft (from over-revving) or damage from an upper cylinder component failure.

☐ Engine mounting bolts or nuts loose. Tighten all engine mounting bolts and nuts to the specified torque (Chapter 2).

☐ Crankshaft bearings worn (Chapter 2).

☐ Camshaft chain tensioner defective. Replace according to the procedure in Chapter 2.

☐ Camshaft chain, sprockets or guides worn (Chapter 2).

8 Abnormal driveline noise

Clutch noise

☐ Clutch housing/friction plate clearance excessive (Chapter 2).

☐ Loose or damaged clutch pressure plate and/or bolts (Chapter 2).

Transmission noise

☐ Bearings worn. Also includes the possibility that the shafts are worn. Overhaul the transmission (Chapter 2).

☐ Gears worn or chipped (Chapter 2).

☐ Metal chips jammed in gear teeth. Probably pieces from a broken gear or shift mechanism that were picked up by the gears. This will cause early bearing failure (Chapter 2).

☐ Engine oil level too low. Causes a howl from transmission. Also affects engine power and clutch operation (Chapter 1).

☐ Chain not adjusted properly (see Chapter 1)

☐ Front or rear sprocket loose. Tighten fasteners (see Chapter 6).

☐ Sprockets and/or chain worn. Install new sprockets and chain (see Chapter 6).

☐ Rear sprocket warped. Install a new rear sprocket (see Chapter 6).

9 Abnormal chassis noise

Suspension noise

- [ ] Spring weak or broken. Makes a clicking or scraping sound.
- [ ] Steering shaft bearings worn or damaged. Clicks when braking. Check and replace as necessary (Chapter 6).
- [ ] Shock absorber fluid level incorrect. Indicates a leak caused by defective seal. Shock will be covered with oil. Replace shock (Chapter 6).
- [ ] Defective shock absorber with internal damage. This is in the body of the shock and can't be remedied. The shock must be replaced with a new one (Chapter 6).
- [ ] Bent or damaged shock body. Replace the shock with a new one (Chapter 6).

Brake noise

- [ ] Brake linings worn or contaminated. Can cause scraping or squealing. Replace the pads (Chapter 7).
- [ ] Brake linings warped or worn unevenly. Can cause chattering. Replace the linings (Chapter 7).
- [ ] Brake disc warped. Can cause chattering. Replace brake disc (Chapter 7).
- [ ] Loose or worn knuckle or rear axle bearings. Check and replace as needed (Chapter 6).

10 Coolant temperature indicator light comes on

Cooling system

- [ ] Coolant level low. Check and add coolant (see *Daily (pre-ride) checks* at the beginning of this manual)
- [ ] Leak in cooling system. Check cooling system hoses and radiator for leaks and other damage. Replace or repair parts as necessary (see Chapter 3).
- [ ] Defective thermostat. Check and replace if necessary (see Chapter 3).
- [ ] Bad radiator cap. Remove the cap and have it pressure tested.
- [ ] Coolant passages clogged. Drain, clean the passages and refill with fresh coolant (see Chapter 3).
- [ ] Water pump defective. Remove the pump and check the components (see Chapter 3).
- [ ] Clogged or damaged radiator fins (see Chapter 3).

Engine lubrication system

- [ ] High oil temperature due to operation in high ambient temperatures. Shut the engine off and let it cool.
- [ ] Engine oil level low. Inspect for leak or other problem causing low oil level and add recommended oil (Chapters 1 and 2).

Electrical system

- [ ] Coolant temperature sensor defective. Check the sensor according to the procedure in Chapter 3. Replace it if it's defective.
- [ ] Coolant temperature indicator light circuit defective. Check for pinched, shorted, disconnected or damaged wiring, referring to the wiring diagrams in this manual.
- [ ] Cooling fan not working (Chapter 3).

11 Excessive exhaust smoke

White smoke

☐ Piston oil ring worn. The ring may be broken or damaged, causing oil from the crankcase to be pulled past the piston into the combustion chamber. Replace the rings with new ones (Chapter 2).

☐ Cylinders worn, cracked, or scored. Caused by overheating or oil starvation. If worn or scored, the cylinders will have to be rebored and new pistons installed. If cracked, the cylinder block will have to be replaced (see Chapter 2).

☐ Valve oil seal damaged or worn. Replace oil seals with new ones (Chapter 2).

☐ Valve guide worn. Perform a complete valve job (Chapter 2).

☐ Engine oil level too high, which causes the oil to be forced past the rings. Drain oil to the proper level (Chapter 1).

☐ Head gasket broken between oil return and cylinder. Causes oil to be pulled into the combustion chamber. Replace the head gasket and check the head for warpage (Chapter 2).

☐ Abnormal crankcase pressurization, which forces oil past the rings. Clogged breather or hoses usually the cause (Chapter 2).

Black smoke

☐ Air cleaner clogged. Clean or replace the element (Chapter 1).

☐ Main jet too large or loose. Compare the jet size to the Specifications (Chapter 4A).

☐ Choke stuck (carbureted models), causing fuel to be pulled through choke circuit (Chapter 4A).

☐ Fuel level too high (carbureted models). Check the fuel level and float level and adjust if necessary (Chapter 4A).

☐ Inlet needle held off needle seat (carbureted models). Clean the float chamber and fuel line and replace the needle and seat if necessary (Chapter 4A).

☐ Fuel injection system problem (2009 and later). See Chapter 4B.

Brown smoke

☐ Main jet too small or clogged. Lean condition caused by wrong size main jet or by a restricted orifice. Clean float chamber and jets and compare jet size to Specifications (Chapter 4A).

☐ Fuel flow insufficient. Fuel inlet needle valve stuck closed due to chemical reaction with old fuel. Float level incorrect; check and replace float if necessary. Restricted fuel line. Clean line and float chamber.

☐ Carburetor intake tube loose (Chapter 4A).

☐ Air cleaner poorly sealed or not installed (Chapter 1).

12 Poor handling or stability

Handlebar hard to turn

☐ Steering shaft nut too tight (Chapter 6).

☐ Lower bearing or upper bushing damaged. Roughness can be felt as the bars are turned from side-to-side. Replace bearing and bushing (Chapter 6).

☐ Steering shaft bearing lubrication inadequate. Causes are grease getting hard from age or being washed out by high pressure car washes. Remove steering shaft and replace bearing (Chapter 6).

☐ Steering shaft bent. Caused by a collision, hitting a pothole or by rolling the machine. Replace damaged part. Don't try to straighten the steering shaft (Chapter 6).

☐ Front tire air pressure too low (Chapter 1).

Handlebar shakes or vibrates excessively

☐ Tires worn or out of balance (Chapter 1 or 7).

☐ Swingarm bearings worn. Replace worn bearings by referring to Chapter 6.

☐ Wheel rim(s) warped or damaged. Inspect wheels (Chapter 7).

☐ Wheel bearings worn. Worn front or rear wheel bearings can cause poor tracking. Worn front bearings will cause wobble (Chapter 7).

☐ Wheel hubs installed incorrectly (Chapter 6 or Chapter 7).

☐ Handlebar clamp bolts or bracket nuts loose (Chapter 6).

☐ Steering shaft nut or bolts loose. Tighten them to the specified torque (Chapter 6).

☐ Motor mount bolts loose. Will cause excessive vibration with increased engine rpm (Chapter 2).

Handlebar pulls to one side

☐ Uneven tire pressures (Chapter 1).

☐ Frame bent. Definitely suspect this if the machine has been rolled. May or may not be accompanied by cracking near the bend. Replace the frame (Chapter 8).

☐ Wheel out of alignment. Caused by incorrect toe-in adjustment (Chapter 1) or bent tie-rod (Chapter 6).

☐ Swingarm bent or twisted. Caused by age (metal fatigue) or impact damage. Replace the swingarm (Chapter 6).

☐ Steering shaft bent. Caused by impact damage or by rolling the vehicle. Replace the steering stem (Chapter 6).

Poor shock absorbing qualities

☐ Too hard:
  a) *Shock internal damage.*
  b) *Tire pressure too high (Chapters 1 and 7).*
  c) *Shock setting too hard for conditions (see Chapter 6).*

☐ Too soft:
  a) *Shock oil insufficient and/or leaking (Chapter 6).*
  b) *Shock springs weak or broken (Chapter 6).*

13 Braking problems

Front brakes are spongy, don't hold

☐ Air in brake line. Caused by inattention to master cylinder fluid level or by leakage. Locate problem and bleed brakes (Chapter 7).
☐ Linings worn (Chapters 1 and 7).
☐ Brake fluid leak. See first paragraph.
☐ Contaminated linings. Caused by contamination with oil, grease, brake fluid, etc. Clean or replace linings. Clean disc thoroughly with brake cleaner (Chapter 7).
☐ Brake fluid deteriorated. Fluid is old or contaminated. Drain system, replenish with new fluid and bleed the system (Chapter 7).
☐ Master cylinder internal parts worn or damaged causing fluid to bypass (Chapter 7).
☐ Master cylinder bore scratched by foreign material or broken spring. Repair or replace master cylinder (Chapter 7).
☐ Disc warped. Replace disc (Chapter 7).

Brake lever or pedal pulsates

☐ Axle bent. Replace axle (Chapter 6).
☐ Wheel warped or otherwise damaged (Chapter 7).

☐ Hub or axle bearings damaged or worn (Chapter 6).
☐ Brake disc warped. Replace brake disc (Chapter 7).

Brakes drag

☐ Master cylinder piston seized. Caused by wear or damage to piston or cylinder bore (Chapter 7).
☐ Lever balky or stuck. Check pivot and lubricate (Chapter 7).
☐ Wheel cylinder or caliper piston seized in bore. Caused by wear or ingestion of dirt past deteriorated seal (Chapter 7).
☐ Disc brake pads damaged. Lining material separated from pads. Usually caused by faulty manufacturing process or from contact with chemicals. Replace pads (Chapter 7).
☐ Pads improperly installed (Chapter 7).
☐ Rear brake pedal or lever free play insufficient (Chapter 1).

14 Electrical problems

Battery dead or weak

☐ Battery faulty. Caused by sulfated plates which are shorted through sedimentation or low electrolyte level. Also, broken battery terminal making only occasional contact (Chapter 5).
☐ Battery cables making poor contact (Chapter 5).
☐ Load excessive. Caused by addition of high wattage lights or other electrical accessories.
☐ Ignition switch defective. Switch either grounds internally or fails to shut off system. Replace the switch (Chapter 5).
☐ Regulator/rectifier defective (Chapter 5).
☐ Stator coil open or shorted (Chapter 5).

☐ Wiring faulty. Wiring grounded or connections loose in ignition, charging or lighting circuits (Chapter 5).

Battery overcharged

☐ Regulator/rectifier defective. Overcharging is noticed when battery gets excessively warm or boils over (Chapter 5).
☐ Battery defective. Replace battery with a new one (Chapter 5).
☐ Battery amperage too low, wrong type or size. Install manufacturer's specified amp-hour battery to handle charging load (Chapter 5).

Measuring open-circuit battery voltage

Float-type hydrometer for measuring battery specific gravity

Checking engine compression

● Low compression will result in exhaust smoke, heavy oil consumption, poor starting and poor performance. A compression test will provide useful information about an engine's condition and if performed regularly, can give warning of trouble before any other symptoms become apparent.

● A compression gauge will be required, along with an adapter to suit the spark plug hole thread size. Note that the screw-in type gauge/adapter set up is preferable to the rubber cone type.

● Compression testing procedures are described in Chapter 2.

Checking battery open-circuit voltage

⚠ **Warning: The gases produced by the battery are explosive - never smoke or create any sparks in the vicinity of the battery. Never allow the electrolyte to contact your skin or clothing - if it does, wash it off and seek immediate medical attention.**

● Before any electrical fault is investigated the battery should be checked.

● You'll need a dc voltmeter or multimeter to check battery voltage. Check that the leads are inserted in the correct terminals on the meter, red lead to positive (+), black lead to negative (-). Incorrect connections can damage the meter.

● A sound, fully-charged 12 volt battery should produce between 12.3 and 12.6 volts across its terminals (12.8 volts for a maintenance-free battery). On machines with a 6 volt battery, voltage should be between 6.1 and 6.3 volts.

1 Set a multimeter to the 0 to 20 volts dc range and connect its probes across the battery terminals. Connect the meter's positive (+) probe, usually red, to the battery positive (+) terminal, followed by the meter's negative (-) probe, usually black, to the battery negative terminal (-) **(see illustration 1)**.

2 If battery voltage is low (below 10 volts on a 12 volt battery or below 4 volts on a six volt battery), charge the battery and test the voltage again. If the battery repeatedly goes flat, investigate the vehicle's charging system.

Checking battery specific gravity (SG)

⚠ **Warning: The gases produced by the battery are explosive - never smoke or create any sparks in the vicinity of the battery. Never allow the electrolyte to contact your skin or clothing - if it does, wash it off and seek immediate medical attention.**

● The specific gravity check gives an indication of a battery's state of charge.

● A hydrometer is used for measuring specific gravity. Make sure you purchase one which has a small enough hose to insert in the aperture of an ATV battery.

● Specific gravity is simply a measure of the electrolyte's density compared with that of water. Water has an SG of 1.000 and fully-charged battery electrolyte is about 26% heavier, at 1.260.

● Specific gravity checks are not possible on maintenance-free batteries. Testing the open-circuit voltage is the only means of determining their state of charge.

1 To measure SG, remove the battery from the motorcycle and remove the first cell cap. Draw some electrolyte into the hydrometer and note the reading **(see illustration 2)**. Return the electrolyte to the cell and install the cap.

2 The reading should be in the region of 1.260 to 1.280. If SG is below 1.200 the battery needs charging. Note that SG will vary with temperature; it should be measured at 20°C (68°F). Add 0.007 to the reading for every 10°C above 20°C, and subtract 0.007 from the reading for every 10°C below 20°C. Add 0.004 to the reading for every 10°F above 68°F, and subtract 0.004 from the reading for every 10°F below 68°F.

3 When the check is complete, rinse the hydrometer thoroughly with clean water.

Checking for continuity

● The term continuity describes the uninterrupted flow of electricity through an electrical circuit. A continuity check will determine whether an **open-circuit** situation exists.

● Continuity can be checked with an ohmmeter, multimeter, continuity tester or battery and bulb test circuit **(see illustrations 3, 4 and 5)**.

● All of these instruments are self-powered by a battery, therefore the checks are made with the ignition OFF.

● As a safety precaution, always disconnect the battery negative (-) lead before making checks, particularly if ignition switch checks are being made.

● If using a meter, select the appropriate ohms scale and check that the meter reads

3

Digital multimeter can be used for all electrical tests

4

Battery-powered continuity tester

5

Battery and bulb test circuit

6

Continuity check of front brake light switch using a meter - note cotter pins used to access connector terminals

infinity (∞). Touch the meter probes together and check that meter reads zero; where necessary adjust the meter so that it reads zero.

● After using a meter, always switch it OFF to conserve its battery.

Switch checks

1 If a switch is at fault, trace its wiring up to the wiring connectors. Separate the wire connectors and inspect them for security and condition. A build-up of dirt or corrosion here will most likely be the cause of the problem - clean up and apply a water dispersant such as WD40.

2 If using a test meter, set the meter to the ohms x 10 scale and connect its probes across the wires from the switch **(see illustration 6)**. Simple ON/OFF type switches, such as brake light switches, only have two wires whereas combination switches, like the ignition switch, have many internal links. Study the wiring diagram to ensure that you are connecting across the correct pair of wires. Continuity (low or no measurable resistance - 0 ohms) should be indicated with the switch ON and no continuity (high resistance) with it OFF.

3 Note that the polarity of the test probes doesn't matter for continuity checks, although care should be taken to follow specific test procedures if a diode or solid-state component is being checked.

4 A continuity tester or battery and bulb circuit can be used in the same way. Connect its probes as described above **(see illustration 7)**. The light should come on to indicate continuity in the ON switch position, but should extinguish in the OFF position.

Wiring checks

● Many electrical faults are caused by damaged wiring, often due to incorrect routing or chafing on frame components.

7

Continuity check of rear brake light switch using a continuity tester

● Loose, wet or corroded wire connectors can also be the cause of electrical problems, especially in exposed locations.

Continuity check of front brake light switch sub-harness

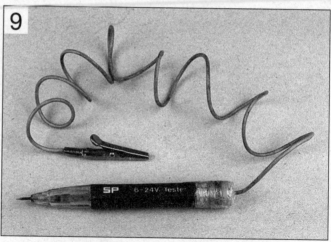

A simple test light can be used for voltage checks

A buzzer is useful for voltage checks

Checking for voltage at the rear brake light power supply wire using a meter . . .

1 A continuity check can be made on a single length of wire by disconnecting it at each end and connecting a meter or continuity tester across both ends of the wire **(see illustration 8)**.

2 Continuity (low or no resistance - 0 ohms) should be indicated if the wire is good. If no continuity (high resistance) is shown, suspect a broken wire.

Checking for voltage

● A voltage check can determine whether current is reaching a component.

● Voltage can be checked with a dc voltmeter, multimeter set on the dc volts scale, test light or buzzer **(see illustrations 9 and 10)**. A meter has the advantage of being able to measure actual voltage.

● When using a meter, check that its leads are inserted in the correct terminals on the meter, red to positive (+), black to negative (-). Incorrect connections can damage the meter.

● A voltmeter (or multimeter set to the dc volts scale) should always be connected in parallel (across the load). Connecting it in series will destroy the meter.

● Voltage checks are made with the ignition ON.

1 First identify the relevant wiring circuit by referring to the wiring diagram at the end of this manual. If other electrical components share the same power supply (ie are fed from the same fuse), take note whether they are working correctly - this is useful information in deciding where to start checking the circuit.

2 If using a meter, check first that the meter leads are plugged into the correct terminals on the meter (see above). Set the meter to the dc volts function, at a range suitable for the battery voltage. Connect the meter red probe (+) to the power supply wire and the black probe to a good metal ground on the motor-cycle's frame or directly to the battery negative (-) terminal **(see illustration 11)**. Battery voltage should be shown on the meter with the ignition switched ON.

3 If using a test light or buzzer, connect its positive (+) probe to the power supply terminal and its negative (-) probe to a good ground on the vehicle's frame or directly to the battery negative (-) terminal **(see illustration 12)**. With the ignition ON, the test light should illuminate or the buzzer sound.

4 If no voltage is indicated, work back towards the fuse continuing to check for voltage. When you reach a point where there is voltage, you know the problem lies between that point and your last check point.

. . . or a test light - note the ground connection to the frame (arrow)

A selection of jumper wires for making ground checks

Checking the ground

● Ground connections are made either directly to the engine or frame (such as sensors, neutral switch etc. which only have a positive feed) or by a separate wire into the ground circuit of the wiring harness. Alternatively a short ground wire is sometimes run directly from the component to the vehicle's frame.

● Corrosion is often the cause of a poor ground connection.

● If total failure is experienced, check the security of the main ground lead from the negative (-) terminal of the battery and also the main ground point on the wiring harness. If corroded, dismantle the connection and clean all surfaces back to bare metal.

1 To check the ground on a component, use an insulated jumper wire to temporarily bypass its ground connection **(see illustration 13)**. Connect one end of the jumper wire between the ground terminal or metal body of the component and the other end to the vehicle's frame.

2 If the circuit works with the jumper wire installed, the original ground circuit is faulty. Check the wiring for open-circuits or poor connections. Clean up direct ground connections, removing all traces of corrosion and remake the joint. Apply petroleum jelly to the joint to prevent future corrosion.

Tracing a short-circuit

● A short-circuit occurs where current shorts to ground bypassing the circuit components. This usually results in a blown fuse.

● A short-circuit is most likely to occur where the insulation has worn through due to wiring chafing on a component, allowing a direct path to ground on the frame.

1 Remove any body panels necessary to access the circuit wiring.

2 Check that all electrical switches in the circuit are OFF, then remove the circuit fuse and connect a test light, buzzer or voltmeter (set to the dc scale) across the fuse terminals. No voltage should be shown.

3 Move the wiring from side to side while observing the test light or meter. When the test light comes on, buzzer sounds or meter shows voltage, you have found the cause of the short. It will usually shown up as damaged or burned insulation.

4 Note that the same test can be performed on each component in the circuit, even the switch.

A number of chemicals and lubricants are available for use in motorcycle maintenance and repair. They include a wide variety of products ranging from cleaning solvents and degreasers to lubricants and protective sprays for rubber, plastic and vinyl.

• **Contact point/spark plug cleaner** is a solvent used to clean oily film and dirt from points, grim from electrical connectors and oil deposits from spark plugs. It is oil free and leaves no residue. It can also be used to remove gum and varnish from carburetor jets and other orifices.

• **Carburetor cleaner** is similar to contact point/spark plug cleaner but it usually has a stronger solvent and may leave a slight oily residue. It is not recommended for cleaning electrical components or connections.

• **Brake system cleaner** is used to remove brake dust, grease and brake fluid from the brake system, where clean surfaces are absolutely necessary. It leaves no residue and often eliminates brake squeal caused by contaminants.

• **Silicone-based lubricants** are used to protect rubber parts such as hoses and grommets, and are used as lubricants for hinges and locks.

• **Multi-purpose grease** is an all purpose lubricant used wherever grease is more practical than a liquid lubricant such as oil. Some multi-purpose grease is colored white and specially formulated to be more resistant to water than ordinary grease.

• **Gear oil** (sometimes called gear lube) is a specially designed oil used in transmissions and final drive units, as well as other areas where high friction, high temperature lubrication is required. It is available in a number of viscosities (weights) for various applications.

• **Motor oil** is the lubricant formulated for use in engines. It normally contains a wide variety of additives to prevent corrosion and reduce foaming and wear. Motor oil comes in various weights (viscosity ratings) from 0 to 50. The recommended weight of the oil depends on the season, temperature and the demands on the engine. Light oil is used in cold climates and under light load conditions. Heavy oil is used in hot climates and where high loads are encountered. Multi-viscosity oils are designed to have characteristics of both light and heavy oils and are available in a number of weights from 0W-20 to 20W-50.

• **Gasoline additives** perform several functions, depending on their chemical makeup. They usually contain solvents that help dissolve gum and varnish that build up on carburetor and inlet parts. They also serve to break down carbon deposits that form on the inside surfaces of the combustion chambers. Some additives contain upper cylinder lubricants for valves and piston rings.

• **Brake and clutch fluid** is a specially formulated hydraulic fluid that can withstand the heat and pressure encountered in break/clutch systems. Care must be taken that this fluid does not come in contact with painted surfaces or plastics. An opened container should always be resealed to prevent contamination by water or dirt.

• **Chain lubricants** are formulated especially for use on motorcycle final drive chains. A good chain lube should adhere well and have good penetrating qualities to be effective as a lubricant inside the chain and on the side plates, pins and rollers. Most chain lubes are either the foaming type or quick drying type and are usually marketed as sprays. Take care to use a lubricant marked as being suitable for O-ring chains.

• **Degreasers** are heavy duty solvents used to remove grease and grime that may accumulate on the engine and frame components. They can be sprayed or brushed on and, depending on the type, are rinsed with either water or solvent.

• **Solvents** are used alone or in combination with degreasers to clean parts and assemblies during repair and overhaul. The home mechanic should use only solvents that are non-flammable and that do not produce irritating fumes.

• **Gasket sealing compounds** may be used in conjunction with gaskets, to improve their sealing capabilities, or alone, to seal metal-to-metal joints. Many gasket sealers can withstand extreme heat, some are impervious to gasoline and lubricants, while others are capable of filling and sealing large cavities. Depending on the intended use, gasket sealers either dry hard or stay relatively soft and pliable. They are usually applied by hand, with a brush or are sprayed on the gasket sealing surfaces.

• **Thread locking compound** is an adhesive locking compound that prevents threaded fasteners from loosening because of vibration. It is available in a variety of types for different applications.

• **Moisture dispersants** are usually sprays that can be used to dry out electrical components such as the fuse block and wiring connectors. Some types an also be used as treatment for rubber and as a lubricant for hinges, cables and locks.

• **Waxes and polishes** are used to help protect painted and plated surfaces from the weather. Different types of pain may require the use of different types of wax polish. Some polishes utilize a chemical or abrasive cleaner to help remove the top layer of oxidized (dull) paint on older vehicles. In recent years, many non-wax polishes (that contain a wide variety of chemicals such as polymers and silicones) have been introduced. These non-wax polishes are usually easier to apply and last longer than conventional waxes and polishes.

A

ABS (Anti-lock braking system) A system, usually electronically controlled, that senses incipient wheel lockup during braking and relieves hydraulic pressure at wheel which is about to skid.

Aftermarket Components suitable for the motorcycle or ATV, but not produced by the manufacturer.

Allen key A hexagonal wrench which fits into a recessed hexagonal hole.

Alternating current (ac) Current produced by an alternator. Requires converting to direct current by a rectifier for charging purposes.

Alternator Converts mechanical energy from the engine into electrical energy to charge the battery and power the electrical system.

Ampere (amp) A unit of measurement for the flow of electrical current. Current = Volts ÷ Ohms.

Ampere-hour (Ah) Measure of battery capacity.

Angle-tightening A torque expressed in degrees. Often follows a conventional tightening torque for cylinder head or main bearing fasteners **(see illustration)**.

Angle-tightening cylinder head bolts

Antifreeze A substance (usually ethylene glycol) mixed with water, and added to the cooling system, to prevent freezing of the coolant in winter. Antifreeze also contains chemicals to inhibit corrosion and the formation of rust and other deposits that would tend to clog the radiator and coolant passages and reduce cooling efficiency.

Anti-dive System attached to the fork lower leg (slider) to prevent fork dive when braking hard.

Anti-seize compound A coating that reduces the risk of seizing on fasteners that are subjected to high temperatures, such as exhaust clamp bolts and nuts.

API American Petroleum Institute. A quality standard for 4-stroke motor oils.

Asbestos A natural fibrous mineral with great heat resistance, formerly used in the composition of brake friction materials. Asbestos is a health hazard and the dust created by brake systems should never be inhaled or ingested.

ATF Automatic Transmission Fluid. Often used in front forks.

ATU Automatic Timing Unit. Mechanical device for advancing the ignition timing on early engines.

ATV All Terrain Vehicle. Often called a Quad.

Axial play Side-to-side movement.

Axle A shaft on which a wheel revolves. Also known as a spindle.

B

Backlash The amount of movement between meshed components when one component is held still. Usually applies to gear teeth.

Ball bearing A bearing consisting of a hardened inner and outer race with hardened steel balls between the two races.

Bearings Used between two working surfaces to prevent wear of the components and a build-up of heat. Four types of bearing are commonly used on ATVs or motorcycles: plain shell bearings, ball bearings, tapered roller bearings and needle roller bearings.

Bevel gears Used to turn the drive through 90°. Typical applications are shaft final drive and camshaft drive **(see illustration)**.

BHP Brake Horsepower. The British measurement for engine power output. Power output is now usually expressed in kilowatts (kW).

Bevel gears are used to turn the drive through 90°

Bias-belted tire Similar construction to radial tire, but with outer belt running at an angle to the wheel rim.

Bleeding The process of removing air from a hydraulic system via a bleed nipple or bleed screw.

Bottom-end A description of an engine's crankcase components and all components contained therein.

BTDC Before Top Dead Center in terms of piston position. Ignition timing is often expressed in terms of degrees or millimeters BTDC.

Bush A cylindrical metal or rubber component used between two moving parts.

Burr Rough edge left on a component after machining or as a result of excessive wear.

C

Cam chain The chain which takes drive from the crankshaft to the camshaft(s).

Canister The main component in an evaporative emission control system (California market only); contains activated charcoal granules to trap vapors from the fuel system rather than allowing them to vent to the atmosphere.

Castellated Resembling the parapets along the top of a castle wall. For example, a castellated wheel axle or spindle nut.

Catalytic converter A device in the exhaust system of some machines which converts certain pollutants in the exhaust gases into less harmful substances.

Charging system Description of the

Cush drive rubber segments dampen out transmission shocks

components which charge the battery: the alternator, rectifer and regulator.

Clearance The amount of space between two parts. For example, between a piston and a cylinder, between a bearing and a journal, etc.

Coil spring A spiral of elastic steel found in various sizes throughout a vehicle, for example as a springing medium in the suspension and in the valve train.

Compression Reduction in volume, and increase in pressure and temperature, of a gas, caused by squeezing it into a smaller space.

Compression damping Controls the speed the suspension compresses when hitting a bump.

Compression ratio The relationship between cylinder volume when the piston is at top dead center and cylinder volume when the piston is at bottom dead center.

Connecting rod bearing The bearing in the end of the connecting rod that's attached to the crankshaft.

Continuity The uninterrupted path in the flow of electricity. Little or no measurable resistance.

Continuity tester Self-powered bleeper or test light which indicates continuity.

Cp Candlepower. Bulb rating commonly found on US motorcycles and ATVs.

Crossply tire Tire plies arranged in a criss-cross pattern. Usually four or six plies used, hence 4PR or 6PR in tire size codes.

Cush drive Rubber damper segments fitted between the rear wheel and final drive sprocket to absorb transmission shocks **(see illustration)**.

D

Degree disc Calibrated disc for measuring piston position. Expressed in degrees.

Dial gauge Clock-type gauge with adapters for measuring runout and piston position. Expressed in mm or inches.

Diaphragm The rubber membrane in a master cylinder or carburetor which seals the upper chamber.

Diaphragm spring A single sprung plate often used in clutches.

Direct current (dc) Current produced by a dc generator.

Decarbonization The process of removing carbon deposits - typically from the combustion chamber, valves and exhaust port/system.

Detonation Destructive and damaging explosion of fuel/air mixture in combustion chamber instead of controlled burning.

Diode An electrical valve which only allows current to flow in one direction. Commonly used in rectifiers and starter interlock systems.

Disc valve (or rotary valve) An induction system used on some two-stroke engines.

Double-overhead camshaft (DOHC) An engine that uses two overhead camshafts, one for the intake valves and one for the exhaust valves.

Drivebelt A toothed belt used to transmit drive to the rear wheel on some motorcycles. A drivebelt has also been used to drive the camshafts. Drivebelts are usually made of Kevlar. V-type (non-toothed) drivebelts are used in the transmissions of some ATVs.

Driveshaft Any shaft used to transmit motion. Commonly used when referring to the final driveshaft on shaft drive motorcycles or ATVs.

E

ECU (Electronic Control Unit) A computer which controls (for instance) an ignition system, or an anti-lock braking system.

EGO Exhaust Gas Oxygen sensor. Sometimes called a Lambda sensor.

Electrolyte The fluid in a lead-acid battery.

EMS (Engine Management System) A computer controlled system which manages the fuel injection and the ignition systems in an integrated fashion.

Endfloat The amount of lengthways movement between two parts. As applied to a crankshaft, the distance that the crankshaft can move side-to-side in the crankcase.

Endless chain A chain having no joining link. Common use for cam chains and final drive chains.

EP (Extreme Pressure) Oil type used in locations where high loads are applied, such as between gear teeth.

Evaporative emission control system Describes a charcoal filled canister which stores fuel vapors from the tank rather than allowing them to vent to the atmosphere. Usually only fitted to California models and referred to as an EVAP system.

Expansion chamber Section of two-stroke engine exhaust system so designed to improve engine efficiency and boost power.

F

Feeler blade or gauge A thin strip or blade of hardened steel, ground to an exact thickness, used to check or measure clearances between parts.

Final drive Description of the drive from the transmission to the rear wheel. Usually by chain or shaft, but sometimes by belt.

Firing order The order in which the engine cylinders fire, or deliver their power strokes, beginning with the number one cylinder.

Flooding Term used to describe a high fuel level in the carburetor float chambers, leading to fuel overflow. Also refers to excess fuel in the combustion chamber due to incorrect starting technique.

Free length The no-load state of a component when measured. Clutch, valve and fork spring lengths are measured at rest, without any preload.

Freeplay The amount of travel before any action takes place. The looseness in a linkage, or an assembly of parts, between the initial application of force and actual movement. For example, the distance the rear brake pedal moves before the rear brake is actuated.

Fuel injection The fuel/air mixture is metered electronically and directed into the engine intake ports (indirect injection) or into the cylinders (direct injection). Sensors supply information on engine speed and conditions.

Fuel/air mixture The charge of fuel and air going into the engine. See **Stoichiometric ratio**.

Fuse An electrical device which protects a circuit against accidental overload. The typical fuse contains a soft piece of metal which is calibrated to melt at a predetermined current flow (expressed as amps) and break the circuit.

G

Gap The distance the spark must travel in jumping from the center electrode to the side electrode in a spark plug. Also refers to the distance between the ignition rotor and the pickup coil in an electronic ignition system.

Gasket Any thin, soft material - usually cork, cardboard, asbestos or soft metal - installed between two metal surfaces to ensure a good seal. For instance, the cylinder head gasket seals the joint between the block and the cylinder head.

Gauge An instrument panel display used to monitor engine conditions. A gauge with a movable pointer on a dial or a fixed scale is an analog gauge. A gauge with a numerical readout is called a digital gauge.

Gear ratios The drive ratio of a pair of gears in a gearbox, calculated on their number of teeth.

Glaze-busting see **Honing**

Grinding Process for renovating the valve face and valve seat contact area in the cylinder head.

Ground return The return path of an electrical circuit, utilizing the vehicle's frame.

Gudgeon pin The shaft which connects the connecting rod small-end with the piston. Often called a piston pin or wrist pin.

H

Helical gears Gear teeth are slightly curved and produce less gear noise that straight-cut gears. Often used for primary drives.

Helicoil A thread insert repair system. Commonly used as a repair for stripped spark plug threads **(see illustration)**.

Installing a Helicoil thread insert in a cylinder head

Honing A process used to break down the glaze on a cylinder bore (also called glaze-busting). Can also be carried out to roughen a rebored cylinder to aid ring bedding-in.

HT (High Tension) Description of the electrical circuit from the secondary winding of the ignition coil to the spark plug.

Hydraulic A liquid filled system used to transmit pressure from one component to another. Common uses on motorcycles and ATVs are brakes and clutches.

Hydrometer An instrument for measuring the specific gravity of a lead-acid battery.

Hygroscopic Water absorbing. In motorcycle and ATV applications, braking efficiency will be reduced if DOT 3 or 4 hydraulic fluid absorbs water from the air - care must be taken to keep new brake fluid in tightly sealed containers.

I

lbf ft Pounds-force feet. A unit of torque. Sometimes written as ft-lbs.

lbf in Pound-force inch. A unit of torque, applied to components where a very low torque is required. Sometimes written as inch-lbs.

IC Abbreviation for Integrated Circuit.

Ignition advance Means of increasing the timing of the spark at higher engine speeds. Done by mechanical means (ATU) on early engines or electronically by the ignition control unit on later engines.

Ignition timing The moment at which the spark plug fires, expressed in the number of crankshaft degrees before the piston reaches the top of its stroke, or in the number of millimeters before the piston reaches the top of its stroke.

Infinity (∞) Description of an open-circuit electrical state, where no continuity exists.

Inverted forks (upside down forks) The sliders or lower legs are held in the yokes and the fork tubes or stanchions are connected to the wheel axle (spindle). Less unsprung weight and stiffer construction than conventional forks.

J

JASO Japan Automobile Standards Organization JASO MA is a standard for motorcycle and ATV oil equivalent to API SJ, but designed to prevent problems with wet-type motorcycle and ATV clutches.

Joule The unit of electrical energy.

Journal The bearing surface of a shaft.

K

Kickstart Mechanical means of turning the engine over for starting purposes.

Technical Terms Explained (REF•46)

Only usually fitted to mopeds, small capacity motorcycles and off-road motorcycles.

Kill switch Handebar-mounted switch for emergency ignition cut-out. Cuts the ignition circuit on all models, and additionally prevent starter motor operation on others.

km Symbol for kilometer.

kmh Abbreviation for kilometers per hour.

L

Lambda sensor A sensor fitted in the exhaust system to measure the exhaust gas oxygen content (excess air factor). Also called oxygen sensor.

Lapping see **Grinding**.

LCD Abbreviation for Liquid Crystal Display.

LED Abbreviation for Light Emitting Diode.

Liner A steel cylinder liner inserted in an aluminum alloy cylinder block.

Locknut A nut used to lock an adjustment nut, or other threaded component, in place.

Lockstops The lugs on the lower triple clamp (yoke) which abut those on the frame, preventing handlebar-to-fuel tank contact.

Lockwasher A form of washer designed to prevent an attaching nut from working loose.

LT Low Tension Description of the electrical circuit from the power supply to the primary winding of the ignition coil.

M

Main bearings The bearings between the crankshaft and crankcase.

Maintenance-free (MF) battery A sealed battery which cannot be topped up.

Manometer Mercury-filled calibrated tubes used to measure intake tract vacuum. Used to synchronize carburetors on multi-cylinder engines.

Tappet shims are measured with a micrometer

Micrometer A precision measuring instrument that measures component outside diameters **(see illustration)**.

MON (Motor Octane Number) A measure of a fuel's resistance to knock.

Monograde oil An oil with a single viscosity, eg SAE80W.

Monoshock A single suspension unit linking the swingarm or suspension linkage to the frame.

mph Abbreviation for miles per hour.

Multigrade oil Having a wide viscosity range (eg 10W40). The W stands for Winter, thus the viscosity ranges from SAE10 when cold to SAE40 when hot.

Multimeter An electrical test instrument with the capability to measure voltage, current and resistance. Some meters also incorporate a continuity tester and buzzer.

N

Needle roller bearing Inner race of caged needle rollers and hardened outer race. Examples of uncaged needle rollers can be found on some engines. Commonly used in rear suspension applications and in two-stroke engines.

Nm Newton meters.

NOx Oxides of Nitrogen. A common toxic pollutant emitted by gasoline engines at higher temperatures.

O

Octane The measure of a fuel's resistance to knock.

OE (Original Equipment) Relates to components fitted to a motorcycle or ATV as standard or replacement parts supplied by the manufacturer.

Ohm The unit of electrical resistance. Ohms = Volts ÷ Current.

Ohmmeter An instrument for measuring electrical resistance.

Oil cooler System for diverting engine oil outside of the engine to a radiator for cooling purposes.

Oil injection A system of two-stroke engine lubrication where oil is pump-fed to the engine in accordance with throttle position.

Open-circuit An electrical condition where there is a break in the flow of electricity - no continuity (high resistance).

O-ring A type of sealing ring made of a special rubber-like material; in use, the O-ring is compressed into a groove to provide the sealing action.

Oversize (OS) Term used for piston and ring size options fitted to a rebored cylinder.

Overhead cam (sohc) engine An engine with single camshaft located on top of the cylinder head.

Overhead valve (ohv) engine An engine with the valves located in the cylinder head, but with the camshaft located in the engine block or crankcase.

Oxygen sensor A device installed in the exhaust system which senses the oxygen content in the exhaust and converts this information into an electric current. Also called a Lambda sensor.

P

Plastigage A thin strip of plastic thread, available in different sizes, used for measuring clearances. For example, a strip of Plastigage is laid across a bearing journal. The parts are assembled and dismantled; the width of the crushed strip indicates the clearance between journal and bearing.

Polarity Either negative or positive ground, determined by which battery lead is connected to the frame (ground return). Modern motorcycles and ATVs are usually negative ground.

Pre-ignition A situation where the fuel/air mixture ignites before the spark plug fires. Often due to a hot spot in the combustion chamber caused by carbon build-up. Engine has a tendency to 'run-on'.

Pre-load (suspension) The amount a spring is compressed when in the unloaded state. Preload can be applied by gas, spacer or mechanical adjuster.

Premix The method of engine lubrication on some gasoline two-stroke engines. Engine oil is mixed with the gasoline in the fuel tank in a specific ratio. The fuel/oil mix is sometimes referred to as "petrol".

Primary drive Description of the drive from the crankshaft to the clutch. Usually by gear or chain.

PS Pferdestärke - a German interpretation of BHP.

PSI Pounds-force per square inch. Imperial measurement of tire pressure and cylinder pressure measurement.

PTFE Polytetrafluoroethylene. A low friction substance.

Pulse secondary air injection system A process of promoting the burning of excess fuel present in the exhaust gases by routing fresh air into the exhaust ports.

Q

Quartz halogen bulb Tungsten filament surrounded by a halogen gas. Typically used for the headlight **(see illustration)**.

Quartz halogen headlight bulb construction

R

Rack-and-pinion A pinion gear on the end of a shaft that mates with a rack (think of a geared wheel opened up and laid flat). Sometimes used in clutch operating systems.

Radial play Up and down movement about a shaft.

Radial ply tires Tire plies run across the tire (from bead to bead) and around the circumference of the tire. Less resistant to tread distortion than other tire types.

Radiator A liquid-to-air heat transfer device designed to reduce the temperature of the coolant in a liquid cooled engine.

Rake A feature of steering geometry - the angle of the steering head in relation to the vertical **(see illustration)**.

Steering geometry

Rebore Providing a new working surface to the cylinder bore by boring out the old surface. Necessitates the use of oversize piston and rings.

Rebound damping A means of controlling the oscillation of a suspension unit spring after it has been compressed. Resists the spring's natural tendency to bounce back after being compressed.

Rectifier Device for converting the ac output of an alternator into dc for battery charging.

Reed valve An induction system commonly used on two-stroke engines.

Regulator Device for maintaining the charging voltage from the generator or alternator within a specified range.

Relay A electrical device used to switch heavy current on and off by using a low current auxiliary circuit.

Resistance Measured in ohms. An electrical component's ability to pass electrical current.

RON (Research Octane Number) A measure of a fuel's resistance to knock.

rpm revolutions per minute.

Runout The amount of wobble (in-and-out movement) of a wheel or shaft as it's rotated. The amount a shaft rotates "out-of-true." The out-of-round condition of a rotating part.

S

SAE (Society of Automotive Engineers) A standard for the viscosity of a fluid.

Sealant A liquid or paste used to prevent leakage at a joint. Sometimes used in conjunction with a gasket.

Service limit Term for the point where a component is no longer useable and must be replaced.

Shaft drive A method of transmitting drive from the transmission to the rear wheel.

Shell bearings Plain bearings consisting of two shell halves. Most often used as connecting rod and main bearings in a four-stroke engine. Often called bearing inserts.

Shim Thin spacer, commonly used to adjust the clearance or relative positions between two parts. For example, shims inserted into or under tappets or followers to control valve clearances. Clearance is adjusted by changing the thickness of the shim.

Short-circuit An electrical condition where current shorts to ground bypassing the circuit components.

Skimming Process to correct warpage or repair a damaged surface, such as brake discs or drums.

Slide-hammer A special puller that screws into or hooks onto a component such as a shaft or bearing; a heavy sliding handle on the shaft bottoms against the end of the shaft to knock the component free.

Small-end bearing The bearing in the upper end of the connecting rod at its joint with the gudgeon pin.

Snap-ring A ring-shaped clip used to prevent endwise movement of cylindrical parts and shafts. An internal snap-ring is installed in a groove in a housing; an external snap-ring fits into a groove on the outside of a cylindrical piece such as a shaft. Also known as a circlip.

Spalling Damage to camshaft lobes or bearing journals shown as pitting of the working surface.

Specific gravity (SG) The state of charge of the electrolyte in a lead-acid battery. A measure of the electrolyte's density compared with water.

Straight-cut gears Common type gear used on gearbox shafts and for oil pump and water pump drives.

Stanchion The inner sliding part of the front forks, held by the yokes. Often called a fork tube.

Stoichiometric ratio The optimum chemical air/fuel ratio for a gasoline engine, said to be 14.7 parts of air to 1 part of fuel.

Sulphuric acid The liquid (electrolyte) used in a lead-acid battery. Poisonous and extremely corrosive.

Surface grinding (lapping) Process to correct a warped gasket face, commonly used on cylinder heads.

T

Tapered-roller bearing Tapered inner race of caged needle rollers and separate tapered outer race. Examples of taper roller bearings can be found on steering heads.

Tappet A cylindrical component which transmits motion from the cam to the valve stem, either directly or via a pushrod and rocker arm. Also called a cam follower.

TCS Traction Control System. An electronically-controlled system which senses wheel spin and reduces engine speed accordingly.

TDC Top Dead Center denotes that the piston is at its highest point in the cylinder.

Thread-locking compound Solution applied to fastener threads to prevent loosening. Select type to suit application.

Thrust washer A washer positioned between two moving components on a shaft. For example, between gear pinions on gearshaft.

Timing chain See **Cam Chain**.

Timing light Stroboscopic lamp for carrying out ignition timing checks with the engine running.

Top-end A description of an engine's cylinder block, head and valve gear components.

Torque Turning or twisting force about a shaft.

Torque setting A prescribed tightness specified by the manufacturer to ensure that the bolt or nut is secured correctly. Undertightening can result in the bolt or nut coming loose or a surface not being sealed. Overtightening can result in stripped threads, distortion or damage to the component being retained.

Torx key A six-point wrench.

Tracer A stripe of a second color applied to a wire insulator to distinguish that wire from another one with the same color insulator. For example, Br/W is often used to denote a brown insulator with a white tracer.

Trail A feature of steering geometry. Distance from the steering head axis to the tire's central contact point.

Triple clamps The cast components which extend from the steering head and support the fork stanchions or tubes. Often called fork yokes.

Turbocharger A centrifugal device, driven by exhaust gases, that pressurizes the intake air. Normally used to increase the power output from a given engine displacement.

TWI Abbreviation for Tire Wear Indicator. Indicates the location of the tread depth indicator bars on tires.

U

Universal joint or U-joint (UJ) A double-pivoted connection for transmitting power from a driving to a driven shaft through an angle. Typically found in shaft drive assemblies.

Unsprung weight Anything not supported by the bike's suspension (ie the wheel, tires, brakes, final drive and bottom (moving) part of the suspension).

V

Vacuum gauges Clock-type gauges for measuring intake tract vacuum. Used for carburetor synchronization on multi-cylinder engines.

Valve A device through which the flow of liquid, gas or vacuum may be stopped, started or regulated by a moveable part that opens, shuts or partially obstructs one or more ports or passageways. The intake and exhaust valves in the cylinder head are of the poppet type.

Valve clearance The clearance between the valve tip (the end of the valve stem) and the rocker arm or tappet/follower. The valve clearance is measured when the valve is closed. The correct clearance is important - if too small the valve won't close fully and will burn out, whereas if too large noisy operation will result.

Valve lift The amount a valve is lifted off its seat by the camshaft lobe.

Valve timing The exact setting for the opening and closing of the valves in relation to piston position.

Vernier caliper A precision measuring instrument that measures inside and outside dimensions. Not quite as accurate as a micrometer, but more convenient.

VIN Vehicle Identification Number. Term for the vehicle's engine and frame numbers.

Viscosity The thickness of a liquid or its resistance to flow.

Volt A unit for expressing electrical "pressure" in a circuit. Volts = current x ohms.

W

Water pump A mechanically-driven device for moving coolant around the engine.

Watt A unit for expressing electrical power. Watts = volts x current.

Wet liner arrangement

Wear limit see **Service limit**

Wet liner A liquid-cooled engine design where the pistons run in liners which are directly surrounded by coolant **(see illustration)**.

Wheelbase Distance from the center of the front wheel to the center of the rear wheel.

Wiring harness or loom Describes the electrical wires running the length of the vehicle and enclosed in tape or plastic sheathing. Wiring coming off the main harness is usually referred to as a sub harness.

Woodruff key A key of semi-circular or square section used to locate a gear to a shaft. Often used to locate the alternator rotor on the crankshaft.

Wrist pin Another name for gudgeon or piston pin.

Trail rules

Just when you're ready to have some fun out in the dirt you get slapped with more rules. But by following these rules you'll ensure everyone's enjoyment, not just your own. It's important that all off-roaders follow these rules, as it will help to keep the trails open and keep us in good standing with other trail users. Really, these rules are no more than common sense and common courtesy.

• **Don't ride where you're not supposed to.** Stay off private property and obey all signs marking areas that are off limits to motorized vehicles. Also, as much fun as it might be, don't ride in State or Federal wilderness areas.

• **Leave the land as you found it.** When you've left the area, the only thing you should leave behind are your tire tracks. Stay on the trails, too. There are plenty of trails to ride on without blazing new ones. Be sure to carry out all litter that you create (and if you want to do a good deed, pick up any litter that you come across). Be sure to leave gates as you found them, or if the gate has a sign on it, comply with whatever the sign says (some people don't close gates after passing through them. Others may close gates when the landowner actually wants to keep them open).

• **Give other trail users the right-of-way.** There has been an ongoing dispute amongst trail users as to who belongs there and who doesn't. If the off-roading community shows respect and courtesy to hikers and equestrians, we stand a far better chance of being able to enjoy our sport in the years to come, and to keep the trails open for our children. When you ride up behind hikers or horses, give them plenty of room and pass slowly so as not to startle them. When you approach an equestrian from the opposite direction, stop your machine when the horse nears you so it won't get frightened and bolt.

• **Don't scare the animals!** Whether it be horses, cattle or wild animals like deer, rabbits or coyotes, leave them alone. Remember, you're visiting their home, so treat them with respect. Besides, startling animals can be dangerous. Loud noises or your sudden appearance can trigger an animal's defensive instinct, which could mean bad news for you.

• **Don't ride "over your head."** Sometimes the trails start to resemble ski runs, with a few irresponsible riders going so fast that they're barely able to maintain control of their vehicles. They'd never be able to stop to avoid another trail user if they had to. Most collisions on the trail are caused by such individuals and the results are occasionally tragic. You should only ride fast in areas where you can clearly see a good distance ahead - never on trails with blind corners or rises high enough that prevent you from seeing what's on the other side.

• **Be prepared.** Carry everything you think you may need to make minor repairs should your machine break down. Know how to make basic repairs and keep your vehicle in good mechanical condition to minimize the chances of becoming stranded. Always let someone know where you're going, and ride with a friend whenever possible.

Note: *References throughout this index are in the form, "Chapter number"•"Page number"*